CHARLES BEAN, working then on the *Sydney Morning Herald*, was elected
by his fellow Australian journalists as the correspondent to accompany
the Australian troops during World War I.

Probably no Australian knew more of the troops than Bean. He went
with them to Gallipoli and to France. He constantly visited them in
the front line and as a journalist he had the freedom to go where
the action was. He determined to observe every significant battle in
which the Australians participated.

After the war, Bean accepted the task of writing and editing the
Australian official history of the war, a series remarkable for its scope
and range. Bean's history is rightly acclaimed as one of the finest
achievements in Australian historical writing.

A man of great vision and dedication, Bean is also regarded as the
founder of the Australian War Memorial. He died in 1968.

GALLIPOLI
MISSION

C. E. W. BEAN

Formerly Australian Official War Historian

an
ABC
BOOK

Published by ABC Enterprises in association with
the Australian War Memorial for the
AUSTRALIAN BROADCASTING CORPORATION
20 Atchison Street (Box 8888) Crows Nest NSW 2065

First published 1948
This edition first published 1990
Reprinted 1991

National Library of Australia
Cataloguing-in-Publication entry
Bean, C. E. W. (Charles Edwin Woodrow), 1879–1968.
  Gallipoli mission.

  Includes index.
  ISBN 0 7333 0022 7.

  1. World War, 1914–1918—Australia. 2. World War,
  1914–1918—New Zealand. 3. World War, 1914–1918—Turkey.
  4. World War, 1914–1918—Campaigns—Turkey—Gallipoli
  Peninsula. 5. World War, 1914–1918—Battlefields—
  Turkey—Gallipoli Peninsula. I. Title.

940.425

Photographs reproduced with permission of
the Australian War Memorial
Printed and bound in Australia by Australian Print Group, Victoria
2.55-1-1995

·FOREWORD·

Of all Bean's books, this is the hardest to put down. After thirty
years as Australia's official Great War historian, gracing that
work with his balance and thoroughness, Bean writes here about
his most passionate cause. His return to Anzac, and this book
about that return, were journeys of the heart. "Do you know
. . .", he confessed to his brother John from Lemnos on 3 February
1919, "I am as homesick as can be for Anzac". Three days later
he stood straining for a glimpse of Anzac's distant coast as his
ship rounded Cape Helles for Constantinople, and after a week
of impatience in the Turkish capital and on the road back to
Gallipoli he could not stay to help set up camp, but hurried
forward, past the old Turkish rear defences, up to Lone Pine
and, despite increasing rain, down to the Beach. As the familiar
landmarks appeared, his heart "bounded". Here was a man with
a mission.

"Mission" was Bean's choice. In November 1918 he arranged
to have his Gallipoli "team" officially named the Australian
Historical Mission, and in 1947 he called this book first *Mission
to Gallipoli*, then *Gallipoli Mission*. The word can mean diplomats
sent to foreign country, or envoys sent with a message, or
preachers sent among unbelievers. Each of these could describe
some part of Bean's work in Turkey. He went back to locate
sites and to answer puzzles about the Anzac fighting, some
of which had taunted Australians since the day of the Landing,
to collect relics for a national war museum, and to report on
the condition of Allied war graves. In Constantinople he gladly
accepted a fourth purpose: to obtain Turkish accounts of the
campaign.

For Bean this work was a mission in a sense first recorded in 1805: "that which a person is designed or destined to do; a duty . . . in life". He meant the word to join other non-secular but not quite religious words and phrases already being used about Anzac: "sacred shore", "hallowed", "pantheon", "temple", "pilgrimage". He wanted to pay homage to the Anzac dead, and to use their faith and fire to inspire his fellow Australians to national greatness. His mission was not only to Gallipoli in 1919, but in Australia for the rest of his life.

Few Australians responded when *Gallipoli Mission* first appeared, just too late for Anzac Day, 1948. The book sold slowly. Only 4115 copies were printed, and the last was not sold until late 1959, after strenuous promotion by J. L. Treloar, Director of the Australian War Memorial and Bean's old assistant. Even he wrote in 1948, "It has only been a wish to render a service to Dr Bean that has caused me to accept the work entailed in the publication of this book." No commercial publisher would have touched it, he went on, because war books were dead, especially those which in 1948 related to the last war but one.

Yet this book will live on. It is not a war book. It means more to veterans and students of Anzac than to others, because you need to know Anzac's story before you can truly admire the master solving its puzzles. But *Gallipoli Mission* is about Australian nationality. For Bean, Anzac's puzzles needed answers in order to set the national record straight, the relics needed collecting because they were "intensely important for the national tradition of my country and its posterity", the graves demanded care because they were also monuments.

This is the voice of an Australia almost vanished, but Anzac still means something. It still helps shape the mission of Australians concerned with the past and the future of their country.

BILL GAMMAGE
Australian National University, Canberra
March 1990

•CONTENTS•

vii

·CONTENTS·

·CONTENTS·

CONTENTS

·ILLUSTRATIONS·

xi

·ILLUSTRATIONS·

·ILLUSTRATIONS·

·DRAWINGS·

·LIST OF MAPS·

LIST OF MAPS·

·PREFACE·

to First Edition

This book was planned with the intention merely of passing on to general readers in Australia experiences which seemed too interesting to be stored in a few fading memories and in semi-official records.

The writer is, however, conscious that it may be used as a source book, in which case its authorship could be criticised for lack of scholarship, for example, in the unscientific transliteration of Turkish names and in the failure to point out all discrepancies between the information given to us by Zeki Bey and that which is now available from other sources, including the answers kindly supplied by the Chief of the Turkish General Staff and here printed in an appendix. An attempt has been made to indicate some of the discrepancies; but in the spelling and translation of the place names the course adopted in the *Official History of Australia in the War of 1914–18* has been generally followed here also, namely to leave them as Zeki Bey and I thrashed them out between us on the spot in February 1919.

In recording the narrative of our Turkish friend, I have made him speak in the first person. Much the greater part of his account was taken down by me in longhand at our mess-table nightly, after dinner, by means of question and answer; that is, in precisely the same way in which I had recorded the evidence of hundreds of Australian, New Zealand and British soldiers in the previous four years, except for this—that I questioned him, and he answered, in French, the resulting narrative being written down by me there and then, but in English and in the third person. My notes, however, followed so closely his actual phrases that I feel the adoption of the first person to be justified, affording, as it does, often a literal translation of what he said and a much more vivid picture of our little friend's personality. The reader is, however, asked to bear in mind that Zeki Bey and I spoke in a langauge foreign to each of us, and my translation may be inaccurate; and that though my note followed generally the wording of his answers it was not actually verbatim, and here again error may have slipped in. And I must add that where our conversations covered the same ground more than once, and I have therefore two or more notes on one subject, I have combined them here into a consecutive account.

For all these reasons it would be unwise and unjust to criticise Zeki Bey for having used any phrase here attributed to him; any error may be mine. But, needless to say, where he is recorded as speaking in the first person to any of his fellow Turks, or they are reported as so speaking to him, the conversation here set down is an exact translation of his words. In a very few instances I have relied on my memory of some phrase used by him which impressed itself beyond possibility of forgetting.

The reader may be interested as to the subsequent history of the team of mainly-young Australian enthusiasts whose names appear in these pages. The oldest of us, George Lambert, after busy and anxious years of really great work in his studio at Randwick Military Hospital, Sydney, died in 1930 partly as a result of overstrain in riding a mettlesome horse. Harry Gullett became the first Director of the Australian War Memorial, wrote the magnificent history of the Palestine Campaign, became Director of Immigration, and later, for twelve years before his death in a tragic air-crash at Canberra, was minister in successive Federal Governments, playing a large part in the framing of the Ottawa Agreement. Major (later Lieutenant-Colonel) J. L. Treloar succeeded him in 1920 as Director of the War Memorial, and has made the establishing of the memorial his life's task. Except when detached to organise Australia's share in the Wembley Exhibition, and, in World War II, to organise and command the Military History Section of the Australian Army, he has, since 1920, played by far the chief part in planning and organising it.

Captain G. H. Wilkins has since become a famous Arctic and Antarctic flier and explorer, besides leading for the British Museum an expedition among the wild Australian blacks (employing generally Stefansson's method of "living off the land") and now has his home in America. C. E. Hughes, after finishing his task with the position of chief administrative officer of the Imperial War Graves Commission in the Middle East, became Australian Government Commissioner in Egypt; H. V. Howe between periods as private secretary to Mr W. M. Hughes and military secretary to successive Ministers for the Army (in World War II), has been secretary of the Chamber of Manufactures of New South Wales, and finally exchanged the wild West Coast for an orchard near Sydney; W. H. James became a colonel of Light Horse; H. S. Buchanan, after alternating private with government practice, is Deputy Chairman of the Federal Contract Board, and has lately given some thrills to his old comrades as a member of the national radio quiz team; G. H. Rogers, when last I heard from him, was a manufacturer of refrigerators; J. Balfour and A. W. Bazley, my chief assistants in the history of World War I, are now in important positions respectively with the historian of World War II and in the Department of Immigration. Balfour was present at the signing of the armistice with Japan. Of others mentioned in these pages, T. H. E. Heyes (like A. W. Bazley after him) acted in charge of the War Memorial during the Director's absence on war service, and is now Secretary of the Department of Immigration; and S. W. Gullett is a prominent Melbourne businessman.

I am especially indebted to Mrs Lambert's excellent biography of her husband (*Thirty Years of an Artist's Life*, published in Sydney by the Society of Artists, 1938, and which should certainly be reprinted). His letters to her from the Mission have been freely quoted in these pages. Other books to which reference has frequently been made are: *Under the North Pole* by Sir Hubert Wilkins; *Gallipoli Today* by T. J. Pemberton, and *Crosses of Sacrifice* by J. C. Waters—both these relating to the cemeteries; H. C. Armstrong's vivid biography of Mustafa Kemal (*Grey Wolf*); Philip Graves' *Briton and Turk*; Toynbee's *Conduct of British Empire Foreign Relations since the Peace Settlement*; and our Mission's much-thumbed Baedekers (*Konstantinopel und*

Kleinasien, and *Palestine and Syria*). References to the Gallipoli graves have also been checked and amplified by perusal of the reports of the Imperial War Graves Commission through the courtesy of its Australian headquarters in Melbourne and of the Australian War Memorial, which last is also the guardian of the writer's diaries and of the papers of the Mission. Where "Official History" is cited, the reference is to the *Official History of Australia in the War of 1914–18.* The British Official History of the Gallipoli Campaign also has been of great assistance.

The drawings are traced from the writer's field-books and diary. Where necessary for clearness the place names on the originals have been added to, enlarged, or replaced by letters, and a very few other slight alterations made. Some of the best photographs taken at the time of the Mission's visit were used to illustrate the Official History. These, except in a few cases, have not been reprinted here but hitherto unpublished photographs selected instead. Many references are, however, made to plates in the Official History illustrating points in the present work. Except where otherwise stated, the photographs here printed were taken in 1919.

The pictures given of the cemeteries do not represent their present condition, cameras having been banned there since 1936 when the Dardanelles again became a military area. For the same reason adequate maps of the cemeteries are difficult to obtain. The maps are from the Official History and Australian War Memorial with alterations carried out by Mr W. H. G. Guard. The index is by Miss Mary Ordish.

C. E. W. BEAN
1st February, 1948

GALLIPOLI MISSION

THE AUSTRALIAN HISTORICAL MISSION IN TURKEY.
Five members of the Mission in one of the trucks which served as their living
quarters on the railway over the Taurus Mountains, March 1919. Above, left to
right: Lieut. J. Balfour, Capt. G. H. Wilkins; below, Lieut. Mackinnon (Railway
Control Officer at Eregli), Staff-Sergt. G. H. Rogers, Capt. George Lambert,
Lieut. H. S. Buchanan. *G2138*

Chapter
· I ·

THE RIDDLES
OF ANZAC

THESE events happened a number of years ago. Their hitherto unwritten story lies in the faded diaries and rain-and-mud-stained field-books beside me as I work.

It is the story of an attempt to decipher, mainly from marks left for several years on the ground, some of the events of a famous campaign; to trace them from relics which we came upon—sometimes exactly where we expected to find them, sometimes quite unexpectedly—a pierced water-bottle in the scrub on this ridge, a line of spent cartridges or clips on that, some hurriedly scratched rifle-pits, barely begun, on a third; at one or two points a length of parapet studded with bullets like a cake with currants; often the poor relics of a line of men of one side or the other, lying where they died.

Our Mission happened in this way:

When the Allies left Gallipoli at the turn of the year 1915-16 after from five to nine months' occupation of the narrow footholds at Cape Helles, Anzac and Suvla, they had already sent away with their regimental war diaries much of the material for writing the history of that famous episode. Yet they left behind them many riddles which no one could then answer.

For us who had been at Anzac, these uncertainties dated from the first hour of the campaign. There was no exact record of where the first troops—the first wave of the covering force which was to seize a foothold for the rest—had landed, though of course the general location

1

was well established; nor was it known how far this advanced force thrust or how the foremost parts fared. The general report was that the first Australians in wild enthusiasm, after driving back the Turkish garrison from the heights above the Beach, had rushed much too far, regardless of plan or control, until some almost reached the Dardanelles, and that they had then suddenly found themselves cut off or nearly so by the Turkish reserves, and had to come back as fast as they had advanced. The commanders and staff officers responsible for writing reports after the battle had little time to investigate; and many of those who knew the facts were either killed where not even their bodies could be reached, or were wounded and scattered to hospitals in Egypt, Malta, England and Australia. But a number eventually came back to the force; and in 1916-18 the writer, working as Official War Correspondent, often came across them. Together we spent hundreds of hours tracing out their tracks and doings. Many were uncertain as to the ridges and valleys they had fought over, for until after the first fight most of these places had no names, or none known to us; and, as that ground was afterwards largely behind the Turkish lines, few of the men who went farthest had any opportunity to check on the spot their recollections.

But from these talks, of which I recorded about 200, I had become certain that the accepted story of the Anzac Landing was far from the truth. I had gradually realised that, although there was much confusion in the Landing and the fight that followed—indeed, owing to the boats being carried by current in the dark to a wrong and terribly rugged landing place, the covering force was shuffled like a pack of cards—yet, in the first advance, planned efforts were made under capable leaders to seize the extensive goal set for the covering force; that in several directions organised forces reached and held, though only for a short time, ground far beyond that held at the close of the day or afterwards; but that in not one instance was the goal for the covering force overstepped. Indeed, it was borne in upon me that, in the circumstances, the goal had been too distant and too extensive to be reached by more than a comparatively few troops at a few points.

It was not, however, only the Landing that had left its train of unsolved questions. Almost every stage of the campaign involved similar puzzles. Where did our various forces get to in the second great attempt to reach the heights commanding the Dardanelles? And when, four months later, in two nights we stole away from Anzac (and the British from Suvla Bay), and, later still, the British left Cape Helles—how much had the Turks known or guessed of our intentions? and what was their reaction when they found we had gone?

Then there was the secret of the Turkish positions, into most of which we had never penetrated. What could they see of us from there? and what could we have seen if we had captured them—from Achi Baba peak, in front of the British and French at Cape Helles, for example? For many months it had seemed almost the main goal of the expedition. But of all the riddles that interested men and officers at Anzac I think the chief one was—where had been the Turkish guns that had plagued Anzac Beach by their fire from the southern flank. The Anzacs had personified them by the name of "Beachy Bill"; and they had puzzled our artillery by the way in which, though often silenced by our guns or the Navy's, they had always opened soon after from the same position, behind a slight fold in the low open country to the south-east. One leading battery-commander told me that he believed they were on rails, and after firing were run back into shelters behind steel doors.

Obviously the answers to some of these questions we could get only from the Turks, when, and if, they should ever supply us with them. Other answers we might obtain after the war from Australians who had been captured by the Turks—but these prisoners were very few, and some had died, and the rest might be difficult to contact. Many of the riddles might, however, be solved by visiting the ground as soon as it was possible to do so, and following whatever traces the events had left there. In some cases these might give the only sure answer,[1] since neither Turks nor prisoners might have observed or recorded the locations of troops and movements more definitely than we at Anzac had.

Most leaders of the Australian, and indeed of the British, forces that had fought on Gallipoli were as interested in these riddles as I. But I had been charged by the Australian Government with writing or editing the history of Australia's part in the war, and both Lieutenant-General C. B. B. White, the chief-of-staff of the Australian Imperial Force, my very close friend, and General Birdwood, its commander, were as determined as I that its records should be complete and accurate.[2] I had discussed with them the possibility of getting back to Gallipoli while the ground was almost unchanged; and so it was that, as soon as it appeared certain that the war was in its last days, I obtained General Birdwood's authority to visit London and arrange for my return to Australia by way of Gallipoli, taking with me such officers and others as I considered necessary for securing the required records on the old battlegrounds. From Gallipoli I would return with most of the party via Egypt to Australia where the Australian Government wished me to complete arrangements for the history and initiate those for the eventual establishment of the nation's memorial to those who fell in that war.

---

[1] Those interested in the philosophy of history may note that in this section of our work on the Australian Official History we almost necessarily followed the method of "question and answer" discussed by the late Professor R. G. Collingwood of Oxford. I suspect that in our investigation of "antiquities" only four years old some of our problems were not dissimilar to his concerning the traces of the Roman Wall from the Tyne to Solway.

[2] As had been General W. T. Bridges, its first commander, killed on Gallipoli.

4

A secondary object of the expedition was to help complete this memorial by collecting, while they could still be obtained there, relics of the occupation of Gallipoli. It had always been in the mind of many Australian soldiers that records and relics of their fighting would be preserved in some institutions in Australia, and to several of us it had seemed that a museum housing these would form the most natural, interesting, and inspiring memorial to those who fell. General Birdwood, General White and some others probably derived their interest in such museums from the Royal United Service Institute in London, with its Nelson and other relics. My own interest dated from when, as one of a young family brought by its parents from Australia, I lived for two winters in Belgium and frequently visited with my father the old battlefield of Waterloo. There, waiting to lunch in the airy dining room of the Hotel du Musée, we youngsters had steeped ourselves in the contents of the museum room, behind the glass double-doors just across the tiled hall, where the walls and glass cases were crowded with relics largely found on the battlefield—caps of Napoleon's Old Guard, casques of French heavy dragoons and of British dragoons, a cuirass with a grape-shot hole, a British infantryman's red coat, round cannon balls (not unlike the Dutch cheese that we would presently be enjoying); old muskets, bayonets, pouches, sabre-taches, lances, ram-rods; a curious leathern instrument of music known as a "serpent" from a British band; many round lead bullets, some of them deep in tree-trunks; even a soldier's skull chipped by a sabre (was he one of Napoleon's cavalrymen or ours?); some of Napoleon's kitchen utensils left with his baggage in the rout, and much else of absorbing interest which made the old battlefield live again. They had been collected by Sergeant-Major Edward Cotton of the 7th Hussars, who had fought in the battle. He afterwards acted as guide and owned the hotel and wrote a history (which lies before me) of the fight, and his nieces then ran the hotel. Anywhere in the district you could buy "Waterloo bullets" (specially manufactured, it was said, in Birmingham[3]); but the relics in that museum, including the few purchasable ones, were strictly and proudly authentic. We could not afford to buy, and in any case it was far more exciting to pick up near Hougoumont a piece of rusty chain (probably from some farm harness) and imagine that it once jingled upon a British gun-team.

I often discussed the notion of a memorial museum with General White; and when, in 1916, the Australian Government agreed that the historical records of our forces, till then preserved by the British services, should be transferred to an Australian authority,[4] and the Australian War Records Section was formed to take them over, the new authority was also charged with collecting and preserving war relics (with us the objective was always relics more than trophies, even where "trophies" were spoken of) and photographs. General White gave to the section, as its organiser and commander under Brigadier-General Tom Griffiths in London, his very able young confidential clerk, Captain J. L. Treloar. Griffiths, then Commandant at A.I.F. Headquarters, Horseferry Road, was himself as enthusiastic as the youngest of us; and under him in 1917 Treloar rapidly extended the collection of Australian records and relics through France, Egypt and Palestine. That year, as advice concerning historical records was regarded as within my province, I finally, with the approval of our leaders, urged upon the Minister for Defence, Senator G. F. Pearce, that our forces should be commemorated in Australia by their

---

3 Generally, just as in Egypt and Palestine, those who bought antiquities had to beware of the influx of manufactured "relics".

4 We were helped by Sir Max Aitken (afterwards Lord Beaverbrook) who had secured such a transfer for Canada.

own collection of records and relics worthily installed in the then unbuilt federal capital at Canberra.

This was approved and the Government's decision was announced to the troops at the front. It happened that at this juncture one of Australia's finest journalists, Harry Gullett, was transferred from the artillery to be our official war correspondent in Palestine, and came first to the Western Front for experience. He was commissioned by Treloar to visit the divisions and explain the plan for the memorial and the need for greater attention to the records. Treloar also built up for the front an enthusiastic staff, headed in France by Gullett's cousin, Sid (whose health had suffered in the Passchendaele fighting) and Sergeant "Tas" Heyes[5] and in Egypt by Hector Dinning. From the first announcement the troops worked with enthusiasm at building up this collection in memory of their dead comrades and of their regiments. Exhibits poured to the bases by road and rail—eventually truck-load upon truck-load. Even tree trunks from certain famous corners, and dugout timbers, were transported by night from under the enemy's nose until the volume of traffic became almost a scandal. Some exhibits had to be returned—old cannon, for example, taken from a French chateau. But at the War Office Trophies Committee Treloar, youthful, fair-haired, pink-cheeked captain, representing Australia at a table surrounded by titled and beribboned generals and heads of departments, fought our case so well and wisely that the truck-loads, even if temporarily stopped at the French ports, eventually come through. To raise his status in that august though friendly company, General Griffiths had him promoted forthwith to major.

The ideas for the collection were thrashed out partly in London, where early in 1918 Treloar and I lodged together, partly at our little Australian war correspon-

---

[5] The original member of the staff, Corporal E. L. Bailey, was killed by an accidental bomb-explosion while at his work in France.

dents' headquarters in France, between Harry Gullett, Fred Cutlack, Will Dyson the artist, Hubert Wilkins and Frank Hurley, official photographers, myself and others. It was team-work from the start. I particularly remember that over one meal at our billet someone started a discussion as to what was the most interesting form of exhibit of former wars. "The models at the United Service Institution," replied someone (I think Dyson) at once. We agreed. It was certainly Dyson who suggested: "You could get them done by a good sculptor; Derwent Wood, I'm sure, would advise us." And there and then was born the notion of what we called the "picture-models" and "plan-models"—the former to be sculptured scenes, the latter raised maps. They were to be records as truthful as art and labour could make them. The object of us all was to ensure that the historical record of the "Diggers" should engage the interest of everyone who saw or read it. We had no doubt this could be done; someone said: "With a team of young Australian brains, planning beforehand with imagination and working with enthusiasm, this memorial may stand out even among the famous memorials of the world."

The main planning fell on Gullett, Treloar and me. Gullett went to Palestine to follow that campaign (of which he would be historian) through 1918 and incidentally to help the collection there. But there was one serious gap in the exhibits: of the episode most famous for the Anzacs, the Gallipoli Campaign, the Australian War Records Section had practically no relics; when the idea was conceived Gallipoli had already been evacuated; except for any private souvenirs that might be handed over, the campaign would apparently be unrepresented. But our visit to the Peninsula for purposes of the history would also give the opportunity of collecting such relics as might still be obtained before the Turks or visitors "souvenired" them or weather destroyed them.

This, therefore, was included among the original

objects of the Mission. In addition Treloar's section, through Harry Gullett and others in the Middle East, had arranged for an Australian officer to revisit the Peninsula with the first troops to return there, and to take photographs of all the positions and collect war relics. As General Griffiths happened to have returned to Australia I telegraphed on November 26th to the Defence Department asking that he should be consulted as to the need for the Mission, and the Minister gave it his approval.

At this stage a third object was added. While in London arranging with Captain H. C. Smart, of the High Commissioner's Office, Australia House, for an artist to come with us to obtain sketches and notes for a picture of the Gallipoli Landing for the memorial, I saw another enthusiast, Alan Box, the Official Secretary. Among many other tasks, Box was acting in place of his chief, Andrew Fisher, whose health was then failing, as Australia's representative on the newly formed commission to control all graves of British and Dominion soldiers in the various theatres of war, among which an important element was the graves in Gallipoli. These, including nearly fifty cemeteries at Anzac alone, had at the Evacuation been left to the Turks—a cause of deeper regret to the troops and their people at home than any other implication in the abandonment of the Peninsula. During the later years of the war their thoughts had constantly turned back to these places; and the Imperial Conference of 1917 had not only (on a memorandum from the Prince of Wales) decided to form the War Graves Commission to ensure that neglect of soldiers' graves was this time avoided, but, the Turks being reputed as neglectful of graveyards, it had urged that the parts of Gallipoli in which the cemeteries lay should, by the Peace Treaty with Turkey, be vested in the Commission in perpetuity. This Commission represented the whole British Commonwealth of Nations and was the first self-governing administrative body set up jointly by those nations.

During the war the anxiety about the Gallipoli cemeteries was eased through the mediation of the Pope, whose delegates were allowed by the Turks to make a visit to the Peninsula in 1916 and were shown some of the graves. The envoys returned satisfied that the cemeteries were being respected. Nevertheless two years later, as soon as it became clear that the Turks, beaten back through Palestine and Syria, must shortly seek peace, A.I.F. Headquarters in Cairo was ordered to send an officer to Gallipoli, when fighting stopped, to report to the Australian Government upon the condition of the cemeteries. The old surveys and plans of the cemeteries and the lists of those buried and of all who died on Gallipoli were sent out from our London headquarters for his information. The British War Office agreed, and attached him to a Graves Registration Unit then being formed at Salonica for despatch to the Peninsula. In addition, the Australian and New Zealand interest in the Peninsula being so keen, General Allenby, British Commander-in-Chief in Palestine, arranged with the Australian commander there, Lieutenant-General Sir Harry G. Chauvel, that the British garrison of the Peninsula under the terms of the Armistice with Turkey should comprise two Anzac regiments, the 7th Australian Light Horse and the Canterbury Regiment of New Zealand Mounted Rifles, both of which, after serving unmounted in Gallipoli in 1915, had fought mounted through the campaign from Egypt to Aleppo.

The British Graves Registration Unit, to which the selected Australian—Lieutenant C. E. Hughes of the 1st Field Squadron, Australian Engineers—was attached, landed on Gallipoli on 10th November 1918; and the staff officer in charge at once reported that the condition of the cemeteries was far different from that which the Pope's envoys had described two years before. "Practically all the British and French graves at Cape Helles and large numbers elsewhere have been systematically desecrated," he said. He added that this had been done deliberately, the spade marks being clear. British officers from the monitor *Mersey* landing at Cape Helles—the old British landing place at the toe of the Peninsula—on November 5th had seen a party of Turks filling in graves that had previously been opened. This applied chiefly to the graves at Helles, which were mainly British and French; but on December 3rd A.I.F. Headquarters at Cairo telegraphed that Lieutenant Hughes reported that there had been desecration at Anzac also—the crosses being removed and a number of bodies dug up.

A report of this reached the newspapers and caused deep concern, not least to the newly established Imperial War Graves Commission

The British Graves Registration Unit on Gallipoli had the duty of carrying out all preliminary tasks of finding, identifying, recording and temporarily protecting every British, Dominion, or Indian grave, burying any unburied dead, and charting the cemeteries. It would then hand them over to the Commission, who would plan and establish—and, it was hoped, be authorised by the Peace Treaty to control—the final cemeteries and memorials. The Australian Government was strongly supporting the proposal that the Gallipoli cemeteries should be handed over in perpetuity to the Graves Commission. Both Sir Fabian Ware, its vice-chairman, and Alan Box were most anxious about the situation in this distant region, and desirous that the work of identifying and restoring the cemeteries there should be capably and vigorously done. Also Box wished to be sure that Australia's interest in this should be protected by right measures from the start. He therefore advised the High Commissioner to cable to his Government asking that I should be directed to report by telegram as soon as possible both to it and to the High Commissioner on the graves in Gallipoli "from the Australian aspect". On December 3rd the Government agreed. The instructions given to me by Box were: "to report without delay on the situation on the Peninsula as it affects the Australian cemeteries"; in particular as to the preliminary work to be done to ensure immediate identification of graves and prevent further dilapidation; to advise "as to what may best be done to fulfil Australian sentiment in the permanent memorial of Australian dead there"; and to give my views as to the possible planting of Australian and New Zealand trees and shrubs, and "as to any improvements which might be needed for facilitating visits by Australian citizens and the general preservation of the site". He added that the Graves Registration Unit, in which Lieutenant Hughes had charge of an Australian section, would make a final report to the Graves Commission as to what should be done in the Gallipoli area.

The High Commissioner, Mr Fisher, gave me two letters shortly explaining the two main objects of the Mission and asking for every help and courtesy—each letter with the big red paper seal of the Australian Commonwealth attached; and Brigadier-General T. H. Dodds, then Commandant at headquarters of the A.I.F. in London, telegraphed to our headquarters in Cairo, and, through the War Office, to the British commander at Salonica, telling of our Mission and asking for help on our journey, and requesting certain facilities from Hughes and from Lieutenant-Colonel J. D. Richardson of the 7th Light Horse, on whose camp it was intended we should base our operations. I told General Dodds that we would call ourselves the "Australian Historical Mission". He spoke of us as such in these cablegrams, and from that time the Australian Historical Mission we became.

During December and early January the admirable Naval Transport Branch under Commander C. A.

Parker arranged for our journey—it was then thought
that we would go via Taranto and Salonica to Chanak in
the Dardanelles, whence I would make a short visit to
Constantinople while the others set up camp at Anzac
where I would join them. While such arrangements were
being made I went a last round of every Australian infantry battalion in France and Belgium, filled in the gaps
in my records of the war, and packed most of those records
in a dozen deed boxes to be picked up by us eventually
in Egypt and taken to Australia. For use in Gallipoli I
held back a few typed volumes of my diary, of which
other copies existed. In some crowded days Treloar and
I drew up the scheme for the picture-models and plan-
models. Already, through the support of the A.I.F. leaders, he had his two sculptors—Web Gilbert, and Wallace
Anderson, a young veteran of the scenes he would work
on—ready to go to France. Harry Gullett cabled that he
would come from Egypt for a last minute conference
with us. Meanwhile the members of the Historical
Mission finished their war jobs and then gathered in
London themselves and the materials for their work.
With a scramble we were ready by the date on which the
War Office arranged for us to leave, Saturday, 18th
January 1919; and on that afternoon there pulled out
from Victoria Station by the 4.30 boat train for
Southampton an eager party of eight on a Mission in
which, it is safe to say, a hundred thousand other Aus-
tralians would have given a good part of their deferred
pay to have changed places with them.

Chapter
· II ·
THE AUSTRALIAN
HISTORICAL MISSION

THE Mission assembled for the first time at the boat train—six officers and two sergeants. Needless to say, being Australians, we travelled together, lodged together, and ate together throughout our journey; and from first to last we had no batmen. I myself (then thirty-nine years of age, lean, active, and with an accurate memory) represented "war records"—fortunately we did not have to carry many books as my memory covered most of the history that we would need to know. Lieutenant John Balfour, compact in body and mind, and Staff-Sergeant Arthur Bazley (formerly my clerk), then both on Treloar's staff, had served throughout the occupation of Anzac, and were to be my main assistants in the compilation of the Official History; on the present Mission they would help me with the records. Lieutenant H. S. Buchanan, a young construction-engineer of the Victorian Railways, who had had charge of the mapping section of the Australian Corps in France, and one of his most capable sergeants, G. Hunter Rogers, would make or check our maps.

To help us in tracing what had happened at the Landing I had applied for the help of the officer who, in all the force—with the possible exception of Major-General E. G. Sinclair-MacLagan—could best, I thought, have helped us to work out the events of the first few hours, especially of the attempt to reach the intended positions on the main range to the left (or north-east) of the landing point. This was Brigadier-General E. A. Drake-Brockman, since well known as judge of the Federal Arbitration Court. As a major of the 11th (Western Australian) Battalion, he had been among the first to reach the top of the first height, and, taking charge there, after narrowly escaping a rush by three Turks, had, more than any other survivor of that day, directed and controlled the first advances towards the main range. Needless to say Drake-Brockman was eager to come—indeed it was probably he who suggested it; but General Birdwood, to whom Brudenell White referred my request, anticipated that this might necessitate the appointment of another brigade-commander, a step he wished to avoid. It happened that I had lately met a young scallywag of an intelligence officer, Lieutenant Hedley Vicars Howe, who as a private in Drake-Brockman's company, had been among the first to land, and had since done well in the Army. He was a fair-haired, blue-eyed lad with plenty of brains and a gift for description. Since leaving school he had lived an adventurous life on the north-west coast of Australia where, when war broke out, he owned and was working a couple of pearling luggers. If he could only have written, as he told them to us, his experiences between Australia and the islands with that variegated, polyglot crowd, his name would be famous as an author long since. He had a lively memory of the first day's fighting at Anzac, and would be able to identify his landing place and the direction of the first thrusts. I was fortunate to obtain his help without difficulty.

Most of these members of our small party had their careers still ahead of them. But the two others, our photographer, Captain George Hubert Wilkins, an athletic figure, rather over middle height, at that time clean-shaven, with eyes and brow that reminded me a little of Lord Kitchener's, and a pugnacious chin, and our artist, George Washington Lambert, with the golden beard, the hat, the cloak, the spurs, the gait, the laugh and the conviviality of a cavalier, were already notable men. As Lambert waved good-bye to his big eighteen-year-old son, Maurice (afterwards well known as a sculptor—the younger, Constant, to become famous as a composer and conductor, was still in short pants); as he settled himself into his niche in our well-packed carriage, pulled out his pipe, and with a cheery dig at me (whom he insisted on calling "skipper") began to pull the legs of us all; as he rolled out one after another of his store of good yarns from a mental cellar stocked by experiences of dukes and Diggers and broached with rich appreciation of their humour; as his teeth gleamed, and his nostrils expanded, and his cavalier's beard was thrust out in each quivering prelude to his "robustious" laughter—one could not help wondering whether he did not consciously mould himself on the contemporaries of Van Dyck and Velasquez whose art so evidently influenced his own.

But one soon realised that he was simply himself—transparently honest, devoted, as a religion, to truth as he saw it. Curiously enough, while Lambert was often ready to make clever fun of anyone or anything, his seriousness (which also could be most interesting) was sometimes reserved, with devastating effect, for ceremonial occasions which everyone was hoping he would brighten by the flicker of his usual wit. Wilkins, on the other hand, could at any time be led into deeply serious discussion of almost any subject—with rare hints of a whimsical background showing through. Both men were well worth listening to.

Being two fairly senior men, both full of ideas and experienced in the big world, they established a firm friendship during our journeys. They had come by their experience in typically Australian ways. Wilkins, one of a large family, born on a remote South Australian farm, was educated as much by watching the habits of animals and plants and the fickle weather as at the bush school, which was all that his parents could afford for him. However, by getting a job in Adelaide—to which his parents moved—he was able to attend the School of Mines by afternoon and night; and the knowledge of engineering which he there picked up was eventually to give him an opening to the career which—next to that of a singer—he most longed for. It was characteristic of him that, though always moved by some reasonable utilitarian purpose, he invariably sought his goal through adventure—the more dangerous the more acceptable; indeed I sometimes doubted whether any course of action was for long agreeable to him unless it led eventually to danger. He had begun, while still a boy at Adelaide, by bolting to Sydney by steamer—I believe as a stowaway—and obtained work there as electrician in a theatre; and this introduced him to the cinema, then hardly out of its teething troubles. The next step found him in Europe as a cameraman, making films for Gaumont Frères and photographs for the London *Daily Chronicle*. By simply poking his nose into Hendon aerodrome he managed to get some experience in flying; and by meeting Sir Ernest Shackleton he obtained a promise that he should be taken on the next polar expedition of that explorer. But at that juncture there broke out the war between Turkey and Bulgaria and the chance of obtaining for his firm, for the first time, some genuine moving pictures of battle came straight into his lap. He hurried thither and for many weary weeks experienced, along with Philip Gibbs, Percival Phillips, Ashmead Bartlett, Henry Nevinson and other well known war correspondents, the heartbreaking frustration resulting from the fear of staffs, commanders and governments on both sides that the press might see and tell the truth. His idea of filming the war from a motor-cycle, which probably would have involved the first use of the internal combustion engine in warfare (at all events by a war correspondent), was overruled by the Turkish staff. When he wheeled his machine, after vast trouble, up to the Pera Palace Hotel at Constantinople, with a movie camera bolted below the handle-bars and a still life camera on top of them, and a side-car full of spare parts, negative, food and camping gear, he had, as he himself says,[1] "a complete one-man unit, self contained. But it was also the laughing stock of the drago-men, interpreters, and the Turkish staff officers", from whom he had to secure his permit to go to the front; they insisted on each correspondent's having two servants, four horses, and two months' food supply.

Nevertheless when, eventually, the trainload of war correspondents did push off into the appalling confusion of a Turkish army which was being driven back on itself, Wilkins succeeded, one day, in getting some interesting and gruesome pictures at close range; and as the only other movie camera in the theatre of war happened to be broken down and out of action during this precious opportunity, Wilkins sent off his film in the proud knowledge that he had secured a historic "scoop" by making the "first motion pictures ever taken of an actual war and in the front line".

To his amazement what he received in return was a furious message from his firm and newspaper saying that he had been disgracefully beaten—"the opposition had a picture of the battle running in the halls two days before . . ." And—as Wilkins immediately grasped when he hurried home to see it—what a picture! Just what the public wanted! Precisely what it thought war was like! Only, when once Wilkins got to work he easily proved it to have been acted and filmed just outside Paris. Wilkins' film, showing precisely what he saw, was much less exciting to audiences. However, when both were exhibited the faking was so plain that audiences and producers at once recognised it.

I have described this episode because it was typical

---

[1] In his book, *Under the North Pole*, describing his later project of submarine exploration in the Arctic.

of Wilkins' work when I was associated with him from 1917-19. By then he had greatly added to his experience by exploration in the Arctic. While filming the cocoa industry in the West Indies he learnt of a filibustering expedition in Brazil, and was on his way to film that also when he received from London a cable containing what he had long hoped for—an invitation to join an expedition to the Arctic. At the time he thought it came from Shackleton, but actually it was from the Canadian-born Vilhjalmur Stefansson, commander of the Canadian Arctic Expedition, which was to leave British Columbia in June 1913 for four years' exploration. From that master, and from the Eskimos, he learnt the method that he always afterwards employed in exploration on the ground, not only in the polar regions but in the wilds of North Australia—to live off the country in the same way as its natives did. Using this method in the Arctic, Stefansson and two companions made an immense journey on foot across the Beaufort Sea. During his long absence the local trappers, whalers and Eskimos gave up all hope of his return; but Wilkins was under orders to meet the party with a small ship, and whether they were dead or alive he was determined to go on until he did so. He managed to work the ship to within walking distance of the intended meeting point, and then pushed ahead on foot until on Banks Island he noted on a certain hill a beacon which had not been there the day before. It had been put there by Stefansson for his two comrades. All three arrived, in the pink of condition, as also were their dog-teams.

It was while in the Arctic in 1916 that the party first heard of the Great War that had been raging since 1914. Wilkins hurried to Australia and obtained a commission as pilot in the Australian Flying Corps; but on reaching England he was debarred, through a supposed defect in his eyesight, from flying at the front. Instead, as we were just then setting up a team of official photographers and

19

cinematographers separate from the British, it was suggested that he should be one of its two ófficers—the other was Frank Hurley. Both were utterly daring fellows, but in other respects they were almost opposite. Hurley, a rare mixture of the genuine, highly sensitive artist and keen commercial man, became responsible rather for the publicity side, to which he was devoted; while Wilkins sought to provide our future historians with a record of places and events so accurate that they could be, and often were, relied on as historical evidence. In the Third Battle of Ypres on a number of occasions both of them nearly got themselves killed through their desire to photograph the effects of bursting shells; and, in accompanying the attacks in 1917-18 in order to photograph the infantry fighting, Wilkins at least once had to assume direction of infantry (they happened to be Americans) who through lack of officers were leaderless in a very tight corner, and he emerged from the campaign with a Military Cross and Bar. It was part of the arrangement for our records that, though the official photographers and the official artists were responsible to Major Treloar and the High Commissioner respectively, both worked under my general direction in the field; and so it was that towards the end of that war in France Wilkins came to me one day with a serious face and informed me he was conscious of a gap in his photographic records; he had not yet taken any satisfactory picture of German infantry actually fighting. He hoped to remedy this by getting some pilot to fly him so low down over the German line that he could get a useful set of pictures of the German army in action.

I was thankful that the war ended before he induced any pilot to let him make the attempt. Although his later flights across the North Pole ànd elsewhere in the Arctic and Antarctic—in which he was one of the world's pioneers —succeeded through his extreme care and determination not to take unworthy chances, no amount of care could have avoided German machine-gun bullets. And so here he was, at thirty, completely fit, having tasted life in most countries and capitals—and preferring, at any rate for the present, the simplicity of the Eskimo—and eager to round off his work on the photographic records by this visit to Gallipoli with, probably, the most unadventurous expedition of his life.

Our artist was the even more picturesque George Washington Lambert. Born in St Petersburg in 1873, son of an American engineer who died before his son's birth, and a young English girl (herself daughter of an English engineer, engaged, like Lambert's father, in building the Russian railways), he was brought at two years old to England, whither his devoted and adored mother returned with her rigid, "self-made" father. Despite the stern grandfather's determination to pitch him young into commerce, Lambert's mother encouraged his evident genius for music and art. When the boy was twelve the family migrated to Sydney, and a holiday on the sheep-station of a grand-uncle at Nevertire gave him the chance of revelling in the bush, the riding, and all the life of the back-country people. He soaked in the sunlight, the sights, the sounds, and the characters; and, though he was forced into various clerkships, his whole heart was in a country life. He wanted to be a sheep-breeder, and at seventeen he plunged back into that life as a "station hand", "fencing, butchering, branding, sheep-dipping, shearing, horse-breaking and droving".[2] That year, 1890, happened to be a hard one, with the shearers' strike on and wool prices low. His energy throughout it left him half exhausted in body and mind. Returning to Sydney with a pile of drawings of the bush, and its people and animals, he had one painting most unexpectedly bought by the Art Gallery; he haunted the Sydney water-front, and the then largely virgin coast, but also the Flemington sale-yards, making

---

[2] See *Thirty Years of an Artist's Life*, by Amy Lambert, *p. 17.*

studies of men, animals and dust there—not for sale but rather to show how much he knew of the detail of country life. His drawings were occasionally accepted by the Sydney *Bulletin*; and it was a *Bulletin* artist, B. E. Minns, who finally urged him to "make drawing his profession. You'll never succeed as a sheep-man," said Minns. "You'll always want to paint. Go and see Julian Ashton."

To Ashton Lambert went, and that foremost teacher of Australian painters settled the matter. Lambert joined his school, desperately earnest, supporting himself part of the time by working as a grocer's assistant. His almost religious concentration during hours of study, and his joy in his leisure, fishing, boating, and loafing, were phenomenal. In 1900 a portrait of his mother won him a travelling scholarship, on which he married and went with his wife to Paris, and, in a top floor of the Quartier Latin, put in, among Swedes, Russians, Rumanians, English, Americans, and other Australians, two more years of intense study. From there with his wife and small son—Maurice, afterwards the sculptor—he moved to Chelsea, where, among many congenial fellow artists, he was still living at the outbreak of the First World War. Intensely though he enjoyed society, including high society, Lambert obeyed no master except his artistic conscience, and throughout his twenty years in London as a portrait painter he and his wife often came almost as near to the bread line as in their Paris days. His friends had high hopes of his becoming very prosperous "if only you play your cards well". "I don't play cards," was his simple reply—and he didn't.[3]

The outbreak of the First World War had found him over forty, but partly through his experience of the bush, and partly through the influence of an aristocratic client, he was placed in charge of the felling of timber in some of the Welsh forests. Then came offers from both the

---

[3] *Thirty Years of an Artist's Life, p. 45.*

Canadian and the Australian authorities in London of work as an official war artist. The Canadian terms were better but Lambert chose the Australian, which would take him to Palestine to paint his beloved bushmen of the Light Horse—and their horses. He spent there the first half of 1918, working through Sinai and Palestine; and it was partly the brilliance of his work, partly his almost romantic scrupulousness in carrying it out and handing in, as his contract required, all his sketches and drawings made in the field—117 in number, exclusive of pocket books and notes—that caused Captain H. C. Smart of the High Commissioner's Office to recommend him to me for our Mission to Gallipoli. I had crossed from France to London mainly to see him, and at dinner at the Royal Society's Club he impressed on me that what he wanted was a clear military "operation order" setting out the work to be done. I received then, as on this Mission I always did, the impression that he looked on himself as a soldier fulfilling a directive, and that he would carry it out in every detail. In this respect his attitude was very similar to that of Wilkins.

Chapter
· III ·

TO CONSTANTINOPLE

"WHAT orders, skipper?" I can hear Lambert saying as—veteran that he was, and liked to be—he hitched his pack over his shoulder while the train pulled up panting under Southampton lights.

"Find the Embarkation Officer," say Wilkins and Balfour in one breath.

This time we found two. The first gave us embarkation cards for the steam packet and the second told us that this was wrong and sent us aboard a fair-sized government transport, the *City of Poona*. In view of the admirable efficiency with which R.T.O.'s, N.T.O.'s, Embarkation Officers, Landing Officers, the War Office, Australian Headquarters and everyone else concerned forwarded our small party, it would be ungracious to mention this were it not that we had reason to bless the man who sent us to the *City of Poona*. I wrote to Treloar, as the ship neared Havre next morning, that we had "a beautiful crossing on a very comfortable ship".

That sentence recalls much more than is on the face of it. In the four years of war I had become oppressed—eventually almost obsessed—with the consciousness that all the world's machinery for happiness was being misused for destruction. The little trawlers and occasional bigger craft that we had watched daily from the Anzac hills had reminded one of the constant traffic of busy vessels that one used to watch up and down the Australian coast, or from Dover cliffs, all carrying the good

24

things of the world to people who needed them and would send good things in return. But for four years that busy scene had been robbed of all pleasure by the knowledge that the trawlers were fishing for men, and the big steamers carrying men and guns, or the supplies for them, to destroy men and the things men valued. One had longed for the familiar scene of men and ships busy on their beneficent exchanges.

And here we were in that big, comfortable ship, with portholes open at last, and lights full on. She was still somewhat grim, grey-painted and carrying soldiers, tidying up, as it were, the ugly mess of war. But that feeling of oppression was gone—for ever, one hoped.

Of the Mission's journey across Europe to Taranto and Gallipoli my diary tells little. For four and a quarter years, since the first contingent of the A.I.F. sailed from Melbourne, I had kept a detailed note of what I saw, heard and thought. Often, especially at Gallipoli, I sat at my diary during most of the night because that was the time of least interruption. Sometimes daylight found me still at it—occasionally, by some strange process of mental effort, falling asleep at each full stop and then waking to write each successive sentence. It had required 226 notebooks. Others were added later; but having completed this series, and left it in store for the writing of our war history, for which it was one of several main sources, I could not just then face the task of beginning another series. Consequently, except for bare daily notes, the diary of the Australian Historical Mission dealt with business only—the solution of the riddles that we had come to solve.

So, unfortunately, I have little record of Lambert's stories, or Howe's, which were quite as good. They could always tempt Wilkins into discussion on the aims and happiness of mankind (in particular of the Eskimos, the simplicity of whose wants, he contended, gave them the highest degree of happiness); on the virtues of all races and

the futility of international strife and suspicion; on
music; on means of foretelling the weather and so perhaps enabling men to avoid the effects of drought that
he had known too well as a child. Both Wilkins and
Lambert had, in childhood and since, read what they
could in science—Lambert largely from a rebellious interest in the universe and whatever laws controlled both
it and him; Wilkins with the almost passionate desire of
applying science to help men everywhere. Once, years
later, I heard Wilkins criticised as an adventurer rather
than a scientist; but never was a more superficial judgment. You had not to live with him a day to discover
that the increase of knowledge for the benefit of men
was the burning impulse of his life.

At Paris we spent one very bright night, as harmless
as a Sunday-school treat, at the Folies Bergères—an experience which we were to repeat at Rome and Constantinople. We reached Italy by train via the Mont Cenis
tunnel. In Rome we experienced, as did most other
travellers at that time, certain results of the extraordinary
demoralisation among Italians after the war. We asked
the porter of our hotel to look after our luggage piled in
his office while we went round the city and to hear
Carmen at the opera. In the morning I found my
haversack neatly crammed and fastened as I had left it—
but someone (possibly the porter) had been through it
and taken my razor. I bought another razor and locked
it in my suitcase, which we left that evening with the
rest of our luggage in our compartment of the train for
Taranto, paying a porter to look after the compartment
while we had dinner at Rome railway station. On our
return Howe's suitcase and mine were gone—certainly
stolen by the staff of the railway, possibly passed through
the window by the man whom we had paid

The razor was easily replaced—I bought a third at
Taranto, and used it daily till it wore out a generation
later. But in the suitcase were also parts of my Anzac

26

diary, brought with us for reference in Gallipoli. Howe, too, had lost things that he valued. I accordingly asked him to stay in Rome for another day to see if he could retrieve them, and follow us to Taranto. The police advised him to issue a public appeal to the thieves to return articles of little use to them but of special value to us. He did so, but without result. Fortunately my lost diaries were copies—two other complete sets existed, and my memory was sufficiently good for most of the purposes for which the lost volumes were being taken to Gallipoli. A much more important casualty that occurred at Rome was the sudden sickness of one of our sergeants, Arthur Bazley. We were visiting St Peters when he was seized with a shivering attack. Pneumonic influenza was then raging, and with a very anxious heart I had to leave him at the Rest House for British troops in Rome. Fortunately he found there the wife of an old friend of ours, Colonel Mason of the 59th Battalion; she looked after him like a mother, and he was well and waiting for us when, two months later, we arrived in Egypt.

At Taranto, at midday on January 25th, we were transported from the train to a dreary rest camp four miles outside the town, almost a replica of the bleak, muddy camps we knew so well in France. But the arrangements made by the transport section at Australia House in London and their good friends at the Admiralty seemed to run like clockwork. No sooner had Howe arrived from Rome than we were embarked in the old enclosed harbour of Taranto aboard the British naval sloop *Asphodel*, and sailed, to our surprise, for Malta.

At this stage the smooth running temporarily ended. From the old basin of Taranto, crowded with craft, you pass through a narrow opening into the open Gulf of Taranto—that is to say, from still water into whatever the Mediterranean has in store for you. The officers of the *Asphodel* treated us with hospitality which I should certainly have described as extraordinary if, in common

27

with other Australians, I had not experienced it at the hands of British naval men whenever we came across them in that war. What the officers of the *Asphodel* had heard about our rather curiously assorted party and its mission, I do not know; but they gave up to us their wardroom at night as sleeping accommodation; fed us there (including our sergeant) at all meals; and let us fill the small open space outside it almost to the deck above with our baggage.

Unfortunately we were not long in a condition fully to appreciate this kindness. The wardroom of the *Asphodel* was at her extreme stern, exactly over her one propeller which, in the head sea into which we increasingly plunged, hoisted itself clear of the sea every ten or fifteen seconds, and seemed to shake itself—and us— much as a dog shakes itself on similarly emerging from water. The few of us who survived dinner felt pretty confident that we could weather any test. Wilkins had seen wild weather in craft of all sizes in many oceans, including the Arctic, and had never yet been seasick. I was camped near our baggage and was doing well until, during the night, I heard a crash of our cases as one of the *Asphodel's* most vigorous plunges brought down the pile of it. As two of the party had nested among it I got up to see if they needed help—and that was the end of me. It was a real consolation to learn from Wilkins that his record was broken that night.

The one who made the journey in most comfort was Lambert. He early made friends with one of the *Asphodel's* engineers, a hospitable Scot, by name Cameron, who first tried to settle Lambert's troubles with one or two stiff whiskies, and then gave him his bunk and himself slept elsewhere. "Was sick in one of the engineers' cabins," wrote Lambert afterwards.[1] "He seemed to regard it as an honour." George repaid the kindness in two ways—first with a pencil drawing of his

---

[1] *Thirty Years of an Artist's Life*, p. 99.

host; and second by speaking nothing but Scotch for the next four days—in fact until he said good-bye to our hospitable friend at Malta. When I say that George Lambert spoke Scotch I mean that he spoke it in such a way that Scots who heard him thought that he was one of themselves. For George, in addition to his power and habit of deep and keen thinking—especially in the No-man's-land between science and philosophy—had a capacity for mimicry greater than that of any human being I have met. It was partly the outcome of a sympathy which went beneath mere sounds and actions of men and animals and in some degree penetrated their feelings; and I am sure that, along with other qualities, it was intimately connected with his power as an artist.

It was on the journey through France that we had first noticed this one of his many facets. When he spoke to the train-guard or the porter, or to the waitress at the buffet, I observed that, though his French vocabulary was not large and to my mind he overdid the accent and gesture, the French people he spoke to were all excitement and friendly smiles. One told him his accent was perfect, and I think they were puzzled as to his nationality and why he ever seemed at loss for a word. And now, when some whim caused him to adopt the Scots' accent I am not sure that even the good Cameron realised that he was acting. For a good part of three days they could be found at the Malta Club with a group of cronies, all speaking—and drinking—Scotch. All members of the Mission were convinced that Lambert was born in Glasgow.

Lambert was (I afterwards found) a keen philosopher, outspokenly sceptical as to all formal religions. I read later that, on this journey, he put me down as "very interesting but not scientific. But," he charitably added,[2] "how can a man be scientific after seeing through the events of the last few years!" He was not, I think, so deep

2 Ibid.

a thinker as my other close war-artist friend, Will Dyson, who first introduced me to the (as he maintained) misunderstood conceptions of Nietzsche. Dyson hated militarism with an intensity foreign to Lambert's happier nature: I can remember Dyson, as we drove across the wilderness of the Somme battlefield, regaling us for a quarter of an hour with an imaginary speech by the Kaiser expatiating on the blessings that his Government was pressing upon a reluctant humanity. Dyson usually shunned high military circles even in our own force, though some of their members largely agreed with his views. But he simply could not feel comfortable there—he vastly preferred to share a snow-and-mud-covered shelter with Ben from Ballarat or Mike from Mullumbimby. Lambert revelled in both societies—he was as brilliant and eager with his stories sitting with cooks, grooms and batmen round the cookhouse fire as in the generals' messes. The extra stripes and stars exhilarated him; but so did the scars on men's hands, the patches in their old tunics, and the creases in their faces and hats. He became solemn only when he thought that the company expected, or required, some expatiation on the principles of art.

Waiting for the first ferry to the Dardanelles we spent three days at Valetta. We stayed at the Hotel Santa Lucia (nine shillings a day all inclusive!) and put in one night at the opera, *Fedora*. At garrison headquarters I happened to mention my instructions as to the Gallipoli graves, and the adjutant-general's staff suggested that I should visit those of Australians buried at Malta. They kindly drove me to the Pieta and Adolorata cemeteries, in which we found 202 graves of Australians who had died in hospital between 8th May 1915 (a fortnight after the Gallipoli Landing) and 27th June 1916, evidently from wounds or sickness incurred on Gallipoli. The graves were cut into solid rock and were eight feet deep: but three men had been buried in each, one above the other, with two feet of earth separating their coffins. Their names were on slabs of soft Maltese stone above each grave. As in all British cemeteries that I had seen, the officers lay among the men, and the graves were carefully tended. The Malta stone tends to blacken when exposed to damp and these graves would probably require special attention as time went on.

After another busy day[3] our party left in the small steamer, *Princess Ena*, formerly a ferry between South-ampton and St Malo, but for the last two years the regular ferry between Lemnos and Salonica. She would probably go on to Salonica, but at Lemnos we were to be transferred to some ship for the Dardanelles. After the wild journey from Taranto we basked in the Medi-terranean sun on the small deck, Lambert still in full uniform and spurs. I talked over with the Mission the programme for our search on Gallipoli. We would ap-proach Anzac from what, during the campaign, was the Turkish side, our ship probably calling at the small harbour used by the Turks opposed to us at Anzac (it was only three miles behind them). There we would drop our main party to pick up tents and a few helping hands whom Colonel Richardson of the Light Horse had been asked to provide. While this party set up camp at

3 I spent it in writing a report for General Brudenell White on Australia's claim to a share in the profits of the War Office Cinema Committee—a claim based on the refusal of the British command in France to let us operate our own cinema until almost the end of the war. The War Office eventually treated Australia most generously in this; but the cinema industry, to which the War Office left the carrying out of all the technical tasks—or possibly Australia House which should have supervised the work—let Australia down quite shockingly. From parts of the British film (taken of our troops and theirs in France) an Australian film had been carefully compiled, the cuts and captions marked and listed, and instructions left for its completion and forwarding to Australia. Evidently these were lost or mislaid, and, without explanation, an extraordinary hotchpotch, without interest, value, or even meaning, was shipped to Melbourne instead, and of course rejected there. Not till some years afterwards, when helping to edit the Australian film in Melbourne, did we become aware of this through finding the rejected rubbish. It had been intended to use the film in support of the war effort in Australia, and the receipt by the Defence Department of this nonsensical stuff had shocked the Minister.

Anzac, Wilkins would come on with me to Constantinople. On our return the Mission would work first, probably for ten days, at Anzac, and then for two days at
the old British and French positions thirteen miles away
at the toe of the Peninsula.

The *Ena's* voyage was broken by a night at Suda Bay,
Crete. Here we noted a large steamer canted over on the
rocks near the entrance. She was the ship from which
Balfour and I had landed on Gallipoli four years before
—with others of the staff of the Anzac Corps and 1st
Australian Division—the fine Atlantic Transport liner
Minnewaska (13,000 tons). She had since been torpedoed
and beached. To our eyes she seemed little damaged but
efforts to salvage her failed. We left Suda Bay next day,
and on the following afternoon, February 3rd, eagerly
gazing, we saw on the horizon the hills of Lemnos. Lambert, Wilkins, Buchanan and Rogers had not been at
Anzac, but the other three had described to them the
wonderful harbours of these Aegean Islands. Yet, as the
Princess Ena made for the entrance of the great basin of
Mudros, it was not on that opening that our eyes were
fixed, but on the horizon, far away over the open sea to the
north-east, where, under a line of clustered clouds, could
be faintly seen some low grey hilltops over fifty miles
away. They were the hills of the Dardanelles, and at that
moment I, for one, was poignantly homesick for them.

That scene was soon blotted out by the harbour
entrance, and we found ourselves passing swiftly in
through the channel, now free from the barrier against
submarines, to the great basin itself. It was filled with
a lesser gathering of ships than those we remembered;
but the same four windmills stood out on the bare hill
behind the small town, with another twelve, like a row
of toy blocks, studding the low distant neck that made
the northern end of the harbour. The last time I had
visited that neck was a few days before the Landing, when
the 3rd Australian Battalion from the old German liner

Derfflinger was carrying out a practice landing there. I had a mental picture of my brother, the original medical officer of the 3rd, standing on the beach with his little button-like peaked cap (such as our officers and men mostly wore in those days) and his pack on, among the crowd of Diggers waiting to return to their ship; his concern at the moment was to ship safely back to the *Derfflinger* one of the landing party to several of whom the Greeks had managed to sell raw cognac.

On the second of the Mission's two days at Lemnos, which we spent in visiting the war cemeteries and walking to the old hot baths and the twelve windmills, we strolled back to camp to find an urgent message from the military landing officer: the *Ena* was to sail for the Dardanelles and Constantinople in an hour's time. He had a steamboat waiting and our baggage already on it. Four years earlier three of us, Howe, Balfour and I, had been in the ships that left Lemnos at about the same hour on just such a beautiful evening. The *Princess Ena,* apparently in order to avoid the British minefields laid since the campaign, must have taken during this night the same course that we had followed on our way to the Anzac Landing, for at dawn next morning, February 6th, Imbros Island with its rugged volcanic hills was close on our right and, after we had doubled round the northern and eastern sides of it, there opened up, ten miles to our left—that is, to the east—the dim coastline we knew so well. On some spot, indistinguishable at that distance, on the slopes directly to our left, was the patch of a square mile or two that for eight months had been our home. Just north of it would be the old British foothold at Suvla Bay. The *Ena,* however, headed south to pass round the end of the Peninsula thirteen miles ahead, where its toe formed the northern entrance of the Dardanelles Straits and the British and French had had their main foothold. The *Ena* rounded it quite close, passing the old ships that had been sunk during the occupation so as to form breakwaters at the two main landing places. At the second of these, "V" Beach, close beneath the cliffs south of Cape Helles, the old French battleship *Massena* linked with a transport still formed the northern arm, and the big, stubby collier, *River Clyde*, stranded high in shallow

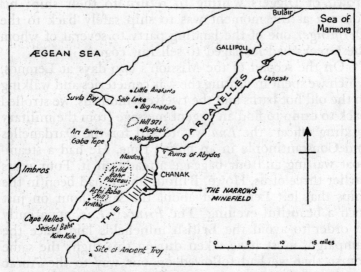

THE GALLIPOLI PENINSULA AND THE STRAITS

water, the southern. Her starboard side, which was all to have been painted yellow to puzzle the Turkish gunners firing from the southern shore of the Straits, was still piebald—the hurried job had to be left unfinished by the painters whom we had seen four years ago dangling on ropes from her bulwarks in Lemnos harbour. Just beyond her, on the actual turning into the Straits, were the stone walls, battered by our fleet, of the fortress built by the Turkish sultans some 250 years before to help in closing the Straits to unwanted ships. Next we passed the trenches held by the French during the campaign, still clearly visible, straggling all over the gentle spur that led down to the small Kereves Gully; and, beyond them,

34

and on the spur after that, the Turkish trenches, line after line. Here, behind each high shoulder of land that swam by, were shelves and ledges, huts and shelters, that had once held the Turkish garrison and its reserves, their stores, hospitals and headquarters. All were now, of course, deserted, but otherwise apparently unchanged, and our hopes rose high of finding Anzac also as it had been.

Next the steep, dark side of the Kilid Bahr Plateau, the massive upland which lay like a huge fortress, four miles square, between Achi Baba (the never-achieved first-day goal of the British at Helles) and that other hill-mass which we also failed to capture at Anzac. Near the far corner of Kilid Bahr, where the Straits closed in to the Narrows, stood on either side of the water the old white stone fortresses built there by the Turks 450 years before, only nine years after they drove the Greek emperors—the last vestige of the Roman Empire—from Constantinople. The shores on either side now closed to within almost a quarter of a mile of the *Ena*, which was moving up what seemed to be a long river channel between the rugged, barren Peninsula on the left and the gentler, cultivated coast of Asia Minor, backed with high mountains of Asia, on our right. The two massive stone castles were like teeth in the jaws through which any naval threat against the sultans must penetrate. The northern one, Kilid Bahr ("Closure of the Sea"), a massive keep within a heart-shaped wall, appeared to be un-damaged by the bombardments of the campaign; the southern, Kale Sultanieh ("Sultan's Fortress"), seen across the water low and square against the houses of Chanak, had a big shellhole through its battlemented keep. Beside these ancient defences, and at intervals each way along both shores of the Straits, were the unobtrusive grassy ramparts of modern forts which, together with the minefields and mobile batteries, had of course been the real defences in the recent campaign.

We had known well what we should see, but had hardly time to take it in before Kilid Bahr was sliding past, opening up on the left the lower ground which led to Anzac hidden on the other side of the Peninsula. But the *Ena* headed to the right where lay the white buildings, gardens, and piers of Chanak, the little town of 20,000 people on the low Asiatic shore, where during the campaign the German, Liman von Sanders, commanding the Turkish Army at the Dardanelles, had his headquarters. A tender took us ashore.

Here a disappointment awaited us. The two Anzac regiments, 7th Light Horse and Canterbury Mounted Rifles, which we expected to find on the Peninsula, had gone. At headquarters of the 28th British Division at Chanak, where I reported, we heard that our troops were too thinly clothed to withstand the intense cold of winter there following the heat of Palestine. After a short stay in old Turkish huts at Kilid Bahr, they had been withdrawn.

Chanak looked to us like a small Italian sea-side resort, with its comfortable, rather flimsy, villas backing on to the Straits, private piers, boat- and summer-houses in the jimcrack, fretwork Turkish style, and a few cheap shops. The more crowded centre of the town had been burnt by naval shelling in the campaign. One fairly comfortable villa had been turned by the British occupation force into an Officers' Rest House, temporarily named the "Red Lion"; and leaving our main party here for the gear and other help which the 28th Division, instead of the 7th Light Horse, was kindly providing, Wilkins and I went on by the *Ena* to Constantinople. As we passed up the Dardanelles I could see several of the summits about Anzac looking at us over the nearer hills, as our army—if we had won them as intended—would have looked down on vessels moving there. Towards dusk a little farther on we passed, near a gap in the hills, the small harbour of Ak Bashi, where the Turks had landed a great part of

THE ANZAC HILLS FROM THE TURKISH SIDE, SEEN FROM CHANAK, 2nd FEBRUARY 1919

The distant hills, seen above Kilia Liman and Mal Tepe, are part of the main range which the Anzacs tried to capture. The part of the range captured in April 1915 is farther south, hidden by the ridges behind Maidos, but the first visible height, Chunuk Bair (above the K in Kilia Liman), was the scene of fighting in August. The two low summits north of this, Q South and Q North (above the word Liman) were not taken though troops fought on their farther side. Hill 971 was never approached, though the crest as far as that point was part of the first day's objective on April 25th and was again aimed at in August.

Mal Tepe was to have been seized by the Anzacs in a thrust immediately following the original landing. Actually it became the temporary Turkish headquarters when their reserves hurried south from Gallipoli after the landing. Mal Tepe and the hills shown farther north were all spurs of 971. Boghali, between which and Maidos lay Mustafa Kemal Bey's division, the 19th, is in the valley immediately behind Mal Tepe.

their troops and supplies for the campaign. From the water beside the pier there stuck up the masts of two sunken steamers; and high above, on a promontory against the skyline, lay the irregular ruins that once were the Greek city of Sestos where, 2400 years before, another army—of Xerxes I of Persia—took (it is said) seven days in crossing the double bridge of boats which his master-builders, after some of them had been executed for a preliminary failure, managed to establish there.

After steaming all night through the Marmora we reached Constantinople on the worst of possible days for real appreciation of it. It was February 7th, bitterly cold, blowing, raining, dull-grey, and so misty that we might almost have been entering London. Yet as the steamer rounded the building-covered hills and the gardens of the old Ottoman palace—with the great mosque, once cathedral of Saint Sophia and the centre of the Christian world, above and the battlemented and turreted line of the ancient Roman walls below—no lover of history could escape a thrill. After all, here perhaps for longer than at Rome, for longer even than the English or French nations have yet existed, was the home and centre of Western civilisation; and in that great church there still proceeded, though with a different creed and language, the daily worship which began there in the days of the Emperor Justinian.

From the quay, in the heart of the city, Wilkins and I drove up the winding modern high street of the European suburb of Pera where, only a quarter of a mile away, the old German Teutonia Club with its roomy grounds had been turned into a comfortable Officers' Rest House. The week that Wilkins and I spent in "Constant" (as all Anglo-Saxons in the Middle East then seemed to call it) was crowded with interviews; first with the staff of General Headquarters of the British forces formerly at Salonica (later known as the Balkan Army) under Lieutenant-General Sir G. F. Milne, and then with several friends in Constantinople whose advice would be valuable.

The British staff was helpful to the point of making the task of the Mission its own, especially Major Cameron of Milne's intelligence staff. I told him that there were many questions which I would like to put to the Turkish staff if I could obtain the privilege of doing so.

"It would be grand if you could get some Turkish officer, who fought at Anzac, to go over the ground with you," he suggested. I agreed, and he sent me to the Turkish War Office, in which two outstanding British intelligence officers, Lieutenant-Colonels R. Crawford and C. C. R. Murphy, were then working on terms of friendship with the Turkish General Staff. I arranged to leave with them a list of questions which Crawford kindly undertook to have translated and then to lay before the Turkish staff with an intimation that I would be grateful if it could see its way to supply answers. At the same time Cameron asked General Milne if he would kindly write to Kiazim Pasha, Chief of the Turkish General Staff, inquiring whether some Turkish officer might, "on terms of mutual respect", stay at our camp and go over the battlefield with us.

"The Turks are very proud of their record there," Crawford and Cameron told me, "and as a historical record they compiled a splendid set of maps—far better and bigger than any of ours. It was done after the campaign, by their own survey corps under Shefket Pasha. You simply must have a set of those—you mustn't rely on ours!" And these grand fellows undertook there and then to see if they could get them for us. It was only after all this that they thought of asking for my credentials, which I too had forgotten. The letters which I carried satisfied them and I cannot recall their being asked for again by anyone during the existence of the Mission.

That week in Constantinople it snowed heavily, but we barely had time to heed this. On the day of our arrival we noticed a few British troops on guard along the sweeping, rather stately high street, evidently keeping the way clear for some expected grandee; and then up the hill from the direction of the quay came several motor-cars, in the chief of which was General Allenby, whose army had conquered the Turks in Palestine and Syria. His entry to the Turkish capital attracted little more attention than would the humblest funeral, but despite his victorious march from Sinai to Syria, he was not the Allied commander in Turkey itself. On the following day the same street was lined on both sides with blue-coated French infantry. The paths and the windows of the houses were crowded with excited people. The wide sweep of the cobbled high road had been sanded, and up the curve came, this time, a procession of which the leading figure rode a stout, champing, ambitious bay cob, with tautly arched neck and a French soldier on each side holding the horse's bit. On the cob—and rather like it—with broad back, square shoulders, and a huge square chin—and with one hand in his waistcoat and the other loose at his side, sat, like a conqueror of old, General Franchet d'Espérey, the French Commander-in-Chief from Salonica ("Desperate Frankey" the British here called him). He was then still the Allied Commander-in-Chief in the Constantinople area. From many windows Greek girls showered flower petals. Every other house seemed to be flying the blue and white Greek flag—indeed it was impressively predominant in Constantinople in those days. The Greeks have always been numerous there, and friends in Constantinople told us that the Greek people had hopes (as they naturally have had ever since their metropolis was taken from them 450 years before) that it would be returned to them. They were therefore doing all they could to impress the Allies with the strength of their claim or hopes.

There was no doubt of their excitement. But I wondered whom it was that Franchet d'Espérey was trying to impress; there could hardly be a greater contrast than between his entry and Allenby's.

The French had about one division in Turkey to enforce, if necessary, the Armistice terms, while the British had two—the 27th and 28th—the 27th being out near the Caspian with the object, I think, of limiting a possible advance by the Bolsheviks in, or from, the oil region. We liked the French soldiers wherever we met them; the officers were happy, pleasant fellows, and there was something in their company that reminded one of an Australian mess-table. Yet despite Franchet d'Espérey's pomp, and the absence of anything like it on the British side, the French army was losing reputation in the Middle East at that time owing to its rather high-handed way with the inhabitants, and the British Tommy, who went quietly amongst the people, asked for little, and carefully paid for everything that he got, was winning respect and popularity wherever he went. We heard later that even the Syrians, who had many ties with the French, were beginning to wish that theirs was a British connection.

Wilkins and I saw Allenby again during that visit. We were in Saint Sophia, gazing up at the wonderful dome and pendants where the mosaics of the old Christian church—huge figures of seraphim, with their wings hiding their faces, feet and bodies—were most clearly discernible under the Turkish whitewash. Everywhere you could see the relics of the Christian symbols, the figure of Christ and of the cross, the figure of the Virgin over the main entrance, defaced but easily recognisable. In the vestibule were camped Turkish troops, with their camp-fires burning—a regular garrison—a precaution taken, I believe, in the expectation that the Greeks might rush the great building and hold a Christian service there. As I say, we were beneath the dome, gazing at the mosaics, when three British officers came silently to a point near us, and they, too, stood for a while gazing up. One was Allenby; you couldn't mistake his clipped moustache and big chin—not an unworthy successor of other conquerors who must have stood there, beginning with Belisarius. I wonder if any ever stood there as modestly as he.

We saw relics earlier than Christianity in the great church too, for Justinian built it partly with the loot of temples, including tall green marble pillars from Greek Ephesus.[4] Not far from Saint Sophia's, in the New Museum in what used to be the Sultan's gardens, was the most perfect example of painted Greek sculpture that I had seen. It is said that all Greek sculpture was painted or tinted, but usually the paint has long since disappeared. However, on the so-called "sarcophagus of Alexander", a large, temple-shaped, marble sarcophagus on which Alexander is shown hunting and fighting, the old Greek colouring remains, possibly toned down by age, and, to me, surprisingly beautiful. Also close to Saint Sophia's was the long park or cavalry parade ground, which, in the heart of the city, still lies open, as it was for century after century when the Greek people, divided in war and peace between the "green" and "blue" factions that cheered the chariot races on this Hippodrome, furnished history with the frightening spectacle of a civilisation that had lost its soul.

I had dinner with a Constantinople man, Harold E. Woods, who had served with us as an intelligence officer at Anzac. He was the son of a retired British naval officer who had lived in Constantinople and who became admiral of the Turkish Navy. Woods was now Food Controller in Turkey, and told me of the dreadful plight of the Turkish soldiers then returning to Constantinople for demobilisation. The Sultan's Government there was doing its best to carry out the terms of the Armistice,

---

[4] The four red porphyry pillars brought from the Temple of the Sun at Baalbek apparently date from 200 years after Christ.

after an initial period in which, as Captain Cyril Falls, the British Official Historian, states, Turkish staff officers in faultless uniforms and shining boots kept politely explaining why nothing that was ordered could be done That was being changed; soldiers, disarmed in Asia Minor, were arriving by the thousand at Haidar Pasha railway station just across the narrow Bosporus Strait from Constantinople. Many were starved and sick, and they were dying on the journey and even on the wharf at Constantinople, but, as always, with fatalism and without a murmur. Later, as will be told, we saw some of the background to these events.

I also met Brigadier-General W. H. Deedes, whom I had known as a captain on Sir Ian Hamilton's intelligence staff, and Philip Graves, a fellow correspondent in Cairo in 1914-15. I almost blush to quote the following from a letter to my parents: "He (Graves) told me how a certain Lawrence—a mere boy, who used to be junior intelligence officer in the Cairo War Office when we were there . . . has developed into Colonel Lawrence who ran the Arabs during the war—organised the army for the King of the Hedjaz and ran their whole campaign." The diary adds that Lawrence had been a junior member of a party of archaeologists who were carrying out excavations in Arabia before the war, with whom was another Oxford man, C. L. Woolley. "Woolley," I was told in Constantinople, "was taken prisoner on some wild little expedition on his own with two or three men in a rowing boat against a gun on the Syrian or Palestine coast."[5] I had seen them early in 1915 when they were sitting side by side in the Intelligence Office collating information as to the Turkish columns which were then several hundred miles away dragging big guns and iron pontoons across the Sinai Desert to attempt the

---

[5] My note about them is inaccurate in other respects and may not be accurate in this—a fact for which my memory, and not my informants, would be to blame.

43

crossing of the Suez Canal. Lawrence, then in his early
twenties, with pale thin face and long, wayward fair hair,
seemed to me very young, academic looking and physi-
cally callow and delicate. I remember thinking them
plucky and enterprising to tackle at once a job in the
army. I had never dreamed that this was the man with
whose name the world was beginning to ring. Woolley
(now Sir Leonard) also has achieved fame as an
archaeologist.

I was now anxious to get back to the Mission. Our
"two days" in Constantinople had already strung out to
nearly a week. As a final task I wrote out over a hundred
questions on which I hoped for information from the
Turkish staff and Crawford told me that, if we returned
there after our work on the battlefields, he hoped that
the answers might be ready for us. The Turkish maps,
which would help us at Anzac, he would try to send
us by the Turkish officer—if an officer was lent to us.
Meanwhile the weather had been bitter, with heavy
snow. Wilkins and I at "Constant" noticed it little; the
few gaps in our days we filled in partly with morning
or afternoon tea at a pastry shop near the Teutonia Club,
where a tall, handsome Greek waitress reserved for us
every day a delicious sweetmeat—Wilkins thought it was
made from mare's milk; and one vacant evening we spent,
as long as we could stand it, at the local music hall, a
tawdry French and Greek place. But we had visions of
the rest of the Mission perhaps already in camp at Anzac
amid the snow storms. Accordingly we secured berths
in the British steamer *Kapurthala,* kicked our heels
aboard for a day, and arrived at Chanak on the 14th to
find our party just embarking on one of the steel motor-
lighters that had been used for the Suvla Bay landing,
and was now to ferry them across the Straits.

ANZAC
THREE YEARS AFTER

GREAT was the excitement of our party that day. The delay had been trying for those held idle in Chanak. "Snow, blizzards, ice and general discomfort," wrote Lambert to his wife. "No coal or wood, and a damp, gloomy, fifth-rate house called the Lion Hotel." Yet he found the southern side of the Straits "very beautiful and fertile" and "the Turks a most murderous looking lot, awfully like Gilbert and Sullivan opera". Moreover on at least one evening the party were guests at what Lambert described as "a jolly good imitation revue by remarkably able soldier actors" of a 28th Division concert party. Also Lieutenant C. E. Hughes—henceforth a fairy godfather of our Mission—had come over from his small Anzac section of the Graves Registration Unit; and, with his help and that of Major-General Croker of the 28th Division—and particularly of Major Collis of the divisional staff—Balfour had managed to obtain, from that hospitable division and the Graves Registration people five good riding horses, a limber, four mules, and eight British soldiers to help us as grooms, working party, and cook. It was something like a small expedition that disembarked from the old steel motor-lighter and made its way a couple of miles northward along the coast-road between the Narrows and Kilid Bahr heights to the old Turkish hospital camp at Cham Burnu, which the Light Horse had recently left and French troops had taken over. We slept there that night—the Graves Registration

Unit, whose "headquarters section", under a New Zealand officer, Captain C. V. Bigg-Wither, was at Kilid Bahr, kindly lending us a second limber to carry part of our gear, photographic supplies, stationery rations, forage and firewood, in the morning.

At dusk we had noticed four crosses not far from our camp and, walking over to them, found a large Turkish cemetery with the graves of, apparently, four Christians (marked by crosses) and about 3000 Turks. Turkish cemeteries we could usually recognise at a distance by the few thin cypresses near which you would presently descry the grey wooden monuments, like small totem-poles, standing at the angles of pins on a pincushion. On the crosses in this cemetery we made out the names of three German "Pioneers" (military engineers) and one Greek doctor. The presence of only three German graves among those of 3000 Turks was evidence that the average Australian soldier during the campaign had overestimated the number of Germans in the forces facing us. Turkish officers, because of their neat uniforms and often fair complexions, were, when seen, almost always assumed to be German.

On the morning of Saturday, February 15th, the Mission set out for Anzac, Hughes having come to help us complete our kit and guide us over. He was a tall, thin, breezy Tasmanian, country-bred and gifted with that easy confidence in tackling men and situations that seems to be more easily acquired in the Australian bush than in most environments. We wound along the coast road, "with the full marching outfit, mule teams and limbers, pack mules, chargers and the whole issue, quite a picturesque little lot," wrote Lambert[1] who, with revolver on hip, could imagine himself on a filibustering expedition. Skirting a small plain enclosed by a northern outlier of the Kilid Bahr heights, and passing the Straits-side village of Maidos—a small Greek town in which the

---

[1] See *Thirty Years of an Artist's Life*, p. 101.

fires started by our battleships' guns had left only half
a dozen houses standing (I well remember seeing the
smoke streaming over the hills from that direction a few
days after the Landing)—we came round a steep promontory to the gentle green lowland, a mile or two wide,
leading sharp to our left to Gaba Tepe and Anzac, just
over four miles across the Peninsula. Close ahead, beneath the nearest hills, lay the tiny Straits-side port of
Kilia Liman, and here we turned off at right-angles, our
track winding across the lower, gently sloping ends of
the rugged scrub-covered hill mass to the north of us
which had been the goal of our Anzac efforts. Quite soon,
after crossing a couple of these lower rises, we came in
sight of the longer and more rugged and prominent
spur on which, from beginning to end of the campaign,
the Turkish defence at Anzac had been based. Most of
the Turkish guns used to fire from behind its crest, and
for that reason we had quickly named it Gun Ridge;
but looking back to the early days of the expedition,
when this, the third ridge from our landing beach on
the Aegean Sea, had been the objective set for most of
our troops on the first morning, we thought of it as
the Third Ridge. But it was never ours; from the first
morning the front had ebbed back on to the top of the
second ridge from our landing place. The Turks also
had reached the Second Ridge that evening. The two
sides then, and for the rest of the campaign in this sector,
had faced each other across the top of it; and along it lay
the trench systems of both sides, ours on or cresting
the almost precipitous western slope; the Turkish on
the somewhat less steep fingers and ravines of the eastern
slope. The Turkish reserves and headquarters and guns
had occupied the Third Ridge; and there it now lay
before us, rugged and scrub-covered, its long even crest
forming the horizon just as, when seen from the other
side during all those months at Anzac, it had formed the

main barrier closing us from all view of the Straits (though
we could see the mountains of Asia beyond).

Part of the way up Third Ridge now lay a small
camp. It was that of Hughes and his Australian section
of the graves unit—and it was a piece of Australia, popu-
lated by breezy, hearty light horsemen, among them
Sergeant Woolley, another engineer, who was then assist-
ing Hughes. Hughes insisted on our having some tea
with them, and then, as I wished to camp nearer to the
old Anzac lines, took us over the hill and down into
the long Legge Valley separating the Third Ridge from
the Second Ridge. Here, on the green flat just this side
of the creek that edged the foot of the Second Ridge,
was a well near which we could conveniently camp.

As we topped Gun Ridge to look down into this
valley, and saw before us for the first time the rear of
the Turkish lines that had faced us so closely all along
the Second Ridge, my heart bounded. The place seemed
to have been abandoned only yesterday. There, crowd-
ing the eastern slope of Second Ridge opposite, were the
shelves on which the Turkish supports and reserves had
been crowded; the huts, stablings and water tanks behind the deeper slopes; the maze of rear trenches leading
up towards the front on the hilltop. The whole side
of the ridge was scarred with them and with the paths
leading to them. I at once recognised the main knuckles
opposite us as the two halves of the 400 Plateau, a height
very famous in the history of Anzac, the southern half
being the scene of two terrific fights, first at the Landing,
and three and a half months later when we made our
second great attempt. On the top of that hill in the early
days of the campaign there stood a single dwarf pine-
tree,[2] which was soon destroyed but gave its name to the
hill, Lone Pine, by which also the second of those battles
was known. I saw now, with something of a shock, stand-

---

[2] A pine from seed found there now grows near the War Memorial at
Canberra.

ing out near the site of the vanished tree, a white obelisk
—a monument (Hughes told us) put up by the Turks
to mark the spot at which they had stopped the terrific
August thrust. Away on the ridges nearly a mile beyond
it, at The Nek where also we had been stopped, we could
see another monument (and we afterwards noted a third,
near North Beach). Obviously the Turks were very
proud of their achievement. And, we reflected, those
who stopped the invading spearheads on Gallipoli well
deserved commemoration as soldiers and patriots.

I had a vivid memory of having, from one of our
loopholes near where the Turkish memorial now stood,
had a glimpse of this rear slope of the plateau, crowded
with shelters which had been hidden from us before the
Lone Pine assault in August 1915. The Turks had not
yet realised that we could see them there, only 350 yards
away, and, beside me, that fire-eater, Lieutenant-Colonel
"Pompey" Elliott of the 7th Battalion, was sniping at
some inoffensive Moslems—probably cooks or batmen at
some headquarters, who were surprised by the sudden
crack of bullets at their kitchen door. In memory I could
still see two of them, with their bronzed cheeks and
khaki skull-caps, peering foolishly towards us over a
water cask under a low brush roof. Luckily for them
Elliott was not one of our regular snipers.

It was on the green flat at the foot of this remembered
slope that the Mission was to camp. Balfour was in
charge of the camp, and as he had ample help I left him
to get it up and rode on with Lambert and Wilkins up
a road which wound from Legge Valley on to Pine Ridge
(a southern spur of the plateau) and thence on to the
level summit of "the Pine" and into the heart of the
Old Anzac position. This road had been made by the
Turks since the Evacuation—previously there had been
only a few goatherds' or fishermen's tracks in the Anzac
area and this road followed one of them. Reaching the

plateau it led over part of the maze of trenches, which still deeply fringed the whole summit of the Second Ridge. We found the trenches worn by rain and a little overgrown but otherwise almost unchanged except that all wood—whether supports or roofs or other fittings—had been taken from them. This reticulation, still six or eight feet deep, and so intricate that Lone Pine looked like an anthill, would have made riding there (as indeed on most parts of the Second Ridge except along No-man's-land) impossible if the road had not crossed the trenches on bridges of pine trunks. On reaching the old No-man's-land, which of course lay along the whole crest of the Second Ridge, the road turned northwards along it, with the Turkish trenches lying on one side and the Anzac ones on the other, the two fronts approaching each other as one went northwards and the ridge narrowed, until at Quinn's Post they almost met. The summit of the ridge had always provided the only practicable track even before the campaign and the trenches now made it still more obviously so.

Thus as we rode northwards along this road the trenches were never, except where a gully broke them, more than about fifty yards away on either hand; and as we passed the northern posts in Monash Valley, with that dark ravine behind them, there was hardly room for a strip of scrub on either side of the track. It gave a strange thrill to ride along this space in front of Steele's, Courtney's and Quinn's where three years before men could not even crawl at night. The bones and tattered uniforms of men were scattered everywhere, though not so thickly as we found them at some points that I will mention later. Lambert and Wilkins were deeply moved.

"Much the most impressive battlefield I've seen," said Wilkins.

"At one place," wrote Lambert next day, "only about thirty yards were between the opposing Jacko and us;

a perfect rabbit warren, and too ghastly for me to people with the image of fighting."[3]

The road led on still following some original foot-track right up the crest of the range north of Anzac; but at Quinn's we turned and rode back along the same road to where, immediately north of the 400 Plateau, a gully runs in from the Turkish side so deeply that its end meets the end of the still steeper gully on the Anzac side, and creates a little nick in the narrow summit of the Second Ridge, bridged only by a short dipping neck or razor edge of gravel, too narrow to be entrenched. There existed, therefore, at this point, a gap in our line which could only be filled with a tangle of barbed wire. The ravine on the Turkish side was for that reason called Wire Gully. The line was quite safe, with strongposts to right and left of the gap; but I remember hearing of the surprise of our men, bivouacked on the steep Anzac side of the hill, when early one morning a Turk, festooned with his comrades' water-bottles, and evidently returning to the front after filling them, suddenly appeared in the wire close above their heads, gazing down as surprised as they. He dived back down the eastern slope and disappeared.

Down the more abrupt gully on the Anzac side of the wire our engineers had in the early days made a very steep but excellent road known as "Bridges' Road", and the gully also took that name. This track, probably following an old Turkish pad, zigzagged down to Shrapnel Gully, the deep ravine running behind most of our "Old Anzac" front line—Old Anzac being all the area that we held until the second thrust, in August. And now we found Bridges' Road almost as the final parties had left it[4] when, on the last night of the Evacuation in December 1915 they had padded secretly down it to Shrapnel

[3] See *Thirty Years of an Artist's Life, p. 102.*

[4] A photograph of this road during the campaign is in *Vol. XII,* plate 78.

Valley on their way to embark at Anzac Beach. From
Bridges' Road and Shrapnel Valley Anzac Beach was of
course invisible, the steep, scrubby side of the First
Ridge intervening.

Lambert, Wilkins and I found the road down Shrapnel Gully quite good, the drain dug four years before
in anticipation of the winter which we never spent there,
having kept the track passable. Even here it seemed a
presumption to be riding—of course the Indian pack-
mules and carts used to go up there with their loads
during most of the campaign; but except for an occasional messenger to Suvla Bay no one ever rode at Anzac.[5]
The commander-in-chief, Sir Ian Hamilton, and even
Lord Kitchener when he came, had to stump along the
beach and up the ridges just as did the water and ration
parties, the reliefs for the trenches (who mostly lived like
sand-martins on the hill-slopes behind the posts), the
stretcher-bearers, miners, engineers, beach parties, and
all other workers of that once crowded population. The
experience was obviously a great pleasure to Hamilton
and Kitchener, and it was Birdwood's delight. All three
could reach the top without stopping for breath. Yet
most of the slopes were too steep and rough for horses;
even our Mission in peacetime only rode to the general
area of each day's task and then dismounted and worked
on foot.

But Bridges' Road was passable, and so we wound
our way down to Shrapnel Gully, past the cemetery near
its mouth, still clearly recognisable as a graveyard though
all wooden crosses had disappeared; thence down to the
shore and then, turning northward along it, round the
low sandy rise of Hell Spit and, suddenly, out on to
Anzac Beach. This half mile of cove, with a big knoll at

5 There was one other exception; when a Turkish envoy came on horseback from Gaba Tepe along the beach to arrange for burial of the dead,
Major S. S. Butler, chief of Birdwood's intelligence staff, rode out to meet
him and bring him in. (*See* photograph in *Anzac to Amiens, p. 97*.)

each end and the much higher and steeper First Ridge[6] connecting and backing the two, had been known to all who were there as a hive of activity for eight months, a place as busy as Broadway or Charing Cross; scene of our Landing, site of our headquarters, stores, clearing stations, and all the transport and directing activities. Now nothing stirred except the waves gently lapping on the shingle, and a few of the piles of our old piers gently swaying in the swell. Gone, of course, were the heaps and mounds of stores, the tarpaulins, the piers and steamboats, the crowd of tethered small craft. Anything movable left by us had been cleared by the Turks, even the posts for the roofs of the few shelters that had possessed any, and the crosses from Hell Spit Cemetery just beside us. But there were a few of the stranded barges; and two white steel lifeboats—originally belonging to transports and used to land troops. There was the concrete condensing plant set up to provide water for the Gallipoli winter that we never experienced; and there was the hole made in it by a shell from "Beachy Bill" before it was ever used. Two features were new—a road leading around the foot of the slope from one end of the Cove to the other, and, parallel with it, a continuous belt of fairly strong barbed wire—both obviously constructed by the Turks after we left Gallipoli. The road followed one that our engineers had made around the Cove shortly before we left, but it had been lengthened both ways and now went on to Suvla Bay, four miles to the north. It was clear at a glance that in other respects the ground had not been interfered with. The rain had rounded a little the edges of our diggings, and the scrub had begun to increase again on the hillside that we digging shelters and grubbing for firewood had left half bare; but in the main Anzac was unchanged, and the hopes for our coming investigations were well founded.

---

[6] Generally known as MacLagan's Ridge—which culminated in Plugge's Plateau.

Naturally I was eager to discover, if possible, the niche where I had lived, worked, slept and eaten, from the first month of the campaign to the last. From the middle of the Beach we turned up Anzac Gully. Several ledges, one of which I recognised with fair assurance as the site of General Birdwood's old shelter, were on our left. We clambered two hundred yards up the washaway to the two tracks or ledges, one above the other, that used to hold the old 1st Division's staff. They were still bordered by the row of niches that had contained the offices and bivouacs. There, 150 feet up, each of us used to sit at his evening meal, looking out on those glorious sunsets over the sea and the distant mountain tops of Imbros and Samothrace, with the hospital ship in the Cove below us like a beautiful memory of peace, and, closer in, the crowded Beach. The shelters were now just holes in a bank, bereft of the roofs of waterproof sheet or iron, and of the biscuit box furniture. I found it hard to pick out which hole had been mine.

None of these dugouts were subterranean; but, wishing to show Wilkins that the underground defences of Anzac were as extensive as those he knew on the Western Front—indeed with our underground trench-lines they were by far the most extensive I had seen anywhere[7]—I bethought me of the big chamber prepared to safeguard the Anzac bomb-supply against both winter and the expected arrival of German or Austrian howitzers. Our bombs—crude missiles improvised from jam-tins filled with high-explosive and scrap-metal—had been manufactured by a group of seamen and Diggers lower down that gully, near General Birdwood's home. (Many Australians will remember the afternoon when a mule, loaded

---

[7] The underground line made in the chalk by the 3rd Aust. Tunnelling Company at Lens in France was the nearest approach to them that I had seen in France; the "Catacombs", a dugout made by the 1st Aust. Tunnelling Company under Hill 63 near Messines, to hold two battalions, would also bear comparison with the Anzac preparations for winter—but the latter were only slightly timbered when at all. A photograph of some of them is in *Vol. XII, plate 140.*

with two panniers of them, became refractory. He scattered everyone near with his heels, and then in a flash was himself scattered, together with shreds of metal and saddlery, about the sides of the gully.) The final bomb store was on the slope perhaps sixty feet below our row of shelters. I had seen parties working on it for some time before the decision to abandon Gallipoli, but being busy on our Christmas magazine, *The Anzac Book,* and in visiting the posts that we were soon leaving, I had barely seen the place though I heard that 40,000 bombs were stored there. Wilkins, Lambert and I quickly found the entrance, leading into a dark chamber in the gravel. Outside it lay an extensive heap of jam-tins, tumbled in all directions and embedded in a mass of what looked like apple jelly, which apparently had oozed from them. Clearly the Turks after we left had emptied the store, and if, as we guessed, the jelly was the explosive from the bombs, there seemed to be enough to bring down the gully side. We therefore struck no matches; and, as I knew that in hardly any of the extensive dugouts tunnelled at Anzac against the winter had the walls or roof been supported by timber, I would not allow our Mission to explore beyond the entrance of any of them. Some had fallen in; and to trust the unsupported gravel, without more experience than we had, would have been to risk burial alive. What happened to that heap of bombs after our visit I do not know.

As rain now began to fall we turned back to camp. On the road around the Beach we met two horsemen, coming from the north. They were Lieutenant W. H. James of the 1st Light Horse Regiment and his sergeant, who were photographing the area for the War Records Section and collecting some of the larger relics. James had done it admirably. He camped with Hughes and his work did not duplicate that of Wilkins, who used to accompany me on my searches and photographed the scenes and evidences of the particular events that we had come to investigate.

Back at camp the tents were up. The eight members of the Mission slept at one end of the marquee and messed at the other. Late that night we were waked by a distant wild chorus of yells coming from far up the range to the north. Hughes told us that the only Turkish military post now on this part of the Peninsula was a corporal's squad guarding a 6-inch gun which the Turks had emplaced on the first main summit of the range, known to us as Baby 700 (that is, the smaller and nearer of two summits each 700 feet odd in height). Half awake I wondered whether these men—or possibly some villagers from Anafarta or Kojadere—might be thinking of descending on our camp.

"There they go," said Lambert's voice in the dark. "Go on, yell you little blighters." And then in explanation, "My friends, the jackals. There they go again," as another chorus of fluty jabbering wavered down the valley.

"I'll get some of the little bastards yet," he swore. It appeared that they had often robbed him of his sleep in Palestine. As they were said occasionally to have sneaked off with men's boots we laced the tent door, but though they came nightly close down the creek I never heard them actually in the camp. So far as I know they had never been seen or heard by our men during the campaign; probably the shooting, which had hardly ceased from the moment of our Landing, scared them away.

Chapter
·V·

THE BATTLEFIELD
CEMETERY

As the Government had asked for the earliest possible report on the cemeteries at Anzac, and Hughes was anxious for me to see the problems, which were serious and pressing, I decided, though it was still raining, to go round the graves with him next day, February 16th. We started at the southernmost cemeteries and worked round to the northern ones.

The Anzac cemeteries had been begun on the day of our Landing on Gallipoli. The men who were killed in or leaving the first boats, which had clustered round the foot of Ari Burnu knoll at the northern end of the Beach, were buried that evening in the scrub on the foot of the knoll, just above the Beach; and the graves there were gradually increased as men were brought down dead or dying to the New Zealand Field Ambulance sheltered from bullets[1] under the foot of the Knoll. At the other end of the Beach, those who died among the vast crowd of wounded brought down from Shrapnel Gully and the 400 Plateau—a crowd that covered the sand there for perhaps a hundred yards by ten on the first afternoon—were similarly buried on the corresponding knoll (Queensland Point) at the south end of the Beach, above Hell Spit. Those who fell in Shrapnel Valley, under the small shells that pestered it in the early days, or whose bodies were reverently brought from the posts high along

---

[1] It was not sheltered from shell-fire; a shell once burst there during an operation, doing, however, no harm except by scattering dust. Men were sometimes killed there by shrapnel pellets.

the edge of Monash Valley (in which Shrapnel Valley ended) or on the 400 Plateau, were buried far down the Valley itself, near its opening to the sea, on the wide, scrubby inland slope of this same hill. Men killed in the first day's advances inland over the ridges lay, of course, where they fell, and the ebb of those advances left many dead behind the Turkish lines; but most of those who fell that day lay thickly in or close in front of the line held at dusk. Many could not be reached and their bodies still lay there when on May 19th the Turks threw in the greatest attack made by them at Anzac, in which 10,000 Turks were said to have been hit, 3000 being killed, in this same No-man's-land. Both sides were glad to arrange an armistice for their burial, and at 7.30 a.m. on 24th May 1915 all firing at Anzac ceased. A line of sentries of each side was stationed down the centre of No-man's-land, and Australian and Turkish burial parties (supposed to be the only other men allowed out of their trenches) sought out and buried the dead in their own half of it. The Anzac battalions chose for this job their biggest men, and we had the impression that the Turks did the same. The dead were buried where they lay, often in the rifle-pits that they had scraped. Several inconvenient trenches were thus filled in, especially at Quinn's, much to the relief of each side; and the Turks, who had by far the greater task, sometimes collected the bodies in the nearest washaway that scored the steep gully sides, and shovelled the banks of it over them. A Turkish captain said to General Godley's intelligence officer, Aubrey Herbert, who had largely helped to arrange the armistice and was superintending the arrangements: "At this spectacle even the most gentle must feel savage, and the most savage must weep." Another Turk pointing to the graves said, "That's politics," and pointing to the dead, "That's diplomacy." Before 4.30 p.m. when the time came to withdraw, the two sides in some places shook hands or exchanged cigarettes. Some Australian, says Herbert, called to one of the Turks near him, "Good-bye, old chap; good luck!" The answer came in Turkish, "Smiling may you go and smiling come again!"[2] Parties waved good humouredly to each other and retired to their trenches. The shot that resumed the battle was fired by a Turk at 4.45.

Those men of both sides who fell in No-man's-land during the rest of the campaign still lay in No-man's-land in 1919, very thickly in some parts, especially in front of Quinn's and Pope's Posts, and at The Nek. And several of the washaways filled in by the Turks during the armistice had been uncovered by the rains and were literally white with Turkish bones. One such gully lay on the side of German Officers' Ridge, in front of Steele's Post, but the most noticeable example was near the southern end of the line, where from the day of the Landing until May 19th Turks had many times tried to reach our line by charging across a small wheatfield on the summit of Bolton's Ridge. These Turks were swept away by machine-gun and rifle fire and by the field-guns of Major F. A. Hughes' battery, thrust right into the front line by the sturdy brigade commander, Lieutenant-Colonel C. Rosenthal, and their bones filling a neighbouring crevice could be seen a mile away as a broad white streak down the ravine. We could recognise the skulls of Turks by the flatness of the back of the head—a feature which, in life, had contributed to the common impression of our men that the Turkish officers whom they saw were German. "I could tell a ―――― squarehead anywhere," said one of the Beach hands to me as the Turkish major, Kemal Bey,[3] who came to

---

[2] Aubrey Herbert's account in *Mons, Anzac and Kut*, pp. *122-6*, from which these details are drawn, is the best description of this incident known to me. Photographs of the parties at work are in *Vols II* (*pp. 138-9*) and *XII* (*plates 72-3*).

[3] Not, so far as I know, the famous Mustafa Kemal, though it has been stated that the latter worked as a stretcher-bearer during the armistice in order to get a better view of our positions. Photographs of this envoy's arrival and departure under unusual conditions are in *Vol. XII*, *plate* 70 and *Anzac to Amiens*, *p.* 97.

arrange the burial-armistice, was led blindfold along the
shore to General Birdwood's shelter. The Turks had
not buried their men as well as we did, but now I noted
three Turkish cemeteries at Old Anzac—two on the
southern side of Wire Gully near its opening towards
Legge Valley, one of these well-kept, the other a single,
dishevelled trench. A third lay in Legge Valley itself, and
there were also a few scattered tombs.

At the southern end of Anzac a number of our cemeteries had gradually grown behind the lines wherever any
open space made a suitable site. Southernmost, high on
Bolton's Ridge where the flank neared the sea, was Shell
Green, originally a fair-sized cotton field on which at the
time of the Landing was a thin crop of bushes flecked
with the white cotton tufts. These were soon trampled
down, and when last I had seen the Green there was in
progress the only game of cricket that I watched at
Anzac, with Major George Macarthur Onslow fielding
at cover-point.[4] The cemetery was on a corner of it overlooking the sea. Another was in Victoria Gully, deep
down near the beach behind that sector. Two others
were high at Brown's Dip near by, where the 400 Plateau
began to sink towards the seaward slope of the Second
Ridge—the Dip used to be a regular hub of the traffic
that moved behind the lines along Artillery Road, especially when the Lone Pine battle was being fought on the
plateau only 150 yards east of it. Other cemeteries were
at the 3rd Battalion's "Parade Ground", a partly soldier-
made shelf a little farther north, behind the lines that
faced the Turks holding Johnston's Jolly; and just north
of this again the 4th Battalion's cemetery. The cemeteries
of Old Anzac thus ran in two chains, one far down near
the beaches, the other high up along, but just in rear of,
the front line on the Second Ridge. Along this ridge also
many leaders and others had been buried in isolated
graves or in groups of a few together.

4 This game is shown in *Vol. XII, plate 153.*

The little cemeteries at Anzac had been carefully tended throughout the campaign, crosses being made by men's mates, mostly from biscuit boxes, with the names painted on them or punched into small plaques of tin-plate which were then nailed to the cross. In December 1915, when it became known that Anzac was to be evacuated, the little enclosures were never without in-dividual men or parties, "tidying up" or otherwise tend-ing the graves of their particular mates. With most sol-diers the leaving behind of these graves hurt more deeply than any other implication of the Evacuation. By the fore-thought of Generals Birdwood, White and others, a care-ful survey of the cemeteries had been made. This task they entrusted, as they did many others where the per-sonal interests of the troops were a main consideration, to Chaplain W. E. Dexter, formerly a sea-captain in the rugged trade of carrying shiploads of Moslem pilgrims up the Red Sea.[5] With a surveyor from among the troops he carefully mapped the graves, and Hughes now had Dexter's plans and the general statistics of deaths at Anzac; more detailed records were then in Egypt. We now know that about 8000 Australian soldiers were killed in the campaign, or died of wounds. Of these about 3000 were buried in the Anzac cemeteries, and 3500 were missing—some of these buried during the May armistice, but yet more unburied, beyond the lines. Of the rest nearly 1000 died on hospital ships, and were buried at sea, and others died in Lemnos, Egypt, and Malta. But in addition many New Zealanders and British and Indian soldiers had fallen in the Anzac area, espe-cially in the second offensive, in the rugged hills north of Old Anzac, where an enormous proportion of those who died were missing. Thus, in the cemeteries and No-man's-land of Old Anzac there would be found not only the Australian dead but, perhaps, another 1200 of

---

[5] His son was chosen to write a volume of the Official History of World War II.

New Zealanders and British, and in the ridges north of Old Anzac possibly 3000 who were not Australians, including several hundred Indians. Moreover about 650 Australians and New Zealanders were killed fighting beside the British and French in the Cape Helles area at the toe of the Peninsula, and their case raised a separate problem with which Hughes intended to grapple later. The position as to Anzac was that, of approximately 12,000 men who had fallen, about a third lay in the cemeteries or in known graves, nearly a half were unburied in No-man's-land and about the ridges, and the rest were buried at sea or at the bases.

Hughes had only his small Australian section of the Graves Registration Unit and a 28th Division party with which to tackle his huge task. The Unit, the great majority of whose personnel was British, was also responsible for the Suvla and Helles areas where three times as many British soldiers had fallen. The officer in charge, a major of the 29th Division, was turning his attention first to Helles. The New Zealand officer attached to the Unit, Captain Bigg-Wither, who I have no doubt was eager to get on with the work on the New Zealand graves, had to remain in charge of the Unit's headquarters and supply centre at Kilid Bahr.

We started our inspection at Shell Green cemetery and Hughes explained to me what had happened to the cemeteries since we left them in 1915. I had already noted that even from a distance the main cemeteries were easily recognisable, and, as one reached them, the well ordered mounds seemed to have been tended with some care in the years of our absence. . . . Only, there was something strange about them. I knew that the crosses would not be there, but the mounds seemed much larger than those that we remembered, and all had similar borders —different from the little individual edgings built up by the hands of a thousand colourful mates. Hughes told me how, furthermore, as soon as he began to compare the cemeteries with the plans, he found no correspondence between these rows of big graves and the graves marked on his maps—the visible graves were much fewer than they should have been and the rows of them ran in quite different directions from those on the charts. Clearly the rows of mounds had been made up by the Turks in order to give the impression that the cemeteries were well tended. But this had happened only at certain well known cemeteries; of most of the smaller, out of the way ones Hughes on first arrival saw no obvious trace. Thus at Brown's Dip, where the old cemetery had two parts, the northern part had been made up with mounds, altogether out of place, but the southern part was covered with deep, thick grass. Only when you examined it closely did you discover that the lines of old graves were still there, marked by a slight unevenness in the ground, with the old wire fence still round them.

Hughes judged that, as soon as our army had left, the Turkish forces occupying the area had quickly used up all the pinewood crosses for their fires, just as they had stripped all dugout and trench timbers for their shelters. The graves thus became unmarked, except by the few inscriptions on stone or tin, and, as the grass grew in the following spring, most of the graveyards became hidden by it. At some time in 1916—possibly when the Pope began to ask questions—the Turkish War Office was led to inquire and, discovering that the cemeteries had disappeared, sent down in haste an officer and a working party to tidy them up. Where this party either remembered or discovered the sites, it probably tried at first to identify and mark with stones the individual graves. Finding this impossible, it made up the cemeteries anew, neatly but irrespective of the actual graves. Any inscriptions on stone or metal that were found it set in the centre of the graves. The Pope's good envoy came, and saw, and went away satisfied.

After this most of the cemeteries were left alone. But

at some time the villagers of Anafarta, four miles to the north near the Suvla area, and doubtless, individual Turkish soldiers also, had prowled over the whole area, searching and rifling the many bodies that lay out on the ridges, especially north of Anzac. Australian and New Zealand soldiers who took part in the Landing and the advances in August mostly carried their pay in gold coin in their pockets; and how long, in any country including our own, would the money upon dead men go untouched? Here in Gallipoli the prowlers had rarely missed anything of value, and in most of the cemeteries that they discovered they had dug up some of the graves—the bones were lying in the disturbed earth in or beside the graves. But the overgrown cemeteries, which the Turkish "tidying up" party had missed, were generally missed by these people too. This interference with graves occurred after most Turkish troops had been withdrawn; and, at Anzac, only a small proportion of the graves in any Australian cemetery had been touched. At the first cemetery that Hughes and I visited, at Shell Green, he pointed out to me that, in digging a new trench after the Evacuation, the Turks had avoided digging through a corner of the cemetery.

At the time of our visit Hughes had been trying to locate the actual cemeteries beneath the sham graves, and to find all graves in cemeteries that the Turks had missed; and he and his men had been extraordinarily successful. He found that, by probing with a steel rifle rod, the real graves could be easily detected, the rod sinking with little resistance where the grave lay but being strongly resisted by the hard ground around it. In this way he had been able quickly to discover the boundaries of each cemetery, whereupon his charts showed the position of each row and grave—running at quite different angles from the Turkish mounds in the remade cemeteries; and he then tested these rows and graves by the same method. He had thus succeeded in finding even the little outlying groups, and single graves, where their general location was known. He told me that he had already located 2500 graves, and would probably be able to locate with certainty four out of five of those of which there was any record. Practically all the cemeteries at Old Anzac had been thus rediscovered, and he was now searching for isolated outlying graves.[6]

I was able to gain some estimate of this work as we went round the two strings of cemeteries, near the beaches and on the heights. In Beach cemetery—one remade by the Turks—there stood in the centre the small bronze memorial tablet that had marked the grave of Captain Brian Onslow, Birdwood's fine young A.D.C. who was killed by a shell from Beachy Bill while sleeping on the roof of his shelter one hot night. (I still remember the burial there at dusk of another splendid member of Birdwood's staff, Major C. H. Villiers-Stuart, the chief of intelligence, who was caught by a Turkish shell when sketching at one of the posts. The groups silhouetted on the hillside against the evening sky would have given a rich haul to any sniping shell from Gaba Tepe promontory which jutted into the sea, clearly visible, two miles to the south. But in that light the Turkish observers could not see us.) The tablet to Brian Onslow was not in its original position, but Hughes had already located his grave among the 378 others in that cemetery.

As we went round, Hughes asked me if I could give him any detailed information as to the position of two single graves—those of Colonel Henry MacLaurin, the young commander of our 1st Brigade, and Lieutenant-Colonel A. J. Onslow Thompson of the 4th Battalion, two of the best leaders we ever had, both of whom were killed within three days of the Landing. As it happened, I remembered well the graves of both. They were high on the Second Ridge. Onslow Thompson had been killed on the day after the Landing when, in constant expecta-

---

[6] A grave was easily distinguished from other diggings by its dimensions and other signs.

tion that the advance would be resumed, his battalion
had mistaken an order for straightening the line and had
wheeled forward, in a brave but useless advance, right
across the summit of Lone Pine and on to the edge of
the northern lobe of the same plateau, Johnston's Jolly.
An hour or two later, just as the sun was setting, Onslow
Thompson, realising that the position reached was impossible to hold, had tried to walk across the flat surface
of the Jolly to the Australian line. Turkish machine-guns
opened (an officer who was near him still recalls seeing
the sunlight gleaming on the stream of machine-gun
bullets that sped across the plateau towards the setting
orb) and Onslow Thompson was killed. His adjutant,
Lieutenant R. J. A. Massie, carried him as far as he could;
and four weeks later, during the armistice, the body was
found and was buried. Soon afterwards the Australians,
who were constantly sapping forward to deepen their
foothold, cut one of their trenches almost through this
grave. A plate was then put up on the side of the trench
to mark it, and I well remembered seeing this during
frequent visits to my brother's battalion, the 3rd, which
long held this part of the line.

To reach the place I led Hughes up the steep Bridges'
Road and thence half-right through the old sap through
which I had often climbed to my brother's aid-post (he
had been wounded, but soon returned). The trenches here
and elsewhere seemed as deep as when we had left them
but the aid-post was now represented only by the widen-
ing of the sap. Next we passed another niche, that had
been the shelter of the chaplain, Dean Talbot of Sydney;
and then the 3rd Battalion's Parade Ground, a level
patch dug by our troops on the steep side of the valley
a little below the crest on which the maze of trenches
lay. The Parade Ground was probably the only place
where choral singing was heard at Anzac during the
campaign. The good Dean held his services there, and
my brother, always a missionary in any good cause, and

with an enthusiasm for music, sent to Cairo for some hymns and anthems and supported his friend by trying to train a number of his Diggers to sing them. I remember hearing music at only one other place on Gallipoli—towards the end of the campaign, in one of the deep gullies below Chunuk Bair, where a New Zealand battalion commander thought to enliven his troops one Sunday with a concert by their band. The instruments must have been specially brought from Lemnos or Egypt; but the Turks, opening at once with a field-gun somewhere behind the ranges, and feeling for the band with their shells, quickly ended the concert. The 3rd Battalion's Parade Ground, in the Old Anzac area, was much closer to the Turkish line than that, and church parade had once or twice to be stopped or postponed through shell-fire. But I think this was only the normal "strafe"; the choristers' bass and tenor, if the Turks heard them, brought not even a trench-mortar bomb.

My last visits to that Parade Ground had been at the time of the August offensive. As a prelude to this the 1st Brigade (to which the 3rd Battalion belonged) was to attack Lone Pine, which lay close in front of the next sector to the south. On the evening before the battle I found the battalion's officers gathered on the Parade Ground, their colonel, E. S. Brown, in the midst discussing with them the final arrangements for the attack. As I arrived he had just reached the question of the rum ration—should it be issued before the attack or after? "I believe," he said, "the issue will be a good tonic to them in their present condition" (they were very worn with work and sickness) "but I don't like the idea of giving it to them just before they go into action." He then referred to my brother, who said the issue should be made just after the fight, as a tonic for the tiring hours ahead; and so it had been arranged. Next afternoon I had watched the battalion and its fellows filing along the road to Brown's Dip[7] and then went with them into the deep

[7] A photograph then taken is in *Vol. XII, plate 104.*

trenches from which, and from a tunnelled line still further forward, the attack was to be launched. Within a few hours the Turkish trenches at Lone Pine had been captured, but nearly every officer that I had seen on the Parade Ground was killed or wounded—my brother and the Dean among the wounded, the Colonel among the killed. When a few days later I saw the Parade Ground it was empty, no men, no movement in the shelters around it; the 3rd Battalion had lost 21 of 23 officers and two-thirds of its men.

And there was the Parade Ground now, almost as I had seen it then. I led Hughes to where I believed Onslow Thompson had been buried, and then to where I had seen and photographed Colonel MacLaurin's grave, high above Monash Valley, the side of which here, just north of the gap at Wire Gully, was called MacLaurin's Hill. There, on the third day, he was sniped, not knowing that ten minutes earlier, 100 yards farther north along the ridge, the same Turks, firing from the head of Monash Valley, at least 600 yards to his left rear, had killed his brigade-major, Major F. D. Irvine of the Royal Engineers. Many of the Turkish infantry, after their two wars in the Balkans, were deadly snipers.

Within three days of my showing Hughes its general position he and his men had found this grave and later they found Onslow Thompson's. This day's inspection impressed me more than ever with the spectacular interest of this battlefield. "One gets the situation at a glance," Lambert had said; and as Hughes and I went round the cemeteries, and among the relics of men lying along the line of posts—Bolton's Ridge, Lone Pine, the Jolly, MacLaurin's, Steele's, Courtney's, Quinn's, Pope's, The Nek—it seemed to me that the finest memorial of these men was that they lay where they lay, marking the lines of that astonishing struggle. We did not know whose relics these were but we could ascertain the names of all men missed in that area. To an Australian soldier what did it not mean that, say, George Simpson fell at the Pine, or Frank Armstrong at Quinn's? If men could only be buried where they lay, and their names, so far as known, commemorated there, no one who ever visited Anzac could fail to appreciate their achievement.

This battlefield was even in peacetime a No-man's-land. There was not, and probably never would be, any human habitation worth considering in these wild hills; their denizens were one or two occasional fishermen, and a few herdsmen who at some seasons brought their sheep and goats down here from Bulgaria. Except to pillage what remained of our men or stores no one would normally be drawn to the place, and in this fairly dry area the signs of our occupation would probably remain for generations, not indeed so unchanged as we saw them that day but, especially if marked, easily recognisable.

Hughes, too, I think, was fired with this idea, that the whole of Anzac was one great cemetery, though, of course, his duty was to carry out whatever plan the Empire governments and Graves Commission should adopt. I was greatly impressed by the way in which this young Tasmanian was handling his task. At a time when the general work on the Gallipoli graves had barely been begun, he had already broken the back of the task at Anzac, which, when he and his few Australians came to the area a few weeks before, must have seemed overwhelming.

After seeing the last of the Old Anzac cemeteries—there were a few others on the ridges and flats to the north that I did not see that day—we trudged back through the rain to find the Mission's camp in Legge Valley equipped with numerous improvements. Wilkins, who needed a dark-room for his photography, had noticed a ship's tank among the Turkish shelters behind Lone Pine, and had it rolled down to the old well on the flat, where it thenceforth became his dark-room and workshop. Lambert had been out, sketching the gravel cliffs

from North Beach and found his way back at dark much
to the relief of his temporary English orderly, who, till
he could see the camp lights, thought Lambert (who was
a good bushman) had lost himself. Balfour, Buchanan
and Rogers had a cookhouse built near the tents of
our fatigue party, using timbers from old Turkish huts
below the Pine. Our Welsh cook would have much preferred to carry on his work in the old huts themselves,
but Hughes had warned us that they swarmed with fleas
in numbers unknown on our side of No-man's-land during the campaign. In our marquee a table and benches of
the same timbers had been set up, and it was there that,
after dinner and a talk with Hughes, I wrote my first report to the High Commissioner and the Australian Government. It was sent next day to Chanak for cabling as
follows:

"The Gallipoli graves have for the past month been
worked on by a small section of the Graves Registration
Union [sic] of which the headquarters is temporarily
under a New Zealand officer at Kilid Bahr, one small
party under a British officer at Helles and a second small
party under Lieutenant Hughes, Australian Engineers,
with Sergeant Woolley, his assistant, as surveyor, at Anzac.
The Australian party, working with great care and
ability, has located 2500 graves, of which all have been
identified. It will probably locate with certainty eighty
per cent of those of which there is any record. But it will
need much ampler means if the graves, once located, are
to be properly kept up. Reasons are given below for the
advisability of finishing the work quickly."

I then explained the disappearance of the crosses, the
overgrowing of the cemeteries, the "remaking" by the
Turks, the interference with a small proportion of the
graves, and the great success of Hughes in discovering the
old cemeteries.[8] The report states: "In the three Vic-

---

[8] The parts of the report here omitted are reprinted, together with
the final report, in *Appendix V.*

toria Gully cemeteries, and the Bridges' Road, Parade Ground, Scott's Point and Pope's Hill cemeteries all graves have been identified, besides numerous isolated graves on the hillsides; also small groups of four or five graves, of which I would have deemed the identification impossible had I not personally examined the spot."

Though the remains of our men lying in the scrub could be recognised as Australian by their kit, the names could seldom be determined. But the report states:

"In almost all cases it is known opposite which post men died. I recommend that the bodies of these men[9] be collected at the post before which they lie, and a simple monument be erected at each site, giving the name of the post and the names of all men known to have lost their lives before it.

"Hughes is now engaged (1) finding and (2) surveying in order to establish and record the position of each grave within a few inches. This, involving a constant check by the records, means a further three months' work. To put the cemeteries in complete order, and make up the few necessary paths, is impossible with the present staff, consisting of a fatigue party of a dozen British soldiers. The Anzac site appears to be the property of several Turkish and Greek farmers, who are now returning. The preservation of the trenches would need continuous labour of many thousands of men and is therefore quite out of the question. But the upkeep of a few paths around the Anzac position probably does not need great labour. While nothing can save the trenches, if the positions are marked, the lines will be recognisable for centuries.

"The site contains, besides the graves, the most wonderful battlefield in the world. It is also a vast store of relics ranging from lifeboats and gun-carriages to innumerable shell fragments from which the local proprietors will make profits unless the Australian Government anticipates them.

---

9 The meaning is: "of all our men found near any particular post".

"I recommend that the peace terms ensure that the complete Anzac site, including the Turkish trenches on the reverse slope adjoining it, be vested in the Graves Commission, with an Australian and New Zealand representative on the Graves Authority for this theatre, resident in Egypt or Constantinople; that all the cemeteries and isolated graves be kept up on their present sites; that memorials be erected at all posts as suggested; that Hughes be allowed by arrangement with the Graves Commission to choose a party of five Australian officers and N.C.O.'s and 100 Egyptian labourers to carry out the work (this is urgent because both storms and the returning inhabitants will inevitably destroy the present traces); that this party, besides finishing the above work, should completely salve the area for relics which will be divided between Australia, New Zealand and Britain (the relics, after disposal to museums, to be retained at Government museums for sale or exchange); that the cemeteries be planted with certain Australian plants, but so as to avoid alteration of the appearance of the battlefield; that arrangements be made for the Graves Registration organisation to answer inquiries without occupying those charged with the actual work; that arrangements be made, on completion, to send the relatives a photograph of every grave; that no visitors except those making official inspection be allowed until the whole work is finished; and that the completion of the work should be made as quick as possible and should involve arrangements for the best facilities for visitors—visits would possibly be via Chanak, from which, if the roads can be kept up, Anzac can be visited within a day during the summer months.

"I am indebted to Lieutenant Hughes for assistance enabling the making of this report; I will report later respecting the roads, and also as to the graves at Cape Helles."

Chapter
· VI ·

WE FOLLOW THE STEPS
OF THE LANDING

WHEN we went to bed on January 16th we little
dreamed that we had introduced a Trojan Horse into our
tent. But we soon discovered it. In the timbers from the
Turkish shelters there had come a swarm of fleas which,
having suffered several lean seasons since the Turks left
Anzac, leapt upon us as a gift from the gods. From that
night until we left Anzac our rest was tortured by them.
The flea powder for which we hurriedly sent to Chanak
seemed at first merely to embitter their attack. After a
few days, by thickly powdering the inside of our sleeping
bags and rubbing our bodies with kerosene before going
to bed, we managed to reduce their campaign to guerilla
warfare, but we never wholly ousted them. The healthy
exhaustion of each day's work on the Anzac ridges was
our salvation; we slept in spite of the enemy.

We all awoke eager for the first day of the Mission's
main task: this day we were to retrace the first steps of
the Anzac Landing. Howe was to show us, if he could
recognise it, his exact course of April 25th. Lambert
would come with us to obtain, for his picture (now in
the Australian War Memorial), a personal description of
the event; Wilkins would take, or note for future taking,
what photographs were required; Buchanan and Rogers
would mark, on the spot and afterwards on our maps,
whatever topographical points we managed to determine; and Balfour—who, besides being camp commandant, was collections officer, would gather, or note, what-

ever relics would be useful for the memorial collection. On every search all of us would help in the task of collection—as indeed most of us had already done in France; but he was now also responsible for listing and keeping the exhibits, and for handing them over to Lieutenant James, the photographer, who kindly undertook to take them to Australia together with the larger relics that he had already gathered for the Australian Government.

The question we had to solve that day was—precisely where did the boat carrying Howe's platoon touch the Beach? What was that party's course, from there, up the first height? and where, throughout the rest of the first day, did that small element of the original covering party get to? If we could once exactly place one boatload, I would be in a better position to place the rest, for it had been my practice, almost since I first began collecting notes of those events, to get each officer or man interviewed to tell me, incidentally, what other officer or prominent man he remembered having seen near him at each stage; and, as the names of these almost always cropped up in other narratives (often I myself sought out the men so mentioned and obtained their recollections), given a few certainties of place and time it was possible to fit together their narratives and reconstruct the story like a jig-saw puzzle.

Howe had been—or thought he had been, for the Landing was made in almost complete dark—in the second boat from the left of the small line of thirty-six rowing boats that had left the transporting battleships an hour before, two and a half miles out on the smooth sea, and had since been tugged by twelve puffing little ship's steamboats (three rowing boats behind each) to where the black shape of land showed suddenly high above them and very close. The steamboats had then cast off the crowded rowing boats, and the four seamen in each boat rowed it with muffled oars straight for shore. Howe's boatload passed the black form of a high jutting

KILID BAHR.
The old fortress, and the foot of the plateau behind it.   *G1858*

SUNKEN TURKISH TRANSPORT
and other vessels at Ak Bashi Liman, Dardanelles.   *G1780*

CONSTANTINOPLE, SEEN FROM GALATA TOWER,
looking across part of the Golden Horn above the Old Bridge. The mosques are
those of Sultan Mehmed and Sultan Selim.   *G1783*

THE MISSION DISEMBARKING AT KILID BAHIR.
Chanak in the distance.   *G1880*

KILIA HARBOUR IN THE DARDANELLES,
the nearest port to Anzac. The Anzac Heights from Chunuk Bair to Hill 971 can
be seen on the horizon, and Mal Tepe on the right.   *G1773*

HUTS OF A TURKISH REGIMENTAL STAFF
at the back of Lone Pine. These huts, which were opposite the Mission's camp, were of mud bricks and roofed with layers of pine logs, earth, and corrugated iron covered with more earth. Most had brick or wooden floors and fireplaces. In front stood a summer-house. *G1796*

BRIDGES' ROAD.
The nick of Wire Gully can just be seen at the top on the left.   *G2016*

SHRAPNEL GULLY.
The view is from near its mouth. The cemetery is in the left foreground.
Opposite is the slope leading to the Jolly. Beyond this comes in Bridges' Road
valley, running down from Wire Gully, of which the nick can just be seen on the
horizon. Left of the nick is MacLaurin's Hill, ending in the bare cliff of Steele's
Post. On the extreme left is the bare nose of Dead Man's Ridge, with the Bloody
Angle next to it, both held by the Turks during the campaign, and looking down
Monash Valley (the upper part of Shrapnel Gully) behind our posts. This valley
was our only line of communication to these post.   *G1772*

THE ROAD ALONG NO-MAN'S-LAND.
The view is along the Second Ridge southwards, from Quinn's to Lone Pine. In the foreground is the No-man's-land opposite the centre of Quinn's Post, with the Australian trenches on the right and the Turkish on the left. One of the shallow tunnels has broken through and made a hole in the road. The gully beyond this is Mule Valley, beyond which are the German Officers' spur, Wire Gully and then the 400 Plateau (Johnston's Jolly and Lone Pine—the latter marked by a double beacon). Monash Valley, which was very steep, lies behind the near crests on the right, the first indentation being the right of Quinn's Post, the next Courtney's and, near the skyline beyond it, Steele's. On the extreme right beyond Monash Valley are part of Russell's Top and then the First Ridge (Plugge's Plateau and MacLagan's Ridge).   *G1931 A and B*

ANZAC COVE IN FEBRUARY 1919.
In the foreground is part of the belt of wire erected by the Turks since the
Evacuation. In the middle distance Ari Burnu; on the horizon the hills beyond
Suvla Bay. *G2084*

VALLEY.
Third Ridge on the left.   *G2039*

LIEUTENANT HUGHES AND SERGEANT WOOLLEY
marking out graves in Brown's Dip Cemetery. At the back can be seen the old
rubbish tip.   *G1935*

THE BEACH CEMETERY IN FEBRUARY 1919
showing graves as remade by the Turks. *G2085*

MacLAURIN'S GRAVE
when rediscovered and re-marked by Hughes in 1919. MacLaurin was shot on
27th April 1915 on the crest close above the grave. *G1853*

TEMPORARY TURKISH MONUMENT
near the edge of The Cup, Lone Pine.   G1752

TURKISH CEMETERY IN CHATAL DERE
(behind Mortar Ridge).   *G1826*

TEMPORARY TURKISH MEMORIAL ON NORTH BEACH.
This was near No. 1 Post. (The farther of the stranded boats was the tug
Marsden).   G1808

THE HEIGHTS FIRST STORMED.
From the left to right, part of Walker's Ridge, The Sphinx, and part of Plugge's Plateau as seen from the top of the saddle joining Ari Burnu with Plugge's. This saddle is about half-way up the first height, which was first reached near the extreme right of the picture. A few boat-loads landing father north reached Russell's Top (the long hill behind The Sphinx) by climbing Walker's Ridge or the cliffs south of The Sphinx. *G1872*

ARI BURNU,
where Australians first reached the shore, as seen from the heights beside The Sphinx. The road around Ari Burnu point was made by the Turks after the Evacuation.   *G1835*

THE RAZOR EDGE
leading from Plugge's Plateau to Russell's Top. The cut paths and the ledges
for bivouacs of troops in reserve were, of course, not there at the time
of the Landing.   *G1871*

MONASH VALLEY,
as seen from the Turkish trenches next to Quinn's. The main front lay along the
heights to the left. The drain was cut in the autumn of 1915. On its left is the
valley bed, used as the sole avenue of communication till late in May when the
communication trench (partly V-shaped) on its right was dug. Monash Valley
turns to the right around Braund's Hill, and thence left again (as Shrapnel
Valley) direct to the sea.   *G1765*

cape immediately on their right, and then grated on the shingle about 200 yards north-east of it. The shape of another boat could be seen going in about 100 yards farther north.

Howe led our party—all, of course, on foot—to the exact spot as far as he could recall it; it was on North Beach, just north of the hill—Ari Burnu—that formed the northern boundary of Anzac Beach. Almost all the other boatloads had landed at the point of Ari Burnu or south of it. Howe's platoon had run across the Beach and thrown off its packs at the bank where the shingle ended and the low scrub began. The night sky had begun paling with grey dawn, and they could make out the form of Ari Burnu leading up to a much bigger and steeper hill—the lower was 150 feet high, the higher (Plugge's Plateau[1]) over 300. Just before the boats touched shore the silence and tension had been broken by shots, growing quickly to a continuous uproar, from the higher hill. Obviously the active enemy in this sector was on top of the higher plateau, though no Turk could be seen; and the men from that boat therefore began immediately to climb one of the scrubby ridges or ribs which led steeply, like a buttress, direct to the higher summit.

We followed Howe's track up this rib. He showed us from about where, as they climbed, they noticed against the growing dawn two men moving on the edge of the plateau above—the first Turks they saw; and then where, two-thirds of the way up, they came on a shallow trench (which we found) with a Turk lying in the bottom of it, whom they made prisoner and sent down the hill with one of them as guard while the rest climbed on.

After, in all, some fifteen minutes' stiff climbing through the low prickly holly scrub they had reached the top of the height. The leading men of other boatloads were then just reaching the same hilltop at other points.

---

1 Pronounced Pluggey's.

Plugge's Plateau—the hilltop—was a bushy, diamond-shaped flat, tilted upwards to their left front, and about the size of a small cricket field. It ended everywhere in almost precipitous slopes except at two opposite corners — the north-east, where a gravelly neck, truly described by its name, the Razor Edge, joined it to the next summit of the principal chain (Russell's Top) about 300 yards away, and the south-east, where it continued in the sharp, scrub - clothed MacLagan's Ridge, quickly dropping down obliquely through Queensland Point to Hell Spit. Behind the troops and far below, between Hell Spit and Ari Burnu, lay the curved shore of the Cove.

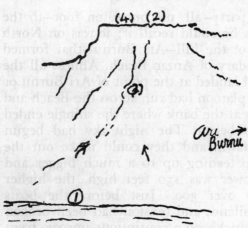

WHERE DRAKE-BROCKMAN'S COMPANY LANDED, BELOW PLUGGE'S PLATEAU

1. *Where L/Cpl Howe's boatload came ashore. Where its men climbed is shown by the two arrows above.*
2. *Point of Plugge's Plateau where two Turks were first seen.*
3. *Situation of shallow trench containing a wounded Turk.*
4. *Point where Captain Annear was killed.*

As Howe and his companions reached the summit, Turks were running back across it. A yard or two beyond its nearest edge lay a trench;[2] but many Australians on

[2] A photograph taken at this point later in the day of the Landing is in *Vol. I, p. 302*; and another taken at the same time looking down on the Beach at *p. 251*.

this first morning had the impression, which had been common in Britain and Australia, that in this war trenches might be mined. Consequently some of the men lay down behind the low parapet, firing over it at the running Turks, and a few of the Turks turned at the far edge of the plateau and similarly blazed at them. Howe showed us where, so far as he knew, about fifty yards to his left, Captain W. R. Annear, one of the first climbers to reach the top, was shot as he lay behind this parapet, the first Australian officer killed in the campaign. But these Turks were quickly shot or plunged down the farther side of the plateau in flight, and for the time being their fire ceased.

Most of the first wave of the covering brigade (3rd), comprising the thirty-six boatloads, had by then climbed the slope of the First Ridge at Ari Burnu and Plugge's or just south of them and the second wave, brought in on seven destroyers on a much wider front, was just landing. At this stage Howe's path, and story, began to separate from that of three-quarters of this covering force. Among the first eager officers and men to reach the plateau had been his company commander, Major E. A. Drake-Brockman. Seeing that the Turks on the plateau were making away towards the right front—that is, directly inland—and knowing that it was the task of the 9th and 10th Battalions, then reaching Plugge's, to strike out to the right front and centre respectively, he set himself to direct his own battalion, the 11th, to the left, north-eastwards, up the principal chain of heights.

Accordingly, after sorting out men of the 9th and 10th, and leaving them to follow the running Turks, which some were already doing, he ordered his own men to the left front where, for the moment, they would reorganise in the nearest valley, just beyond Plugge's Plateau. Howe showed us where he himself crossed the plateau to its north-eastern corner. Two shallow communication trenches wound across it, through the bushes.

It had been then half light, and two Turks jumped from the scrub, shot and mortally wounded a comrade beside him (Private E. A. Batt), and dived into the gully beyond. Reaching the edge the men looked down the almost sheer slope. The gully, 280 feet deep, was only a small amphitheatre, with the Razor Edge on the left forming its back, and its wide mouth on the right opening into the much longer valley (called Shrapnel Valley there, and Monash Valley higher up) which ran past the inland side of Plugge's Plateau, and ever afterwards formed the main communication avenue of the Old Anzac position. Its farther side was made by the steep, corrugated slope of the Second Ridge, which shut out all view except to the north, where rose the main chain, and the south, where lay the belt of lowlands backed by the massive Kilid Bahr tableland, and Gaba Tepe jutting into the sea, and the distant head and shoulders of Achi Baba near Helles.

In the long even skyline of Second Ridge there was clearly visible, opposite Plugge's, the nick made by Wire Gully; and, in the valley below, some retreating Turks could be made out trundling towards it along a faintly marked zigzag path through the scrub. Evidently that was the direction from which they were accustomed to come to their outposts on Plugge's and Ari Burnu, and, as usual with fleeing men, ran back along the track they knew best. Farther south, where the expanse of the 400 Plateau formed part of the Second Ridge, part of the 9th and 10th from the destroyers could be seen making up the side of the ridge.

Drake-Brockman's company halted for a moment at the north-east corner of Plugge's. Two Turks lay in the scrub beside them, one dead, the other with his brain exposed, but apparently conscious, reaching for his water-bottle. An Australian put it in his hand while Drake-Brockman tried to give him morphia. Two paths zigzagged down the gravel cliffs into the amphitheatre, and by these the company descended. They had spent, Howe thought, half an hour on the top, while Drake-Brockman directed other companies to their destinations; and now another half hour was occupied in reorganising in this gully (Rest Valley). While there they noticed the first enemy shell most of them had ever seen burst in a fleecy white puff and scatter its shrapnel upon the gravel of the Razor Edge.

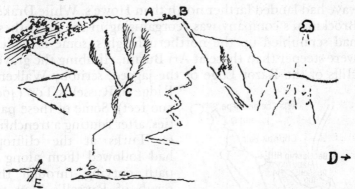

INLAND SLOPE OF PLUGGE'S PLATEAU, DOWN WHICH TROOPS NEXT PLUNGED

A. *Exit of Turkish trench on summit.*
B. *Where Drake-Brockman began to reorganise his company.*
C. *A dead Turk had rolled to here from the summit.*
D. *Where Drake-Brockman's company finished reorganising.*
E. *Where pick-handle was found, near creek-bed.*
(The sketch also shows two Turkish tents on the slope, and the first shrapnel shell throwing its pellets on to the Razor Edge as described to us by Howe. The pick-handle and tents had, of course, disappeared early in the story.)
A photograph of this height showing the paths is in Volume I at p. 260.

They were next directed by Drake-Brockman to various parts of the range north of them. The platoon of which Howe was a member wound out of the amphitheatre into Shrapnel Valley, and made to the left (north-

wards) up its deep, winding course towards those heights.
At the junction of the valleys was a pick-handle stuck in
the ground. Through the early fear of mines every man
carefully left this alone.

By that time the fight had, for the moment, passed
beyond these particular troops. From my previous inquiries I knew that a number of boatloads of the second
wave had landed farther north than Howe's. While Drake-
Brockman's company was reorganising in the gully these
had scrambled up the northern heights, some of which
were steeper than those at Ari Burnu, climbing the gravel
cliffs of the Razor Edge or the jagged, scrubby Walker's

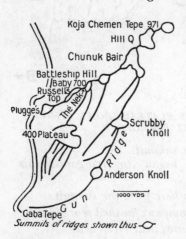

Ridge to Russell's Top (400-
500 feet). Some of these parties, after routing a trenchful
of Turks at the clifftop,
had followed them along a
path curving through the
scrub of Russell's Top towards the narrow green
saddle afterwards known as
The Nek, where the crest
veered east and then north-
east again up the first main
summit of the chain. This
was a rounded, rather bald,
hilltop which, rising to 700

feet, was known as Baby 700; a bigger summit known
as Big 700 (and later as Battleship Hill) lay hidden just
beyond it, and was the 11th Battalion's main objective
for that morning—and beyond that again, in the next
mile-and-a-half, were three other higher summits,[3]
Chunuk Bair, Hill "Q" (itself comprising two summits

---

[3] Strictly speaking there should perhaps be only one "summit" in the
chain—and that would be the highest, and last, Hill 971. But each successive
hill was definitely the summit of the ridges that ran from it on either
side as ribs do from a backbone.

of equal height), and Hill 971. The Turks were not immediately followed across the saddle; Colonel L.
F. Clarke, the elderly commander of the reserve battalion
(12th), who in spite of his fifty-six years had been one of
the first to scramble up the gravel cliffs, kept his men
well in hand. He was standing by the curved track at its
junction with another path which came very steeply out
of Monash Valley on his right, and was pencilling a quick·
report to his brigadier, when a shot from some Turkish
party invisible in the scrub on Baby 700 ahead killed
him. At the same spot other shots immediately afterwards
hit his batman and Major C. H. Elliott.

Clarke's men, a little
farther on in the scrub
near the beginning of The
Nek, were much better
sheltered. Immediately
after his death the junior
officers with him decided
to push on, and sent across
The Nek two scouts[4] to
see if the way was clear.
Part of the force on Rus-
sell's Top belonged to the
11th Battalion, and these

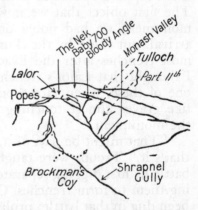

then pushed on across The Nek; but Captain J. P. Lalor[5]
of the 12th, as that battalion was to be the forward reserve, kept his men at the beginning of The Nek, setting
them to dig a semicircular trench the ends of which would
look down into the gullies on either side of the saddle.

As I have indicated, all this advance up the beginning of the main range had happened while the men of
Drake-Brockman's company were, first, assembling in

[4] One of them was Private G. Vaughan, who afterwards won a Military
Cross, and thirty years later was headmaster of the preparatory school at
Newington College, Sydney.
[5] Grandson of Peter Lalor, of the Eureka Stockade. For his colourful
story see *Vol. I, p. 291.*

Rest Valley, and, afterwards, winding their way up the depths of Shrapnel and Monash Valleys, with the noisy fusillade of the battle again resounding far above their heads. Time was wasted in searching the valley sides for snipers who were imagined to have been left there. But, as will be seen later, Howe's party eventually climbed up the end of Monash Valley on to The Nek close to where the semicircular trench lay, and I therefore asked him to show the Mission its site. I rather expected to find that the trench had been dug over and obliterated by either the Turks or ourselves when sapping our later positions on or near The Nek. The first object that we now saw at The Nek was the monument we had noted on the day of the Mission's arrival, put there by the Turks between their two foremost trenches after the Evacuation. After some search I thought that Lalor's trench must have been erased by one of these, when Howe pointed to a few pits shaped like graves almost touching the south-western edge of the monument.

"That might be part of it," he said. " . . . Yes, I think that's it." Troops were taught to establish their line in battle by first digging separate shelter pits, and then joining them to form trenches. Certainly these rifle-pits had been dug in that battle; probably the rest of them, reaching across The Nek, sheltered the Turks in the later stages of the battle (which at The Nek lasted three days) and had then been converted into the Turkish front line.

However on the morning of 25th April 1915 this trench was the position only of the reserve company on that flank under Captain Lalor. Advanced troops had early gone beyond Lalor and on to Baby 700. But I had discovered no one, including survivors of those bodies, who knew precisely where that advance had ended—indeed few Australians, infantry or staff, had heard of it—until towards the end of the war I happened to meet in France the officer who, as second-in-command of a company of the 11th Battalion, had made the first, and certainly the farthest, advance.

This was Captain E. W. Tulloch, in peacetime on the staff of a Melbourne brewery. As the story of his advance was perhaps the most important that I had come to Gallipoli to investigate, and as it directly links with Howe's story of the fight on Baby 700—which, however, touches only the beginning and ending of the episode—I hope the reader will bear with me while I describe, as Tulloch and others described it to me, this incident and its immediate background. It forms only one spoke, as it were, of the wheel of that great battle, but it was the one that we most closely inquired into; and our search for the evidence on the ground, of which I shall tell immediately afterwards, gives perhaps the best example of the Mission's work.

Chapter
· VII ·

TRACING THE FIGHT
UP THE RANGE

TULLOCH and Lalor had landed with several boatloads far up North Beach; had zigzagged in scrambles and rushes up the steep Walker's Ridge to near The Nek; and had seen Colonel Clarke fall 100 yards away. Like Lalor, Tulloch reorganised those troops who were with him in several provisional platoons under good leaders.

Three years later, in France, Tulloch had given me a map (torn from *The Anzac Book)* on which he had since traced what he believed to be his course—the map lies beside me as I write. Leaving Lalor in reserve, as ordered, he had headed across The Nek, intending to seize "Big 700", on which his battalion (11th) was to rendezvous. Crossing The Nek, he was held up by a nasty fire from the opposite side of the head of Monash Valley— that is, from the upper end of the Second Ridge, where it ran into Baby 700.[1] A few Australians, however, working round The Nek, fired into these Turks from the flank and quickly dislodged them, and the advance continued. Tulloch sent Lieutenant S. H. Jackson with a platoon along the nearer, or seaward, side of Baby 700 to keep away interference from that side of the range while he with the remainder advanced along its inland side. His party was caught up by Lieutenant Mordaunt L. Reid (an engineer of Coolgardie and an inspiring leader, older

[1] From one point of view the Second Ridge, running up to Baby 700 through the "Chessboard" might be considered as the prolongation of the main range; generally, however, the range was considered as continuing (though with a westward kink at The Nek) through Russell's Top and the Razor Edge to Plugge's Plateau.

than most subalterns) with a party of thirty; and the combined body on this side of the range pushed on in line, extended to seven or ten yards between men, over the long, undulating slope where, first, the Second Ridge and, next, Mortar Ridge ran up to it. On the second of these rises they were met by stiff fire from about sixty Turks 400 yards away in the scrub part of the way up the next spur. A machine-gun was firing from somewhere behind the Turks, but the Australians beat down the enemy fire with their own and advanced again, having by this time had about ten men hit.

They now again pushed on without a shot fired except that, whenever they crossed a rise, there came from somewhere far on the ridges on their right half-spent bullets which lisped, almost like buzzing bees, into the dark knee-deep scrub under the bright blue sky. The Turks ahead melted away but, after the line reached and crossed the spur these had been shooting from, it was again met by sharp fire from some force exceedingly well hidden in the scrub of a larger hill. The crest of this seemed to be 500 yards away, and Tulloch took it to be his objective, "Big 700".

Here a long contest for superiority of fire took place. Each side was well hidden in the scrub, and it was only when the Australians moved or tried to use their entrenching tools that they brought on themselves a storm of rifle-fire. The Turks had machine-guns also firing, but at very long range. While lying here Tulloch noted that on the "northern shoulder" (apparently of a farther hill, in front) was a solitary tree, and by it stood a man, to and from whom went messengers. Tulloch fired at him, estimating the range at 800-900 yards, but the man did not stir.[2]

On an order passed along the line, the Australians crawled on their stomachs another 100 yards down the slope. "The men were doing everything they had been

---

[2] For this whole incident see *Vol. I. pp. 287-90.*

taught," Tulloch told me, "firing only as directed, con-
serving ammunition." During a lull, by passing word up
and down the line, he found that their water-bottles were
practically untouched, a sign of high discipline. Ten
minutes after the Australians had crawled forward, the
Turks opened heavy fire on the ground that had just
been left.

They fought here for, Tulloch estimated, half an
hour, the crest-line of the range running a short distance
away on their left, and scrub-covered ridges and valleys
succeeding one another on their right as far as the Third
Ridge, half a mile away. Possibly part of the water of the
Narrows was in view in that direction—Tulloch could
not remember, three years later, whether he had noted it
or not. Many in the line had now been hit, including
Mordaunt Reid, who crawled to the rear alone, refusing
assistance. To the right the Australians could see a line
of Turks almost in the same alignment as themselves but
facing the other way and firing at other Australians, who
were digging in half a mile south of Tulloch—probably
on Mortar Ridge. These Turks were so intent on the
troops facing them that they did not seem to notice shots
fired at them by Tulloch's men in direct enfilade.

At this stage, however, shots began to come to the
Australians from their left, from the crest of the range—
at first only a few but increasing in number and at short
range. Obviously the Turks were creeping along the
other side of the range. The sound of fierce firing now
came from that direction. Clearly the Turks, already
around the right of Tulloch's force, were now passing
round his left, where Jackson had been sent. Turks were
also gathering in a hollow close in front of Tulloch. His
men, spaced among the bushes, were tightly pinned down
by fire from in front, which chipped the leaves of holly
scrub above their heads and scattered the fragments down
the collars of their tunics. They could now do little to
stop the Turks, who were evidently gathering to attack.

Accordingly, just in time, Tulloch withdrew his force
by stages, alternate sections covering the others by their
fire. They shouted Mordaunt Reid's name as they passed
the ground in rear, but no answer came and he was never
heard of again. Crossing the summit of Baby 700 Tulloch
left there half of his party with orders to delay any Turkish advance. With the rest, including Jackson who here
rejoined him, he withdrew down the seaward side of Baby
700, where fighting was then going on and the Turkish
shell-fire was very fierce.

The oncoming Turks were now clearly seen, pressing
along the seaward slope from Battleship Hill. But the
Australians were being reinforced by bodies of New
Zealanders who arrived up the steep gullies there straight
from the Beach 500 feet below, staff officers down there
showing the way. The effort here was to build up a line
with which again to beat down the Turkish fire and then
reoccupy the seaward side of Baby 700. Pending this,
Tulloch and those with him withdrew to Happy Valley,
near Lalor's old trench. He then heard that Lalor had
been killed; and soon afterwards, recrossing The Nek to
see the position for himself, Tulloch himself was hit.

Much had happened since his improvised company
had gone forward leaving Lalor on guard at The Nek.
Major S. B. Robertson of the 9th, losing his way with a
few of his men,[3] had come up to Lalor's troops at the
semicircular trench. So, presently, had Drake-Brockman,
who, after directing other parts of the reorganised 11th
Battalion to various positions near the upper end of the
Second Ridge, brought up parts of his own company
towards Baby 700 itself.

That long, rather bare hill rose beyond The Nek
without sign of life, and shutting out the view of the
higher summits beyond, though its own seaward slope
could be seen for nearly half a mile. The only fire on
Lalor's troops at that stage came from somewhere lower

---

[3] The 9th was intended for the southern flank.

down on that side, which sloped at first gently, and then precipitously by four jagged spurs, to the sea. It was clearly urgent to occupy Baby 700, and the leaders therefore at this stage took their small force across The Nek. Part, with Lieutenant I. S. Margetts, a master at the Hutchins School, Hobart, went straight up and over the summit; but Lalor, still mindful of his duty as reserve, held his own troops part of the way up the slope, agreeing with Drake-Brockman to stay there and make certain of Baby 700. Major Robertson, either then or soon after, made for the seaward slope whose scrubby expanse jutted out beyond the very deep gully which made the north side of The Nek (Malone's Gully).

This advance had ended at precisely 9 o'clock, just when Tulloch—unknown to these leaders and out of sight, must have been making the last 100 yards of his advance. But it was not long before the same Turks who penetrated along the seaward slope and turned Tulloch's left flank began also to press with their fire the Australians on the seaward slope of Baby 700. After Major Robertson and many others had fallen, the Australians there were forced back to Malone's Gully. At about 10 o'clock Margetts' line was driven from the top of the hill.

But far south near the 400 Plateau Colonel MacLagan, commanding the covering brigade (3rd), saw this withdrawal and telephoned urgently to General Bridges, commander of the 1st Australian Division, pressing for reinforcements to retake this hill; otherwise the Turks would thrust on behind the line on the Second Ridge, along which the main Anzac position now lay.

The reply was immediate. The reserve brigade, the 1st (N.S.W.), had by then mostly landed; and, one after another, its first three battalions were sent, by Bridges and other leaders who knew MacLagan's wishes, up Shrapnel Valley or Russell's Top towards the hard pressed line near Baby 700. In Monash Valley some of

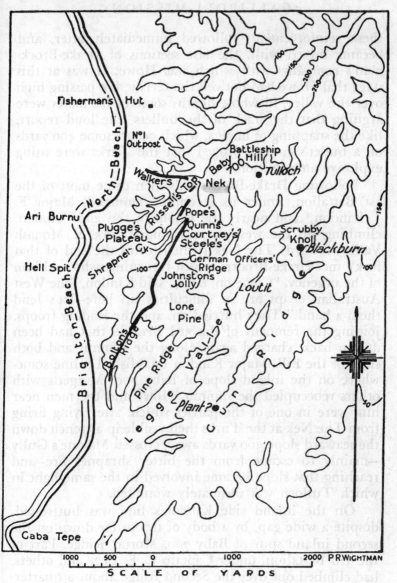

The "OLD ANZAC" POSITION

The line held by the Anzac forces after the Battle of the Landing is shown in black; the farthest points reached are marked by black dots.

these reinforcements followed immediately after, and became mixed with, the last sections of Drake-Brock-man's company—with which was Howe. It was at this stage that Howe had noticed the terrific fire passing high over the valley, in whose depths some of his mates were arguing that the crack of the bullets (the loud report, like the snapping of fingers, which occurs some 400 yards on a bullet's course) proved that the Turks were using explosive ammunition.

Following Drake-Brockman's men came most of the 1st Battalion, under its second-in-command, Major F. J. Kindon,[4] and nearly the whole of the 2nd. Kindon, climbing up the western and longest fork of Monash Valley, towards The Nek (which forms the end of that fork), met Drake-Brockman just returning, who told him of the urgency. "Come on, boys," said Kindon, "the West Australian chaps are in difficulties up here—let's lend them a hand." They hurried on, and the leading troops, joining the remnant of the 3rd Brigade that had been driven back, charged again along the summit and both sides of the hill. Major Kindon established a line some-where on the inland slope of Baby 700. Margetts with others reoccupied the summit. Howe and the men near him were in one of the parties which, after lying firing from The Nek at the Turks then visible in a trench down the seaward slope 300 yards away, crossed Malone's Gully —mainly to escape from the bitter shrapnel fire—and reaching that slope became involved in the same fight in which Tulloch was ultimately wounded.

On the inland side Kindon's line was buttressed, despite a wide gap, by a body of troops far down on the second inland spur of Baby 700, Mortar Ridge. Part of the 3rd Battalion, under Captain C. E. Leer and others, had climbed out over the Second Ridge about a quarter-

---

4 Part of the 1st Battalion had already been sent in farther south; and the 3rd, while moving up the valley, was diverted by urgent calls for help to the posts high on the right, lining the edge of the valley.

of-a-mile from its upper end, and crossed the next valley to this spur. Probably some of the 3rd Brigade—perhaps the line that Tulloch saw south of him—had already been there; here in the story may exist a gap that will never be filled. Leer was not as early as Tulloch, for Turks were already reaching the other side of Mortar Ridge when he arrived there, and his troops advanced no farther. Instead, the opposing fire became always heavier. Eventually the Turks drove past on either flank; by 5 o'clock, Leer and many others were dead. For these troops the most dangerous fire came from the rear: Australians on the Second Ridge continually shot at them, regarding their shouts of "Don't shoot—we're Australians!" as a Turkish ruse. Lieutenant R. O. Cowey then commanding the troops on Mortar Ridge accordingly chose an opportunity to withdraw them to the Second Ridge immediately in rear, at what was later Quinn's Post. On their left the Turks drove through to the upper end of the Second Ridge which later was so criss-crossed with their trenches that it was named the Chessboard.

Meanwhile, during the late morning and first half of the afternoon, the Australians had again retaken the summit of Baby 700 two or three times. But even the keenest men seldom saw many Turks to shoot at, whereas these rushes showed the Australian line to the Turks. "They made a lying-down fight, and we made a standing-up fight of it," said Lieutenant "Alf" Shout of the 1st Battalion afterwards. Kindon's line on the inland slope had clung steadily. "We were faced with a machine-gun on the flank, and shrapnel in front, and rifle-fire," he said long afterwards. "We were up against a trench and couldn't shoot much—we could simply lie there, and they couldn't come on whilst we were lying there." So Kindon had lain, puffing his pipe, an example to his troops. From noon onwards, following the 1st Australian Brigade, company after company of New Zealand infantry

91

arrived. At about 2.30 Kindon noticed two New Zealand machine-guns set up seventy-five yards behind him. To obtain their help, and to avoid the fire from his right, he withdrew his troops (then mainly New Zealanders of the Waikato company) to the alignment of these guns.

On the other slope of Baby 700, overlooking the sea, the fighting had swayed as it did on the summit. The slope of Baby 700 beyond Malone's Gully was a scrub-covered expanse undulating with the gentler upper ends of the four scraggy fingers that broke from it lower down. The Turkish trench at which Howe had fired ran through this scrub, and into it the Turks filtered thickly from farther along the range. Three times the Australians—largely 2nd Battalion—rushed it, strengthened on the last occasion by a New Zealand company which had climbed Malone's Gully. But each time a machine-gun higher up the hill, in a position to fire down this trench, shot them out and they recoiled to the good shelter of the top of Malone's Gully. At times the Turks were helped by a false report which persisted among the Australians in this part of the line, that Indian troops were helping on that flank; as the swarthy strangers moved on, fire was withheld.

About 3.15 p.m., when word reached Lalor that the troops on that flank were hard pressed, he at last moved his men thither, after sending Margetts to the Beach for further reserves; and soon afterwards, rising to lead a charge across the scrubby spur, Lalor was killed.[5] On the other side of the hill Kindon handed over control of his line to the New Zealand officers, whose troops now composed it, and went to report to Colonel MacLagan. Just afterwards a new reinforcement, half the Canterbury Battalion of New Zealanders under Lieutenant-Colonel D. McB. Stewart, appeared coming from the rear towards The Nek and lined out in the scrub a little on the Anzac

---

[5] For Lalor's ending see *Vol. I, pp. 308-9.*

side of it. Seeing troops ahead, beyond The Nek, Stewart decided to bring his line up to them.

But at that moment, about 4 p.m., the worn out Australians on Baby 700 saw that a formidable Turkish force was moving against Baby 700 and both its flanks. Hitherto all the Turks there had been khaki-clothed. Now some force of blue-coated men had joined them. Major D. Grant, the New Zealand officer in charge of Kindon's former line, and Colonel Stewart were killed. The much strained remnant of the front line came running back in panic over these supporting elements. "Get to beggary!" said the running men. "The Turks are coming on—thousands of 'em!" The rear lines rose and withdrew with the front line. The little group clustering in the head of Malone's Gully was one of the last to retire; and last among them, waiting till the Turkish leaders were 150 yards away, in plain view and hearing, were a New Zealand corporal and Howe. Howe shot the officer leading the Turks, and then ran back across the head of Malone's Gully.

This party saw that the reserve line on Baby 700 had gone; the hill was bare of Australians. Most of the troops had withdrawn down the valleys. But Howe, recognising the lie of the land, kept on Russell's Top, and his party found the semicircular trench still held by fifty men, mostly New Zealanders, under a sergeant with three machine-guns. The party stayed with them, and messengers sent by them for reinforcements found a line of men —probably the survivors of Stewart's companies—some way in rear. A note arrived from these, promising reinforcements. But, though the troops in the semicircular trench held on for three hours, no help came. Night had descended. The Turks with cries of "Allah! Allah!" had crossed The Nek and been stopped by fire from the semicircular trench now two feet deep; but Turkish shouts could be heard on either flank; and when another messenger, sent to the rear, returned to say that the line there

had gone, the party decided that there was nothing for it
but to withdraw until they got in touch with their own side.
They retired along Russell's Top by the white track on
which Colonel Clarke had been shot early that morning.
Beside it lay his pack, which Howe picked up. Finally
they stopped in a small Turkish trench near where the
Top dipped suddenly into Rest Valley. The Turks followed them, but were easily stopped. At dawn next day
Howe's party was still there with the Turks 100-200 yards
away in the scrub. It was on that morning that the British
battleships off Anzac opened heavy fire in this direction;
a staff officer came at 6 a.m. and warned the party to
withdraw, but the last men had not left the trench before
a naval shell whizzed low overhead and burst close
beyond. The guns lengthened range and apparently scared
the Turks from that end of Russell's Top. In the next
two days Australians and New Zealanders gradually retook most of the Top.

* * * * * *

That was the story—or rather the part material to
the Mission's search; other details which bring back the
atmosphere of these events, and of others equally important that were occurring elsewhere, are told in Volume
I of the Australian Official History.[6] The part of the
story which concerns Tulloch's advance was not checked
by our Mission until the second day of our search.
But as that advance started with the early events at The
Nek, as to which our researches have already been described, confusion may be avoided by describing at this
stage our search for traces of Tulloch's operations.

Tulloch himself was not sure what ridge he had
reached. His map places his farthest point on the southernmost spur of Chunuk Bair, whereas in his description
to me he spoke as though the hill which he finally faced
was "Big 700" (Battleship Hill). It seemed to me that our

---

[6] See pp. 252-574 of that volume.

best method would be to try, first, to discover his farthest point, and then work back from it.

Accordingly, on the morning of February 18th Wilkins, Buchanan and I, together with Lieutenant James and a sergeant with a pack mule, rode straight up the crest of the range, along the road (which, as a track, had existed before the Landing) to Battleship Hill. Beyond us the range continued in a long, open, rising "hog's-back" to the next main summit, Chunuk Bair, about 1000 yards away. In this long crest a curious nick (something like that caused by Wire Gully but less abrupt) marked the division of the two hills. We rode on to the first short, inland spur of Chunuk Bair, and then searched the spur carefully, on foot, for any evidence of infantry's having fought there. The whole wide upland of dark, crumpled spurs, sloping down to the south, was as silent, breathless, and apparently empty as it had been during some early parts of that morning nearly four years before. In a gutter at the head of the valley beyond this spur were the poor remains of a Turk; and all along that edge of the spur were scraps of white linen, evidently from Turkish soldiers' clothing. It was hard to say what this indicated—possibly that wounded men might have been attended to there.

We had extended our party into a line with eight or ten paces between men, and then walked slowly through the prickly, knee-deep holly scrub with our left on the edge of this gully. It was deep, and lower down on its opposite side were three big, sandy washaways, of the shape of three huge oyster shells side by side. I well remembered these "sandpits" as a ranging point ("Target C") for the field-guns of Colonel George Johnston, of Johnston's Jolly fame. How often he had fired on some suspected Turkish activity there was shown by the tiny craters made by our shrapnel shell exploding "on graze" all over the top of the spur. The nearer side of the gully along whose edge we were moving was also steep and broken, but the top of the spur was gently rounded and clothed with the low scrub we misnamed holly.[7] We presently found slightly on the Turkish side of the summit numbers of small, torn, cardboard ammunition packets with Turkish labels. Clearly a line of Turks, here just sheltered by the spur and possibly massing for attack, had opened their ammunition cartons. A little farther south were a number of spent Turkish cartridge cases. About 150 yards farther south still this edge of the spur rose slightly in a small hummock, from which Turks lining it could have fired at the next spur southwards (the easternmost finger of Battleship Hill). Behind the edge here were little clusters of fired Turkish cartridges; and on that part of the spur we found "our bullets everywhere".[8]

It was certain that, at least, the firing of those Turkish cartridges must have occurred on the first morning of the campaign; the fighting had never since been within effective rifle range, or probably even sight, of that position, which lay three-quarters of a mile from the line we afterwards held.

The top of that spur was some 200 yards wide. We found there no trace of Australian uniform, weapons, or kit except one tiny shred of web equipment which, I thought, might have been carried there by a bird or jackal. Towards the Anzac side of the spur were several pear-shaped craters, apparently made by big naval shells; the biggest I noted, very rashly, as "the only *Queen*

---

[7] It was really a dwarf oak, only knee or waist high. Two bushes, grown from acorns sent from the Peninsula, are growing at Geelong Grammar School in Victoria but, probably through careful tending and watering, they have reached the size of trees.

[8] So says the note in my field-book. In writing up the diary I noted: "Some of our bullets lying near the Turkish cartridge cases, showing where our men had fired in reply. (Got specimens for Museum.)" That was written at the time, and the conjecture that these Australian bullets were fired by Tulloch's line may have been justified by some evidence not recorded. But looking back, it seems to me more likely that they were fired later in the campaign when this hummock near the sandpits may have been a nightly target for indirect machine-gun fire.

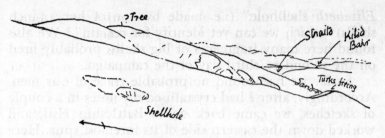

POSITION OF THE TURKS WHO STOPPED TULLOCH'S
COMPANY

*The view is along the inland side of the main range, looking
from the southernmost spur of Chunuk Bair towards the
southern shoulder and summit of that hill. It shows the
valley with the three "quarries" and the point from which
Turks had fired.*

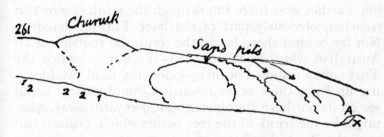

CHUNUK BAIR FROM ITS SOUTHERNMOST SPUR, SHOWING
WHERE WE FOUND THE FOLLOWING TRACES AND RELICS

A. *Turkish spent cartridge cases.*

X. *Holes of Australian shrapnel shellbursts.*

1. *Turkish clothing (everywhere along this edge).*

2. *Turkish cartridge packets (along this line).*

97

Elizabeth shellhole" (i.e. made by one of her 15-inch
shells) "which we can yet identify for certain".[9] We also
found here many fragments of big shells, probably fired
on the second or third day of the campaign.

So far we had found no probable trace of our men.
Accordingly, after I had crystallised my notes in a couple
of sketches, we came back on to Battleship Hill, and
worked down the eastern side of its foremost spur. Here
too, at first, we found traces only of Turks, evidently
killed there. Then, immediately after passing a bend, we
came upon three small trenches—one with the parapet
on the west, two with the parapet on the east. I noted
that they were "probably made by the Turk". But on
the parapet of the northernmost lay a blue enamelled
water-bottle, certainly Australian, with bullet holes
through it. Near it was part of an Australian boot, and
also of an Australian uniform. Twenty-five yards west of
it Wilkins found an Australian cartridge case, fired. Close
behind, an Australian mess-tin had been picked up on
the previous day. Ten yards farther south was an old
Turkish trench, which might have dated from the Landing. Farther west there ran through the scrub one or two
trenches, obviously part of the later Turkish defences.
Not far behind there lay in the scrub the remains of an
Australian who had been burnt—the way in which the
Turks often disposed of their opponents' dead. And looking up from these relics towards Chunuk Bair I could
see on its northern shoulder, about 900 yards away, what
might be the trunk of the tree beside which Tulloch had
seen the Turkish officer.

I should here note that our subsequent experience on
these searches was that almost invariably, when we
examined ground over which our men had certainly

9 Hers were the biggest guns used in the campaign. Wilkins photographed
the crater. But it was so big that later thought has sometimes suggested
to me that it might have been made by the explosion of an ammunition
dump. Yet why should a Turkish dump have been placed on our side of
the spur?

attacked, we found clear traces of them; whereas on ground which they had not fought over we seldom found any of their material except, occasionally, such articles as bully-beef tins—which might reasonably have been carried there by Turks who would find them in the haversacks of our dead or in the huge dumps that we left on the beaches at the Evacuation. This same morning we

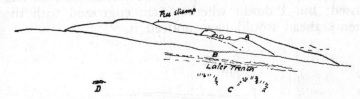

WHERE WE FOUND PROBABLE TRACES OF TULLOCH'S COMPANY

(The view is from the inland side of Battleship Hill, looking at the spur from which the two previous sketches were made.)

A. *Point from which Turks had been firing (as shown in previous sketch).*

B. *Close to edge of spur we found an Australian water-bottle and boot.*

C. *An Australian cartridge here.*

D. *Cremated remains of an Australian.*

had found a few ration tins on the spur of Chunuk Bair, but disregarded them for that reason.[10] Even an undamaged Australian water-bottle might well have been carried by a Turk. But a bottle with holes through it was of no use to anyone. These relics were 300-400 yards from the ground on which we found the line of Turkish ammunition packets and cartridges. The fire of these

[10] Near the road on Battleship Hill we also found, that day, on the remains of a Turkish salvage or supply dump, the web equipment of an Australian. The cartridges from his pouches had been opened, possibly by a Turkish villager, to extract the cordite. On Scrubby Knoll we afterwards found a heap of our cartridges similarly opened.

Turks, I noted, "must have been against Tulloch's men" (no one else on our side came near the place); and I felt sure that the traces of Australians that we now saw showed where Tulloch's company had crawled through the scrub in the last 100 yards of its advance. Probably the streak of the Narrows could have been seen far down to the right, as it certainly could from Baby 700 and from the upper part of all the spurs over which Tulloch had passed; but I doubt whether men engrossed with the enemy ahead would have noticed it.

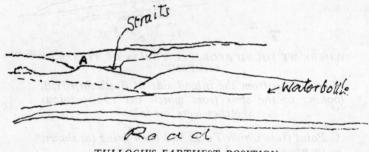

TULLOCH'S FARTHEST POSITION

The view is from the road (formerly a track through the scrub) just inland of the summit of Battleship Hill.

A. Point from which Turks fired (as shown in previous sketches).

Water-bottle marks point, in bend of spur, where traces of an advanced Australian party were found.

We next searched the westernmost spur of Battleship Hill. On the hill itself the remains of Turks lay everywhere through the scrub, but most of these probably fell two days after the Landing, when the warships' guns caught Mustafa Kemal's attack moving over that summit in full daylight and threw on the lines moving down it the sudden bombardment which gave the hill its name. Wilkins, however, as we passed, noticed a Turkish skull with a bullet hole, a probable relic of the Turkish counter-attack against Kindon's and Margetts' line on Baby 700; and 200 yards down the spur we began to meet undoubted signs of that counter-attack—a line of Turkish cartridge cases, metal clips, and torn ammunition packets, in little collections every few yards along the crest of the rise. Each man had fired 20-50 rounds. They were probably fired by the line of Turks which had followed up

THE POSITION OF THE AUSTRALIAN LINE ON BABY 700, LOST ABOUT 4.30 p.m., 25th APRIL 1915

Seen from the inland slope of Battleship Hill where we found the spent cartridges of a line of Turks which had lain there firing at the Australians and New Zealanders four years earlier. We found the relics of Major Kindon's line to the left of the 6-inch gun emplaced by the Turks on this hill after the Evacuation. (Beyond the hills here shown was the sea.)

Tulloch's withdrawal. Straight ahead of them, visible 400 yards away through frequent gaps in the low scrub, lay the long open shoulder of Baby 700 where Kindon's line would have been, and at this (or at troops near it) those cartridges were certainly fired.

The Mission had already, on the previous day, searched with Howe for the position of Kindon's line, which comprised men of the 1st and 2nd Battalions and New Zealanders; Howe thought that, though he himself finally went to the seaward slope, he had noticed a line of men on the inland slope. At the time of our visit there stood, in an open patch on the inland side of the summit

101

of Baby 700, a solitary 6-inch gun with a few shells—the only armament then remaining at Anzac, and still guarded by three Turkish soldiers. This gun, standing out on the hillside, had, of course, been placed there by the Turks since the Evacuation—during the campaign no gun could have shown its nose except to peep from good cover. It now served as a useful landmark, high near the summit, above where Mortar Ridge ran in, with Battleship Hill just across the next valley. On the slope south of its enclosure we found, beginning 150 yards away and extending for another 150, a line of some thirty graves of men buried by the Turks, certainly during the armistice of 24th May 1915, and almost certainly exactly where they fell. Parts of their clothing still lay about—on one sleeve was an arm patch of the 1st Battalion, on another an arm patch of the 2nd. On a piece of kit I could make out the mark, either 1st or 12th. Some seventy yards behind was another line of perhaps a dozen graves, and here we found badges of the 16th (Waikato) company of New Zealanders, and the badge of a New Zealand major. In a later search along both of these lines I found a number of our spent cartridges or clips.

These men could only have been killed on April 25th; we had never approached that position again. I had no doubt, therefore, that these were the positions of Kindon and of the Aucklands close behind him. Farther up the hill, just on the north-west side of the gun, I found later the remains of another twenty or thirty Australians, perhaps more. They had evidently thrust just over the top of Baby 700, facing Battleship Hill—the position which Margetts told me that he had reached.[11] One of the two who lay farthest appeared to be a New Zealander, for the cover of a New Zealand entrenching tool lay beside the little patch of torn clothes and human remains. Part of the Narrows was clearly visible from this summit.

[11] See Vol. I, pp. 291-9 and 307.

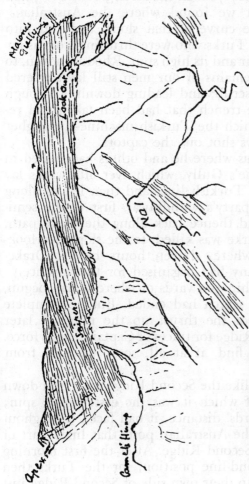

THE SEAWARD SLOPE OF BABY 700 AND BATTLESHIP HILL SHOWING THE
FARTHEST POINT AT WHICH WE FOUND EVIDENCE OF THE AUSTRALIAN
THRUST THERE ON THE DAY OF LANDING

X. The farthest point on this slope apparently reached by Australians.
The Nek is on the summit just beyond the right of the sketch.
Above Snipers' Nest can be seen the eastern shoulder of Chunuk Bair,
with the southern shoulder of Chunuk, and the Pinnacle, just north of it.
The western slopes of the range, especially above the sea, were much more
eroded than the eastern, and were generally steeper.

It was on the first day of the Mission's search that Howe and I with Wilkins and Buchanan examined the seaward slope of Baby 700. In the scrub about 200 yards below the summit we found where the Australians, advancing over the curve of that slope, had run into heavy fire from the Turks who were thrusting from as far back as Chunuk Bair and its high spur, Rhododendron, to meet them. The remains of our men still lay scattered thickly under the scrub; and leading downhill through the bushes ran the trench that had been taken and re-taken, but from which the Turkish machine-gun higher on Baby 700 always shot out the captors.

Howe showed us where he and others had rallied in the head of Malone's Gully, which ever afterwards lay mostly behind the Turkish line; and then led us along the course of his party's withdrawal, first to the semi-circular trench, and thence back along the white path, where Colonel Clarke was killed, to the slope overlooking Rest Valley where, sixteen hours before, Drake-Brockman's company had organised for the advance.

Here, back within 500 yards of where it had begun, the Mission's first search had ended. But, to complete our investigation of the thrust up the range, I later examined Mortar Ridge for traces of Captain Leer's force. These we should find, if at all, some distance from Kindon's right.

Mortar Ridge, like the Second Ridge itself, ran down from Baby 700, of which it was the easternmost spur; and, at 300-500 yards' distance, it had faced throughout the campaign all the Australian posts that lined part of the upper end of Second Ridge. After the first morning it was only a second-line position, for the Turks then trickled ahead on to their own side of Second Ridge just west of it. But it had been fortified as a very strong second-line position, and the maze of trenches which scored much of its western edge obliterated most traces of the first day's battle.

But I found that its scrub-covered and rather wide summit behind those trenches had not been much disturbed. Up it ran a sandy gutter about two feet deep, possibly following the line of an old foot-track; and along the whole length of this were the remains of Turks; and also, at intervals of two or three yards all along the gutter, small heaps of empty Turkish cartridges or clips. The men who fired them were shooting, almost certainly on the first day and night, at our men on the Second Ridge at Quinn's, Courtney's, Steele's and MacLaurin's Hill;[12] and these Turks themselves had been under heavy fire. At one point six lay together.

This Turkish line ended opposite Quinn's, where a succession of small spurs broke the western slope of Mortar Ridge. From descriptions by those who were with Leer, I felt sure that the second of these minor spurs was his position, but I could find no trace of his presence. This was one of the few exceptions to the rule that where troops attacked we would find traces of them. The gully between there and Quinn's had afterwards been crowded with the bivouacs of the local Turkish garrison and its headquarters; and they had probably cremated or buried the dead and salved the kit and cartridge cases.

Searching for traces of Australians I went to the head of Mortar Ridge, 400 yards farther north. This section of it was beyond the northernmost Australian post on the Second Ridge (Quinn's). As previously related the Turks had driven through to here on the first afternoon and had afterwards dug there the trenches known as the Chessboard. The corresponding part of Mortar Ridge was comparatively little entrenched; but I found no trace of an Australian on it till I reached a clear patch near its head. Turks surveying (possibly Shefket Pasha making his maps after the Evacuation) had placed a "trig" station there, and on this patch was a piece of Aus-

---

12 At the same time our posts were receiving sniping fire from The Nek in rear.

tralian kit. Next, 150 yards north-north-east of the trig
was the body of an Australian, and, near it, a red cross
from one of the field medical-panniers carried by our early
battalions. Then, 200 yards north of the trig, I began to
find, along a sandy path—or perhaps merely an accidental
streak of bare gravel, in the scrub—the fired cartridges
and the graves of the line of New Zealanders seventy
yards behind Kindon's position. The gap between Kindon's right and Leer's left would be 400-600 yards. It was
the Turks who drove through there who sniped that
afternoon into the back of the Australian posts along
Monash Valley.[13] Most of the Australians and New
Zealanders from Baby 700 fell back into the valleys at
the Anzac end of that hill. Of these, the heads of the
Bloody Angle on the inland side, and Malone's Gully on
the seaward, lay afterwards behind the Turkish lines;
Turkish patrols could then creep into the upper parts of
them at night and our patrols into the lower. I had heard
that Malone's Gully was "thick with the bones and traces
of our men" who had fallen back through it on this day
of the Landing. I decided to test this report by climbing
Malone's Gully to The Nek on my way back to camp
from a search at North Beach.

The gully is very steep, and for that reason probably
few people, if any, had been up it since the campaign
ended. All the way up I kept coming upon spent Turkish
cartridge cases—those lower down possibly fired on April
25th, those higher up certainly left by snipers who from
the high ground regularly shot at our No. 1 Post (on a
steep knoll above North Beach); the bullets fired back by
our snipers in No. 1 lay there also. But I found no trace
of any Australian until almost at the top. The men who
climbed there on April 25th were reinforcements, not at
that moment in action; apparently none were killed there

---

[13] Among others they wounded a man on the 3rd on the valley side at Steele's Post,
and then wounded my brother who ran out to attend to him. Two days later they killed
MacLaurin and his brigade-major.

and no gear dropped, as happened when men were fighting. The only sign of an Australian was a water-bottle or some such article at the very head of the gully, whither it might have rolled from The Nek, which was littered with the relics of later fighting, as will presently be told. On the inland side of The Nek, in the Bloody Angle and other gullies, we found many traces; but they also seemed to be those of later fighting, in which Baby 700 was again attacked, first a week after the Landing, and again in August, and our troops and those with them were terribly repulsed.

Incidentally, the climb up Malone's Gully gave me a better notion of the task that faced the troops on the first day. I was bringing back to camp, as we constantly did on these searches, a number of relics for the memorial collection; but so steep was the gully that at one time, though a strong walker, I wondered whether I should be able to carry them to the top of that nearly 500-feet climb. Yet, I reflected, I was probably not so heavily weighted as were the New Zealanders who climbed that gully on April 25th.

The result of the Mission's first two searches had been encouraging beyond our expectations. Those of our questions which related to the thrust up the main range on the day of the Landing had been almost completely answered. Some of the evidence for those answers lies in the show cases of the War Memorial at Canberra today; and whenever I see them I still wonder, as I did when we first came on them on those ridges—of what high morning hopes, what grim midday obstacles, and what final tragedy do those cartridge cases or that torn fragment of uniform tell?

Chapter
· VIII ·

GEORGE LAMBERT
SETS TO WORK

GEORGE Lambert had not come with us on our second day's search, on Battleship Hill. He had received the "operation order" for which he constantly asked, which in fact amounted to my having discussed with him the subject of the big pictures which he would be commissioned to paint for the future memorial—one of the Landing of Australians on April 25th; one of the heroic charge of the Light Horse (dismounted, of course—they could not bring their horses to Gallipoli) at The Nek on August 7th, at the climax of the second offensive of the Allies; and possibly a third of the advance of the 2nd Australian Infantry Brigade, sent to help the British at Cape Helles, on May 8th. In our first day's work, with Howe as guide, Lambert had been over the ground both of the Landing and (though that had been a much later event in the campaign) of the charge of the Light Horse[1]—indeed he had obtained his bearings there with me on the day we reached Anzac. Lambert was, I think, more sensitive than the rest of us to the tragedy—or at any rate the horror—of Anzac. At The Nek, in the last effort to seize Baby 700 or part of it, four lines of Australians charged successively to practically certain death in order to pin the attention of their opponents to that supposedly vital point, and so give the New Zealand infantry, then climbing the just visible heights of Rhododendron Spur, 1200 yards away,

---

[1] Not to be confounded with their mounted charge, two years later, which tipped the scale of Allenby's first campaign at Beersheba in Palestine, and which Lambert also painted.

the supreme chance of winning the real goal, Chunuk
Bair summit, and with it, possibly, the campaign. Unfortunately the New Zealand leaders, whose tired men by
a wonderful effort then had the summit almost within
their grasp and practically unoccupied, allowed the
chance to slip. But that was unforeseen by the Light
Horse who flung themselves across the narrow strip of
The Nek in face of the seven or eight Turkish trenches
that rose, tier after tier, across it and up the face of Baby
700 beyond. We found the low scrub there literally
strewn with their relics and those of earlier Turkish
attacks over the same ground. When shortly after our
visit Hughes came to bury the missing in this area, he
found and buried more than three hundred Australians
in that strip the size of three tennis courts. Their graves
today mark the site of one of the bravest actions in the
history of war.

"Descriptions are all too true," wrote Lambert[2] to his
wife. "Evidence grins coldly at us non-combatants. . . .
From the point of view of the artist-historian The Nek
is a wonderful setting to the tragedy." The grim, rather
beautiful landscape of distant ridge-tops surrounding this
upland would be his background, his foreground the
patch of level scrub with the line of charging men shown
at the moment when, a few yards out from their trench,
the full force of the Turks' rifle-fire struck them. As he
says, he regarded himself in these works as the artist-
historian, and he purposed in this picture to show the
reaction of different types of Australian to this shocking
experience. There was to be the larrikin; and the gently-
bred type; the fair-haired Scandinavian-Anzac; the lean
countryman, and so on. You see them all in the picture
which he painted some years afterwards in Australia from
the landscape studies begun that morning on Plugge's
Plateau and The Nek.

I had been answering Lambert's questions as to our

2 *Thirdy years of an Artist's Life, pp. 103-4.*

men's equipment and dress at the Landing when Balfour reminded me that the men of the 3rd Brigade, which landed first, had been told to roll up their sleeves to the elbow so that in the half-light they might be distinguished from the Turks. Like Balfour, I thought this might add something to the vigour of the picture, though I did not say so when I mentioned the fact to Lambert.

"How disgusting," was all he said. I think he sensed that we were expecting him to paint something like the flamboyant illustrated-newspaper pictures of the Anzacs which seldom failed to show their forearms bare. "You know," he once said to me, "we constantly picture Australians as tall, wiry men, whereas the average Australian —if there is one—is short and stout. Look at them next time you're in the street."

However, the original Anzacs were big men, and Lambert did not make the mistake of painting them otherwise. But nothing could have induced him to turn up the sleeves of that landing brigade. In his great picture, of all the scores of climbing men who, in the flat morning light, almost blend into the colour of the scrub, every one has his sleeves down to his wrist, and every one wears an Australian hat, though Lambert knew that they landed in the little round peaked caps which were the general wear of Australian infantry in that great battle.

"I suppose some wore hats, skipper?" he asked.

"Certainly," I said, and that was enough for him.

But in his picture of the charge at The Nek he gave the men exactly the uniform they would have worn—shirts with sleeves cut above the elbow, shorts, slacks, anything— the "Anzac uniform" in fact. He often asked me how I thought a man would fall if hit on one side and spun round; Lambert used to jerk himself forward as he imagined this charging man would, and as you see one figure falling in the centre of the picture today. It is a rather terrible work and meant to be so. Yet Lambert did not hate war so fiercely as our even more prolific war artist, Will Dyson, who once told me: "I'll never draw a line to show war except as the filthy business it is." Nothing could have induced either of these artists to swerve a hair's breadth from what he believed to be the truth—their integrity was absolute.

Lambert had been allotted a bell tent to store his materials and for a studio on the worst days, but it had to be pretty wet or snowing to keep him from the field. He carried his field-gear in a case which the Mission called "Lambert's coffin"; and, to carry it, from this morning onwards, Hughes or James kindly allotted him a pack mule from their camp, with a light horseman named Spruce, from Port Stephens in New South Wales, to look after the mule. Lambert wrote to his wife:[3] "I sit perched on the edge of what you would call a precipice and wait for the sun to shine, getting in a dash now and again. My bad temper is kept under by the presence of a dinkum Australian lent by the Hughes-James camp . . .(He) accompanies me, carrying my painting gear, himself, and odd bits of salvage on a pack mule, a female of character. I ride a very ugly plug, a small draught horse which, though unspeakably plain, is useful and has a fondness for the mule. The mule breaks away every fifteen minutes or so when we camp for painting, and the Dinkum shows the stuff he is made of by sliding down the side of the precipice and catching her, tethering her by some special stunt which he says will make her feel as happy as a Jew on the hobs of Hell. Then he climbs laboriously back to me, and by the time he reaches the summit she is off again; quite a good circus for a grey day. If the weather serves we move on, after mungaree, to The Nek, and I swat at painting leaves and small pebbles into the sketch of The Nek."

Since his first holiday in the Australian country as a boy, Lambert, when opportunity occurred, had never ceased to play at being bushman, at which his quick

[3] *Thirty Years of an Artist's Life, p. 104.*

111

intelligence made him tolerably expert. The same propensity caused him to dramatise his situations. Something he had heard or read led him to believe that there should still be a few stray wolves among these hills, and it would have given him even more pleasure to use the revolver, which he still carried, on a wolf than on a jackal. It happened that on the evening of February 18th, after returning from Tulloch's tracks, I went out by myself on to the ridges behind our camp in my eagerness to get at least a preliminary answer to some of the problems of Scrubby Knoll, the main summit there, the goal of most of the searches described in the next chapter. As I was wandering through the scrub up the Third Ridge (Gun Ridge), towards that summit, I heard some kind of report, and a bullet buzzed through the air near enough for me to hear it and wonder at its sound, rather like that of a bumble-bee. I thought somebody must be out shooting with an old Martini Henry rifle, when almost at once the felt hat and puggaree and eager face of Lambert appeared bobbing up and down as he hurried through the bushes.

"By God, skipper," he said, "did you see that chap? Wolf or something—I didn't get him, he cleared off through the scrub; I think he lost a bit of fur though! Damn good job I didn't get you either, now I come to think of it—what?"

Back in camp he set about devising a wolf or jackal trap on the lines of the traps for wild dogs and dingoes which he had learnt to make in his bush days. He constructed a second one later. A year afterwards, back in Australia, we heard from Hughes that Lambert's trap was still there—and still virgin.

Lambert worked like an assiduous student, and the rest of us also were occupied by night as well as by day. Buchanan and Rogers had their maps to check and trace; Wilkins his negatives to develop; Balfour supplies to order as well as the collections to list and pack. Almost every day he led a party of six or eight British helpers to search systematically the ground already examined for the purposes of history. Their duty was to bring back everything that might be useful for the memorial collection. It was a rule that this party should never work over ground which I had still to examine; they searched for particular articles in special places—remains of bomb-screens and other signs of trench warfare at Quinn's Post where bombing had never ceased during the campaign; shrapnel pellets in the bed of Shrapnel Valley; fragments of battleships' shells on Battleship Hill. Sometimes, if the find was likely to be heavy, the limber was taken. The British soldiers generally enjoyed this work; and when, on about our fifth day, there arrived a relief party of six men, both parties asked to remain with us, which the 28th Division most kindly permitted. We had work for them, and our camp would have grown to about twenty-five members had it not been for illness. Unfortunately Howe, who had not been well throughout our travels, had to leave us after sticking it out till he had done his job, and several of the 28th Division men sickened with malaria contracted at Salonica and had to be sent back. Hughes with his Australian section, however, was keenly interested in our investigations, and often helped us by coming with us and by lending us some of his men.

Naturally these fellow-countrymen were the most interested in our searches; but, apart from that, the outlook of the "colonials" increased their helpfulness to a degree that impressed us all. Whereas the British orderly or groom would do faithfully what you told him, the Australian could be trusted, almost without instructions, to turn up with the right equipment for himself, you, and the horses, and not infrequently with suggestions for the day's work, whether it was that of Hughes seeking for graves or of Lambert making sketches. Lambert noted that his light horseman-muleteer, Spruce, "says he has always had a leaning towards art and beauty, and he

113

thinks that Port Stephens is the most beautiful place in the world. When I told him that he would never be as good a painter as a mule-catcher, he replied that a man doesn't value the gifts that are handed to him at birth."[4]

After our second day's search (February 18th) a splendid piece of news was waiting for us. The 28th Division at Chanak had sent a copy of a telegram received from G.H.Q., Constantinople, saying that Major Zeki Bey of the Ottoman General Staff would leave there in the s.s. *Maryland* next day to meet me. General Milne directed that "although a certain formality is to be observed, everything possible is to be done to make this officer's visit pleasant and comfortable". The 28th Division was to make arrangements for his accommodation and transport. To my delight the message concluded: "Tell Bean Major Zeki Bey has maps"—that meant, of course, the large scale Turkish historical maps which Crawford and Cameron so admired.

It was indeed a wonderful advantage that these loyal British friends had secured for us. At that time the outside world knew almost literally nothing of the Turkish side of the campaign, and seemed, indeed, unlikely ever to hear much. I had scores of questions to which I was anxious to obtain even the most general answer. And now general information, at least, should be obtainable; from a staff officer we could hardly expect much detail. It was therefore with much interest that I arranged to ride to Kilid Bahr on the evening of the 19th in order to bring back our visitor next day. General Croker of the 28th Division had most kindly offered to put me up at Chanak, but I was so eager to get quickly back to our task that I refused. Meanwhile we filled the evening of the 18th and morning of the 19th with two important searches towards Scrubby Knoll.

---

[4] *Thirdy Years of an Artist's Life, p. 112.*

"FARTHEST IN"

OUR searches on Scrubby Knoll and the fingers of the Third Ridge leading to it were aimed at answering another question relating to the Landing: how far did parts of the covering brigade penetrate inland?

The thrust in that direction was made at the same time as Tulloch was thrusting northwards, mainly by somewhat similar bodies of the 9th and 10th Battalions. The 11th Battalion, as already stated, was to seize Battleship Hill, on the northern flank; but it was also to establish itself on the northern part of the Third Ridge, whose long curved watershed left the main range at Chunuk Bair and swept southwards and then south-westwards enclosing the First and Second Ridges, to end in Gaba Tepe promontory. The right of the 11th was to rest on Scrubby Knoll, the most prominent hump in the northern part of the Third Ridge. The 10th (South Australia) would occupy the central part of the ridge, from there southwards. The 9th (Queensland) would capture the southern part, from another hump (Anderson Knoll) to and including the strongly fortified cape of Gaba Tepe itself.

What part, if any, of the Third Ridge had been reached in either of these sectors was in doubt. It was certain that in the central sector some parties had reached one or other of its spurs, beyond Lone Pine or Johnston's Jolly. These parties had been met on the Second Ridge by Major (afterwards Major-General and Senator) C. H.

Brand, then brigade-major of the covering force, who urged them to "keep going"—which indeed was their orders. A little later they had been sighted high up on a spur of the Third Ridge; and when the commander of the covering force, Colonel MacLagan, decided that it would be impossible for his troops to reach and hold the Third Ridge that day, and that the bulk of them should dig in where they then were, on the Second Ridge, he also decided to let these foremost parties stay out in front for the time being, as a screen for the troops digging the main line. Shortly afterwards it was reported that the advanced line was being driven in. Whatever position it had occupied lay far beyond the Anzac line from that morning onwards.

Not till three years after that event had I, to my knowledge, met any member of those advanced troops, and so had an opportunity of ascertaining where they had been and what had happened there. The officer whom I then met, Lieut.-Colonel N. M. Loutit, had in the meantime risen to command a battalion at the age of twenty-four years; but at the time of the Landing he had been just twenty-one, a platoon commander of the 10th Battalion. Before the war he was an engineer student. He told me that while the crowd of troops was assembling on Plugge's Plateau, he had hurried on with some of his men, chasing a party of Turks through the depths of Shrapnel Valley, and then climbing the Second Ridge near the nick at Wire Gully. Clambering up the steep hillside they were joined by Major Brand whom MacLagan had sent to do what he could in keeping track of and co-ordinating the forward troops. As they reached the edge of the 400 Plateau they saw several of the Turkish field-guns, which airmen had reported to be emplaced in a fold of this plateau. The guns were about 300 yards south-east of them on that scrubby expanse. Turks were hurrying up mule teams to the battery and, despite snap shooting from Loutit's party, guns, mules and men quickly disappeared into some hollow which evidently divided the northern and southern halves of the plateau.

It was the first duty of the 10th Battalion, on its way to its sector of the Third Ridge, to capture the reported battery or batteries on this plateau, and Loutit headed for this valley, afterwards named Owen's Gully, striking it some way down its course, but found there only a small camp of deserted tents. Small eastern lamps were still burning inside them, and Loutit's men began ransacking them for small articles. He had to drag his troops away and then press on down the valley. Lieutenant J. L. Haig of the 10th and a few men of the 9th, 10th and 11th joined and went on with him, thirty-two all told.

They hurried on to where the gully debouched into the green flat of Legge Valley, with its sandy creek, scattered olive-trees, a few more tents behind Lone Pine, and a small stockyard with some horses, but no other sign of the battery. Accordingly Haig and Loutit made for their objective, the Third Ridge, whose spurs formed the far side of the valley. They climbed first a small hill, and then a higher ridge. The battle had ceased except for odd rifle shots coming from every direction, evidently from individual Turks scattered in the scrubby hillsides. Like all the rest the ridge they were now mounting was covered with scrub, and from its crest they looked over a gully to a similar ridge 400 yards away. On it were Turks in large numbers, who opened heavy fire; and the Australians after passing slightly over the crest of their ridge had to fling themselves down and shoot from behind bushes; the opposing fire was much too hot to allow them to dig. Looking back, Loutit could see, over both his right shoulder and his left, Australians "cruising about" in the scrub on the 400 Plateau in rear of Legge Valley. Brand had told him that he would send other parties up to him but none arrived; as has already been stated, the orders had been changed, but Loutit knew nothing of this, and sent back to a party which he saw to his right rear, asking it to come up. It turned out to be a platoon under Captain J. F. Ryder of the 9th, who duly brought his men across and into line on Loutit's right.

The Turkish fire, however, was finding one after another of the Australians. The Turks had worked round to the north; and thence from 400 yards away, they were firing down the length of the Australians' line. Ryder, after summoning reinforcements by sending back a sergeant on one of the horses found in the valley, decided to withdraw. He sent a message to Loutit and then fell back with his men towards his former position on the 400 Plateau. Loutit had "dashed hard work" to prevent his men from taking the same direction, but managed to withdraw them, by alternate sections each covering the other, from spur to spur until they reached a "small mound" just on the Turkish side of the creek. The Turks quickly followed them to the ridge that Loutit had just left, and as the enemy carried with them a machine-gun the fire was very hot. During the next retirement the pursuers reached the abandoned position before the Australians got to cover and for a moment the situation was tenser still.

But Loutit was now in touch with a few of his own side opposite the mouth of Wire Gully. The adjutant of the 11th, Captain J. H. Peck, had received Ryder's message and hurried down that gully with a few men to help them. Here at 10 o'clock exactly (as he himself noted) Peck was wounded; but they managed, in one long stage, to cross the flat and climb Wire Gully; and near the top of this at 11 o'clock Loutit posted himself with seven men on one side, Haig with another seven on the other, with three advanced sentry groups farther down the valley—these posts together serving during the next few days, with other troops added, as the "battle outposts" that played a famous part in the fighting there. Their precise position was an uncertainty which the Mission had also, if possible, to solve.

Loutit told me that "the water of the Dardanelles was clearly seen" from his fathest point; and he had thought, for that reason, that "they must be a very long way in". They had advanced "very fast". Much the same report had been made by many of the advanced parties that day, and it represented the genuine impression of many of the survivors. Yet before I returned to Gallipoli inquiry into many cases had made me certain that the distance actually traversed in that wild country was usually far less than the troops thought. On the other hand a leader of Loutit's type would be minutely accurate in his statements.

When, on the Mission's arrival, I told Hughes that we should be searching the Third Ridge for traces of these parties, he told me that he had already had it searched but his men had found no trace of Australians on the ridge itself. They had, however, found a few pieces of Australian kit on one of its spurs which lay at the back of our camp.

Now, assuming that Loutit and Haig after coming into Legge Valley had hurried along it for a hundred yards or two southwards, as they probably did when looking for the guns and camps, and had then turned eastwards to climb the Third Ridge, the part of it that faced them would be a spur about a mile long running down from the southern shoulder of Scrubby Knoll to a point just at the back of our camp. Its top would be reached by climbing first over the lower folds of a shorter spur, and then about 200 feet up its own scrub-covered side. It was up this spur that I was searching on the evening of February 18th when Lambert shot at his "wolf" and (according to the good yarn that he afterwards told), narrowly missed his leader. Next morning with Wilkins, James and Buchanan, ten days later with Balfour and half a dozen men, and finally with Wilkins on March 6th, the day before we left Anzac, I searched that spur as well as part of those near it.

I shall not describe those searches with the minute-
ness with which I have followed our invetigation of the
traces of Tulloch's company. The reader will now be
familiar with our methods and interested chiefly in their
results. These seemed definite. Over the southern end
of that spur (which, Zeki Bey told us, was called Adana
Bair—that is, Adana Ridge) the Turks, at some time
during the campaign, had cut a very deep, wide communication trench, through which probably their mule
train with supplies, and certainly their relieving infantry, could pass unseen and, except for the dust they raised,
unsuspected. Near this sap, which of course was not there
on the day of the Landing, we found, in the scrub along
the summit of the spur, Australian cartridges, some of
them opened by the Turks, and a mess-tin. Several hundred yards farther north, along another section of its
crest, were similar traces, including an Australian puttee,
and close behind them an Australian tunic; and on the
ridge to our rear of it (called by Zeki Bey Fondaluk Sirt,
"Brown Hill") Balfour found an Australian cap, exactly
between the point where the tunic was found and the
mouth of Wire Gully. Men lying where we saw the first
traces above-mentioned would look across a valley to the
Third Ridge itself, exactly 400 yards away; farther north
the spur came rather closer to it. And along the part of
the crest where we found the more northern traces there
were also a line of spent Turkish cartridges or clips and
the remains of a few Turks. These almost certainly
marked the place at which, after the disappearance of
whatever Australians had fought there, the Turks had
reached the crest and lain for a time firing at someone
(probably the retiring Australians) on the next ridge
towards Anzac. There seemed very little doubt that the
traces we had found were those of Loutit's and Ryder's
men. Loutit's retirement would be across the lower ends
of the successive spurs—the little open knoll opposite the

mouth of Wire Gully was one of them, and near it Balfour had found the cap.

But there was one great difficulty in accepting this solution. From the positions where these relics were found the Dardanelles could not be seen. The Third Ridge was higher than the spur, Adana Bair, and shut out all view beyond. Farther north Adana Bair rose more steeply, with a marked shoulder; and it was not until we had climbed 300 yards along this, and almost reached a second and final shoulder leading to Scrubby Knoll, that a sharp dip in the Third Ridge suddenly opened to us a view of the Straits about Kilia Liman. From farther north, on Scrubby Knoll itself, the Narrows, of course, lay wide open.

Despite this fact, I felt sure that we had found Loutit's and Ryder's positions, and there must be some explanation, as yet unknown to us.

After returning to Australia I wrote to Loutit, sending him a sun-print from the Turkish map, telling him our difficulty, and asking him to trace his course on the map as well as he could remember it. His answer cleared all doubt. He said that from the position of his men he had not been able to see over the Third Ridge. So, taking two companions, he had gone farther up the ridge, just as we had done except that he kept just behind the crest until, where it rose towards Scrubby Knoll, he obtained a clear view of the Straits. On this prominent height, how-ever, the three Australians were immediately seen by the Turks and were heavily fired on. In a few moments one of them was hit. Loutit and the unwounded man[1] carried him back to their party. On the map that I sent him, which I refer to as I write, Loutit marked the position of his line and Ryder's exactly where we had found the two groups of cartridges and other relics; and the red ink line showing his retirement runs across the foot of succes-sive ridges, including the small knoll and the slope where

---

[1] Pte (afterwards Lieut.) R. O. Fordham, killed two years later in France.

Balfour found the Australian cap. Up the ridge north of it (Fondaluk Sirt) we found where a line of Turks had lain shooting, probably at Leer's men on Mortar Ridge. These Turks would have come over Scrubby Knoll, north of Loutit, just as he described. And my diary says that in the valley there, Usun Dere (Long Valley) near the remains of a Turkish camp, Balfour and I "found some of our kit evidently taken with unfired cartridges in it; for in it were many empty clips; and one fired cartridge, and one not fired, were not far away. These possibly mean that some man got into the Usun Dere—possibly one of the men who lost themselves."[2]

At the time of the Mission's visit we had no word of any party's having been so close as Loutit's to Scrubby Knoll. But some years after the story of those events had been published in the Australian Official History I received a letter from a distinguished citizen-soldier in South Australia, Lieutenant-Colonel A. S. Blackburn,[3] who afterwards, as Brigadier, commanded the Australian force which, in the Second World War, had to be left to its fate in Java, where eventually he was captured by the Japanese. In 1916 as a lieutenant he won the Victoria Cross at Pozières, but at the Landing had been a private and scout of the 10th Battalion. His letter stated that with a fellow scout, Lance-Corporal P. de Q. Robin, he had been sent from the Second Ridge to reconnoitre the Third. Going very fast they reached it where its top was wide and level, just north of Scrubby Knoll, and, finding few signs of Turks yet there, they circled southwards round the knoll. At that moment, however, numbers of Turks began to appear in a valley east of the Third Ridge. They therefore moved back over Third Ridge south of the

---

[2] The alternative would be that the Turks had carried the equipment to this place, which is unlikely. As to what lonely man was there and what was his end, there is no gleam of evidence.

[3] An Adelaide solicitor, and brother to Sir C. Bickerton Blackburn, physician, Chancellor of the University of Sydney.

knoll, noting, as they did so, a line of Australians—presumably Loutit's and Ryder's—south-west of them.

So these two men came closer even than their three comrades of the 10th, closer, so far as we know, than any other soldiers of the Allies, to the objective of the Gallipoli Expedition. The Straits were about three miles away. There was, however, at least one other party which had gone inland very fast and far—and had to come back, if anything, faster. This was a handful of the 9th Battalion under Captain (now Major-General) E. C. P. Plant, a young regular officer, formerly A.D.C. to General Bridges. Plant, whom I remember having seen on the Beach after his return, could only tell us that he had gone "a hell of a distance", until he looked over open country. My impression was that he said that at his farthest point he looked out on the Kilid Bahr Plateau; but he could not be sure that they had seen any part of the Straits. The place he had been intended to reach would lie somewhere on the southern portion of the Third Ridge, between its second hump, Anderson Knoll, and Gaba Tepe. I now assumed that if he had directly looked out on the water of the Straits he would never have forgotten the sight; and therefore we expected that any traces of his party would be found, if at all, where the Third Ridge afforded a view over the open country to Kilid Bahr but no sight of the water of the Narrows.

We found (to quote my diary) that on the crest of Third Ridge, "anywhere from about fifty yards south of Anderson Knoll for about 500-600 yards, a man not quite getting over the skyline would have this view; and on the southern shoulder of the knoll he cannot see the Dardanelles even when he is on the crest. You cannot see over green fields anywhere except from this section of Gun Ridge." It was from the direction of these flats that, between 9 and 10 a.m. a column of Turks, a battalion or two with guns, reached just this section of Gun Ridge and began marching steadily northwards up the track

along its crest, the first large body of Turks to be seen
by the Anzacs. Possibly it was the danger of being cut
off by some of these troops that necessitated the speed of
Plant's retreat.

At all events the lie of the ground seemed to agree
with that described to me by Plant, so far as I could remember his words. But here we could find hardly a
trace of Australians to confirm our conjecture that this
was the place he had reached. This was not surprising,
considering that his party was small and had to retire
almost at once. That Australians in numbers, first of the
9th Battalion and then of the 2nd Brigade had reached
the next ridge in rear, Pine Ridge (an advanced spur of
the Second Ridge), I knew well; and the ample evidence
of this will be described later. But all that we found of
Australian gear on or near this part of Third Ridge was
a single spent Australian cartridge case found by Balfour
a little farther down the crest. Much stronger evidence
was the discovery of several clips from Turkish cartridges
fired near the top of the ridge *but on the Turkish side of
it.* Judging from their position I noted, "They may have
been fired at someone either a little south of the knoll
or 600-700 yards south of it."

I appreciated that even Australian cartridges might
have been fired since the Evacuation, by some Turk with
an Australian rifle, or even by one of our light horsemen during their recent visit, shooting at a hare. The
balance of probability, however, was that these articles
were left there at the time when there was known reason
for their presence there; and, as I have said before, it was
remarkable how regularly such traces were found where
our troops were known to have fought, and how rarely,
if at all, where they had not. Balancing the evidence I
concluded that Plant had probably reached Gun Ridge
at this point.

by warships alone, had been stationed on the Peninsula,

Chapter
· X ·

ZEKI BEY

ON the afternoon of February 19th I rode to Kilid
Bahr and crossed to Chanak to meet Zeki Bey. At headquarters of the 28th Division I was disappointed to hear
from Major Collis that the ship had been delayed until
the 21st. However the delay disconcerted me alone; the
rest of the Mission would be only too glad for a chance
to catch up with their work.

On the 21st our visitor duly arrived by tender at
the pier where a staff officer of the 28th Division and I
were waiting for him. He proved to be a smartly but
quietly uniformed officer, of perhaps slightly under average height. He spoke to us in French, and his very quiet
voice and reserved manner closely matched his appearance. He had the complexion of a pleasantly browned
European, a slight, dark moustache, deep brown eyes
and a quick smile. His uniform was not unlike the German field grey, with red shoulder patches, black gaiters,
and a Turkish helmet of dark felt material. After making
arrangements with the British staff at Chanak, I crossed
with him to Kilid Bahr, and there and on our ride to
Anzac I had the opportunity of learning from him something of his Gallipoli experience.

He was a Salonica Turk of, I should say, about 29
years. At the outbreak of war he had been an officer on
the regular staff of the Turkish Army, but later, when
some new battalions were being formed,[1] he had volun-

---

[1] From the fourth companies of existing battalions.

teered for command and had been given the 1st Battalion
of the 57th Turkish Regiment, which was brigaded with
two Arab regiments, the 72nd and 77th, to form the 19th
Division of the Turkish Army. This was the division
which, in the redistribution carried out by the German
General Liman von Sanders after the failure of our Navy's
attempt on March 18th to force the passage of the Straits
by warships alone, had been stationed on the Peninsula
a little north of Kilid Bahr as reserve for the southern
end of the Peninsula. Zeki Bey and his battalion had
formed part of the force which was thrown in to bar our
advance on the day of the Landing. He had been wounded
in that fight, but had returned a month or so later and
taken over with his battalion the position at German
Officers' Trench. After a long term at that post he was
rushed with his troops as the first reserve to meet our
thrust at Lone Pine; and after fighting through that
battle he was given command of a regiment—the 21st—
whose leader had been killed on August 9th near Hill
60. Through malaria Zeki Bey missed the main fighting at
Hill 60 in August but he commanded there for the rest
of the campaign and at the Evacuation.

I had never dreamt of being able to obtain information of the Turkish side from an authority with such experience. Here was one who, from his close association
with the staff, could speak with knowledge of the major
plans, and who at the same time could give us at least a
battalion commander's personal account of the most
important incidents of the campaign, so far as these
concerned Anzac. I had yet to learn the degree to which
Zeki Bey had actually taken part in the fighting, and of
his close association with the greatest commander on
Gallipoli. That he should have been selected to visit us
was not, of course, mere good luck; it was due to the
help of Cameron, Crawford, Murphy and the head of the
Turkish General Staff, Kiazim Pasha, whom I had not
yet had the privilege of meeting

The two winters spent as a youngster in Belgium had made French a fairly easy medium for me; and by the time Zeki Bey and I, and an English groom with our visitor's spare horse, rode over Third Ridge, and into the valley, so familiar to him, in which we camped, I had obtained most of this information, and much besides. He had not, I think, seen Lone Pine since the days of the critical struggle there—certainly not since the months following the campaign, and he was intensely interested. Accordingly, after a cup of tea we climbed up there, and he began the graphic account given in the next chapter.

Much the greater portion of his narrative of that and other events was taken down by me, from that evening onwards, as we sat over our mess-table after dinner. The mess-tent was lighted by a couple of hurricane lamps whose rays barely reached its corners, and in the snow-storms and sleety nights the tent was very cold. We had only tea to warm us. But Zeki Bey, sitting on the bench beside our table, let me cross-examine him for hours at a time, just as I had done throughout the war with officers of the A.I.F. Wilkins would be in his dark-room tank; Balfour writing up his records; the others working or yarning. The evenings were so cold that Rogers suggested building a fireplace, and eventually got leave to do so. He and Lambert spent a day making it of bricks from parts of the Turkish trenches, with some bits of galvanised iron for the chimney. They were helped by a fatigue party of our 28th Division men, "whose greatest effort," Lambert wrote to his wife, "was making exclamations of admiration." That night Lambert in his studio-tent could hear them "discussing where we learnt to make so many gadgets. They have placed me," he wrote,[2] "as a chap who rose from navvy to artist (quite right) and Sergeant Rogers as an architect who descended from a high position for the purpose of helping his country." I suppose it was by Rogers' skill and not by pure luck that our mar-

2 *Thirty Years of an Artist's Life, pp. 107-8.*

quee survived the fire that we thenceforth enjoyed; anyway it became a much better place to work in.

The answers of Zeki Bey to my questions proved
absorbingly interesting from the start, at least to us
Anzacs. I must here repeat the warning which I have
given in the preface to this book, that in writing Zeki
Bey's narrative here I have made its order consecutive,
often combining several conversations that dealt with a
single subject, and have made him speak in the first person, whereas my notes are in the third. Also in a few
places I have amplified my notes from memory, where
my memory is certain. In any case my original diaries
will be in the War Memorial for any authentic student
to read.

Needless to say I did not begin my interrogations with
pencil and notebook in hand (as in a portrait which
George Lambert some years later did me the honour of
painting), firing questions at Zeki Bey and expecting him
to answer them. Never since my earliest days as a reporter
have I produced a notebook or pencil at the beginning
of such an interview. One must, of course, let one's subject know that he is speaking for publication, but if one
also starts by bringing out this apparatus any but the
most hardened public person is immediately scared.
Any statement elicited is frozen by self-consciousness. On
the other hand it is easy to turn the conversation in some
direction that requires a sketch-map, and then say, "Hold
on—I don't quite follow; I take it you mean this—perhaps we'd better have a diagram." Out comes your pencil
with some scrap of paper. "Here's where you were standing . . ." and you mark down this or whatever other point
you seize on to illustrate, "and the other man was over
there . . ." Your man may correct you, but whatever he
says you note it down on the diagram: "Smith here, other
man there . . ." and the ice is broken. You may then sit,
as I have often done, for three-quarters of the night taking down word for word the rest of the story of your new

friend (which he usually becomes) in an atmosphere of complete ease. Anyway, that was the atmosphere in which Zeki Bey and I, side by side under the lantern at our mess-table, fired our imperfect French at one another, mutually eager to thrash out the story.

I should say here that our visitor was given one of the three bell tents for himself. To serve as his batman and orderly, Hughes had suggested that we should obtain one of the Turkish soldiers guarding the 6-inch gun on Baby 700; they seemed to look upon Hughes as both commander and protector. Next evening two of them (I had asked only for one) reported to our camp. "I fancy they, poor devils, come in for a feed," wrote Lambert that night,[3] "as the Turkish officer doesn't seem to remember any order that was issued commanding them to report. However, they will make excellent models. One of them has a uniform of which at least six square inches is of the original material." Actually the guard on the gun seemed to have been forgotten by the Turkish War Office. (I have known larger units forgotten by our own command.) They told Zeki Bey that the officer formerly in charge of the gun had left for Constantinople some weeks earlier, after telling them that the British would shortly be taking over the gun. They had been given three weeks' Turkish rations and told that no more would be coming as the British would take charge of "the fort" before that time ended. They had since heard no more, and as their rations were nearly finished I reported the position to the 28th Division. I fancy they lived largely on rations from Hughes' camp and did small services in return.

Before Zeki Bey retired for the night I gave him an outline of our daily arrangements: call time, 7.30 a.m.; breakfast, 8; start for the field, 9 o'clock, unless otherwise arranged, always taking our lunch with us. Dinner, 7

[3] *Thirty Years of an Artist's Life. p. 105.*

p.m. I had, of course, given orders that no food that was
prohibited to Mohammedans should be included in our
meals while he was there. When he left us that night for
his tent the verdict of the Mission, as the nightly five
minutes of gossip flew over the six of us in our sleeping
bags or blankets in the dark of the big marquee, was that
we had gained a pleasant and interesting companion.
Strangely enough the one who throughout, while con-
versing cheerily in French, maintained longest an
inward non-committal attitude towards our visitor, was
Lambert.

Next day we were to begin with Zeki Bey a systematic
survey of Anzac from the north southwards. But as his
nightly answers to my interrogations illuminated nearly
all the problems for these searches, I shall interpose here
his account of the Landing and return later to our work
in the field.

ENTER
MUSTAFA KEMAL

"My battalion was on parade when the news of your landing came to us," said Zeki Bey, in reply to my first question on the point. "It chanced that there had been ordered for that morning an exercise over the ground, especially towards Koja Chemen Tepe [Hill 971]. There had been previous exercises of that sort, and our regiment, the 57th, had mustered early for this one. It was at that moment that the report came.

"The regiment had been camped at Boghali [about two miles north of Kilia Liman on the Dardanelles and exactly four miles directly east of Anzac Cove]. The commander of our division, the 19th, had received about dawn a report from the commander of the 9th Division [which was guarding the coast] that a landing had occurred at Ari Burnu.

"There was one battalion of the 9th Division between the Asmak Dere [two miles north of Anzac] and Kum Dere [three-and-a-half miles south of Gaba Tepe]. I think it was the 1st Battalion of the 27th Regiment; at all events it was one battalion of that regiment. Its other two battalions were west of Maidos [just four miles from Gaba Tepe]. The other regiments of that division were farther south.

"The Turkish staff and commanders concerned did not expect a landing at Ari Burnu, but they had given a great deal of thought to Gaba Tepe, and that was why the two reserve battalions of the 27th Regiment were placed east of Gaba Tepe. Little thought was given to Ari Burnu because it was too precipitous.

131

"The message from the commander of the 9th Division said: 'About one battalion has landed at Ari Burnu, and this battalion has gone in the direction of Koja Chemen Tepe.' The message then asked the commander of the 19th Division to send one battalion against Ari

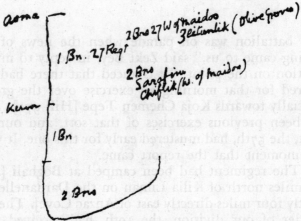

DIAGRAM MADE DURING A TALK WITH ZEKI BEY, SHOWING DISTRIBUTION OF THE 9th TURKISH DIVISION, GARRISONING THE SHORES INVADED

(Apparently three battalions, not two, were at Sarafim Farm.)

Burnu from Boghali—because the troops at Boghali were closer to the threatened points than were the 9th Division troops.

"The commander of the 19th Division was Mustafa Kemal Bey—'Bey', that is, I think, equivalent to your 'Major'."[1]

---

[1] Zeki Bey added that a Pasha would probably be "Colonel". He was certainly thinking of the German majors and colonels, whose commands were much higher than those of most British officers of those ranks. Actually (as Zeki Bey told me later) Effendi, Bey and Pasha were titles rather than ranks, and the rank of Mustafa Kemal at this time was apparently equivalent to Lieutenant-Colonel. (The present writer is in error in *Anzac to Amiens*, p. 115.)

This is the first time, so far as I remember, that I heard Mustafa Kemal's name.[2] I may, perhaps, have seen it in one of the intelligence reports at Anzac—"The prisoner gave the name of his divisional commander as Mustafa Kemal Bey." Military intelligence at the British War Office in February 1919 would, of course, have known much better. I fancy they would have said: "Let's see . . . that's the chap that's been commanding the Seventh Turkish Army." Our Light Horse commander Lieutenant-General Sir Harry Chauvel, whom we saw a few weeks later at Aleppo, knew still more—Chauvel had just had some troublesome dealing with him over the prescribed demobilisation of the Turkish forces in Syria, and spoke of him, with a twinkle, as "my friend Kemal". But the world in general outside his own country, including war correspondents from the Western Front, was not then aware of his existence. So far as the Mission was concerned Zeki Bey's next words changed all that.

"The regiment was assembled when the order came. Mustafa Kemal came himself, and ordered the regiment and a battery of artillery—mountain guns—to intercept the 'English' who had landed. He reasoned: 'If this force has gone in the direction of Koja Chemen Tepe, the landing is not a mere demonstration—it is the real thing, the landing of a main force.'

"For that reason he took, not one battalion, as the commander of the 9th Division had asked, but the whole regiment. They went at once straight across country towards the south of Koja Chemen Tepe—towards Chunuk Bair—Kemal himself leading."

This was vigorous action; how vigorous I only began to realise when Zeki Bey made clear the distribution of responsibility under the plans of Liman von Sanders, German commander of the 5th Army guarding the Dardanelles. "The 19th Division," Zeki Bey told me, "was

<hr />

[2] A photograph of Mustafa Kemal, apparently taken at Anzac, is in *Vol. I* at *p. 449*.

absolutely in reserve under the order of Liman Pasha; it was reserve of the Fifth Army. The XV Army Corps was holding the southern part of the Peninsula; the III Army Corps was holding the north. North of the 9th Division the coast was guarded by gendarmes; and about the same time as the commander of the 9th Division sent word of the Landing to Mustafa Kemal Bey, the gendarmes sent news of it to the III Corps commander, Essad Pasha. He was at Gallipoli [at the northern end of the Peninsula], and he and part of his staff came south to Maidos about 10 a.m.

"But Mustafa Kemal Bey had not waited for that. Although his division was in reserve under the direct orders of General Liman, and had not yet even been allotted to Essad Pasha [as it was soon after], he decided at once to use the 57th Regiment; and later in the day he put in both the other regiments, the 77th and 72nd, which were camped between Boghali and Maidos. All that first day General Liman did not send reinforcements from Gallipoli, because he had always in his head the belief that the real attack would come in the north near Bulair."

The town of Gallipoli lies twenty-five miles north-west of Anzac and Bulair is about ten miles north of that again, where the Peninsula narrows to a neck before joining the mainland; and here during the Crimean War French and British engineers had constructed the famous fortifications known as the "Bulair Lines". By seizing this neck an invader could cut off the Peninsula and all its defences from the mainland of Turkey; and to give the impression that this was his intention, the Allies' commander, Sir Ian Hamilton, had arranged that the transports of the Royal Naval Division, which was not to land for some days, and the other transports when they had finished emptying out their troops at Anzac, should steam along the coast to near Bulair, and make an appearance of preparing to land troops there. This (according to Zeki Bey) confirmed Liman in his belief that the real thrust would be at Bulair.

"When Liman Pasha received the report of the landing at Ari Burnu, he said: 'It's a demonstration, not the true landing.' Seeing the vessels sail for Bulair he said: 'The real landing will be at Bulair.' But those on the spot saw that the ships were empty before they sailed for Bulair."

Zeki Bey impressed on me that, down near Boghali where the 57th Regiment was paraded, Mustafa Kemal had gone off straight across country for the threatened point without awaiting leave or instructions from any-one. The regiment was headed by its 1st Battalion under Zeki Bey. Mustafa Kemal ordered a company to advance 200 yards ahead of the battalion; and with this company he went himself, a small map in his hand; and beside him Zeki Bey.

"Probably," Zeki Bey told me, "Mustafa Kemal didn't know where Ari Burnu was; on the little maps which we then had it was not marked by name. 'Bee Point' was perhaps the name given to it by the garrison of the 27th Regiment. Decent maps were then being prepared, but they weren't ready." However, Kemal *was* impressed by the importance of Koja Chemen Tepe—or of Chunuk Bair, which was practically the same position. He directed the march so as to meet the "English" before they could get there.

On reaching a valley south of Chunuk Bair (that is, one of the deep ravines behind Third Ridge some way north of Scrubby Knoll), Zeki Bey said, they met Turkish soldiers who came tumbling down the side of the valley. These men told Mustafa Kemal that they had been pushed back, and that numbers of troops had landed about Ari Burnu.

"Mustafa Kemal Bey had then two battalions ahead, 1st and 2nd, and one—the 3rd—in rear. He had lost the commander of our regiment, who had gone in another direction, and so he gave the order directly to me—that my battalion, the 1st, must without losing a minute vigorously attack the troops who were coming up the main hill-range, and push them back into the sea. At the same time he placed the mountain battery in position, just north of Kemal Yere—that is Kemal Hill—as it was afterwards called [Scrubby Knoll]. The 2nd Battalion was to advance on the right of mine; he kept only one battalion, the 3rd, in reserve.

"At this time we were only under the fire of the warships. But the advance was very difficult because we had come straight across country, and by the time when Mustafa Kemal Bey told me to attack my men were scattered and it was possible to get at only part of them. It was when I was searching for them, looking out from Third Ridge near Chunuk Bair, that I first saw the Australians. There was a line of them on the inland slope of Dus Tepe [Straight Hill, i.e. Battleship Hill] and they were advancing. Some soldiers of my battalion had crossed one of the valleys between me and the Australians —I think it was Dik Dere [Deep Valley, i.e. the valley in which lay the three sandpits, and along whose edge our Mission had found the spent ammunition of a Turkish firing line] and had attacked the Australians so closely that it seemed as if the bayonets might be used. I could see a line of men of my battalion on the spur. Opposite them was a line of Australians and near the upper end of this line an officer was standing, pointing with what looked to me like a sword—though it may have been a stick. He was pointing at the men of my battalion opposite him, who were retiring. A lieutenant of my battalion was there, holding on; I could see him, and saw him fall and his men retire. His men came back into Dik Dere. I shouted to the men with me to shoot at the Australian who seemed to be encouraging his men to go forward after my retiring men. On reaching the valley my soldiers moved southwards along it. Presently I saw

THE ANZAC POSITION, VIEWED FROM WHERE MUSTAFA KEMAL BEY SAW IT ON THE MORNING OF 25th APRIL 1915. (HE PLACED HIS HEADQUARTERS AT THE POINT FROM WHICH THE SKETCH WAS MADE, JUST NORTH OF SCRUBBY KNOLL, AND STATIONED A MOUNTAIN BATTERY BESIDE HIM. LATER THE HEADQUARTERS BECAME THAT OF ESSAD PASHA, COMMANDING THE "NORTH-ERN GROUP", AND THE OBSERVATION POST SHOWN IN THE FOREGROUND WAS CONSTRUCTED)

W.G. Wire Gully (nick in skyline).

C. Courtney's Post.

M.R. Mortar Ridge.

B. 700. Baby 700.

B'p H. Battleship Hill.

T. Tulloch's farthest point.

X. Point from which Turks fired.

160. Hill 160 (or 261), southern shoulder of Chunuk Bair.

S. Su Yatagha, eastern shoulder of Chunuk Bair.

U.L. Western branch of Usun Dere.

U.R. Eastern branch of Usun Dere.

the Australians, who were in a little bunch, take cover in the scrub.

"I myself had then been wounded; I was shot through the arm while I was standing up. But I could not have the wound attended to yet, as the situation was critical. I went down into Dik Dere to see what had happened to my soldiers. When I got there I found that the soldiers, who had retired on the right and gone down through the dere to the left, were not demoralised; but they had come under the fire of their own mountain battery—I think that is what prevented your troops also from advancing. The lieutenant whom I had seen wounded had been hit through the neck but was holding on, and his troops whom I had seen retiring were reinforcing the line farther south in the dere and were quite unshaken.

"The two battalions of the regiment drove your advanced troops back from Battleship Hill. I was sent away to hospital at 4 o'clock or 4.30.[3] In the afternoon the fighting had become severe. At first our soldiers met only weak troops and pushed them back. The guns were able to do good work. They couldn't fire on the Beach because it was too steep, so they fired down the long slope on your troops. The 2nd Battalion of our regiment attacked between my battalion and the sea and got to about the Fishermen's Huts. At the time when I left the 3rd Battalion was just coming up in reserve behind the left of my battalion. Farther south was the 27th Regiment. The battalion of the 27th[4] had all its company commanders hit, three killed, one wounded but still carrying on; and most of its younger officers were dead or wounded. The leading company of my battalion had one officer killed and one wounded.

"At dusk the 3rd Battalion of my regiment was

---

[3] I suspect that, as constantly happened, Zeki Bey thought he had been with the troops longer than he actually was.

[4] I think this refers to the battalion which had garrisoned the coast at Anzac and Gaba Tepe.

ordered to attack between the 1st and 2nd and to carry the attack to the sea. The 2nd Battalion, attacking on the seaward side, got, as I said, to the Fishermen's Huts or near them but didn't come back. The commander of this battalion himself went forward during the night to find his men and came back to report that there were only 'English' ahead, his own men were all gone. The regimental commander, Ahuni Bey, was rather upset by this report. But at that moment there came in also a report from the C.O. of the 3rd Battalion which had got to Jessaret Tepe [Hill of Courage, Russell's Top at The Nek]. He said that he was well ahead with his troops. They were weak, about 80 or 90 men, and he was a bit anxious lest, if attacked, they might not be able to hold: he needed reinforcements. But he added that things were then fairly quiet about there, and he thought that the 'English' were too exhausted to attack. His report was made with coolness; the general impression was that the commander of the 2nd Battalion had lost his head, while the C.O. of the 3rd Battalion, Hairi Bey, had kept his. At regimental headquarters—in Usun Dere [Long Valley][5] Ahuni Bey was greatly reassured by this report.

"That same night the 77th (Arab) Regiment came in to the south of the 57th, between it and the 27th Regiment. The two battalions of the 27th which in the first instance had been camped west of Maidos to resist any landing at Gaba Tepe, had early been ordered to send their troops straight towards the sea. They had come into the fight farther south than the 57th Regiment. In the night, the 77th Regiment coming in behind and between the 57th and 27th began to fire before it reached the

---

[5] On the Turkish map given to me by Zeki Bey, Usun Dere is the valley next behind Dik Dere and immediately in front of the northern end of Third Ridge. On the other hand my note of Zeki Bey's account of these events says that Usun Dere "forks to the right of Chatal Dere into Battleship Hill". That would be the valley at the head of which Mustafa Kemal afterwards had his divisional headquarters close to the nick between Battleship Hill and Chunuk Bair. He probably took over the old regimental headquarters.

front line. The 27th Regiment coming under this fire, and thinking that the 57th was shooting into it, was all night crying out to the 57th not to fire; and the 57th in the same way was calling to the 27th. The 77th was an Arab regiment, and the Arabs understood neither of the others. For this reason there was a panic and a lot of disorganisation—and the 77th was later sent to the Gaba Tepe end of the line, because that flank was quiet and the regiment had not much value.

"Towards evening of that first day there was sent up to the right flank the 72nd Regiment—the other regiment of the 19th Division. This regiment, too, was composed of Arabs. They were brought up towards Dus Tepe [Battleship Hill] to reinforce the 2nd Battalion of my regiment, which was by now pretty weak. That first day no reinforcements came from Gallipoli in the north because Liman Pasha thought the 5th Division up there would be needed at Bulair. They got ready the ships, however, to bring troops down if necessary. Essad Pasha, commander of the III Corps, came down, as I said, from Gallipoli to Mal Tepe. He approved what Mustafa Kemal had done. All the troops were under Mustafa Kemal Pasha that day and Essad merely helped him."[6]

I think Zeki Bey mentioned to me that at one time on April 25th some Turkish commander reported that the "English" at Ari Burnu had been driven back into the sea. At all events it was with reference to some such report that he told me: "Your troops from Dus Tepe [Battleship Hill] retired to the sea shore and remained there covered by the fire of their warships. The Turkish troops got about to Jessaret Tepe [The Nek]. They might

---

[6] General Aspinall-Oglander, in the *British Official History*, says that between 7 and 8 a.m. Liman von Sanders, hearing of the landings at Kum Kale (south of the Straits) and Cape Helles, sent Essad Pasha south to take charge of the 9th and 19th Divisions. Mustafa Kemal, after leading the 57th Regiment to action, hurried back to Essad, received from him approval of what he had done, and was authorised to take the two other regiments (77th and 72nd) from Army Reserve. As to the 72nd, see Zeki Bey's letter in *Appendix III*.

have done better, but the troops on their left were Arabs, and they panicked and came running round behind the 57th Regiment.[7]

"It was also reported to Constantinople that some of the troops who landed at Ari Burnu had been captured. About the third day Constantinople wanted to know when these prisoners were coming along. It was then reported that it was a mistake—there had been some misunderstanding. The Turkish soldiers thought that some of your men were going to surrender; your soldiers thought that some Turks were going to do the same. Some troops had surrendered, but others came up meanwhile—there was a complication, and an inquiry was held afterwards."

This probably was the Turkish interpretation of an incident that occurred on the first night. At the head of Monash Valley a surviving group of the 11th Battalion told Colonel H. Pope of the 16th, which arrived in the dark to reinforce them, that Indians were fighting on their left—a notion which had been current there since 4.30 p.m. and which allowed part of a Turkish battalion (III/57th) to penetrate along that side of Russell's Top. Pope sent three of his officers and men who could speak Hindustani along the edge of Pope's Hill towards The Nek to get in touch with these "Indians". As he could hear talk, and his men did not return, Pope followed them only to realise just in time, from some movement of the strangers in the dark, that these were Turks. He

---

[7] This statement of Zeki Bey's was made, of course, at second-hand; when the events happened he was on his way to hospital. But he possibly heard that Russell's Top had that night lain open to the Turks. He would not, however, know that Walker's Ridge, leading from the Top, near The Nek, down to the sea, was held by a strong and unshaken force of Australians and New Zealanders under Lieut.-Colonel G. F. Braund (vegetarian, theosophist, and invincible) and Brigadier-General H. B. Walker (a cultured Englishman and the one general at Anzac who that day fought like a tiger against any suggestion of withdrawal). In three days' fighting this force finally held the Top against stronger attacks than any previously made.

plunged into the gully, shots following him, and got back to his battalion, but his three envoys were captured. As only one other Australian—a bugler who mistook another gully for Monash Valley, and was clubbed there —was captured, the prisoners referred to by Zeki Bey were almost certainly Colonel Pope's envoys.[8]

OTHER RIDDLES
OF THE LANDING

ON some questions relating to the battle of the Anzac Landing and its immediate sequels Zeki Bey could throw no light. For a month from the first afternoon he had been away in hospital. He was able to tell us, as will be seen later, some details of policy and tactics learnt later from his colleagues or their records; but a number of the questions relating to those days we of the Mission had to settle by the evidence on the ground. I will briefly touch on these before returning to Zeki Bey's narrative of later events.

The first of these questions related to what were called the "battle outposts" which during this battle our infantry established and maintained in front of one section of the line. These included the posts established by Loutit and Haig on their withdrawal from spurs of the Third Ridge to Wire Gully. Those two officers were still in front of the main line, and the posts comprised a weak line above, and down, the southern side of Wire Gully and two or three smaller more advanced posts down its ravine. During the first ten days, while the main line was being dug and connected, they served to keep the Turks at some distance, or at least to give notice of their approach. They were not far from the line but it was most dangerous to attempt to reach them by day. During the fourth night they were taken over by the first troops who relieved their original garrisons. The newcomers were the inexperienced British "Marines" of Churchill's newly-raised Royal Naval Division. The Turks, who were

143

by then creeping forward and establishing themselves on the knuckles north and south of this ravine, shot them out of part of their exposed positions. The Marines in their turn were heroically relieved by Sergeants H. R. W. Meagher and T. D. McLeod of the 3rd Battalion.

Eventually, having proved a death-trap (though the scene of a series of fine actions, including that which brought the first Victoria Cross to be won at Anzac),[1] these outposts were all given up—the last of them on May 5th. Having constantly come on mention of them in early accounts of this sector, I was anxious to ascertain precisely where they were. The most famous incident connected with them happened at dusk on the first day. In the half dark Australians digging in on the crest-line behind Wire Gully saw a large body of troops coming up from Legge Valley towards the knuckle, on the northern side of Wire Gully, afterwards known as "German Officers'". All the afternoon rumours had been flying along the line (passed from mouth to mouth as the troops were then trained to do) that Indians were on the left or right, and other rumours that the British 29th Division was advancing from Cape Helles. A cry of "Don't shoot—Indian troops!" now came along. Not all men believed it, but fire stopped and from the main line at two points officers, one of whom had seen service in India, went to investigate. In the foremost outpost, down the bed of the gully itself, deep in the ravine, Lieutenant G. E. McDonald of the 3rd Battalion, a Sydney signwriter, also went out to make sure. He bent low till a tall figure stood out of the scrub close in front of him, and then pinned the man and rushed him to his post: he proved to be a

---

[1] It was won by a British marine, Lance-Corporal W. R. Parker. Others were deserved, as the reader will see at *Vol. I, pp. 540-2,* and *Preface to 2nd Edition, pp. xix-xxii*; but that battle left the inexperienced staffs far too busy, with the task of rebuilding their units and carrying on, to attend to recommendations for awards; also witnesses were dead or in hospital, and records almost non-existent. For the special difficulties of the Marines, see *Vol. I, pp. 532-4.*

tall, well-dressed Turk with a medical armlet. He was sent back to the line as prisoner; and this incident, and the shooting of Australians who were investigating elsewhere, settled the question. Australian machine-guns opened, and the crowded oncomers—possibly part of the 77th Arab Regiment—threw themselves down or fled. Practically all Australians at Anzac heard the story and most of those who saw it were convinced that the cry "Indian troops" was a ruse of the Turks to enable them to approach with impunity.

Zeki Bey, however, when I told him the story, looked so incredulous that it was clear not only that he had never heard of it, but that he felt—as I had long done—that such a ruse was beyond the capacity of Turkish infantry to carry out. His view was supported by McDonald whom I later questioned in Australia, and who told me that he, in the farthest outpost, was quite sure that the cry came from the Australian line. It seemed to me possible that it arose in, or was repeated by, one of the less advanced battle outposts, in which case Australians in the main line would probably imagine that it came from the enemy.

The position of the main outposts became quite clear to the Mission when we examined Wire Gully; was indeed terribly clear. Near the top end of the ravine there ran up the steep slope forming its southern side (part of Johnston's Jolly) a succession of gravelly gutters or washaways. Along the forward edge of one of these were a number of shelter holes, obviously burrowed into the top of the bank by a line of our men who had held that rib. The gutter was interrupted at the bottom by the steep, V-shaped, twelve-feet deep, channel of the valley-bed; and thence up the northern side (German Officers' knuckle) ran a wide shallow trench, the upper part of which, near the summit of German Officers', was only a succession of rifle-pits, with the partitions not yet completely dug through to form a continuous trench. Both "trenches"

145

were straight and terribly open to fire from the other
side of the ravine, and the northern one was full of the
skeletons and uniforms of the dead—chiefly of
marines in the lower part and valley-bed, and of Australians and Turks farther up. The remains, sometimes
of several men together, lay in the little pits like rags

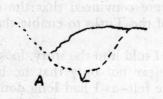

THE "BATTLE OUTPOSTS" IN WIRE GULLY

A. Diagram of the gully, looking east from the Australian
   line, showing the position of the two nearer outposts
   (dotted line) on its southern and northern slopes.
B. Rough sketch of the outpost on the southern slope, with
   washaway behind it apparently used as a grave.
C. Part of battle outpost above the northern slope, showing
   a line of rifle-pits not fully connected and containing
   the bodies of Australians.

poked into drawers. In the "pozzies" along the washaway on the southern side the only relic was the sun helmet
of a marine, but the washaway next behind it was littered
with these helmets, along with jam tins and rubbish
thrown later from our lines. A gutter nearer to the Turkish
trenches was littered even more thickly with the remains

146

of Turks. It was clear that the trenches and gutters, though tenable as long as the Turks were distant, were terribly exposed after the Turks thrust up the summits on either side of the valley; and that the positions had been used as graves in the armistice on May 24th.

Of the foremost battle outposts farther down the gully we could see no sign, unless it was a few pieces of our kit a little ahead of the other posts. But on the summit of the knuckle north of the gully (the MacLaurin's Hill-German Officers' spur) was another abandoned trench, just ahead of the battle outposts. Both these trenches ran northwards into the Australian front trench,[2] which lay about 15 yards in from the edge of Monash Valley. On the southern side of Wire Gully, however, the post originally established by Loutit's comrade, Haig, on the edge of the plateau above the ravine, was isolated so far as surface trenches went; but at some later time our troops had tunnelled out to it and incorporated it in the front line system.

Another problem of the first day's fight was the location of the Turkish guns captured in the advance over or near the 400 Plateau. In all official reports after the battle, so far as I know, they were referred to as "a Turkish battery", and the official accounts of their capture probably came from Major Brand. For the guns which Loutit and Brand had seen on the 400 Plateau, with the Turkish teams hastily limbering up and then vanishing down Owen's Gully, had not escaped, as Loutit imagined. They had turned into a deep hollow leading off that gully (in the Official History it is called "The Cup"), near the top of which were their proper emplacements. Near its eastern rim the guns were presently caught by

---

2 By front trench I mean the open, surface trench; there was an underground front line considerably farther out. The northern end of this battle outpost as seen after the Turkish attack on May 19th is shown in *Vol. II, p. 138.*

other infantry, who tried to burr the screws inside the breeches and otherwise disable the weapons.[3]

Three guns were captured there. They were out of their emplacements, but the Australians could not drag them away, for the rifle-fire sweeping the plateau soon became too deadly. Presumably these guns were recovered by the Turks that night. They were Krupp guns and were thought to be field-guns. But within a few weeks of the Landing, Captain R. M. F. Hooper of the 5th Battalion, a young Victorian afterwards killed at Lone Pine, told me that he had taken part in the capture of "the Turkish battery"; that the guns were Hotchkiss, and were still in their emplacements, and his party and others had held them until late at night. I soon came across other leaders, including Lieutenant A. P. Derham who gave me a detailed and most interesting account of a fight at these guns. Derham was one of a party who held them all the afternoon. At dusk Turks from Third Ridge began to cross Legge Valley and tried to rush the gun-pits, and eventually even to burn the party out, but were beaten partly through the arrival at the last moment of an Australian sergeant who happened to be able to work a Turkish machine-gun.[4]

It was therefore clear that not one battery but two had been captured on or near the 400 Plateau. The Krupp guns were at the depression already referred to as The Cup, behind the solitary pine that gave Lone Pine its name. The Hotchkiss guns were farther south, somewhere on Pine Ridge, the farthest of four ridges that ran southwards like the prongs of a fork from the southern side of the Lone Pine Plateau. Hooper had given me a plan of the Hotchkiss emplacements, and the Mission searched all Pine Ridge for them. Eventually, in a fold at the southernmost end of the ridge Rogers and I found some old trenches associated with three old gun emplace-

---

[3] The incident is told in *Vol. I, pp. 338-42.*
[4] This fighting is described in *Vol. I, pp. 389 and 422-3.*

ments; they seemed to be part of an old system of defence to protect Gaba Tepe from attack from the north. I noted that they "might be" those mentioned by Hooper; and some way farther up the ridge we found the remains of eight Turks in a group together with bones of two horses or mules, possibly part of a gun team. On returning to Australia, however, I interviewed Derham (then

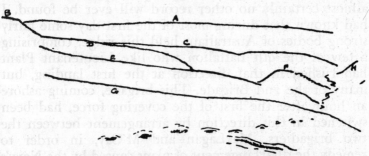

*THE FOUR RIDGES SOUTH OF LONE PINE—THE VIEW LOOKS
EASTWARD ACROSS THEM TO THIRD RIDGE*

A. *Third (Gun) Ridge.*

B. *South-east shoulder of Lone Pine.*

C. *Pine Ridge.*

D. *Weir Ridge.*

E-F. *Snipers' Ridge—Knife Edge (the Knife Edge, bent
 back like a razor blade, is narrower than would appear
 from the sketch).*

G. *Silt Spur, showing part of our underground front line.*

H. *Holly Spur (an off-shoot of Bolton's Hill).*

a young doctor in Melbourne) and he made it quite clear that the Hotchkiss gun-pits had been at the northern end of the ridge, just down the shoulder from Lone Pine, where Pine Ridge sprang from it. Probably they had since been obliterated by many other diggings for headquarters and supports. But I notice that on an old British map that I have beside me, issued by our staff just before the Landing, and marked in purple ink with the Turkish defences seen by Villiers-Stuart and other observers from the air, there is marked at precisely that spot: "7 gun battery".[5] Probably both the Krupp and the Hotchkiss batteries were noted by the observers as near this point.

But if our search of Pine Ridge failed to show where the tense fight at the gun-pits had taken place, it provided us with traces of other struggles just as tense, of which almost certainly no other record will ever be found. I had known that during most of the first day some fairly strong bodies of Australians held this ridge, comprising a few of the 9th Battalion who like Lieutenant Plant had rushed in that direction at the first landing, but many of the 2nd Brigade. This brigade, coming ashore an hour after the first of the covering force, had been switched in this direction by arrangement between the two brigadiers, MacLagan and M'Cay, in order to remedy the disarrangement of plans caused by the Navy's having set the 3rd Brigade ashore too far north. Towards the afternoon young Major H. Gordon Bennett (who twenty-five years later commanded Australian troops in the Malay Peninsula) had organised an advanced line of some 300 men of the 6th, 7th and 8th Battalions there. He was apparently a little south of the party in the gun-pits; but he knew nothing of them or of other parties, under Sergeant A. R. Knightley of the 9th, Lieutenant R. C. G. Prisk of the 6th, and others, which had posted themselves from a quarter to half a mile farther south, near the southern end of the same ridge.

These several bodies kept back the 27th Turkish Regiment on Third Ridge, just across the open green of Legge Valley, until late in the afternoon. But then a movement started which they could not stop. Turkish

---

[5] In some details since ascertained, this map is remarkably accurate. For example, the camps of the 57th, 72nd and 77th Turkish Regiments, and the reserves of the 27th Regiment and 9th Turkish Division are accurately placed; they are not, of course identified by name, but the approximate strength is correctly shown in each case.

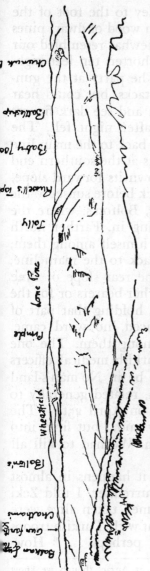

THE TURKISH SIDE OF THE SECOND RIDGE WHICH CONFRONTED THE TURKS MOVING OVER THE THIRD RIDGE

The view is from near the position reached by Loutit, Haig, and Ryder on the day of the Landing. This is the first view of Anzac which confronts anyone coming by road from Kilia Liman on the Dardanelles and over Third Ridge. The Australian advanced parties here were soon outflanked and driven back by Turks swarming over the Third Ridge. These Turks, from their side, looking across Legge Valley, could see swarms of Australians throughout the morning and the rest of the day trying to reach the part of Lone Pine shown in this picture and the long crest of Pine Ridge (in the middle distance on the left). Parties of Australians already were there. Late in the afternoon the Turks began to creep across the valley and drove back or cut off most of the Australians on Pine Ridge. Captains Daly and Hooper, in some captured gun-pits on Pine Ridge near its junction with Lone Pine, beat off the attacks there and were recalled during the night to the main line along the rear edge of the Second Ridge, as were most of the advanced parties on Lone Pine. These gun-pits were on Pine Ridge below the word Pimple. The Balkan gun-pits (on left, beyond "Our farthest South") held no guns.

Lone Pine was temporarily recaptured on the next afternoon by a thrust, consequent upon a mistaken order, from the direction of the Pimple and ending at Johnston's Jolly. Both it and the Jolly were afterwards occupied by the Turks.

skirmishers began to cross the valley to the foot of the ridge, which was clothed by an open wood of dwarf pines similar to the Lone Pine—they somewhat resembled our Australian cypress pine but were shorter, ten feet high, or fifteen at most, and rounder. The party at the gun-pits managed to beat off several attacks, but could hear Turkish officers rallying their men and see dark figures now and again advancing, until after night fell. The troops at the gun-pits were brought back to the main line late that night. Also the Australians at the southern end of the ridge, some of them well down its forward slope, finding Turks behind them, fell back before sunset to the first and highest of the five ridges, Bolton's, where the main line on that flank was digging in. Farther north many of Bennett's three hundred, himself among them, had been hit and had struggled back to the main line, or at least to the washaways on the rear slope of Pine Ridge, where they waited for stretcher-bearers or for the dark. But, of those who were still holding that part of the ridge when the Turks advanced, no word came. Bennett's younger brother was among them. The one shred of information, given by Turkish medical officers to some of ours who happened to be in No-man's-land during the armistice on May 24th, related generally to the Australians who were overrun on April 25th. "The living pretended to be dead," they said, "but fired into us again after we had passed them. We had to kill all those."

Probably it was true of some; it happens in almost every battle where men will not surrender. I told Zeki Bey that our men had heard that men taken alive were mutilated by the Turks. He said that with Turkish troops it could not happen—with Arabs, perhaps . . .[6] How-

---

[6] No sign of such atrocity was ever found at Anzac, though we know from Australian prisoners captured in August that some of them would have been killed had not Turkish or German officers intervened.

ever that may be, none of the many wounded left in our opponents' hands that day survived.

This was all that we knew of the Australians on Pine Ridge until Balfour searched the ridge with a party of his men, and returned with a report which brought himself, Rogers, and me to examine the ground more carefully.

There we found them. From near the northern end of the ridge, just south of where the road climbs it, for about 200 yards southwards along—or rather just in front of—the crest there lay at intervals the bodies of Australians, their bones rather, still associated with the tatters of their uniforms. Far down the slope in front lay a couple more; and about a quarter of a mile down the ridge, on a little knob low down, overlooking Legge Valley, were four or five, grouped in a little half-circle where they had fought it out—a Turk or Turks had been firing from the other edge of the knob, eight yards away. And at the back of the ridge, up near the road, there lay from top to bottom of a small gully the remains of Australians who had lain there wounded or sheltering when the attack caught them. On uniforms, among all these groups, we found the red and purple arm patches or bronze numbers of the 6th Battalion.

The fight in which they died helped to keep the Turks from the troops digging the main line on Bolton's Hill and the 400 Plateau. But the troops on Pine Ridge thought they themselves were holding the main line; and I have often wondered since whether, if the brigadiers and the staff of the 1st Australian Division had known that they were there, and that others were on Lone Pine, they could not have secured Pine Ridge and Lone Pine for the Allies on the first day or night of the campaign, and so won a great advantage for their later offensives. But probably the troops were too disorganised for so quick a development of the modified plan, by which the advance was to stop for the time being at the rear

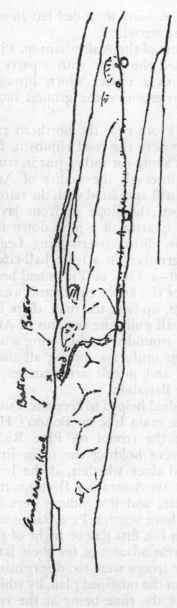

WHERE THE RELICS ON PINE RIDGE WERE FOUND

Pine Ridge is the ridge seen in the middle distance, covered by the stumps of the pines which once clothed it. The Turks were attacking from the foot of the higher ridge (Third or Gun Ridge) beyond. Between the two ridges lay Legge Valley; and at the points marked O-O-O along Pine Ridge were found remains of the 6th Battalion and others.

It was along the top of Gun Ridge that a battalion or two of Turks with guns were seen marching northwards about 9 o'clock. Before then it was possibly reached by a party under Lieutenant Plant—the point marked X, above the road, may have been reached by him. Turkish batteries took position near there from the day of the Landing, and two battery positions were found by the Mission at the points marked.

THE NEK, BETWEEN RUSSELL'S TOP AND BABY 700.
The Nek is marked by the permanent Turkish monument, placed where the
Turkish soldiers, from the evening of 25th April 1915 onwards, stopped all
attempts by the Anzacs to reach the key position, Baby 700 (in foreground). On
the left of The Nek lies the head of Monash Valley, and on the right Malone's
Gully, behind which can be seen Turk Point and, behind it, parts of Walker's
Ridge. The front trenches can be seen beyond the monument, and beyond them
the expanse of Russell's Top. Baby 700 was captured by the Anzacs on
April 25th, but lost towards evening. *G1874*

MALONE'S GULLY,
leading to the seaward side of The Nek. *G1879*

HEAD OF MONASH VALLEY,
leading to The Nek. This is the western branch of Monash Valley. The eastern
branch is divided from it by Pope's Hill (in foreground). *G1882*

AUSTRALIAN RELICS
on the north-easternmost spur of Battleship Hill. This was probably the point
reached by Captain Tulloch's company on 25th April 1915.   *G1887*

TURKISH GUN PLACED ON BABY 700
after the Evaculation. The view is northwards to Battleship Hill. It was south
of this gun that traces of Major Kindon's line and of the Auckland troops
were found.   *G1799*

MAJOR ZEKI BEY
COMMANDANT THE TURKISH REGIMENT
AT GALLIPOLI

LAMBERT'S DRAWING OF OUR GUEST.
Australian War Memorial Collection

THE TURKISH CORPS COMMANDER'S LOOKOUT AT SCRUBBY KNOLL.
In the foreground is a ruined shelter. Essad Pasha's observation post is seen
beyond it.   *G2024*

LEGGE VALLEY, SEEN FROM JOHNSTON'S JOLLY.
This shows the opening of Owen's Gully, between the Jolly and Lone Pine, and
Turkish saps for passage of mules across Mortar Ridge (left) and a spur of Third
Ridge (right). It was a higher section of that spur which was reached on
April 25th by Loutit, Haig and Ryder.   *G1900*

WIRE GULLY,
showing (in foreground) the remains of one of our old battle outposts. In the middle distance is the end of Mortar Ridge, and behind it Scrubby Knoll. It was up the foot of this valley and the slope on the left that the Turks approached in the dusk of April 25th, when the cry of "Indian troops!" was raised.   *G1893*

PART OF A TURKISH SAP
for the passage of mules to Mule Valley. It was the sight of the Turkish mule train crossing this gully towards the "Turkish Quinn's" that gave the valley its name. Elaborate trenches were dug to avoid the consequent losses.   *G1878*

TURKISH MULE· SAP
through the back of Johnston's Jolly to Mule Valley in 1919. It took "months of
work with pickaxe and spade" to build in 1915.   *G2040*

THE VALLEY BEHIND "TURKISH QUINN'S".
This was crowded with bivouacs of reserves and the post headquarters. Up the valley-bed passed troops and mule-borne supplies for Baby 700 and The Nek. It was this part of Mortar Ridge (on the right) that was reached by Captain Leer on April 25th. *G1832*

THE VALLEY BEHIND "TURKISH QUINN'S"
looking south. The Australian and New Zealand trenches at Quinn's were only 100 yards from the top of the slope on the right. The lower part of the valley was known as Mule Valley. Johnston's Jolly and Lone Pine are in the distance. *G1834*

edge of the Second Ridge. However that may be, after the troops had been withdrawn from the Lone Pine Plateau that night, the same plateau was seized again in an unintended and, as things went, useless attack next day, April 26th. This was the operation in which, as mentioned in Chapter V, Lieutenant-Colonel Onslow Thompson was killed. It took place when, in mid-afternoon, the 4th Battalion and part of the 5th mistook an order to straighten the line for a command to make the general advance that everyone then expected. They swept across Lone Pine northwards, and many ended by uselessly lining the northern and southern edges of Owen's Gully and facing northwards across Johnston's Jolly. Even at that stage, possibly, Lone Pine could have been held. But the divisional staff—and a very good staff it was —did not even know that the attack was being made.[7]

The Mission found some of the half-scraped rifle-pits of our men along the edge of the Jolly fringing Owen's Gully, where they lay for an hour or two when this attack stopped, and whence Colonel Onslow Thompson had tried to make his way back while the setting sun glanced from the stream of Turkish machine-gun bullets.

The Anzacs had, by the third day of the campaign, been left holding the rear edge of the Second Ridge and (on the left) of Walker's Ridge, sharply bent back to North Beach, enclosing a narrow triangle of steep ridges and scrub with the Beach as its base. As I have already stated, although Zeki Bey was not then at Anzac, he was able to give us an outline of the Turkish reaction during that critical time. No troops, he said, arrived from the north on April 25th—Liman von Sanders kept them near Bulair for the reasons already explained. "But on April 26th," Zeki Bey said, "battalions began to arrive at Anzac.

---

[7] The making of the unintended attack was not the fault of headquarters but of the dangerous method, inherited from the South African War, or devised after it, of passing orders by word of mouth down the line. The whole incident is explained in *Vol. I, pp. xvi-xix* and *490-8*.

Liman also came south; it was by then known to him that the English transports which had gone up north were empty, and Liman was better satisfied.

"There were complications at Ari Burnu, but the situation at that time was not dangerous there. On the other hand in the south there was very great danger. The 9th Division had only two battalions there and another battalion about Kum Tepe, between the southern zone and Gaba Tepe. The 9th Division had sent the two reserve battalions of the 27th Regiment to Ari Burnu. There remained the battalions of the 9th Division's third regiment, mostly at Serafim Chiflik (Seraphim Farm) on the Kilid Bahr Plateau about three miles south-east of Gaba Tepe. That shows the importance that had been attached to Gaba Tepe—four battalions of the 9th Division's reserves were within reach of it. The consequence had been that there were very few troops in the south. The officer commanding there was sending to Essad for troops, saying that he could not hold; but the authorities could not send him troops. Essad told him that he *must* hold. Essad Pasha was given command in the south and Mustafa Kemal was, for the time being, left in command at Ari Burnu.

"Kemal Bey did not lose his head. By the end of the first day at Ari Burnu he knew that, though the situation was still obscure there, it was not immediately dangerous. The calm reports from the III/57th Battalion at The Nek helped in this result. Kemal Bey knew his troops were tired, but he would not ask for reinforcements. So when the battalions of the 7th Division came down that day, April 26th, from the north to Maidos, the Turkish command was able to send them straight on to Helles, where it now knew the real danger to exist; and the first reinforcements to reach Ari Burnu were a few battalions of the 5th Division, also from the north, which arrived on the night of the 26th or morning of the 27th.

"Kemal Bey knew that the troops he then had at Ari Burnu were not sufficient for a counter-attack. The four regiments there had reorganised on April 26th and a few battalions, possibly of the 5th Division, had been added. He knew that these troops were not sufficient; but he wanted to drive your forces into the sea before they had a firm foothold there, and so he had to counter-attack.

"He did so on April 27th."

At this point I told Zeki Bey that the impression of our troops had been that the Turks tried to counter-attack on the morning of the 26th, moving down over Baby 700, but that they had been caught there by the guns of the battleships, which also happened again on the 27th.

"No," he said. "The movement on the 26th was merely reorganisation; but on the 27th it was a general attack."

I told him that such assaults as had been reported on the 27th happened at different times at different points, and many of the Anzacs did not even realise that they were being attacked that day. On the other hand a very brave attack was made up Mule Gully against our 1st Brigade.

"The general assault was probably ordered for the early morning," he said. "But at the start of the campaign the telephonic communications were not good, and probably the various parts of the operation were not well timed. Probably the attack up Mule Gully was made by the first of the arriving battalions of the 5th Division— their dead lay there afterwards.

"From then until May 19th we made no general attack; only small thrusts were made,[8] on the initiative of local commanders, to gain particular points of advantage.

---

[8] Kannengiesser (*Gallipoli pp. 106-7*), however, makes it certain that the attack on May 1st was intended to be general.

Our right flank [on the high land about Baby 700 and on the slope to North Beach] suffered a lot in the earliest days owing to the direct observation from the warships—but more in morale than in actual losses. Later our troops understood that the warships' guns did little real damage (les canons des vaisseaux ne faisaient pas grandes choses). The machine-guns prevented attacks being made by day."

Chapter
· XIII ·

GERMAN OFFICERS'
TRENCH

WHILE Zeki Bey was in hospital he heard of the great attack made by the Turks on May 19th. Essad Pasha had come back from Helles to take command of that attack. He divided the front between the divisions—the 19th Division under Mustafa Kemal still held the right, as far south as Quinn's; from Quinn's to Wire Gully was the 5th Division; Johnston's Jolly was held by the 2nd Division, Lone Pine by the 16th; and the 77th (Arab) Regiment still occupied the extreme left. There was one regiment in reserve for the zone.

"The attack was late at most places," Zeki Bey told me, "though some parts attacked at the proper hour. The 3rd Battalion of my regiment (57th), which was opposite the right of Pope's Hill, had received six young officers the day before; they had arrived in the evening. They just knew there was to be an attack—nothing else. Five of them that day lay dead on their own parapet, where they had jumped in order to give an example to the soldiers.

"Ten thousand men were killed or wounded in that attack. The 5th Division attacking up Merkez Tepe, ["Central Hill", the Turkish name for German Officers' Ridge] lost most heavily. That hill lay squeezed in between two valleys [Mule Valley, leading to Quinn's, and Wire Gully] and the troops were crowded into a narrow space, with machine-guns firing down each side of the hill. One reason why the Turkish staff chose to attack at Ari Burnu rather than at Helles at this time was that the troops would not be under fire from the

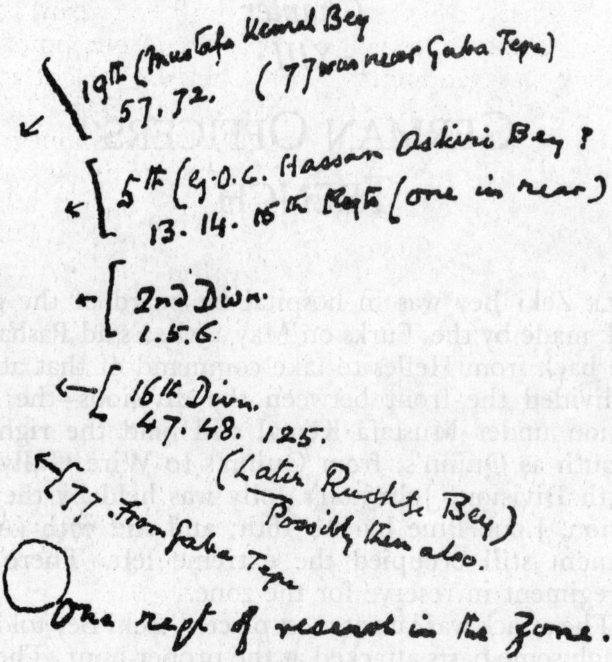

[handwritten annotations:]

19th (Mustafa Kemal Bey
57. 72.   (77 was near Gaba Tepe)

5th (G.O.C. Hassan Askeri Bey ?
13. 14. 15th Regts (one in rear)

2nd Divn.
1.5.6

16th Divn.
47. 48. 125.

(Later Rushti Bey)
Possibly then also.

77. From Gaba Tepe

One regt of reserve in the Zone.

ORDER OF BATTLE FOR ESSAD PASHA'S
COUNTER-ATTACK OF 19th MAY 1915 AT
ANZAC (from the writer's diary)

warships; and also a small advance would suffice to push you into the sea.

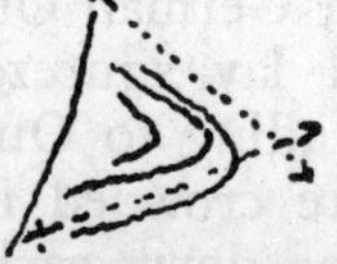

HOW THE 5th DIVISION
WAS CAUGHT BY AUS-
TRALIAN MACHINE-GUNS
AT GERMAN OFFICERS'
RIDGE

"But after that experience the Turkish command knew that it could do nothing at Ari Burnu by attacking, and so the force up there was reduced to three divisions.

"I returned from hospital a few days after that attack, and was given command at Merkez

Tepe [German Officers'].[1] In hospital I had heard that at Ari Burnu the opposing trenches were at one point only from five to seven metres apart. I heard of the attacks at Bomba Sirt [Bomb Ridge, Quinn's Post and the Turkish post facing it], and that your troops were bombed from either side and couldn't get out because of enfilade fire. I would not believe the reports because it was so different when I left.

"When I got back my idea at first was: 'Why don't we attack and thrust these Australians off their position at Bomba Sirt?' I went straight up to Bomba Sirt to see. After a short time I became convinced of the impossibility. The position was held only by the initiative of your men." On several occasions Zeki Bey repeated this comment: The bare foothold on the edge of almost sheer slopes was not a really tenable position; it was only exceptional initiative that enabled his opponents to stay there. The Turkish soldier, though tough and steadfast, could not have held those positions, he said.

Merkez Tepe, the short, steep knuckle running from MacLaurin's Hill down to Legge Valley with Quinn's to the north and Johnston's Jolly to the south, was apparently called "Central Hill" because it lay between those two important positions and was vital to the defence of each, especially of the Turkish Quinn's.[2] It was the machine-guns on the "central" spur which, by sweeping the No-man's-land in front of its neighbours, were the chief protection of those posts. For this reason the Turkish Quinn's and the two posts on either flank of it, at German Officers' and the southern part of the Chessboard, were all held by Zeki Bey's regiment, the 57th, which kept two battalions (the 2nd and 3rd) at the most difficult post, Quinn's, one in line and one in support

---

1 Later Zeki Bey said that by August 6th his unit had been 45 continuous days at German Officers', in which case it must have entered on that tour on June 23rd; but apparently he was there also on June 13th and about May 29th, possibly on a previous tour.
2 The Turkish post facing Quinn's.

changing places every few days. The 1st Battalion, Zeki Bey's, was kept at Merkez Tepe, two companies always in the line and two in support on the rear slope of the hill, these similarly changing places at intervals. The regimental headquarters was now at Edirna Sirt (Adrianople Ridge, our Mortar Ridge) just in rear.

Perhaps the main function of the Turkish post on Merkez Tepe was to keep that machine-gun ready to sweep No-man's-land between the opposing posts at Quinn's. It was the sight of two officers surveying this hill about May 10th that had caused the Australians to call the trench which immediately appeared there "German Officers' ". It quickly spread through the scrub like a molehill, looped around the knuckle from valley to valley.

Raids were made by the Australians to try to silence the machine-gun emplaced at the corner of it nearest to Quinn's. Zeki Bey heard that one night a pair of Australian legs had stumbled into the trench, possibly through its headcover, and had been quickly withdrawn. The raids did not succeed, and it soon became evident that the Australians were resorting to a more subtle means of destroying the position.

It was not the Australians who began mining at Anzac. The Turks opposite Quinn's Post had turned to it very early, possibly before May 10th, as a means of blowing us from our slight foothold there. After the dreadful consequences of their attack on May 19th they began to mine with greater vigour,[3] and on the 29th blew up and captured for a few hours part of Quinn's. That occurrence gave great impetus to the Anzacs' min-

[3] Zeki Bey told me that "mining began after the attack on May 19th". In this he was certainly wrong, see *Vol. II, pp. 98, 105,* and footnote on *p. 199.* The tense struggle in the early mining there is described in *Vol. II, pp. 199-211.* The Turkish staff, in the answers given in *Appendix I,* says that mining began after the attack on May 11th. But there was no such attack; probably May 9th is meant. Zeki Bey said the Turks valued our entrenching tools as the best implement for mining.

ing: on that day men experienced in mining had been
sought out from the infantry to form special units. Tunnels were to be begun like an apron in front of trenches
that the Turks were likely to undermine. The shallow
tunnels, keeping just beneath the roots of the grass, could
be broken through to the surface where desired, to make
new front trenches which were secret at least for a time,
and to steal ground farther in from the valley's edge,
along which the original trenches ran. Longer tunnels
were pushed out from this apron to undermine the
Turkish front line.

This had been the position when Zeki Bey came to
German Officers'. Australian mining activity had already
overtaken the Turkish and was causing keen anxiety;
nothing placed a garrison under greater strain than the
suspicion that it was being undermined and might at
any moment be blown up. "There were twenty-one
explosions at Merkez Tepe before I left there," Zeki Bey
told me. Apparently these occurred in ten weeks. Not
many of these mines actually blew up part of the trench;
some were just outside it, others destroyed Turkish tunnels. "The big explosion," he went on, "was about the
centre of our front. But before that took place you had
tunnelled out and undermined the northern end of my
trenches so badly that, with the constant explosions, the
earth there became friable. We had to use mud bricks to
make the side of the trench stand up." He pointed out
this part to us, and Wilkins photographed it. "Your
trench-mortar bombs also made this corner so dangerous
that the machine-gun could not be kept near it, but was
placed lower down the hill, in the second line, behind an
'island traverse'." Wilkins' photograph showed this also.

"Later still the position of this gun, which was used
only against Quinn's, became so dangerous owing to your
fire, that we emplaced another gun on the far side—the
southern side—of the Merkez Tepe trench system to shoot
over at Quinn's. About this time a third machine-gun,

163

one belonging to the 125th Regiment which held Kirmezi Sirt [Crimson Slope, Johnston's Jolly] was put in

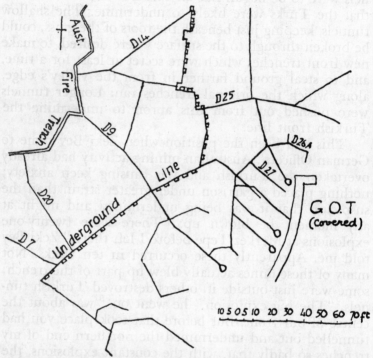

PLAN OF MINE-GALLERIES DRIVEN FROM THE AUSTRALIAN
FRONT LINE AT STEELE'S POST AGAINST THE NORTHERN END
OF GERMAN OFFICERS' TRENCH. AS THEY NEARED THE TURKISH
TRENCH THE GALLERIES WERE 23-24 FEET UNDERGROUND

The plan has been roughly traced from one made by Company-
Sergeant-Major W. Wilson of the 1st Field Company, Australian
Engineers, in July 1915. The "big crater" was too far south to
be shown in this plan.

on the south side of Merkez Tepe to fire towards Kirmezi
Sirt; but that gun was not under my orders but under
those of the 125th Regiment, whose sector was separated
from that of my battalion by Gedik Dere" (Hole Valley,

as the Turks called Wire Gully, the hole being the nick at its upper end). Zeki Bey added that he used few troops, or tired ones, to hold the side of his post bordering Wire Gully because that side was much less dangerous and trying for them than the northern side of it. He illustrated the tension on the northern side by an incident typical of the place.

"The aide-de-camp of the commander of the 125th Regiment was coming up to my sector on Merkez Tepe one day for a reconnaissance, and wanted to look over from the machine-gun position on the northern side of my trenches. You had the gun awfully well marked by then, and it seldom fired. The sergeant with the gun told him not to look over. He insisted on doing so and was hit through the middle of the forehead and killed."

So much for that machine-gun. As to the mines Zeki Bey said: "About the time when I returned from hospital the Turks had exploded a mine"—this was certainly the one that blew up part of Quinn's on May 29th—"and we had heard through our agents in Egypt that you were digging mines everywhere. So an order had been sent out that mines were to be dug by us also everywhere—up to then it had been a matter for individual commanders to decide on.

"When I returned, I found that a tunnel had been dug into the hill, Merkez Tepe, on its northern side. I asked how much had been done. They said, 'Only a few metres, two or three.' I said, 'What is the use of that? Something will happen soon, you will see!'

"A few days later a soldier who was sentry at the northwest corner of the post came running to me. 'There has been an earthquake,' he said. 'There was a shaking of the earth, and little bits of dust rose from the ground like raindrop-splashes.'

"Nothing else had happened. I went to the tunnel. Your mining had evidently been deeper than ours, and you had exploded a mine on hearing our men working, but your explosion had not succeeded in destroying our tunnel. A few days later, however, it was blown in by you."[4]

Soon after this the lull in operations above ground at Anzac was broken by some sorties—nasty, difficult operations—by infantry and light horse on the southern flank at Anzac on June 28th. Their object was to pin down the Turkish garrison at Anzac while the British attacked at Helles. Though all our troops were back in their trenches the same evening—after considerable losses—these demonstrations caused some tension in the Turkish garrison; and when on the next evening, June 29th, shortly after dark, a thunderstorm suddenly swept over the Anzac area, and the wind blew wildly from the Australian area over the Turkish lines, whipping the powdered dust from paths, ledges and shelters in a white dust cloud, thick as fog, across No-man's-land, both sides began an intense fusillade. The Anzac guns or infantry also fired some flares. They were rarely used by us at Anzac, but this time they set fire to the scrub and increased the nervous strain on the Turkish soldiers. When the dust suddenly whirled over and firing started, Zeki Bey at first thought a mine might have been exploded, or that the cloud might be artificial. The weirdness of the scene was augmented by our flares which the Turks saw blurred through the dust. On Mortar Ridge—the Turkish second-line position just behind Merkez Tepe and Quinn's, with a valley intervening—were two Turkish mountain guns, placed in tunnels to fire from openings in the hillside. We had them well marked, just as they had similar guns of ours which shot from an opposite hole in the Second Ridge. By the date of this incident these Turkish guns were almost completely prevented from firing, but they had

---

[4] As Zeki Bey suspected, a charge was fired by the Australians in their gallery No. D9 in front of Steele's Post on June 13th, Turks having been heard at work; but the explosion merely bulged the tunnel walls and the gases leaked back through the tamping of sandbags into our own tunnel. The Australian side of these events is told in *Vol. I, pp. 260, 328.*

standing orders to open in an emergency. And now they did so. In this pandemonium Zeki Bey was called to the telephone.

"An urgent message came from regimental headquarters," he told us, "asking for information. Though I did not know it, Mustafa Kemal, the divisional commander, had an important attack at The Nek planned for next morning, and probably he was most anxious. Our regimental commander, Ahuni Bey, telephoned to me: 'What has happened?'

"I said: 'I don't know—I can only tell you that I see nothing but dust, and there is a great deal of noise!'

"Just then a soldier who had been sent from the right sector of my front trench came in with a report from a young and nervous officer there. It said: 'The English are advancing by bounds.' " (Zeki Bey repeated this to us two or three times laughing, with gestures—as if his enemy were kangaroos.) "I knew this was wrong," he said, "because your men too were shooting—they must have been at their loopholes ready to fire upon any attack by us. But as Ahuni Bey pressed for report, I said: 'I can only send on a report that I have just received from the 12th Company, which I don't believe, but here it is . . .' and I repeated it, and added that I would go up to the front myself and report.

"My headquarters was on the rear slope of Merkez Tepe, and I went up the trench to the front line and saw that nothing of importance was happening. Your men were not in our trenches, but many newspapers were blowing over wildly to our trenches. The soldiers gave them to me and I took them and returned. They were papers of old date.[5] I telephoned that it was only a storm.

"Meanwhile an order had arrived and been written down by my adjutant: 'If the Australians attack,' it said, 'advance and meet them in No-man's-land with the

---

[5] Zeki Bey was interested in them—probably a collection of *Ages, Arguses, Heralds, Ballarat Couriers* and country dailies.

bayonet.' An order had also been sent to one of the battalions on my left to counter-attack at once and re-establish the position. But as there had been no attack there was no counter-attack.

"Some minutes later the C.O. of our sister battalion at Bomba Sirt [Turkish Quinn's] rang me up: 'I've been ordered to attack,' he said. 'Be prepared to help us in an hour or two's time, in case of need—with enfilade fire.'

"I asked the Regimental C.O. about this—what was the reason? His answer was, 'Yes, that battalion at Bomba Sirt is going to make an attack, and the 18th Regiment at the head of Kuruku Dere [Valley of Fear—Shrapnel-Monash Valley] is going to make an attack.' "

I. told Zeki Bey what we afterwards knew of this attack—that it had been made by a regiment fresh from Constantinople, and added that prisoners had told us that it was personally ordered by Enver Pasha, Minister of War and one of the triumvirate who ruled Turkey.

"No," he said, "Enver was down at Ari Burnu at the time, but the attack was made solely on the initiative of Mustafa Kemal. Enver was a bit displeased, as he didn't see the object of it. What happened was that the 18th Regiment had come down to that zone—it was a fine regiment with a fine C.O., a distinguished and brave officer. Mustafa Kemal thought that the state of this regiment and the personality of its C.O. justified the expectation that it would do great things." He had accordingly determined to throw this regiment against Anzac at the point where a short advance might be decisive, that is to say, at The Nek—if successful it should look down on North Beach and Monash Valley. The regiment's fine commander was sniped, Zeki Bey told us, about June 12th; nevertheless the attack took place a fortnight later.

It was the heaviest made against Old Anzac after May 19th, and came against the 3rd Light Horse Brigade in the trenches facing The Nek, the same trenches from which that brigade six weeks later made its even more heroic and disastrous charge. In front of the Australian front line in that sector were a number of shallow tunnels and secret saps on which our engineers and others were nightly working to steal more ground, and which were not yet used as firing-line but guarded only by a few men. The Turks stumbled into these, overrunning or passing beyond most of the workers, and some passed on towards the main line and machine-guns beyond. Zeki Bey told us the tale from the Turkish side.

"The Turks had prepared a tunnel for getting their men secretly into their own trenches near Jessaret Tepe [The Nek]," he said, "but it was not ready and they hadn't the benefit of it. I was on the side of my post nearest to Bomba Sirt. I heard the cry of our troops as they began to charge, at first enthusiastic—'Allah! Allah!' and a few minutes later there came on the telephone the report that the regiment had taken the first line of Australian trenches and two machine-guns, and had reached the second line, and some men had got into it. This report was also given to Essad Pasha, who had his headquarters at Kemal Yere [Scrubby Knoll] and had with him that night Enver Pasha.

"But I noticed that the cries, which at first had been enthusiastic, later became tragic. Lots of flares were being thrown by your side, and I think they fell behind our men, and reinforcements could not reach them. One battalion and a half were lost. Those few who got back said that they fell into trap-doors[6]—from the rest we never heard; we don't know to this day what happened. It was a 'black' night—there were the wounded crying in No-man's-land, and both sides rolling out flares, and no one helping them.

"To help this attack the 3rd Battalion of my regiment, which was at Bomba Sirt [Turkish Quinn's] was ordered to attack as soon as possible. Everything had been

---

6 Evidently our secret saps and tunnels were meant.

very rushed. Our trenches at Bomba Sirt were covered
with planks. Instead of taking these up, the troops lifted
them in order to get out all together. The order was hurried and it was difficult to lift the planks; in places a few
were lifted. Your men knew what this meant and as
many of ours as climbed out were shot. Lots of men were
lost.

"At The Nek, where one and a half battalions had
gone forward and did not return but left the trenches
empty, there was great anxiety; for if you had attacked
then you would have found no one in the trenches
opposite you. Mustafa Kemal brought his headquarters
close up to the front line to defend it and reserves were
rushed into the trenches.

"When the two machine-guns, which were reported
to have been captured, did not arrive, Enver Pasha
wanted to see them. However, the 18th Regiment was
told that, though it had not succeeded, it had occupied
the attention of the 'English' at a critical time. When
some weeks later your troops attacked at Jessaret Tepe
the regiment considered itself satisfied; it had 'got its
own back'."

While Zeki Bey was telling us this there came to my
memory two incidents known to me from our side. The
first had been reported in June by two snipers of the
7th Australian Battalion who daily from behind Steele's
Post fired on a section on the Chessboard, perhaps 600
yards away. They noted that every morning a Turk, who
was clearly an important officer, came to the front
trenches at the Chessboard, looked over, borrowed a
rifle from some sentry, rested it on the parapet, deliberately fired a shot or two down the valley, and handed the
rifle back. "Through the telescope you could almost see
his white teeth as he smiled," they said. He was well uniformed, with gold braid. The snipers "laid for him";
he ignored their first two shots, which struck the earth

very close to him, and was killed by the third.[7] The
other incident occurred after that regiment's brave attack.
The Turkish wounded, lying out, just as Zeki Bey said,
with no one to help, came to the notice of an Englishman
whom I have already mentioned in connection with the
armistice of May 24th, Captain Hon. Aubrey Herbert.
He was a diplomat really, tall, thin, scholarly, untidy,
unassuming, not a soldier though a friend of any soldier
from private to general. Before the war he had been on
the British embassy at Constantinople until he became a
member of Parliament. I could remember him about
1900 as a speaker in debates at the Oxford Union. Having lived among the Turks he felt a responsibility concerning them, and this day, after getting a Turkish
prisoner to shout from our front trenches an explanation to
those Turks who might be within hearing, he walked out
on The Nek and brought in a terribly wounded Turk,
and later sought for another who had been waving a
newspaper in the scrub high on the slope to Monash
Valley. But by then the newspaper had ceased to wave;
when Herbert called, no answer came. The man was
probably dead.[8]

---

[7] The full story is told in *Vol. II*, footnote on *p. 308*.

[8] In *Mons, Anzac and Kut,* Herbert mentions the first incident though
saying nothing from which readers could realise the risk he ran, or that
no one else ever attempted such action at The Nek. I did not know that
he had a rope thrown to another Turk, whom he found shamming to be
dead, and who was pulled in, and that he repeated these acts of mercy
next day.

Chapter
· XIV ·

THE FIGHT
AT THE CRATER

Soon after I met him—probably after dinner on the first evening—Zeki Bey asked me if I knew of an officer of ours who had been killed fighting in one of the mine craters at German Officers' Trench. "He was a fine looking, handsome young man," he said.

I told him that I did not personally know the officer, but I was sure I knew whom he meant. We had made, on July 12th, a raid on a crater there by way of a demonstration to keep the Turks at Anzac busy while the British made their last big attack at Cape Helles. Our infantry did not believe that this crater was as close to German Officers' Trench as the engineers who blew it believed it to be; the commanders thought that, if captured, it might be held by us as a forward position—probably as a bombing post from which to pester the garrison of German Officers'. When volunteers were called for, a newly-arrived officer of the 7th Battalion, Lieutenant N. J. Greig, offered to lead the attempt; and at 8.15 on a bright morning with eleven other volunteers he rushed the crater, in which was a Turkish guard who scrambled out, leaving three killed. Greig and his men were now, of course, lost to sight from the Australian trench; but another party of Australians, who were ready to clear the tunnel leading to the crater, presently heard Greig's voice calling for reinforcements. Half a dozen brave men of the 6th immediately climbed out but charged in the wrong direction—towards the Turkish trench—and were shot back, partly by one of their own side's machine-guns, turned on

172

them in error from Russell's Top. Very soon afterwards most of Greig's men came back, all wounded; he had ordered them to retreat. The last of them said that, when he left, Greig was standing at the tunnel mouth, bleeding from the head, holding back the Turks with his revolver while his men got away. Greig himself did not appear.

Other demonstrations had been made by the Australians on the same day, ranging from the showing of bayonets over the parapet to sorties by infantry and light horsemen into valleys in front of the trenches on the southern flank, these sorties always bringing deadly shell- and rifle-fire in return.

The story of Greig's raid, told from the Turkish side, begins at a slightly earlier date when this crater was blown. "Sometime after you had begun to attack the northern end of our front trench with your mines," Zeki Bey said, "we heard the sound of picks at work underground near the centre also." Zeki Bey had already obtained the advice of some German experts—the Turks not being skilled at mining. This time he himself decided that the only useful action he could take was to dig towards the sound of our picks in the hope of opening a vent through which the explosion might more or less harmlessly direct its force; and to hold his front line with as few men as possible and depend more upon the supports. At the time of the Mission's visit the support trench at the centre of German Officers' ran within two or three yards of the front line— but possibly this support trench was dug after the incident here referred to.

At all events, on the night of July 4th our engineers exploded 150 lb. of ammonal in a tunnel just in front of the centre of German Officers' Trench. Our miners, as soon as they heard the Turks digging, had themselves quickly tunnelled ahead in a slightly different direction. Zeki Bey's precaution by causing this haste had probably averted an explosion directly beneath his front trench.

"All the communication trenches were filled with

173

dust," he said, "and all the men were crouching in their shelters. If you had attacked immediately after that explosion we should probably have lost the trench.[1] A great crater was formed." (It was not great by comparison with those we sometimes saw in France, but about the size of an average bedroom.) "The front part of the trench bordering on it was wholly blown away. The trench had been lightly garrisoned—only fifteen men in that position. Five of these were not seen again.

"We filled up the great gap in the trench wall, where it looked into the crater, with a grid of barbed wire. But I knew that this was not the end of your men's activities, and so [apparently on July 8th] I set about exploring the crater, taking a soldier with me. There were a lot of stones in it, and after pulling these away I came upon two wires leading straight back towards the 'English' lines. They led into a mass of sandbags which I found to be closing the mouth of a tunnel, the bags being packed up from its bottom to its roof. I and the soldier drew the bags away, one by one.

"As we did so, some noise the other side made us think that a sentry with a bayonet was there" (which was indeed the case). "We took away bags until we had made a crevice and could see through. By then no one was in the tunnel. The tunnel led away from us. I wondered what to do. At first I thought, 'I'll blow this place in'; so I had six or seven sticks of explosive brought. But it was the sort of explosive that is used in blowing up railways, and this had failed before in similar tasks; accordingly I decided not to blow the place. I went out again with a man and we pulled the bags away and made an opening. I told the man to go through, and he did so. There was a tunnel leading about ten feet ahead of us. It led no farther in that direction, but then turned at right-angles to the left.

"I told the man to go round the corner. He did so,

1 Why no attempt was made to do this is told in *Vol. II, p. 330.*

and a sergeant with him, I staying at the corner. There were steps leading down to a deeper tunnel, and at the bottom a light could be seen flickering, and someone was there. Then someone from below fired a revolver shot, which hit against the wall at the end of the gallery, where the turn in it was. I afterwards picked up this bullet," Zeki Bey added with a twinkle in his eyes, "and sent it to Kemal and Essad as the first shot fired in underground warfare here.[2]

"When that shot occurred the Turkish soldier came running back, trembling. Then there was some shooting on both sides, with rifles. I accordingly had a parapet of sandbags made a little around the elbow[3] and had the tunnel tamped up. I stationed a sentry behind this tamping in the tunnel, and another farther back in the crater where the tunnel opened into it, with a third man immediately upon his right. A corporal had charge of the three. I gave the most advanced sentry my revolver. An Australian sentry was farther down the tunnel.

"Later, voices were heard coming from behind your sentry. I said: 'The Australians are certainly up to something, not sitting down waiting,' so I had a German expert sent up. He listened with me in the crater, just south of the tunnel mouth, and said, 'Digging is going on two or three metres from here.' We wondered what to do. Measures ought to be taken at once, but we had begun mining later than you, and we knew that the moment we started counter-measures you would blow. We didn't start.

"A few days later there was an explosion. I was in the trenches and was thrown down. I ran along and found

---

[2] It appears likely that it was fired by the well-known Australian leader, Lieutenant-Colonel "Pompey" Elliott—who had rushed into the mine-gallery on hearing that Turks were there, and himself stood on guard and fired. For the Australian side of the story, see *Vol. II, p. 332.*

[3] Presumably by throwing or pushing the bags round the corner. Farther along the tunnel the Australians made a barrier at the same time in the same way.

that your people had exploded a mine. The sentry behind the tamping was not found at all; the sentry at the mouth of the tunnel had been blown back over the parados of our front trench and killed; the sentry on the right of the tunnel mouth was killed. The tunnel was still there from the crater to the bend, but the bend of it had been blown in and a new crater had been made just beyond the bend, beyond where our sandbags had been.

"I still said, 'The Australians won't remain inactive.' So we again cleared away the stones and clods where the elbow had fallen in, until we could see through a crevice between the stones. I myself looked through; and there was a soldier, an Australian, crouching on one knee against the forward edge of the crater[4] with his rifle in one hand on one knee, brushing the earth off the bolt quietly with the other hand, and looking intently over his left shoulder up at me. Perhaps he had heard something.

"My revolver I had lent to our sentry, and it had been lost with him in the explosion. I ran for another. 'I can shoot that man,' I thought. Then I reflected: 'What's the use of shooting him? We will wait for this evening and capture him.' We needed prisoners.

"I intended to send over about midnight a few soldiers from the old crater and capture the man. They tried it, jumping out of the big crater, just south of the tunnel mouth, two or three of them; but immediately the first who jumped out was shot and badly wounded. The others ducked back crouching into their crater and stayed there. Later the sentry told me that the hole where the [Australian] sentry was had been shut[5] and a wire entanglement put in the crater. That was all we could see—not a soldier was then in the crater. A few days later

---

[4] That is, to Zeki Bey's left front.
[5] Probably this means that the Australian end of the tunnel had again been tamped up, which is correct.

our sentries must have been talking—they couldn't keep quiet—and a bomb was thrown at them from your wire and a sentry slightly injured.

"Things remained like this for a few days. Then, one day about noon, some projectiles fell on both flanks of my post—not on the front line but about the second line. The soldiers crouched down in the trenches and did not look over. Kemal noticed this and complained to me. I held an inquiry and found that some had been wounded by the shells.

"I had sent a messenger to find if anything of importance was occurring. At the end of some minutes he returned with the answer. The commander of the 2nd Company, who was at the northern end of the post—he was not my most reliable officer—brought back word that there was nothing doing in the trenches.

"Just then the chief of Essad Pasha's staff got on the telephone to me direct. He said: 'Zeki Bey, the enemy is getting into your trenches. What are going to do?'

"The headquarters of Essad [commanding the Corps in the Ari Burnu zone] were just north of Kemal Yere [Scrubby Knoll]; they were at the top of the reverse slope, near the mountain-gun battery, and he had an observation post there from which he could look down on a great part of the front line; and his chief-of-staff could see from there what was happening.

"I went straight up to the line, and as soon as I reached the second trench I found that bombs were being thrown by my men over into the crater. I came straight on to the front line to see what was doing—to the point where the grid of wire was. At the same time the lieutenant commanding the left front-line company, a brave young fellow, who had saved the situation by getting his men at once to fire down their own front line from the southern end of it, caught my arm and said: 'Don't go there, Zeki Bey. It is dangerous there; they have been exchanging shots.' But I went on to the grid.

177

"A number of my soldiers were at the wire, looking into the crater. At the wire several soldiers of both sides were lying dead. One of your men had laid his rifle and bayonet up against the wire. Your men were apparently getting back, away from the crater. But in the crater was a well dressed young officer, a very fine, handsome man. He had retreated into the tunnel mouth. I called out: 'Don't kill this man—we want to take him!' The men said, 'He will not allow himself to be taken.'

"There was the officer, revolver in hand, against the earth at the far end of the crater, by the tunnel. Then he dropped. He had been hit by a bomb and had both legs broken. I afterwards found that he would not have been able to get back through the tunnel—it wasn't open. My men afterwards were not agreed as to where yours attacked from; some said from the trenches, others from the mouth of the tunnel. Six or seven were dead; one was found in the next crater farther north. Twelve or fifteen rifles were found. None of your men were prisoners—all there were dead. Immediately after this fight there was great quietude in the Australian trenches, no bombs being thrown; probably your men thought their comrades had been captured."

Zeki Bey said to me more than once: "I would have liked to take that officer prisoner; he was a very brave man." He had him buried in the valley behind the lines with more ceremony and care than the Turks usually devoted to their dead opponents.

Zeki Bey told me that he did not think that the demonstration made that day had the effect that our leaders intended. The defeat of the raid on the crater, he said, "did much to cheer up the Turks. We had been getting very anxious for some time—we didn't know what you intended to do. To me it seemed that all your machine-guns were beginning to point at my post, and we expected an attack there. On the day of the attack on our crater bayonets were seen opposite our left flank and on Kirmezi Sirt [Johnston's Jolly], and it was reported that the 'English' were going to make an attack. Afterwards we were able to say the 'English' had made an attempt and had failed—and the fact had considerable influence. Great importance was attributed to this little success by our higher command. I asked why. They said, 'You don't know, but it is important.' Probably our troops in the south had not been having a good time" (Zeki Bey told me in other talks that the strain on the Turkish divisions at Helles at that time was great, and their losses very high) "and probably it was desired to report a success to the newspapers. The young officer [of the left company] who beat the attack was given a medal —the 'Gemish Imtias' medal for courage; it is an important decoration, usually given to older officers."

I told Zeki Bey that, strangely enough, we too, at that time, had been expecting to be attacked. Reports from spies and from prisoners told of preparations; but, above all, it was the time of the Turkish Ramadan fast, and it was expected that the Turkish command would take advantage of the religious devotion of that celebration for some military end. Zeki Bey laughed when I told him.

"We were rather anxious at that time, too," he said, "because so much time was spent by us in visiting our friends in other units when we should have been working. At the feast of El Bairam I went to call on the good old commander of my regiment, Ahuni Bey, at Edirna Sirt [Mortar Ridge]. He told me he had a letter from his home—his children were asking how long this war would last, and whether 'Father' would be with them for the feast, as he had been the year before; they all told him how dreary it was without him. Within two hours of his telling me this, the poor fellow lay dead, killed by a shell from one of your howitzers. It may have been one of your older howitzers—your 6-inch howitzers shot very well indeed, but they may not then have arrived."

I asked Zeki Bey whether they had suffered much from our trench mortars, especially the four Japanese ones. They were the only modern ones we possessed and they threw a flat bomb attached to a metal stick—it contained high explosive and burst with a savage, dry crack and black smoke.

"Yes," he said, " 'Black Cats' we called them. One day one burst in the air over the heads of some reserves assembled in the valley behind my post, and killed or wounded eighty men. Later we found that if we covered our trenches with head-cover these bombs were not dangerous to the men there; a few inches of log cover would render you safe against them. That is why we roofed in those trenches which were most exposed to them. The wood was mainly brought from Constantinople. Later this cover caused terrible trouble.[6] Kirmezi Sirt [Johnston's Jolly] was the worst place for these bombs, though generally that post contained our most comfortable trenches. If you were watchful you could hear the faint report of the mortar and then see the bomb high in the air.

"About that time an old howitzer of ours used to enfilade your trenches opposite my post, dropping its shells on them from up north near Koja Chemen Tepe [Hill 971].[7] We noticed that, when these bombardments were on, your men kept low and didn't fire and we were able to look over the parapet and move about. It was one of these shells falling in No-man's-land in front of my post that disclosed to us that you were digging an underground line there. We saw the shell go in and, later, the earth being shovelled out from below—so we knew that there must be a hidden line there."

Zeki Bey told me that at this time the strain upon his

---

6 By causing howitzer shells to explode *in* the trenches on penetrating the roof—as told in the next chapter.

7 Zeki Bey told us at another time that the position of this howitzer was at Su Yatagha (the Watercourse) near Chunuk Bair. So far as he knew it was a 21-cm. (8-inch) mortar.

battalion in German Officers' Trench was very great. Our mine craters and the underground galleries leading to them had brought us close enough to his trenches for bombing, and the constant fear of being undermined was shaking his men. They had been a very long time in the line but could not get relief from outside. "The 1st and 2nd Companies had to relieve each other, and so did the 3rd and 4th," he said. "The reserves were on the shelves and in the shelters, behind Merkez Tepe. At first the companies relieved each other weekly; later, when the bombs became bad, every forty-eight hours; latterly, every twenty-four hours. Towards the end of our time, in July, even these reserves came under the fire of your catapults.

"At Bomba Sirt [Quinn's] the losses through bombs were so great that at one time our command thought of giving up the post. We had to keep our trenches crowded —we were aware of the grave disadvantage of this, but our men were ignorant, however brave, and could not fight singly. Also they always tended to observe and fire only straight ahead; it was difficult to get them to do otherwise. The two battalions of our regiment at Bomba Sirt sometimes had to relieve each other more frequently than once a week, because incidents occurred which caused great damage. For example, on some days you threw a multitude of bombs, and when you did that the losses were always high. We debated giving up Bomba Sirt and withdrawing the line to Edirna Sirt [Mortar Ridge]; but we decided against it because, if we held on, we might be able with artillery (if that arrived) to drive you back.

"We could see your periscopes, but our soldiers in the line did not have them because they brought bombs.[8] Our soldiers kept watch through loopholes. These were under the logs of the head-cover and were made by leaving spaces between ammunition-boxes filled with earth. We found that some loopholes were dangerous—your men shot into

---

8 Zeki Bey probably meant trench-mortar bombs.

them; so we forbade our soldiers to watch through those ones—others were safe. Sometimes the loopholes would get covered with earth by day, so we used to clear the front of them by night, getting out of the trenches to do so. With these methods we found our losses smaller than in using periscopes. Later we copied the periscope-rifle used by your troops, but found them of no great help to us."

I can recall as if it were yesterday Zeki Bey's quizzical expression as he said: "A constant wonder to me were the signs of the digging done by your troops. I used to watch those heaps and heaps of earth always accumulating and extending, everywhere heaps and more heaps"; and his laugh as he added: "I used to say to myself, 'What *are* they about?' I said, 'These Australians will tunnel to Constantinople!' "

THE TURKISH SIDE
AT LONE PINE

THE nerves of the I/57th at Merkez Tepe were being dreadfully frayed when, one day early in August, after a very long tour without relief at this crucial post, it found howitzer shells dropping persistently, though at big intervals of time, about its covered trenches. This slow bombardment lasted for several days.

"Your howitzer shells occasionally hit my trenches," Zeki Bey said. "Not many hits, but very great damage. On August 6th, [what he actually called it was 'the day of the Demonstration'] some of these shells burst in the trenches. It happened that that day, by order of Mustafa Kemal, a notice had to be exhibited above the parapet of my post saying that Warsaw had been captured.[1] I went up there and put it up myself. We thought that these shells might be an answer to this. From twenty to twenty-four shells had fallen that day around the position, and about five of them had hit the trench direct. The battalion had been suffering so heavily in these last days that our relief had at last been promised; we were to be withdrawn for rest that afternoon. When these shells fell in our trenches I went up to the front myself, and there was the head-cover blown in, and the men lying smashed up and dead. I was very frightened.

"But now, just when we were to leave, the relieving

---

[1] Actually this was done on the afternoon before, but it would give rise to the same inference. Notices at the Jolly and German Officers' said: "Varsaw ash fallin", "Warcheuve est tombe", and so on; probably our Turkish was often worse!

battalion hesitated. "We cannot carry out the relief in this bombardment," they said. The relieving battalion was Arab, one from the 72nd Regiment, in divisional reserve. But I, who had been up to the front line, insisted that they must relieve us. It was always like that, I said[2]— and my battalion had been there forty-five days.

"So the I/57th came out and I went to regimental headquarters. I was with the regimental commander at Edirna Sirt, and we could see the bombardment which was still going on. We could see that both large and small shells were concentrated on Kanli Sirt [Bloody Ridge, Lone Pine]. My battalion had just come out and was at that moment assembled behind Edirna Sirt, and I ordered the officer-in-charge at once to be ready to reinforce as they were the nearest reinforcement to Kanli Sirt.

"From the regimental headquarters at the back of Mortar Ridge[3] you could see clearly. There was a lot of dust raised by the shells at Kanli Sirt. I could not see through it, but when the bombardment there ceased we heard infantry fire—a little—like after thunder you hear the rain beginning; and the observers beside us said, 'The English are getting into our trenches.'

"Our observation of this bombardment had given us the impression that the trenches subjected to it would not be in a condition to repel the attack—there had been much damage, and heavy loss. At that moment an order arrived by telephone from Mustafa Kemal Pasha: 'I/57th, the battalion of reserve, will move at once to 'Kanli Sirt'. The battalion was ready to go. I gave the order to move as fast as possible to Kanli Sirt. On the way, we fixed bayonets; we went in column of route, at the double. While we were going I noticed that all the batteries which were at Kemal Yere [Scrubby Knoll, beside Essad Pasha's

2 Meaning that the bombardment was not unusual; Zeki Bey was fully aware of the exaggeration in this statement.

3 Presumably this would lie behind the rear edge of the ridge, and had an observation post there from which the main length of the Second Ridge with its successive knuckles would appear spread out as on a raised map.

headquarters] had concentrated on No-man's-land in front of Kanli Sirt. I told the leading lieutenant: 'I am going ahead a bit. Follow me. I'll meet you in Djemal Dere' " —that is at Owen's Gully, dividing the two halves of the 400 Plateau, Johnston's Jolly and Lone Pine.

"The moment we turned into that valley we came into fire, from your men at the head of it"—the valley had always hitherto been safe for the Turks. "Near there I met the commander of one of the battalions which had been holding the centre of the Kanli Sirt [Lone Pine] front. His name also was Mustafa Kemal—he was a Kolasi, something between Captain and Major. I asked, 'What has happened?' But he was clearly very shocked. He kept on saying, 'We're lost, we're lost!'

"I said, 'I want you to tell me what the situation is and what you wish me to do.'

"He said: 'The situation is critical. My whole battalion remained in shelter of the trenches after the bombardment. I'm waiting here for the remnants of it—I have no one now under my command. If any survive, I'm here to stop them and take them under my command.'

"But there was no one there except him. I saw it was useless to ask for information from him, and I didn't want to lose time, so I asked him where was the commander of his regiment. He said that the C.O. had withdrawn into the zone of the 125th Regiment"—that is Kirmezi Sirt, Johnston's Jolly, on the north side of Owen's Gully— "and was at the rear shoulder of that hill, where he could see well what was happening.

"At that moment I met half a company of Turkish soldiers lying down in the valley, across the route of my battalion. They didn't know what to do. They had come from the right section of the Lone Pine post, where it bent down into the valley; and they had climbed out of their trenches and got down the gully and were lying there—they had sent to find out what to do. Fire was

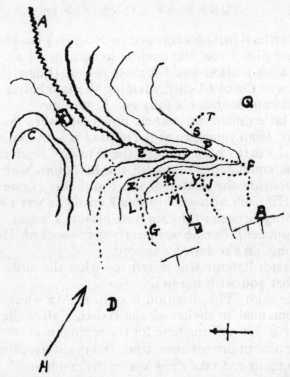

FACSIMILE OF SKETCH-MAP USED BY ZEKI BEY IN DESCRIBING TO THE HISTORIAN THE SITUATION EXISTING WHEN HIS BATTALION WAS RUSHED TO LONE PINE, AND LATER

(The sketch shows roughly the contours of The Cup and of its junction with Owen's Gully. Dotted lines are communication trenches. The compass points have since been added.)

A — *where, turning into Owen's Gully, Zeki Bey met a battalion commander.*

B — *where that commander's battalion had been.*

C — *where the C.O. 47th Regiment had retired to, towards rear of Jolly.*

X — *stables where Zeki Bey met the C.O. of another battalion.*

Z and Y — *headquarters on the edge of The Cup which commanders had left.*

D — *direction from which Australian fire was coming down Owen's Gully.*

E — *point at which Zeki Bey's battalion, climbing up The Cup, was called in by urgent summonses from Z, Y, and F for help.*

(Continued at foot of opposite page)

coming down the valley from somewhere on the southern side of it.

"I found their regimental commander"—he was farther up on the right where Johnston's Jolly began to rise —"I said to him, 'Don't be anxious, Tewfik Bey; I have come with my battalion, which is very well rested and calm. We've come from rest (it was not true of course), and we'll do whatever you want.'

"Tewfik Bey said, 'Give me some men.'

"I asked, 'What trenches do you want them to go into?'

"He then said, 'I'll give you some men. They'll take you to the headquarters of the two battalions and the commanding officers will tell you where they want your men to go.' He was very much upset.

"We went down into the valley, much exposed to the

F — head of The Cup, and point where Australian periscopes appeared looking down it. Turkish troops were congested in the valley head.

ZLG, KM, YJ — communication trenches running towards the front lost by the Turks. Another ran towards D, but was not seized by the Australians and was reoccupied by the Turks.

G — the position held by the Hoja, hard up against the Australians.

J — corner to which Zeki Bey next went, where Australians were bombing, and to which he shortly afterwards led a young Turkish officer.

Y — battalion headquarters where three Australian dead lay.

Between B and G — a flag is shown where one was put up by the Australians to help their artillery.

KL — trench in which Zeki Bey had a firestep dug.

GF — general line of Turkish front when our attack was held.

Z and Y — headquarters reoccupied by battalion commanders. The commander of the 13th Regiment took post at Z.

ZK, KY, YP — sectors into which the front was next divided; Zeki Bey had KY.

M — position of an overhead traverse, where losses were heavy. Apparently it was from here that an attempt was made to rush the position where the Australians had put up the small flag. A machine-gun at B foiled this attempt.

ST — short trench leading towards the southern part of the plateau. Men were ordered to dig towards Q, the position of the III/47th holding the southern part; but a small cannon firing from the direction of H (line of fire shown by arrow) immediately blew the working party out of the trench.

FQ — the Turks eventually made contact here between the troops on the northern and southern sides of the Pine, and Zeki Bey saw them make a short advance at F. The final Australian line lay through B.

fire that came down it. By this time my battalion had got
ahead of me. It was clear that the trouble was at the head
of the branch gully." (That is, the deep, spoon-shaped
hollow which here opened out of Owen's Gully on its
southern side, and, biting more than half-way across the
Lone Pine plateau, formed the immediate hinterland of
the Turkish defences on the Pine; the communication
trenches from the northern half of the position all ran
out into its upper edge, and its slope was seamed with the
shelves for the reserves and headquarters, and the paths
leading to them like the benches and passages of a Greek
amphitheatre. It has been suitably called The Cup.)

While Zeki Bey was hurrying to catch up to his
battalion, he met, opposite the entrance to this branch,
the officers and C.O. of another of the battalions from
Lone Pine. "He was much cooler than the other had
been," Zeki Bey said. "Their headquarters had been on a
terrace high up on the side of the valley just behind the
trenches, one battalion at one end of the terrace, the other
at the other end. Down where we were, opposite the
mouth of this gully, there were some stables partly dug
into the side of Kirmezi Sirt. There were some horses
there and this C.O. had now taken his station at these
stables. I didn't wait to speak to him, but ran on up the
branch gully after my battalion.

"I found my battalion split into about three parts.
What had happened was that, as it climbed up the bed
of the hollow, its head had been met by some young
officers coming from various parts of the front [i.e. from
the summit on its right as it climbed The Cup]. One had
said, 'help is needed at the right'; another 'at the centre';
another 'on the left'. The battalion had gone in those
various directions by the communication trenches leading out of the top of the hollow. There were three of
these trenches, not counting one which led along the
right flank [that is, along the edge of the slope of Owen's
Gully]. My battalion was not in that one but in three

188

which went in from, roughly, the right, centre and left of the top of the slope.

"I went first up the right-hand trench, perhaps thirty-five yards up it. There I found not an officer but only the Hoja—the chaplain—of my battalion. It being the 1st Battalion of the regiment, he ranked as Mufti—the 2nd and 3rd would have an Imam. He was a very brave man and kept his head very well. I went up close to him. He said. 'You can't go farther up here'—there were some dead and wounded of the I/57th and of the line battalion. It was an old trench-bay, rather knocked about. The men told me, 'Behind this place there are English.' Bombs were being thrown from both sides and it was very dangerous. The situation was evenly balanced there, although from somewhere in the north a small cannon [almost certainly on Russell's Top] was enfilading any of our men who didn't know their way about and exposed themselves to it.

"The Hoja Mufti said, 'Don't be anxious about this flank—I'll remain here.'

"It was clear that the danger was higher up towards the centre; so I left the position in the hands of the Hoja and went towards the centre." (A communication trench led towards the centre and then turned at right angles towards the old front line.) "At the corner I met a young officer who said, 'This communication trench is held by the Australians.' There was a traverse[4] there, and above it could be seen the Australian bayonets. Bombs were going over from both sides. In the trench behind me were dead and wounded, and the soldiers were stepping over them. This increased the emotion of the troops; they were in a state of high strain. I said to the young officer: 'You will bar this trench with your fire until we see what is happening elsewhere.'

"I then went out and round to the left, to the extreme

---

[4] That is, one of the buttresses to give protection against enfilade; the trench bent round them and continued.

end of the gully: it was the highest part and the most important. On my way, as I emerged from the communication trench I met some N.C.O.'s and soldiers and asked: 'What is the position? What has happened?'

"They said: 'The English reached even here—see, there are three of their dead here,' and I saw an Australian lying beside me." (On another occasion Zeki Bey told me that this was just beside a battalion headquarters).

"Things were clearly critical; there were few trenches behind, only communication trenches and one cross trench. An officer of one of the line battalions from nearer the centre said, 'The English have entered our trenches and these men won't go into them.' To encourage the soldiers, I said: 'The trenches aren't empty— we hold enough of them. Come with me and show me where these Australians are.'

"The young officer himself took me to the point that I had just visited. I showed him that we had enough troops there, ready with their bayonets. I returned with him to his men and heard later that he went back into the trench and was wounded.

"From the back of the trenches I again looked towards the head of the gully. There were soldiers in the valley there, crowded in the same way as in the other approaches; so instead of going there I went up the central communication trench towards the same point I had visited before, and met there the officer commanding that section. We looked together in the direction of your trenches. What could be observed there? An N.C.O. reported that he could see a man putting up a flag apparently some distance farther along the trench. He asked, 'Is it one of our men or an Englisman?' I said, 'It must be an Englishman.' So he fired at him.

"The attack was at a standstill by then—at that very moment. It was obvious that the situation was critical. If any further attack came, we should lose the whole position. The only trench that we held running across the front was a very deep communication trench, running across the three other communication trenches, but without a firestep from which men could shoot over the top. I said, 'Leave everything else, and quickly put firesteps in this trench so as to give us a defence line.'

"So, with bayonets and entrenching tools they began this at once. I ordered the N.C.O.: 'Tell your men in this trench to fire even if they don't see the English, so as to make a barrage.' The same thing was being done by soldiers on their own initiative, and thus a front line was established facing roughly from the Hoja's position on the right to the head of the gully [The Cup] on the left. The communication trenches were full of troops and nothing more could be usefully done there. After seeing that things were quiet, and noting how close your troops were, I sent a message to the Hoja saying that I was going to Kirmezi Sirt [Johnston's Jolly] and left the position. My whole battalion had by then been absorbed into the trenches and there was no reserve.

"My reason for going to Kirmezi Sirt was to ask the commander of the 125th Regiment there, Abdul Rasak Bey, who could see the situation very well from his headquarters,[5] to turn fire on to Kanli Sirt [Lone Pine] and demoralise the assailants there." (Zeki Bey told me, at another time, that he thought it was probably fire from Johnston's Jolly, together with his men in the communication trenches, that stopped our attack.) "At this headquarters I found the regimental commander of the 47th [which had been holding Lone Pine] and all his battalion commanders. Abdul Rasak said that the Australians on his front too were active—some of the sandbags had been taken down in their trenches [often a preliminary to going over the top] and they were firing

---

[5] This was about in the position where Colonel "Pompey" Elliott and I saw Turks—as already mentioned—looking out from shelters, over some water-barrels.

191

heavily on his trenches[6] and he thought he would be attacked. I said that things were more critical at Kanli Sirt—would he do at all costs what I asked?

"At the same time I noticed that Tewfik Bey, the commander of the 47th, was writing a report to the commander of his division (the 16th) in which he said: 'After the attack by the enemy, the soldiers who have remained under my command have been pushed up again, and have retaken the front lines in my position; but they cannot hold on there—they need large reinforcements, and the troops who have gone up there are not enough.'

"After seeing him sign this, I asked: 'Major, what front line are you speaking of? If you mean the trenches I've just left, the situation there is ...', and I told him what I knew. From what he then said I inferred that he was speaking of the trench running along the side of Djemal Dere [Owen's Gully]—a trench which was never occupied by the Australians. What had happened was that he had received a report from an officer or N.C.O. there: 'We have advanced [along that trench] up to the front line.' But this was only on the extreme right, in Djemal Dere. I said: 'I will go back and do all I can, but you too, on your part, do all you can.'

"By the time I got back to Kanli Sirt night was falling." He had not yet, he told me, been able to grasp the precise position at the head of The Cup. "The half-company of the 47th which we had first found lying in the valley had been sent up in disorder, but had gone.[7] With night, reinforcements began to come, with Ali Riza Bey, the commander of the 13th Regiment (5th Division) from reserve—probably he came with a battalion of his regiment. The commanders of the right and centre battalions of the 47th Regiment also came back to their old headquarters [in The Cup]; they had no troops left, but

---

6 This had been ordered partly as a demonstration, and evidently had some success.

7 Presumably it had either been absorbed or had withdrawn.

could be consulted as advisers. About midnight Ali Riza Bey took up his headquarters near the headquarters of the right battalion. I went to him. His troops, in the dark, filed into the trenches behind those of my battalion.

"Several hours passed in this process, and the position was now fairly stable. About midnight Ali Riza ordered a night attack to be made. He had divided the front into three, each section under a battalion-commander, right, centre and left. I asked the C.O. if I could remain in the central sector, because I didn't know the left [the head of The Cup] but I did know the centre, whereas the new man whom he was putting in the centre knew neither. Throughout the night there was great congestion and disorder in the valley and the trenches.

"The attack was begun—at what hour I could not now say. At the head of the valley the only defences were pits and heaps of earth. The officer formerly in charge, Mustafa Kemal, couldn't tell me how the trenches ran there—actually there weren't any. Your machine-gun fire and flares came from very close. I wanted to do something, but couldn't find my way in that corner. We tried to do something—bombs were being thrown from all sides; we didn't manage to get anything done, nothing till dawn. News came that the right flank had advanced, but it was only another version of the old false report; at dawn the position was unchanged. Especially on the right of the centre there had been heavy losses. At that point the communication trench was crossed by an overhead traverse. As the trench was so deep there we placed men on the top[8]—twenty-five or thirty were hit there by your fire.

"So the night passed—nothing done. With daylight we saw that the most important position you had won was

---

[8] My note says "men were sent overhead there"—Zeki Bey's meaning probably was that he was forced to station them above the trench there. But possibly he meant that this was where the counter-attack "over the top" was made.

on our left, for there were the periscopes of your men visible at the extreme head of the gully. My men asked me, 'Aren't those our men?' 'Of course not,' I said. 'Can't you see—we haven't those things!'

"The whole of this day the attack continued; all the troops who arrived had the same order. Kemal Yere, the headquarters of Essad Pasha, was opposite this sector and saw everything—they didn't want to lose a foot of ground; it was their tactics not to give ground, so they sent troops to push you back.

"The Turkish army in Gallipoli had known there would be a landing by troops of 'Kitchener's Army'—but did not know where. In Liman Pasha's head there was always the idea, 'They will attack in the north.' The original landing had rather upset this idea, but still the reserves were in the north. Your submarines were doing damage in the Sea of Marmora, and so our headquarters wanted to avoid the risk of their communications being cut." Apparently, however, the Turkish troops in the line had not observed that we were nightly landing large numbers of the "New Army" at Anzac.

When we attacked at Lone Pine (Zeki Bey always called that battle simply "the Demonstration") the nearest Turkish reserve was the 5th Division. After the attack on May 19th the 2nd Division had been sent to Cape Helles, and the 5th, which had lost very heavily, had gone into rest and was reserve for the Ari Burnu zone. Its battalions were now the first reinforcements to arrive, two or three of them, from the 12th and 13th Regiments—the 15th was the last to arrive, possibly on the third or fourth day, Zeki Bey said.[9]

"They always came in the same direction, into the

---

[9] The 12th Regiment appears normally to have belonged to the 4th Division. My note, however, makes Zeki Bey state more than once that battalions of the 12th, 13th and 15th were sent to Lone Pine in this battle; and statements of prisoners make it certain that the 12th was present. The 14th, originally part of this division, was guarding the hills north of Anzac.

same gully. They came in, one company, two companies at a time, just as they arrived, during August 7th. These battalions had lost most of their officers on May 19th; a company would be commanded by a sergeant. On coming into the valley they would find themselves exposed to fire from the head of Djemal Dere [Owen's Gully]. They had to pass up the valley where the Turkish dead (brought out of the trenches) were laid out beside the track, four deep. They saw this column of dead men; at the upper end of it were some Australians, including a lieutenant or sergeant, a splendid looking fellow of very great stature, lying there—they had got well down into the position—and the sight 'knocked the stuffing' out of the incoming troops. When they got to the top of the gully there were the Australian periscopes looking over at them, and the fight going on—bombs, rifle-shots. The troops were in bad condition, and they came to a bad situation."

These battalions, Zeki Bey said, and the head of the 9th Turkish Division also, had come up behind Lone Pine by the first night of the struggle; and though many of this immense mass had very soon been sent on elsewhere (as will presently be told) there was constantly a crowd moving up to the Pine or waiting to do so. And still the Australian periscopes looked over the top down into the gully where the Turks were, and bomb after bomb rolled over murderously. The Australians' observation of the head of the valley "made it most difficult to put up sandbags or make any improvements there".

On the second morning Zeki Bey, after seeing these difficulties, concluded that the best chance for a counter-attack lay on the right of the central sector. Standing there with our Mission three and a half years later he told us what happened.

He had put the suggestion to those around him: "Why can't you counter-attack over the top here?"

"But can't you see?" the soldiers said. "There are all

195

those men lying on the top who tried to make an attack over the top there. They were caught by fire the moment they got over. You can't go there."

"I looked," Zeki Bey told us, "and there was a complete line of dead along the top. Then I said: 'Well, you can attack by the left—it is clear that is the way—by the sap leading round to the left'—a communication trench running out of the extreme head of The Cup and curving towards the front.

"They said: 'But how can we do that? The same fire that got our men on the top can get them there.' I said: 'Well, we will put sharpshooters where we can to try to keep down this fire.'" Zeki Bey showed us where he decided to station a number of these men, ensconced on both sides of The Cup, down near its entrance. They were to fire over the heads or past the flanks of his troops, taking something of a risk of hitting them, but, if possible, forcing the Australians to take cover. He proposed to assemble his attacking troops in a sap still farther to the left than that which ran out of the head of the gully. There was a short sap already leading on to the plateau from there; it ran towards another which came in from the direction of the southern side of Lone Pine. A battalion of the 47th Regiment was still holding the southern approaches to the captured trenches, and the regimental commander, Tewfik Bey, had been ordered to co-operate with the troops north of the Pine; the higher staff told Zeki Bey, "If you dig from this side we'll order them to dig from that side."

"I ordered my working party into the sap to begin the work," Zeki Bey told us. "The moment they got into it with their picks they were fired on from the direction of Kirmezi Sirt by a small gun [actually it was one emplaced by the Anzac command on Russell's Top]. It got fairly in among them—two or three men were wounded more or less badly, and the rest came tumbling back to the right of my sector. Your people had put up two red and yellow flags on the trenches your men had reached." These little flags were the normal means by which the Anzac infantry, in such conditions, showed its position to the artillery. To Zeki Bey it had looked as if these flags were right on the edge of the gully, but examining the place now I estimated that they must have been fifteen yards from the lip—a stretch of grass lay between.

"The soldiers who were driven out were not demoralised," Zeki Bey went on, "but bewildered. I went among them under the bank and decided on another method. Riflemen were stationed, as before, to keep down the heads of your men, and I ordered about eight men under a corporal and a fine young lieutenant to attack over the top from about the centre, where three communication trenches led in, and to rush, at all costs, into the position held by your men at the head of those communication trenches. They were to throw as many bombs as possible and then make the rush, about six or seven yards. The snipers were to shoot over their heads, taking some risk.

"Our attacking party tried it; but as soon as they got out a shell from the little gun hit the lieutenant direct— the shellcase did—and badly wounded him, and the others were immediately swept down by a machine-gun of yours, which was right on the top at the very front, and by rifle-fire. Eight or nine—all but one of the party—fell back dead and wounded.

"We then understood that all measures were hopeless. Tewfik Bey of the 47th Regiment had been killed in attempting some similar attack from the other side. He had come in for a lot of blame. [Actually prisoners had told us of this at the time.] He had lost the greater part of two of his battalions (in the original attack), and had made the mistaken report about his troops having regained the front line. At last he became indignant at things that were being said. He said: 'Well, I'll take the troops myself and we'll do something whatever it costs.' On the second night or the third morning he led his men up to close range by a little sap on the southern flank, and there he was killed by a bomb." Zeki Bey showed us his tomb there, where the Australian and Turkish trenches ran extraordinarily close together. It was near there that Colonel R. Scobie of the 2nd Battalion A.I.F. was killed about the same time on the Australian side.

"On the third day I sent a company to attack and it disappeared altogether; I don't know if it was captured or killed, or if it got involved in a panic that happened on the left. Possibly they turned round and attacked their own troops by mistake—the trenches were so involved. But on that night or next day (August 9th) another attack was made from the left flank, the south-east; either your men had retired or they had been killed.[10] Fifteen or twenty Turkish soldiers were put in from just beyond my left. I saw bombs being thrown and then some young Turks get into the trench with the bayonet. The advance was an easy one; they said they came upon several young Australians dead in the communication trench, with their rifles broken. The Turkish bayonets could be seen advancing ten or twelve yards from the head of the gully." Apparently the Australians then lost the position from which their periscopes had stared down the head of The Cup. At all events that advance was final; as Zeki Bey said, "That, to the end of things, was the situation.

"After the check [to his last counter-attack, on August 8th] I had retired to the right-hand section of the position (near where the Hoja had been posted) and collected the relics of my own battalion (I/57th). Ali Riza Bey (C.O., 13th Regiment), who was commanding at the head of the valley after this, always came to me for advice, thinking that I knew more of the position than any of the others. The situation at Kanli Sirt was now better, and it was well known that the danger was elsewhere. Indeed all these days I had been looking over my left

---

10 Possibly by the Turkish fire from Johnston's Jolly.

shoulder[11] seeing your shells bursting on the rear slope of Chunuk Bair. Although the situation at Kanli Sirt was critical I could scarcely keep my eyes on it—I knew things must be happening at Chunuk Bair"—Zeki Bey pronounced it "Dchonk Byre"—"which were more critical by far; and, if you succeeded there, what use would be our efforts at Kanli Sirt?"

Zeki Bey told me that not only the 5th Division, which was close at hand near Kojadere village (a small place high up in the second valley beyond Third Ridge), had been hurried to the Pine on the first evening, but also the 9th Division had been summoned from the south and had arrived there that night, with its 25th and 64th Regiments.[12] But on hearing by dawn next morning that the British had landed at Suvla Bay and that Chunuk Bair and all its rugged foothills north of Anzac also were being attacked, the Turkish command ordered the 9th Division to go on at once to Chunuk Bair—the 5th Division sufficed at Lone Pine.

"A final order was given [about August 9th] to abandon the attempt to retake Kanli Sirt, and to entrench our existing front there. As I have told you, the I/57th had been reassembled at the northern part of the crest [near Owen's Gully] and had been allotted that part to defend. When it was clear that all was safe I wired to the regimental commander: 'If you want this battalion to be entirely worn out and finished, keep us in the trenches.' There had been no time or place to eat. The end of our stay on Merkez Tepe [German Officers'] also had been a very

---

11 I would have expected Zeki Bey to say "right shoulder", but possibly my note is correct. He was constantly occupied with events at the head of The Cup; in that case he would be facing south and Chunuk Bair would be north-east of him.

12 This division, then under Colonel H. Kannengiesser, had in June been stationed south of Gaba Tepe to fortify and hold the coastline at Kum Tepe. Essad Pasha at Anzac was allowed to call on it and he had now summoned these two regiments, with which came Kannengiesser, leaving only the 26th Regiment to defend the Kum Tepe coast. (Since April, the 27th Regiment had apparently been allotted to Mustafa Kemal's 19th Division, the 64th Regiment taking its place in the 9th.)

anxious time, because all the time we could hear under our position the sound of your men digging. The moment we ourselves started digging to meet you, you used to blow us up. After more than forty days in the trenches opposite the Australians I was done up and without sleep.

"On August 9th the I/57th was withdrawn behind Edirna Sirt [Mortar Ridge] again. By the time we left a junction had been made by the troops from the head of the gully with the III/47th·from the southern side of the position. The 12th, 13th and 15th Regiments, mixed up, were between it and Djemal Dere [Owen's Gully], Ali Riza Bey of the 13th commanding them."

That was Zeki Bey's story of Lone Pine. We traced the trenches in the area where Zeki Bey said the final counter-attack had thrust our men back from the edge of The Cup. My note says: "In the trenches leading from our eventual front towards this point there has since been heavy fighting. Our trenches end in an underground sap with a hole covered with a bomb screen. In front of this is a bit of old trench, pretty well square; then a fair-sized crater. On one edge of this were about twenty Turkish pinfire revolver cartridges. Beyond was a Turkish bomb shelter, the wooden posts still remaining. From there the broad trench led down into the Turkish lines. I fancy that to the north of our bomb-stop was the broad trench [Barber's Trench] into which we [afterwards] got by means of the Turkish tunnels." Outside the south-eastern bend of our eventual front line in Lone Pine was a Turkish trench which ran within three-and-a-half to four yards of ours—the tomb of Tewfik Bey was beside it.

The Australian tunnelling in that part of the Pine was, of course, all carried out at a later date. We found one shaft there which Wilkins, by dropping a stone and timing the impact, estimated at 100-120 feet deep. In most parts of this plateau and elsewhere the shallow tunnels had fallen in and looked like trenches without parapets. On the very flat surface of Johnston's Jolly (the plateau north of the Pine) the result was especially interesting. Here one Turkish tunnel ran straight out into No-man's-land, ending in a large shallow dome of bare earth, apparently where some exploded mine had just failed to break the surface. A shallow tunnel of ours ran straight into the other side of the dome. Who had blown the mine we could not judge. Farther south a Turkish tunnel ran straight to a crater, a third of the way across No-man's-land, like a stalk to a flower; and on either side of the stalk there branched shallow tunnels like the sticks of a fan. All these were Turkish attempts to meet our mining.

Behind them was a still more interesting work. Along the whole front of the Turkish line on the Jolly, seven or eight yards out from it, there ran what may once have been a shallow tunnel, but was eventually a wide secret sap, without any parapet to betray its presence to our sentries. Along the centre of this stood iron stakes which looked as though they had been intended to support, and possibly once supported, a tall wire entanglement, which would be hidden from our troops and unlikely to be touched by our shells. If this hidden entanglement existed during the campaign it was unknown to us and would have been a terrible obstacle to meet if, as was once under consideration, we had attacked the Jolly at the same time as Lone Pine. The Turkish front line behind it was another "secret sap"—that is, without parapet, with a well bricked and cemented firestep and ammunition shelf; just behind this again was the old front line, with its high earthen parapet and firestep. We could well understand Zeki Bey's statement that this was the most comfortable Turkish post.

Like the Turkish, the Australian shallow tunnels and tunnelled front line had mostly fallen in, but on the ridges immediately south-west of the Pine—Bolton's Ridge, and the little Silt Spur—we were able to show them to Zeki Bey in something like their original condition, with the tunnels running just beneath the grass and "secret"[13] openings for our sentries at short intervals. The last time I had seen those openings it was from below, with

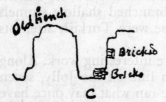

ABOVE: SECTION OF NO-MAN'S-LAND ON THE JOLLY, SHOWING (FROM LEFT TO RIGHT) THE FOLLOWING FEATURES:

C. *Turkish front line dug as a secret sap (the older front line was immediately behind it, just out of the picture).*

B. *Secret ditch, apparently containing a barbed wire entanglement.*

A. *Dome of earth, apparently raised by a mine explosion which did not break the surface.*

D. *Our own "secret" front line (dug from below ground). Some distance to the right of this is an older front line.*

Below (left): Old Turkish front line with newer "secret" front line (C) in front of it.

(right): Rough plan of fallen-in Turkish apron of defensive mine-galleries in front of a section of the Turkish line on the Jolly.

the sentry steadfastly standing with his head below the surface,[14] above which it would have been death to appear —now it was too dangerous to explore below it. Beyond

---

[13] For this remarkable system see *Vol. II, pp. 261-83 and 472 et seq.* The openings were originally intended to be secret, but Turkish patrols found them and, at first, tried to mark them by throwing food tins at them. Later, when the line was no longer secret, small parapets were often made.

[14] Photographs of these men at their posts are in *Vol. XII, plate 88.*

the valley in front of Bolton's, Silt Spur—just south-west of the Pine—had been seized, fortified and held by tunnelling. The openings from the tunnels were still there, both on the surface and at the southern end of the spur, where five of them glared from the gravel cliff down the valley like the gunports of a battleship. That gallery was known as the "Black Hand" and was, of course, obvious to Turkish observers; and it was while looking through one of these loopholes that General Walker, commanding our 1st Division, was badly wounded by machine-gun bullets fired straight into it.

But what still impressed us chiefly about Silt Spur were the heaps of sand from our tunnels spilled over its sides and surface. From one of these heaps, mixed with the old jam and water tins and other rubbish, grew a young tree like an apricot just then in blossom—an astonishing sight at Anzac. It was certainly about three years old, and a few weeks later, when speaking to about 300 Diggers in the well-deck of the *Kildonan Castle*, I told them the story and was adding: "I wondered whether . . ." when the words were drowned in general laughter, amid which a clear voice said: "There were no stones in *that* jam."

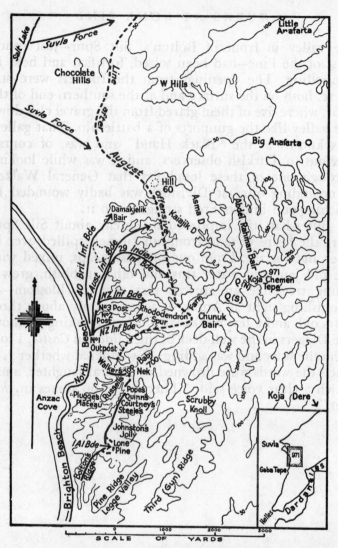

THE AUGUST OFFENSIVE AT ANZAC

This shows the main attack by infantry columns on the night of 6th/7th August 1915, the feint at Lone Pine, and the line ultimately held. It does not show the preliminary seizure of the foothills by the N.Z. Mounted Rifles, or the feints by the Light Horse and others at the head of Monash Valley.

Chapter
· XVI ·

CHUNUK BAIR
AND HILL 60

THE reinforcements from the 9th Turkish Division which, Zeki Bey told us, had arrived behind Lone Pine during the first night of the fighting there, but had been sent elsewhere to meet what was then realised as an even greater danger, were two regiments, 25th and 64th. They had been hurriedly brought up from between Anzac and Helles, under their divisional commander, a German, General Hans Kannengiesser. He had first been sent to Lone Pine, Zeki Bey said, but shortly after arriving behind it he had, in the early hours of August 7th, received the order to pass on to Chunuk Bair, which was the real object of our offensive.

The general situation in which this happened was as follows: At dark on the 6th, after the terrific disturbance created by the Lone Pine assault, which was still furious, the New Zealand Mounted Rifles Brigade (dismounted, of course) had stolen out of the outposts near the shore north of Anzac and, attacking largely in silence with the bayonet alone, had cleared the incredibly rugged foot-hills in the most brilliant operation carried out at Anzac.[1] Thus, after midnight, they had opened the way for three columns, of New Zealand, Indian, and Australian infantry, each a brigade strong, to pass through. Of these, the New Zealanders were to climb up two valleys on to the high spur (Rhododendron) leading to the southern

---

[1] The 40th British Infantry Brigade cleared those on the extreme left flank nearest to the beach. For the New Zealand attack see *Vol. II, pp. 567-77.*

PART OF THE COUNTRY THROUGH WHICH THE AUGUST ATTACK MOVED

The view is southwards from Table Top towards Old Anzac. (Table Top is about 600 feet high.)

A. Chunuk Bair.
B. The Apex.
B-D-F. Rhododendron Spur.
C. Table Top.
E. Battleship Hill.
F. The Saddleback.
G. Baby 700.

H. Turkish Monument at
    The Nek.
I. Walker's Ridge.
J. Snipers' Nest.
K. Destroyer Hill.
L. Camel's Hump.
M. No. 1 Outpost.

N. No. 3 Outpost.
O. Fishermen's Huts.
P. Russell's Top.
Q. The Sphinx.
R. Plugge's Plateau.
S. Ari Burnu.

The New Zealand infantry on the night of August 6th moved out from Nos 1 and 3 Outposts up gullies on either side of Table Top to Rhododendron Ridge and reached about point D at dawn on the 7th. During the 7th they reached B, and on the 8th a point slightly south of A.

shoulder of Chunuk Bair, and seize Chunuk Bair before dawn. They were then to turn southwards and attack down the summit of the range towards Battleship Hill and Baby 700 while the 3rd Australian Light Horse Brigade, breaking out from Russell's Top, attacked from the other direction—from the south northwards—the tiers of Turkish trenches on The Nek and Baby 700. The Indian Brigade, turning into the many folds of the Aghyl Dere, north of the New Zealanders, was to climb the almost precipitous ribs of the range to the twin summits known as Hill Q; and farther north still the 4th Australian Infantry Brigade under General John Monash, was to turn up northern branches of the Aghyl Dere, scramble across a farther valley (Asma Dere) and so on to the lofty and rugged spur, Abdel Rahman Bair, which led to Hill 971 itself, the last and highest summit of the range.

All the Anzac troops (including those who took Lone Pine) were sick with almost universal and continuous dysentery or similar troubles. Their spirits had risen to the attack, but many looked like scarecrows. I have already told how, when the crucial moment of the campaign arrived, at dawn of August 7th, the 3rd Light Horse Brigade at The Nek rose to the occasion by making the bravest charge in Australian history; and how, though hoping to find Chunuk Bair still undefended, the tired New Zealand infantry, two of whose battalions were to have joined each other on Rhododendron Ridge, 1000 yards from Chunuk Bair, was by a tragic decision of its commanders allowed to sit down and wait because only part of those battalions was there. At 7 o'clock the advance was resumed by two battalions (Auckland and Wellington), but at a slight crest (afterwards known as The Apex) in the spur the leading troops were met by shots from the main crest, 400 yards away, and were stopped and allowed to have their breakfast. The summit

could now be seen "bristling with rifles"[2] and when at
11 o'clock the Auckland Battalion tried to advance it was
met by dreadful fire from front and flank and was barely
able, at very heavy cost, to struggle to a further rib of
Rhododendron, 100 yards ahead, afterwards called The
Pinnacle. There it held on during the day and at night
was relieved by the Wellington Battalion. Meanwhile,
the Indian column, which during the night attack had
reached the foot of the range farther north, had climbed
part of the way up it, one battalion reaching a shelf 300
feet below Chunuk, and known to us as The Farm, only
a few hundred yards to the left of the New Zealanders,
who from The Apex looked down across the southernmost
branch of the Aghyl Dere at that ledge. (On the ledge
were, or had been, a low walled enclosure and a hut
which, Zeki Bey told us, comprised the sheepfold, or
"Aghyl" from which this many branched valley presumably got its name.) The northern column, Monash's 4th
Australian Brigade, had to go a distance which, by night,
against even slight opposition, in that rugged country,
was portentous. Like the New Zealand infantry, by dawn
it was half worn-out. It would have needed an ideal
brigadier—a Leane, Rosenthal, Elliott, Gellibrand—to
have lifted it farther; Monash, always nearer to the ideal
of corps-commander, did not by personal reconnaissance
make certain of its position; like most of his subordinates,
he believed that it had reached the spur next to Abdel
Rahman, and he was allowed for the time being to halt
the attack there. All three columns lay short of their
objective, the crest of the range; the New Zealanders
were nearest, the Indians next, the Australians far away—
farther than their commanders realised. All were to make
another effort early next morning, August 8th.

In the early hours of the 8th, Monash's Brigade moved

---

[2] The description is that given by Major (afterwards Major-General) A. C.
Temperley in the *British Official History* by Brig.-General C. F. Aspinall-
Oglander, *Vol. II, p. 205.*

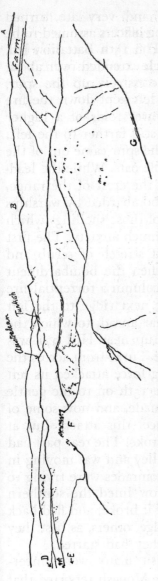

PART OF THE COUNTRY THROUGH WHICH THE AUGUST ATTACK MOVED. THE VIEW IS NORTHWARDS FROM TABLE TOP

A. Chunuk Bair.
B. Abdel Rahman Bair.
C. The "W" Hills.
D. Damakjelik Bair (left flank of "New" Anzac).

E. Bauchop's Hill.
F. Little Table Top.
G. The Chailak Dere (the main route to The Apex).

Cheshire Ridge is in the middle distance with dugouts and trenches.

Aghyl Dere lies beyond it.

On August 7th the New Zealand Brigade reached The Apex (just off the picture, to the right of The Farm and slightly higher); some of the Gurkhas temporarily held The Farm and others were lodged up the slope north of it. The 4th Australian and 40th British Brigades pushed to the ridge indicated by D.

The Australians were to have thrust on up B to Hill 971. They attempted to do so on the 8th, but did not reach B. On that day the New Zealanders and some British troops reached the crest immediately to the right of Chunuk Bair.

On August 9th some Gurkhas and British troops reached the crest immediately to the left of Chunuk Bair but were driven back again.

On August 10th the Turks drove the British from the crest and The Farm.

From that time the front ran from The Apex, northwards along Cheshire Ridge to the point marked "Australian" and thence more westwards to D or, after September 21st, to Hill 60 (in valley below C) where it joined the southern flank of the British Suvla position.

out, across the next valley ahead, and, very late, turned
up the next ridge which its leading officers assumed to be
a spur of Abdel Rahman Bair. The 15th Battalion led,
in a wide column of platoons each extended over about
100 yards' front and moving successively up the spur.
A couple of platoons sent to the left kept down the fire
of some Turks visible on the lower folds of a higher
ridge that ran near and parallel, still farther to the left;
the other platoons marching up the spur came out of the
scrub on to an open field of stubble oats. While the leading troops were crossing this, all the crest of the range,
a mile ahead of them, was being bombarded by warships
and the guns at Old Anzac—one of those shellings which
caused Zeki Bey at Lone Pine so much anxiety. The first
troops had just entered the next stretch of scrub and
run into some Turkish scouts when the bombardment
ended, and there opened on the column a torrential fire
from machine-guns, some on the next ridge to the left
front, others on the main ridge far ahead, to which the
fire of a Turkish field-gun high up near Hill 971 was
presently added. At the same time Turks from across the
valley on the left of the marching force attacked its left
flank. The 14th had followed the 15th on to the gentle
spur up which the advance was made, and now some of
its platoons were detached to meet this attack. But at
that stage the struggling column broke. The rear part had
wisely been turned up the first valley and was moving in
shelter of the spur up which its comrades were trying to
advance. The sheltered troops now lined the southern
edge of this spur. Those on top of it broke, and fled back
in fragments, some to the same edge, others, as best they
could, to the ridge from which they had started.

From that day until our visit many were uncertain where the 4th Brigade got to. Monash reported that
the head of the column had crossed the Asma Dere and

was on a spur of Abdel Rahman Bair,[3] and the diary of the 15th Battalion also says this. Captain W. J. M. Locke, who had guided the column, told me that he afterwards suspected that the valley they crossed was the next one in rear, the Kaiajik Dere; and Colonel C. M. M. Dare and other officers of the 14th said that they were certain of this, and that the ridge up which they fought was the one of which the extreme lowest tip was the swelling known as Hill 60, which two weeks later we attacked with heavy loss and half success.

At the time the one thing of which all were certain was that the left column had tragically failed. The central column, the Indian Brigade, was for this morning's advance to be reinforced by four British "New Army" battalions, but the deep contorted branches of the Aghyl Dere were so confusing and difficult that most of these lost their way. Major Allanson, of the 1/6th Gurkhas, clinging to the side of the main range below Hill Q, managed to get hold of a few of the 7th North Staffords and 6th South Lancashire (some of whom were meant for him and some not) and pushed a little higher up the hillside. The 9th Worcestershire, which also was meant to reinforce him, did not reach him—apparently it was afterwards believed to have come up somewhere on his left.[4]

But in the right column (the New Zealand Infantry Brigade), high on Rhododendron Ridge, observers at The Apex at dawn saw to their surprise the Wellington Battalion march up to the southern shoulder of the Chunuk crest, and then spread along it, without a shot being heard. Unfortunately the silence did not last. As the light grew there swept Rhododendron, from left and right, though not at first from in front, a terrific fire, including direct fire from field-guns due left, on Abdel Rah-

---

[3] Brigade Headquarters and the rear of the column were still in the old Australian lines.

[4] See the British Official History, Gallipoli, Vol. II, p. 305.

man Bair. A New Army battalion, the 7th Gloucestershire, which was to advance on the left of Wellington and seize the actual summit, but was a little late, was decimated by this fusillade, and could not quite reach, or at any rate hold, its objective; and, of the supporting wave, the Maori Contingent was driven down to shelter at The Farm,[5] and the Auckland Mounted Rifles got through to the Wellingtons only at heavy cost.

It was generally believed, after this battle, that the fine farmer-leader of the Wellingtons, Lieutenant-Colonel W. G. Malone, had ordered his troops on no account to move over the top of the ridge but, in accordance with a theory in vogue when the German guns were dominant in France, to dig in just behind it. I knew from survivors that this report was in error: Malone, contrary to his brigadier, did hold that theory, but he did also push out 100 men to dig in beyond the crest while the remainder, about 650 strong, dug on the rear slope close behind them. The Turks had soon counter-attacked, and killed or driven out all the men in the forward trench. But against heavy and constant attacks Wellington, with a few of the Gloucester, held on close behind the crest, and were unbeaten when nightfall, as usual, brought a marvellous alleviation of the strain. The relieving troops, Otago Battalion and Wellington Mounted Rifles, crossed the saddle at The Apex without the least difficulty in the dark and replaced the troops on Chunuk Bair. Wellington had gone in at morning 760 strong and now came out with only 70 unwounded or slightly wounded men.

---

[5] The Gurkhas who reached The Farm during the night of the 6th abandoned it during the 7th; on the Mission's visit to Gallipoli Captain Bigg-Wither told me that he had seen the Gurkhas run from The Farm. I recall this because it helped to prick the inflated notions held by Australians about these very good troops. But the deflation was probably mutual. Some of the more talkative of our men boasted in those days that the Australians were becoming known as "the white Gurkhas". After the attempt on Abdel Rahman a rather shocked Australian said to me: "The Gurkhas have seen us run."

These efforts on August 8th had opened the way for a final attempt to seize Chunuk Bair and Q on August 9th; by then it was realised that Hill 971 was beyond possibility of early capture, and therefore Monash's brigade was not asked to renew its attempt. At dawn on the 9th the New Zealanders on the one hand, and Allanson's Gurkhas and the British elements with them on the other, were to go for the crest ahead of them while a new force, General A. H. Baldwin's composite brigade (which after some shuffling comprised four New Army battalions) was to have assembled behind the New Zealanders and from there would attack the part of the summit lying between those to be seized by the other two forces. Baldwin's was, of course, the main task.

By a string of tragic miscarriages which need not be described here,[6] Baldwin's four battalions had to turn back on their steep climb and take a much more difficult route through the depths of the Aghyl Dere to below The Farm, hoping to climb up thence past The Farm in time to assault Chunuk Bair between the other columns at dawn. But at dawn Baldwin's leading battalion was still working along the bed of the Aghyl Dere far below. The New Zealanders were at that moment repelling another furious attack by the Turks, and as no sign appeared of Baldwin's brigade, they merely maintained their ground. But near Hill Q Allanson's Gurkhas and the 6th South Lancashire clambered to the top, which in that sector had been heavily bombarded by the guns of Anzac and of the warships, and drove the Turks from the summit. Apart from Baldwin's column, Allanson's men were to have been supported on their right by the 2/10th Gurkhas, 9th Warwickshire, 7th North Staffordshire and 9th Worcestershire of the 30th Brigade, but he could see no sign of these troops.

What happened next is described in a note of a talk

---

6 See Vol. II, pp. 688-91 or *Anzac to Amiens*, pp. 162-3.

the writer had with Allanson not long after the event.[7] "When the Gurkhas got on top," he told me, "they saw about 200 Turks who had been waiting down the farther slope for the bombardment to finish—cowering—and who, as soon as they saw the line of heads, ran. There was a flattish bit of scrub, then a dip; then a flattish bit; then another dip; and on the edge of this were the supports [just as we had left ours] about 200 more. The first lot were running and we stood on the parapet and fired into their backs. There was only one shallow, half-dug little Turkish trench there. We stood on the parapet of this and fired."

I knew from other accounts that Allanson and his men had stood for a few minutes as the New Zealanders had done on the morning before, looking down at the distant water of the Narrows and the road winding down the Peninsula. "Then," continues the note, "five shells, high explosive, fell right among us. They fell exactly where naval shells had been falling and looked like naval shells. If our men had been in the trench they might have lain doggo and not been hurt, but these shells did a lot of damage."[8] All Allanson's force ran except Allanson himself, Lieutenant J. W. J. Le Marchand, and two South Lancashire officers and several of their men, twelve in all. These stayed, Allanson told me, until the Turkish supports were within fifty yards, when they fell back on the Gurkha supports, who had stayed firm about 100 yards below. Le Marchand had been killed, and every other officer had been wounded.

Hours late, Baldwin's leading battalion, the 6th East

[7] The writer probably made this note in his diary not during the interview but after return to his bivouac as, by a slip, he refers to the South Lancashires as the Gloucesters. There may be other inaccuracies.

[8] As will be seen in the *Official History*, the writer after studying the other available evidence has concluded that these shells came, almost certainly, not from the Navy but from a howitzer battery at Anzac which a few minutes before had thrown a deadly salvo among the New Zealanders a little farther south. For these tragic incidents and the heroic actions which they occasioned see *Vol. II, pp. 692-3 and 695-6.*

Lancashire, followed by the 10th Hampshire and the 6th Royal Irish Rifles, struggled up to The Farm, lined the edge of the shelf on the steep hillside, and began their hopeless attempts to cross it and climb the 300 feet to Chunuk Bair. Night found them still at The Farm.

That night, August 9th/10th, the New Zealanders—still up on the southern shoulder of Chunuk Bair—were at last relieved by New Army troops, the 6th Loyal North Lancashire and also (at the last moment) by the tired 5th Wiltshire, worn out with four days' loss of sleep. The Wiltshire were too many for the trenches and therefore piled their arms and slept in the head of the Sazli Beit Dere just behind the front. At The Farm Brigadier-General Baldwin, with his headquarters behind the ledge, though helped by his colleague, Brigadier-General R. J. Cooper, had too confused a mixture of units to allow any effective reorganisation or straightening of the line. Precisely what troops, if any, were between The Farm and Allanson's position below Q, or who were immediately north of Allanson, nobody knew, then or afterwards. The 4th Australian Brigade and other troops on the northern flank had been pinned down by heavy Turkish sniping, which caused the New Army battalions many casualties, but, so far as most of the 4th Brigade was aware, no serious action had been launched on that flank by either side since August 8th.

Such was the position when, at dawn on August 10th, the Turkish infantry heavily bombed the western side of the crest at Chunuk Bair, and, after some shelling by their guns, appeared in line after line with bayonets fixed, sweeping over the whole skyline at Chunuk Bair and down the seaward slope. The New Army troops were shot down or broke, many, it was afterwards believed, fleeing down the Sazli Beit Dere between Rhododendron Ridge and Battleship Hill, where the depths were then and afterwards No-man's-land. The New Zealand machine-guns still at The Apex opened a terrific fire, and such warships as were off the coast hurled salvo after salvo into the Turkish lines which nevertheless still trickled on. The Apex was held against them, but everything in front of it was lost, as was The Farm close on its flank. Baldwin, Cooper, and many of the British regimental leaders were killed, and the troops driven into the depths of the Aghyl Dere. The Farm was later reoccupied, but was finally given up as being now a useless and exposed position; and Allanson's Gurkhas, who were not attacked, eventually retired to the best defensive line, on Cheshire Ridge behind the Aghyl Dere.

During the four days on which this intense struggle for the wild, almost unfortified crest-line north of Anzac had been in progress, New Army troops of the IX British Army Corps had landed at Suvla Bay, which lay spread like a map beyond and below the Anzac left flank. They were to have seized a semicircle of hills bringing them into line with the intended position of the Anzacs on Hill 971. The comparative slightness of resistance gave them their chance, but through lack of leadership and training they barely reached by August 10th the foothills of the range. The chance had now passed. Like that of the Anzacs their offensive had failed, and on August 10th the Allies were left holding two separate positions each reaching (except at Rhododendron Spur) only to the foothills. A few days later it was decided to connect the two, the Anzac Corps swinging up its left flank across Hill 60, the last and lowest hill of the spur between the Kaiajik and Asma Deres. At the same time the IX Corps at Suvla Bay would try to keep open the opportunity for further attack from Suvla by seizing two foothills on the plain near Northern Anafarta—the W Hills (so called from the markings on their sides) and Scimitar Hill.

But the time for attacks of that kind, even with such artillery bombardment as the limited guns and shells on Gallipoli could give, had passed. On the afternoon of August 21st, when the effort was launched, the 29th Division and Yeomanry made ground at Suvla but could not hold it; and on their flank the mixed force of Anzacs, Indians, and New Army seized little more than a foothold on Hill 60, by then well entrenched. It chanced that the first troops of the 2nd Australian Division had just reached Anzac—tall, hearty, stout, rubicund men, a marked contrast to the thin, worn men who had been there so long; and with great hopes the New Zealand staff put in next morning one of the newly arrived battalions, the 18th, which had been lent them. It was to clear the rest of the "hill"—a low, broad rise, half covered with dwarf scrub. Most men of the 18th, almost straight from Sydney, had until the last moment the impression that they were merely to go into the trenches—an experience sufficiently exciting under the circumstances. They were then led round in the night and at breaking dawn reached "a gap in a hedge" opposite the extreme end of the hill. From this they attacked; and trying, company after company, to advance up the smooth slope—to what objective they did not know—they suffered terrible loss, and, after gaining a little ground, were able to hold on to only a few yards of the gain. Five days later, on August 27th, a composite force, British, New Zealand and Australian, attacked from the trenches then held, and by the morning of the 29th had seized about half the maze of trenches on the hill, but not its summit.

It was at first mistakenly reported by Anzac Headquarters that the hill had been taken, but the troops themselves knew it had not; and, by first watching both attacks and then crawling about the maze of shallow trenches, the writer also had ascertained for the purposes of the future Australian history what parts of the "hill" had been seized and when. But there remained the question—since the 18th Battalion itself did not know[9]— where did the 18th Battalion attack and how far did it go?

Of the answers to some of these problems of the August offensive the next chapter will tell.

---

[9] Or most who had known had since been killed or wounded.

Chapter
XVII

THE OTHER SIDE
OF THE HILLS

UNTIL our visit we knew nothing of the Turkish side of these events. But Zeki Bey was able to tell us—though not as an eye-witness, as in the case of German Officers' and Lone Pine—much that till then was generally unknown to our side.

He told us that before this offensive the rugged hills north of Anzac were held by the 14th Regiment, which appears to have been detached from the 5th Division of which it was normally part. The 14th "had a very large zone", extending apparently over all the foothills north of Old Anzac up to Abdel Rahman Bair. As I have already mentioned, when news came that our columns had broken out of Old Anzac and were storming those hills, Kannengiesser Pasha, who with two regiments of his 9th Division had been brought up close to Lone Pine, received the order to go on to Chunuk Bair. "With the two regiments, 25th and 64th," said Zeki Bey, "he arrived this day at Chunuk Bair. Before reaching it he was wounded. Another officer was appointed, one who knew that area. These two regiments, helped by fragments of the 14th and other small bits, fought that day at Chunuk Bair. They could not do anything except face the troops who were advancing on[1] Chunuk Bair."

---

[1] My note says "from" Chunuk Bair, which I have assumed to be a slip on my part. On the other hand I think Zeki Bey was under the impression that we reached Chunuk Bair on the morning of the 7th, and he may have believed that these regiments stopped us from coming farther. On another occasion he told me that it was certainly our attack at The Nek that put us on Chunuk Bair: "it held up the reinforcements," he said. We know from Kannengiesser's book, *Gallipoli* and from the *British*

Fortunately Kannengiesser has since written a book relating to these critical events, and the excellent British Official History fills in, from Turkish sources, other gaps. We thus know that the commander of the 9th Division had been at Essad Pasha's headquarters[2] at Scrubby Knoll (Kemal Yere) when, at 4.30 on the morning of August 7th, he was called to Essad Pasha and told of the landing at Suvla. He was to take at once the 25th and 64th Regiments and occupy the crest of the main range north of Anzac, from Chunuk Bair to Hill 971.

Kannengiesser went ahead himself, taking two staff officers. At 6 a.m., under an already hot sun, he climbed on foot up the valley behind Chunuk Bair and, reaching the summit, saw Suvla Bay crowded with shipping, and a British battery crossing the dry Salt Lake; but on Chunuk Bair about him all was quiet. He found a Turkish battery commander there, asleep in his shelter[3] and waked him. There was no one at all on Rhododendron Ridge, but there were twenty Turkish infantry with the battery. Kannengiesser got its commander to open fire on Suvla.

Official History (Gallipoli Campaign, Vol. II, pp. 205-6) that Zeki Bey's account was not correct in all details, for example as to the hour at which Kannengiesser was wounded; he appears also to have been unaware that, immediately on hearing of the Lone Pine attack, Liman von Sanders reinforced the 14th Regiment by bringing to the Asma Dere the only reserve for the small garrison of Suvla. This was the 1st Battalion, 32nd Regiment *(see British Official History, Gallipoli, Vol. II, p. 201)*. It helped to stop Monash's brigade on August 8th and possibly on the 7th. The Turkish General Staff says that on the 8th the attack on Abdel Rahman Bair was opposed by the 4th Division with the 11th Regiment and a battalion each of the 31st and 32nd.

[2] Kannengiesser had first ridden from the south to the headquarters of the 16th Division (which was apparently on the hill behind the camping place of our Mission—the wide, paved trench leading over that hill to it was at the time under fire). There he had received a telephone message from Essad Pasha to say that the 9th Division had been allotted to Essad's (Northern) Group as a reserve, and that he was to report to Essad's headquarters. At Essad's headquarters he found Kiazim Bey (later Kiazim Pasha), Liman von Sanders' chief of staff, who had been cut off there by the barrage.

[3] The battery, four field-guns, was presumably the one whose emplacements the Mission found (as will be told) on the northern side of Chunuk Bair, where the saddle leading to Q (South) begins.

Then, "suddenly," he writes, "the enemy infantry actually appeared in front of us at about 500 yards range. The English approached slowly, in single file, splendidly equipped and with white arm bands on their left arms, apparently very tired, and were crossing a hillside to our flank,[4] emerging in continually increasing numbers from the valley below. I immediately sent an order to my infantry—this was the twenty man strong artillery-covering platoon—instantly to open fire. I received this answer: 'We can only commence to fire when we receive an order from our battalion commander.'

"This was too much for me altogether. I ran to the spot and threw myself among the troops, who were lying in a small trench. What I said I cannot recollect, but they began to open fire and almost immediately the English lay down without answering our fire or apparently moving in any other way. They gave me the impression that they were glad to be spared further climbing."

Thus passed by far the best chance of winning a great campaign.

Kannengiesser goes on to tell how he presently received "an unexpected reinforcement". From Battleship Hill he suddenly saw a column of Turkish troops about to descend to the rear into the deep valley there. They were two companies of the 72nd (Arab) Regiment of Mustafa Kemal's 19th Division, which that great commander had sent to picket Battleship Hill behind his right flank. Kannengiesser ordered, and at last induced, them to stop. Next, the commander of the 1st Battalion, 14th Regiment, reached Hill 971 and Kannengiesser took him under his orders. Thus he established a weak firing front on either flank of the position that he had been ordered to secure. His own two regiments were not yet there, but their commanders had told him that they soon

---

[4] Certainly Rhododendron Spur near The Apex. The view from his position was similar to that in *Vol. II, p. 655.*

would be. In front of him his opponents had now set up a machine-gun[5] and, to prevent its hindering his regiments when they would try to deploy along the crest, he ordered the battery to fire on it. But just when the regiments were due to arrive the machine-gun hit Kannengiesser through the chest. However, his leading troops presently arrived and it was they who shot to pieces the Aucklanders who at 11 o'clock tried to complete the advance.

Of the seizure of the southern shoulder of Chunuk Bair by the New Zealanders on August 8th, or of Q Hill by the Gurkhas next day, Zeki Bey told us nothing—he may have been under the impression that we reached Chunuk on the 7th. What he did tell us was that on August 8th, as the 9th Division had not managed to drive us from Chunuk, Essad Pasha (commanding in the Anzac zone) sent his only remaining reserve, a battalion of the 64th Regiment, to Chunuk Bair "under a staff officer, to be there against all happenings.

"This day," he said, "the 8th Division, with two regiments, arrived at Chunuk Bair, and in the evening it made a counter-attack with one of its regiments, the 24th, but failed. This division had originally, before the Gallipoli Campaign, been stationed at Rodosto [between Constantinople and Gallipoli] but had then been sent to Jerusalem. From there, leaving one regiment behind, for use in Persia or elsewhere, it had come back to Gallipoli with two regiments, 23rd and 24th. The 11th Regiment also was employed on the right flank of the 19th Division [i.e. about Battleship Hill] under Mustafa Kemal Bey.[6] In this way," said Zeki Bey, "Chunuk Bair and its sur-

---

[5] Kannengiesser says the Gurkhas set it up, but it was possibly the New Zealanders. It is most doubtful whether any Gurkhas were then near.

[6] Zeki Bey was not sure where the 11th came from—he thought it had probably been brought up behind Lone Pine. The answers of the Turkish General Staff (see *Appendix I*, Questions 61-80) differ in many respects from Zeki Bey's, but of course the Turkish reinforcements in this crisis were intermixed.

roundings were reinforced. Chunuk Bair and the troops there were placed under the commander of the 8th Division, Ali Riza."

As soon as I mentioned to Zeki Bey the other attack made on August 8th—the disastrous attempt of the 4th Australian Brigade to reach Hill 971 by way of the long spur, Abdel Rahman Bair, and the wrecking of it by machine-gun fire, he said: "I heard much credit given to a machine-gun company for repelling an attack there. It was the machine-gun company of the 11th Regiment which had been stationed out there on a commanding hill, Alai Tepe [that is, Regiment Hill, a high spur of Abdel Rahman Bair]. There would be four machine-guns in the company and there may have been other machine-guns also. These together with parts of the 14th Regiment met and defeated that attack." When he showed us the place the result became clear as daylight—but I must first complete his outline of the main events.

"As the 24th Regiment didn't succeed," he said, "they remained on the defensive. The 'Southern Group' [that is the force in the Helles zone] sent all its reserves northwards, although it was being attacked,[7] and won the admiration of all by doing so. Vehib Pasha, a brother of Essad, commanded in the south; Liman Pasha's headquarters was at Yalova [a port of call on the Sea of Marmora]. This finished the local reserve. The only troops left were the 7th Division in the north by Gallipoli, resting, and the 11th Division. These had been ordered to march, but they were coming to Anafarta.

"The situation was realised. As a result of that realisation, it was intended to check the Anzac troops by making a manoeuvre [against their northern flank], and by throwing in this force by the shortest possible route. As commander of these troops from the north, a staff officer, Feizi Bey (later, I think, military attaché in Aus-

---

[7] It was attacked on August 6th and 7th. It is now known that Vehib Pasha protested strongly against the withdrawal of his only reserve.

tria), had been given the order to make this attack. He reported that his troops were tired by their march, and were still a long way from the front, and that they couldn't make the attack. Accordingly Liman Pasha ordered Mustafa Kemal Pasha to hand over his division, and go to Anafarta and take charge of the troops arriving there. This was on August 8th."

On the following day Mustafa Kemal devoted his attention to the carrying out against our left flank of "the manoeuvre" which, it was hoped, would automatically force us to abandon our hold on the Chunuk heights. "An assault was made against the Asma Dere [sic], the 7th Division, with all its three regiments, attacking on the left and, I think, the 11th (or it may have been the 12th) Division on the right. This attack was not a great victory; it pushed back your line, but it didn't put you off Chunuk Bair by outmanoeuvring you as had been intended. Mustafa Kemal Pasha lost two of his regimental commanders, those of the 20th and 21st Regiments—they lie side by side under the cypresses at Anafarta[8]—and very heavily in men." Actually, as has already been said, the 4th Australian Brigade did not even report that it was being attacked that day; the Turks apparently advanced across the Asma Dere and entrenched upon the Hill 60 ridge, which till then had been No-man's-land. Part of the attack reached the British on our right, but they beat it off despite loss.

"At Chunuk Bair, in the meantime," Zeki Bey said, "nothing important had been done. Mustafa Kemal Pasha, who had been given control there, was directing the Anafarta attack. The situation at Chunuk was very critical because Essad Pasha had no more troops.

"In these days," continued Zeki Bey, "shots from Chunuk Bair hit the stores, kitchens, and waggons and pack animals behind Edirna Sirt [Mortar Ridge at Old Anzac] and in Dik Dere [behind the next ridge to that].

---

8 Cypresses mark the cemetery of every village, Turk or Greek.

223

Some of the transport under this fire was prepared to with-draw and there was disorganisation, especially among the transport. Possibly these shots were indirect—I cannot say whether they were aimed or not; but the incident shows how critical and anxious the time was.

"No one knew what to do; even the Army Corps staff had lost its power to influence events, since it had used its reserve. Ali Riza Pasha, commanding the 8th Division on Chunuk Bair, asked Kemal: 'What are we going to do?' Kemal answered: 'It isn't as important a question as you think. I will come there and we will settle everything. Don't be anxious.' He gave this answer as if everything was in a settled state. The staff officer who told me this was always speaking of Kemal's *sang froid* at this moment.

"Kemal then came to Chunuk Bair [on the 9th]. On the evening that he arrived he studied the situation, and afterwards ordered that next morning, at dawn, they should make a great attack with the bayonet. The troops he already had there were to take part—the 23rd and 24th Regiments of the 8th Division, and then the 25th and 64th of the 9th Division. The order of battle[9] is uncertain. The 23rd had not previously taken part, and was the strongest. The 24th had lost pretty heavily a few days before. The staff didn't know what was on the other side of the crest—a precipice or what—because it hadn't been possible to reconnoitre; but they sent the men over in spite of this because they had to." Actually, at Chunuk Bair itself, it was a naked, almost precipitous slope.

Zeki Bey went on: "This attack was made with the bayonet, and your line was pushed back to where it re-mained to the end. When the light grew the shells from your guns at Ari Burnu fell behind Chunuk Bair, and

---

[9] That is, the order (usually from right to left) in which regiments or divisions were stationed along the battle-front. The Turkish General Staff in its answers (*see Appendix I*) says that the attack was made by the 23rd and 24th Regiments and the 56th Regiment (13th Division), a total of 5000 men. Which, if either, account is right I have no means of knowing.

those of the naval artillery fell in front of it; there was also heavy machine-gun fire. The start of the attack was not costly, because the soldiers in your trenches—the Australians[10]—seeing this wall of soldiers with bayonets coming over the hill and moving down on them, lost their heads and took to flight. But the fire of your artillery and machine-guns prevented the Turkish infantry from taking advantage of this success.

"After this Mustafa Kemal Pasha had his headquarters at Chamla Tepe, or Chambeli ['Pine Hill', or 'Pine Ridge']. His troops were called the Anafarta Grubu, Essad's were known as the Shemal Grubu (Northern Group). On August 21st and 22nd you attacked at Bomba Tepe [Bomb Hill, Hill 60]. Kemal Pasha saw what was wrong with the troops there. They had lost their regimental commander, and were under a battalion commander. He asked Essad Pasha to send him at least two officers whom he, Kemal, knew. He said, 'Your front is normal, mine is not—the need is urgent.' So Essad Pasha sent me—to command the 21st Regiment. Essad wouldn't send Hairi Bey, who had commanded the III/57th and was now acting in command of the 57th Regiment—he was the same who had sent the calm reports from Jessaret Tepe [The Nek] on the evening of April 25th—Essad wouldn't send away both the officers who knew Bomba Sirt [Quinn's] and Merkez Tepe [German Officers']; Bomba Sirt was then a very complicated position.

"When I arrived, Mustafa Kemal said to the commander of the 7th Division: 'I'm sending you an officer—you can put him in the most dangerous position.' He was joking, speaking as if it were a court-martial judgment. I was given the 21st Regiment, at Bomba Tepe [Hill 60].

---

10 Those were Zeki Bey's words, but in this case the soldiers were (as already stated) exceedingly tired troops of the New Army, who had just arrived after a long relief and previous exertions. It will be noted that the Turkish General Staff in its replies said, "The casualties were not heavy." The investigations of our Mission led us to conclude that near Chunuk Bair and The Farm they were considerable.

At that time everything indicated that there was going to be a further push by you.

"Four days later, when I was absent through an attack of malaria, another attack was made there against a company of gendarmerie and two machine-guns. There was a big bombardment first and the 'English' took these machine-guns. From then bomb and mine fighting went on until the end."

Summing up his account to me of the Gallipoli fighting Zeki Bey said: "Kemal's work on the Peninsula was unforgettable. He knew exactly where to attack in the first instance, in the attacks prior to the armistice of May 24th; and at Chunuk Bair again he kept his head.

"The Lone Pine demonstration cost the Turks very heavily, about 5000 casualties. But not only that: it drew in all the troops in immediate reserve, the 5th Division. It drew reserves from the south, and it prevented troops from being on Chunuk Bair when the New Zealanders arrived.[11] If you had got to the top of Chunuk Bair I don't think we could ever have got there; we would have lost the Peninsula." At another time he told me that in meeting the August offensive the Turkish command used its last reserve.

But there were a number of questions as to this fighting which Zeki Bey could not settle for us. Precisely where, for example, did the New Zealanders (and 7th Gloucester and 8th Welsh) on August 8th—or the 6th Gurkhas and 6th South Lancashire on August 9th—reach the crest of the range? In an endeavour to answer that and other questions on Zeki Bey's second full day with the Mission, February 23rd, most of us rode out with him to the last summit but one of the range, Hill Q

---

[11] It probably prevented the 5th Division from being sent early to Chunuk Bair; on the other hand it drew from the south the 9th Turkish Division, which actually met the New Zealanders at Chunuk Bair. *See Vol. II, p. 642 (footnote)* and *British Official History, Gallipoli, Vol. II, p. 202.*

(North),[12] and then dismounted and, in extended order, moved along the crest-line southwards, searching carefully. On the summit of the next height, Q (South), we came upon some Gurkha web equipment and a water-bottle. But it was not until we approached Chunuk Bair that we found, on this and later expeditions, clear signs of the presence of British or Indian troops. In the saddle of the crest between Q and Chunuk, in the bottom of a shallow trench, was British kit, and close by lay British cartridge cases.

The objective of the Gurkhas had been Hill Q, and several reports of their attack had stated that it took place there. The British Official History still records this fight as "The capture and loss of Hill Q", and indeed some men of the Gurkhas may have reached there. But some months after the attack Allanson, in describing it to me, had pointed out the saddle between Q and Chunuk as the place where his Gurkhas and the South Lancashire had reached the crest.[13] I had forgotten this, not having brought to Gallipoli my note of that talk—or Sir Ian Hamilton's despatch, which said the same; and as the signs of the Gurkhas on the Q summits were so slight, we searched that whole area on two more days, after Zeki Bey had gone. Buchanan and I finally climbed down the steep side of Q (North) and then back again up the side of Q (South). In this search Buchanan went to the bottom of the slope while I worked along the hillside about half-way down. On reaching the rib below Q (South) I noted that the lie of the ground there corresponded for the first time with that described to me by Allanson. An old British or Indian trench ran along a ledge and then up a steep rib leading to the southern end of Q (South). Near by lay the first piece of British kit we had seen in

---

[12] On the southern shoulder of Q (North) we found on a later search some traces of English kit.

[13] The point is shown in a sketch made by me at the time, and since reproduced in the *Official History, Vol. II, p. 694.*

our climb. The slope above was by no means unclimbable. The crest there had been very heavily shelled. I concluded that the Gurkhas had climbed here and reached the top at the saddle between Chunuk and Q (South).[14]

Allanson's account, since published, has of course placed it beyond doubt, and our search there is interesting only because it proved that our methods led, in this case, to an unquestionably correct conclusion. Incidentally, Zeki Bey told me that he knew of no report of the

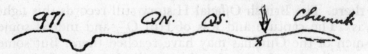

DIAGRAM MADE DURING THE MISSION'S VISIT, SHOWING THE POSITION (X) JUDGED TO HAVE BEEN REACHED BY GURKHAS ON 9th AUGUST 1915

British having reached the crest elsewhere than at Chunuk Bair. I have described this search not because we discovered anything previously unknown, but because it shows that where I was originally in error our methods succeeded in correcting this.

At the southern end of this dip, where the crest began to rise again to Chunuk, we found the emplacements of four Turkish guns, obviously sited to fire direct on the ridges and slopes leading to the crest. Next, just north of the Chunuk summit, we came upon many traces of British soldiers. I noted them as Gloucesters. Clearly they reached here in the dawn of August 8th, beside the New Zealanders, but, being completely open to fire from Q and 971, were shot down or driven off. Slightly to the southern side of the summit we began to find signs of the

---

[14] This conclusion was reached as a result of our last search, on March 4th. Previously I thought the relics found here might have betokened the left of the New Zealanders.

New Zealanders. A few had been buried by the Turks in the hard, stony ground of the crest; and, just below the road that skirted the Turkish side of the ridge-top, was (as my diary says) a "cemetery of them", row after row. "All the bones in the first three rows had been dug up, and were lying on the surface. There were many other graves below, rows of them, untouched. Those dug up—by the villagers or whoever it was—contained our men and Turks, both."

These graves were only a biscuit throw from the crest-line. The position which the New Zealanders had occupied there was determined for us beyond any doubt by Captain Bigg-Wither, the New Zealander with the Graves Unit. By our extraordinary good fortune it turned out that he had been a sergeant in the Auckland Mounted Rifles when they advanced behind the Wellington infantry in this attack. He showed us the old Turkish trench, running along the crest south of Chunuk Bair, into which the two leading half-companies of Wellington and a few of the Aucklanders had settled. It was almost straight and very shallow, hewn out of stony ground. The summit of Chunuk was not 200 yards away on their left; its humped southern shoulder about the same distance on their right;[15] and a third summit, projecting towards the Turkish rear, lay 300 yards to the New Zealanders' right front.

These summits were smooth and largely open. When the New Zealanders reached there in the first light of dawn there was no enemy to be seen; for the moment the Turks had disappeared; apparently some panic had, shortly before, seized those who occupied that section of the crest. Indeed from the starting point at The Apex the New Zealanders had seen no opponents except some machine-gunners who were found asleep near the top of Rhododendron.

---

15 This was shown in our better maps (copied from captured Turkish ones) as Hill 161. The figure was a mistake for 261, the height in metres.

Had the trench on the crest which the New Zealanders took been a good one, or open to Turkish attack
from only one direction, it would have been difficult for
the Turks to recapture; but being straight it gave little
protection against a machine-gun which they rushed
immediately to the summit of Chunuk Bair on the direct
left, and another which was almost as quickly emplaced
on the shoulder to the right. This made it impossible to
show a head above the trench in order to shoot; and
when, after about fifteen minutes, a strong body of Turkish infantry began to advance from the third summit, Su
Yatagha—that is, from the south-east—those New Zealanders who were capable of retiring had to get out and
make the rush back over the crest into the trench which
their main body was digging fifty yards in rear.[16]

Much of the western slope was pestered by the same
enfilade as the front trench, except that here the machine-
gun fire from the right came from a more distant summit, Battleship Hill. Also field-guns somewhere to the
north shelled it in enfilade. But the New Zealand line
here, lying just above the head of the Sazli Beit Dere, and
south of the upper end of Rhododendron Spur, was
slightly favoured by the curve of the hillside. On the
crest ahead of the southern end of this line I again found
traces of the Gloucesters—a man's grave with the helmet
and shoulder strap lying there. Close behind was a small
natural bank under which our men had at one time
sheltered.

The Turks did not actually re-enter their old trench
on the summit until nearly 9 a.m. Then they began to
bowl bombs over the crest, and had to be scared away by
rush after rush with the bayonet. By 4 o'clock the New
Zealanders' trench was so full of dead that they had to
scratch and occupy another trench behind it. This Bigg-
Wither also showed us. It was the trench in which the

---

16 For details of this famous episode see *Vol. II, pp. 668-78,* and the
New Zealand Official History by Major F. Waite, *Vol. I, pp. 219-23.*

THE NEW ZEALANDERS' TRENCHES ON CHUNUK BAIR

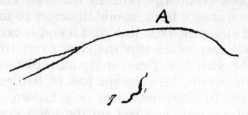

Summit of Chunuk Bair (A) seen from trench captured by Wellington, showing how this trench was enfiladed by Turks from the north.

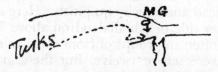

Trench captured by Wellington seen from the north; showing the direction of the Turkish counter-attack upon it, and also the enfilade from the southern shoulder of Chunuk Bair.

Malone's trench just behind the crest, south of Chunuk Bair, seen from the north, showing direction of the enfilade from Battleship Hill.

A. Battleship Hill.
B. Southern shoulder of Chunuk Bair (Hill 160, or 261).
C. The Apex, and Rhododendron Ridge.
D. Malone's trench.

British troops eventually relieved the New Zealanders. I paced the distance from its middle sector to the centre of the road along the crest-line, and found it exactly fifty paces. It was easy to see why the New Army troops had fled into the Sazli Beit Dere; it lay immediately behind them. In its depths, between the foot of Battleship Hill and our line (if these men had only known of it) on Rhododendron, only 200 feet up the steep slope above it, many of them lived for weeks and then perished.[17] We found the valley marked here and there by their bones and by the kit they dropped. The crevices and gullies leading up the side of Rhododendron contained numbers of dead and much equipment. Here and on the crest and other side of Rhododendron above The Apex, the dead lay often in groups of from three to six; in one place there were ten or twelve. But these groups were largely Turks killed in their final counter-attack on August 10th. Between The Apex and The Pinnacle the remains lying thickly were probably those of the Auckland infantry killed on August 7th in the belated attempt to reach Chunuk. Behind the southern shoulder of Chunuk Bair were considerable buildings for the headquarters of a division; and around the front of the summit there had been dug a sunken road or, more probably, a shelf for a wire entanglement.

From Chunuk Bair, on our second visit, we went down the northern side of Rhododendron to The Farm, in order to search for traces of Baldwin's attack. On Rhododendron itself we found only one sign of it—a trench immediately below The Apex, in which were many English dead. On the small open field or terrace of The Farm a few tumbled stones showed where the hut had stood. We noted no traces of men on the terrace itself.

But when we came to its seaward edge, where the valley dipped deep and steeply, as if the shelf had been precariously built up, the remains of men were everywhere. Up

17 *See Vol. II, note on p. 714.*

the slope to the ledge there straggled an irregular shallow trench which tee-d out, at the top, under the seaward edge of the terrace. At the right-hand extremity of this trench, where the terrace dipped to the valley between The Farm and Rhododendron, a soldier had been sniping from behind a stone. From there northwards, says my note, "we came across the remains of men, thick; all below the seaward edge of the shelf. The slope for a hundred yards down was simply covered with them. Those on the right [south] were mostly Royal Irish Rifles; then some Wilts and Hants. As far as the northern edge of The Farm slope [that is, the bank below the shelf] the bodies of Tommies were thick—their helmets everywhere. In some places they had dug themselves little dugouts—scoops in the slope. Only one man, as far as I could see, had got round the left hand [northern] shoulder of the slope.

"From the left of the slope we could see across the valleys northward, and I started with Bigg-Wither and James to see if we could come across any traces of the Gurkhas" (that is, of those who with Allanson reached

THE SLOPES AND RELICS AT THE FARM (FROM THE HISTORIAN'S DIARY, DATED A FEW DAYS AFTER THE VISIT)

the crest on the morning on which Baldwin's brigade was to have been beside them). "We could see the bones of men on two hills ahead of us, somewhat as in the above sketch, and [so we] cut across the valley intervening. We found on both the further heights" (they were steep, lofty

233

spurs, leading to the crest of the range just north of Chunuk Bair) "the remains of the Worcestershire Regiment and a few South Lancashires. Those at the very top seemed to have been attacking a Turkish trench or redoubt on the hilltop. None had got quite to the top; but we found them very near to it, and some of those on top had bombs—old jam-tin bombs—lying near them. Hughes came across what seemed to be a colonel's coat; and the buttons showed that he belonged to the 1st Battalion, Worcestershire Regiment."

It was clear that the Worcesters had been engaged here in a stiff fight of which nothing was known, at least by me. The battalion of the Worcesters which fought in these hills was the 9th; it did not belong to Baldwin's column, but had been ordered on August 7th to reinforce Allanson's Gurkhas. Its commander, Lieutenant-Colonel M. H. Nunn, was killed, apparently on August 10th, when the Turks finally bombed it from its high lodgement.[18] It seems most probable that, despite the discrepancy as to the number on the tunic-buttons, it was his coat that we found among the remains of his men by the hilltop.

For the first time in our mission to Gallipoli, the scenes we looked on that afternoon "got us down". Wilkins, Buchanan and the others felt as I did. For some reason the dissolution of the human remains in that lofty area was not quite so complete as at Old Anzac; and the number that must have been trapped, and the hopelessness of the situation on those steep ridges when once they were caught there, did not bear thinking of. My note says: "I have nowhere, except at The Nek, seen the dead lying so thick, I think, as on these slopes and

---

[18] *See British Official History, Vol. II, p. 307.* To me on this search it seemed likely that the Worcesters were slightly south of Allanson's Gurkhas; I have also noted some evidence that they may have been, as the British historian states, slightly north of him. In any case they were very much farther up the range than has been generally understood, and should certainly be numbered among those who almost reached the summit.

THE EXTREME LEFT OF QUINN'S,
looking across successive valleys to Dead Man's Ridge, Pope's Hill, and Russell's
Top. At this point the Anzac trenches at Quinn's ran into the Turkish one along
the edge of the Bloody Angle valley. (The original trench here had been dug by
our 16th Battalion in an unsuccessful attack on May 2nd. It was afterwards used
probably only by Turkish snipers.) Dead Man's was held by the Turks, Pope's
and Russell's by the Anzacs, and The Nek (just visible on the horizon above
Dead Man's) by the Turks. The valley between Dead Man's and Pope's
(Waterfall Gully) was shallow at its upper end but steep at the lower.   *G1925*

THE HEAD OF MONASH VALLEY
seen from near where on 15th May 1915 General Bridges was shot. The hills at
the end of the valley are (left to right) Pope's, Dead Man's, and the slope of the
Bloody Angle adjoining Quinn's (which is obscured by the shoulder of the
indentation leading to Courtney's). Dead Man's Ridge and the Bloody Angle
were held by the Turks; and during May, until our snipers suppressed them, the
Turkish snipers made passage along the valley-bed most dangerous. A
communication trench was then dug along the left-hand side of the valley.
The excavation up the centre is the drain dug in the autumn to keep the
valley-bed dry for traffic. *G1769*

THE RIGHT OF GERMAN OFFICER'S TRENCH,
commanding No-man's-land at Quinn's. No-man's-land is marked by the track
passing along it and doubling around Quinn's Post (see on extreme right). On
the horizon are (from left to right) Russell's Top, The Nek, Baby 700, and part of
Battleship Hill. In the middle distance are Pope's Hill (with Courtney's Post
nearer to the reader), Waterfall Gully, Dead Man's Ridge, the Bloody Angle (with
the Chessboard above it) and Quinn's. The Nek, Dead Man's, Bloody Angle, and
all the ground above them were Turkish. No-man's-land at Quinn's was
impassable, being commanded by Turkish machine-guns at Dead Man's, the
Chessboard, and German Officers', and by Anzac machine-guns at Russell's Top,
Pope's, and Steele's (just outside the picture, facing German Officers').   *G1919*

CONCRETE EMPLACEMENT OF A TURKISH MACHINE-GUN
on Dead Man's Ridge. Dead Man's is on the right, with the Bloody Angle valley
beside it. Dead Man's Ridge points straight at Quinn's. No-man's-land at
Quinn's lies just above the Bloody Angle, with German Officers' Ridge beyond
it. It can be seen how machine-guns at these two places swept the ground
across which any attack from Quinn's had to be made.   *G1996*

THE SCENE OF GREIG'S FIGHT.
Zeki Bey standing near the blown-in gallery and the mine crater which broke
into German Officers' Trench.   *G1924*

THE SAME GROUND SEEN FROM THE OTHER DIRECTION.
The Anzac trenches ran along the horizon. *G1933*

THE ENTRANCE TO OWEN'S GULLY
into which Zeki Bey led his battalion when rushed to Lone Pine. Lone Pine
forms the left side of the gully and Johnston's Jolly the right. The original
Australian front, on the plateau beyond the head of the gully, is invisible, but
the attack (on 6th August 1915) reached the edge of The Cup (the hollow
branching to the left near the top of the gully and marked by a Turkish
monument). The fighting near the edge of The Cup was desperate, and into
it Zeki Bey and his battalion were immediately drawn. Headquarters of the
125th Regiment, to which he also went, were on the right-hand side of
Owen's Gully. *G1831A*

THE CUP AND THE HEAD OF OWEN'S GULLY.
It was just above the rim of The Cup that the Lone Pine attack was held. A few
Australians reached the Turkish battalion headquarters, which were apparently
on the uppermost ledge shown in the picture. The photograph was taken after a
fall of snow early in 1919.   *G1795*

A SCENE OF SHARP FIGHTING AFTER THE BATTLE.
Beyond the Australian bomb stop here shown was a mine crater, on the edge of
which still lay, in 1919, Turkish revolver cartridge-shells and the remains of a
bombing shelter.   *G1939*

AN OLD AUSTRALIAN SHALLOW TUNNEL
at Lone Pine. Many parts of these tunnels had fallen in by 1919. The one here
shown was possibly part of the old underground forward line dug before
the battle. *G1992*

TURKISH SHALLOW PROTECTIVE MINE-GALLERIES
in No-man's-land on Johnston's Jolly. The circular ceiling was a peculiarity of the
Turkish tunnels. *G1989*

THE SHORE NORTH OF OLD ANZAC,
starting point of the August offensive. The view is from the seaward slope of
Baby 700 (held by the Turks). Below are No. 1 Outpost (hill on the left), Nos 2
and 3 Outposts (hill in centre), and the low Fisherman's Hut ridge (between
them). It was from cover of these that attacking columns marched out after dark
on 6th August 1915 into the valleys beyond these ridges, while the British IX
Corps was landing at Suvla Bay (in distance). Part of one New Zealand column,

from Fisherman's Hut, lost its way, heading by mistake into the main Sazli Beit Dere on the near side of Destroyer Hill (the ridge on the right) instead of into the branch valley between it and Nos 2 and 3 Posts. This contributed to delaying the final New Zealand attack. The dark ridge across the bottom of the picture leads to Snipers' Nest, a Turkish observation post (dimly seen at the end of the dark spur). *G1823 A and B*

THE TRENCH (IN FOREGROUND) REACHED BY THE NEW ZEALANDERS
on the crest south of Chunuk Bair. The New Zealanders had originally climbed
to The Apex (seen in centre) through very steep valleys from Nos 3 and 1 Posts.
On August 8th they attained the trench here shown but were shot out of it by
fire from Chunuk Bair (behind the reader) and from its southern shoulder (on
left of picture). Their support line, however, held on about 50 yards behind the
crest, above the head of the Sazli Beit Dere, the steep depths of which are here
hidden by the curve of the summit.   *G2004*

THE VIEW INLAND FROM THE SUMMIT
of Chunuk Bair. The buildings, trench, and road are almost certainly all of later
date than the New Zealanders' attack. At that time Chunuk Bair was practically
untouched by military works. (The Narrows, here faintly seen, are more clearly
shown in the plate at p. 671 of Volume II.)   *G1914*

CHUNUK BAIR,
and the crest to the right of it where seized by the New Zealanders and 7th Gloucestershire. All the trenches on Chunuk Bair and its shoulder here shown were dug during the later stage of the campaign. The excavation encircling Chunuk Bair seems to have been a shelf for a barbed wire entanglement. The view is from Rhododendron Ridge. *G1916*

THE FARM,
scene of the tragedy of Baldwin's Brigade. The view is from the Turkish position on Chunuk Bair. The depths of the Aghyl Dere (South), up which the brigade approached, are hidden by The Farm. Beyond them is the top of Cheshire Ridge with a Turkish track down it; and behind this again, also mainly hidden, lies the Chailak Dere up which the main body of New Zealand infantry had originally climbed to Table Top (marked by a zigzag track) and Rhododendron Ridge (extreme left of picture). The Salt Lake and Suvla Bay are in the distance. *G2003*

THE SUMMIT OF HILL 971,
seen from the inland side of Chunuk Bair. The hill on the left is Q (South), which
obscures all but a fraction of Q (North). Part of the road on Q (North) is just
visible below the left-hand end of Hill 971. 971 is cut off from Q (North) by a
gorge spanned by a razor edge behind which the road winds.   *G1802*

"THE CYPRESSES OF ANAFARTA"
seen from the top of Hill 971. The valley here shown reaches across the
Peninsula, between the hills, Tekke and Kavak Tepe, which the IX Corps tried to
reach, and Hill 971, which the Anzacs tried to reach. At one end of the valley are
Suvla Bay and Salt Lake, and at the other Ak Bashi Liman, the main Turkish
landing place in this part of the Dardanelles. Little Anafarta lies under Tekke
Tepe, on the distant plain; and Big Anafarta to the right of the cypresses, close
under the spur of 971.   *G1845 C*

THE MISSION AT LUNCH ON HILL 60,
22nd February 1919. From left to right: Lieut. Buchanan, Zeki Bey, Lieut. James,
the writer, and Captain Lambert. In background: Tpr. Spruce with Lambert's
mule. On the horizon are part of Abdel Rahman Bair and Hill 971. The valley
behind the animals is the Kaiajik Dere.   *G1904*

MINE CRATER AT THE NEK,
blown at the Evacuation. It was the firing of this mine and two others at
3.30 a.m. on December 20th that first notified to the Turks that Anzac had been
evacuated. Sixty Turks were killed. The Turkish monument marks the point
where all attempted advances up this part of the range (Baby 700) from the
evening of April 25th onward were stopped by the Turkish soldier. *G1895*

THE VILLAGE OF KOJA DERE.
G1804

ONE OF THE GUN-PITS AT THE OLIVE GROVE,
the emplacement of a 15-cm. howitzer. The western side of the Kilid Bahr
plateau is in the background. *G1971*

THE ASMAK DERE, SOUTH OF GABA TEPE.
George Lambert on his cob, 27th February 1919. The Olive Grove guns were
behind a gentle rise south of this stream. *G1970*

THE SOUTHERN END OF THE ANZAC LINE,
on Harris Ridge. The line was dug by the 2nd Light Horse Brigade. Chatham's
Post is on the rise in the centre. Beyond this the line was dug and tunnelled for
about 100 yards down the next saddle to Wilson's Lookout. Poppy Valley
is in the left foreground, joining with Valley of Despair, Pine and
Third (Gun) Ridges beyond.   *G1761*

A FRUIT-TREE ON ONE OF THE HEAPS AT SILT SPUR.
Lieutenant Buchanan is standing beside it.   *G1951*

those of The Farm. We searched for signs of the general [Baldwin] but could not find any."

On our visits to this northern flank it remained to answer the questions—which was the spur up which the 4th Australian Brigade advanced on August 8th on its intended way to Abdel Rahman Bair and Hill 971, and where was the so-called "gap in the hedge" from which the 18th Battalion launched its hurried attack two weeks later against Hill 60? In two searches, first by most of the party, together with Zeki Bey, and later by Buchanan and myself, we were able to determine both points.

It will be remembered that General Monash, commanding that brigade, believed that his front on August 7th lay on the ridge next to the lofty and rugged Abdel Rahman Bair, and looked down into the valley between the two, the Asma Dere. He believed that his men next morning crossed the Asma Dere and began to climb a spur of Abdel Rahman; and the same was, at the time, the belief of Lieutenant-Colonel J. H. Cannan,[19] commanding the leading battalion, the 15th. Testing their reports, we rode from the south and west around the seaward end of the much lower and gentler spur that ended in Hill 60, and turned into the Asma Dere to begin our search. If Monash was right we should find traces of the brigade on the left-hand (north-eastern) side of the valley as we went up it. But we saw no sign of our men at all until half-a-mile up the valley, where a deep branch forked to the left, enclosing between the branching valleys a steep promontory which stood out as a very prominent spur of Abdel Rahman Bair. Zeki Bey pointed to this spur. It had lain directly behind his headquarters, he said, when he was sent to command the 21st Regiment on this flank. And on top of this hill had been stationed the machine-gun company which had done so much to defeat the 4th Brigade's attack.

---

[19] Probably both he and Monash afterwards realised that their reports were wrong.

235

"It was the machine-gun company of the 11th Regiment," he said. "All the other troops fled" (possibly from our original advance two nights before), "but this company had held on, and was on the hill when your men came towards the Asma Dere. They had great effect because they were not themselves under fire, and could therefore shoot very calmly."

"If this is so," I noted in my diary, "we shall find traces of our repulse on the hill between Kaiajik Dere and Asma Dere," that is, on the more gentle spur leading down to Hill 60. In the Asma Dere we had seen few traces of Australians, and those all from half to three-quarters of a mile along the valley; water-bottle, mess-tin, waterproof sheet—all of them articles which Turks might have taken from the dead, or which might indicate the presence of a few prisoners or wounded men brought behind the Turkish lines after the fight.[20] Certainly in those few relics we had found nothing suggestive of the calamity that befell the 4th Brigade under the fire of those machine-guns.

Wilkins, Buchanan and I returned to this area a day or two before we left. Wilkins was ill with ptomaine poisoning, but insisted on coming as the day was fine though very cold. We left our horses out of the wind, near the fork of the Asma Dere, and then climbed at once the crumpled, but not very steep, slope of the ridge that led down to Hill 60. This must long ago have been a spur leading up to Hill Q, but several upper branches of the Aghyl Dere on the one side and the Asma Dere on the other had broken down the upper half of it, nearest to the main range, leaving there only a chain of high knobs and narrow necks; the lower half began steeply with a small plateau 330 feet high, Hill 100, and then fell, through a gentler swelling, Hill 90, to another such

---

[20] In one case I think some Australian had almost certainly been on the ground on which we found the relics—a clip for cartridges, piece of web equipment and waterproof sheet.

THE HEIGHTS THE 4th BRIGADE WAS SET TO CLIMB ON 7th-8th AUGUST 1915

971—Koja Chemen Tepe, the brigade's objective.

A. Abdel Rahman Bair, the height by which it was to reach Hill 971.

B. Alai Tepe, the height by which it was to reach Abdel Rahman Bair.

C. The height up which it actually moved (Hill 100). Its dead lay at C, caught by machine-guns posted at B.

swelling half a mile lower down, Hill 60, which barely deserved even the name of hill, so gradually did it merge into the Suvla plain. We climbed at once to the upper end of Hill 90 where machine-guns firing from the high spur that Zeki Bey had pointed out to us—just across the Asma Dere—would most effectively have caught troops marching up the wide ridge-top.

Here at once we came on groups of our dead, some with the colours of the 14th Battalion on their sleeves. One group lay as far up the ridge as Hill 100—Australians and Turks together; one had the badge or colour of the 14th Battalion, and one a small bible with the name "H. Wellington" on the fly leaf.[21] The hill on which the Turkish machine-guns were posted—Alai Tepe (Regiment Hill) Zeki Bey called it—was about 600 yards away and 130 feet higher, and the smooth, wide crest up which the 4th Brigade moved was tilted slightly upwards towards it, so that the streams of bullets must have grazed the whole surface. Lower down, the big field of stubble and several smaller open patches were completely bare, and the rest was covered only with scrub ankle- or waist-high. Far down the spur we found in the Asma Dere the graves of a group of Australians buried by the Turks and dug up again by someone; and opposite these, on the lowest spur of Abdel Rahman Bair, a line of Turks had lain firing into the flank of our men as they crossed the stubblefield and headed up the ridge; one Turk (perhaps a machine-gunner) had fired 200 rounds. Doubtless these were relics of the counter-attack which some of our platoons had been diverted to that flank to meet. We found many of our cartridges above the southern side of the Asma Dere and the bodies of Australians (including one of the 15th or 16th Battalion). After the war one of the few Australian prisoners-of-war on return from Turkey said that some small parties on that slope had known nothing

---

[21] Though we noted men of the 14th, the 15th lost more heavily.

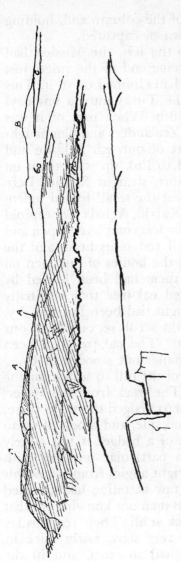

WHERE THE 4th BRIGADE WAS CAUGHT BY THE TURKISH MACHINE-GUNS, 8th AUGUST 1915

A-A-A. Ridge rising to Hill 100 along which the brigade was moving. (The Kaiajik Dere lies
        behind this spur.)

B. Lala Baba, hill south of Suvla Bay.
C. The Salt Lake, adjoining Suvla Bay.
60. Hill 60.

The view is from the position of the Turkish machine-guns on Abai Tepe. (Other features of
Suvla and northern Anzac are not shown on this sketch, though they were visible from that
viewpoint.)

of the retirement of the rest of the column and, holding on, were cut off and shot down or captured.

On our first excursion to the left, the Mission had examined Hill 60 at the extreme end of the ridge, just below where the 4th Brigade had climbed on to it. This "hill" was not occupied by the Turks until a few days after the attempt of August 8th. When part of it was taken from them by the New Zealanders and Connaught Rangers on August 21st, part of our 4th Brigade and some Hampshire troops tried to link up with them on the south by crossing the short, straight Kaiajik Dere ("Valley of the Little Rock") at the small folded indentation marked on the maps as Kaiajik Aghala ("Sheepfold of the Little Rock"). The valley was completely open and swept by deadly fire from Hill 100 at its head, and the attempt failed; but we found the bodies of our men on the whole objective—one of them had been buried by the Turks under the fair-sized oak-tree that originally stood there. The day of the fight had been hot and dry, and the blackened stumps of the scrub set on fire by our shells still marked the slopes.[22] The oak-tree had been burnt in a later fire, but a smaller one stood near by.

We went around the foot of the hill to search for the traces of the 18th Battalion. The track from the Fishermen's Huts (at Anzac) to Anafarta edged the plain there, with a slight bank on its inland side, and a belt of scrub beside it had the appearance of a hedge. It was clearly through the gaps in this, in particular one gap with another "hedge" running at right angles from it towards the end of the hill, that this raw battalion had attacked in full daylight, and most of its men not knowing till that instant that they were to attack at all. Their remains lay there to witness it from the very start, fairly thick in the stubblefield which they had to cross, and in the

---

22 The straight valley and the site of the oak-tree are shown in *Vol. II, p. 734;* the smoke of the fires in *Vol. XII, plate 119.* It was after saving wounded men from these fires that Chaplain A. Gillison was killed. (*See Vol. II, p. 735.*)

scrub on the hillside below the first trench, which they seized,[23] and along which, knowing nothing of bombs but doing their best with some Turkish ones that had been left there, they were presently bombed back.

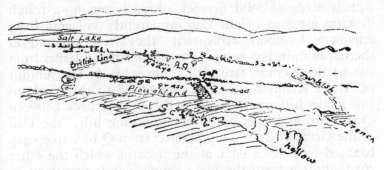

WHERE THE 18th BATTALION WAS CUT TO BITS

The view is north-westwards from the top of Hill 60 (from the crater of the later British mine), and looks along what eventually became No-man's-land on the extreme southern flank of the Suvla zone. In the middle distance are the Asmak Dere and the Chocolate, Green and "W" Hills, and in the distance Kiretch Tepe, beyond the Suvla flats. The 18th apparently attacked through the gap in the hedge, and through the hedge west of it. (The gap, seen from the road, is shown in the photo in Vol. II at p. 735.)

From our two expeditions to Hill 60 we returned by way of Abdel Rahman Bair, the steep spur which dominated the whole of that flank overlooking, southwards, all the ridges to Rhododendron and, northwards, the whole Suvla plain and amphitheatre. Up the side of it that was hidden from Anzac a well graded road[24] ran straight to Hill 971 in which the spur ended. Zeki Bey told us that all the Turkish observation posts on our

---

23 *See Vol. II, pp. 739-44.*
24 Shown in photograph in *Vol. II, at p. 654.*

northern flank were on that ridge; and several field-guns for direct sniping were also lodged up there.

On our first visit we passed on the plain the only Turkish civilians seen by us during the Mission's stay at Anzac, a procession of several bullock waggons with wheels made of solid wooden discs, driven by a rough looking gang in bright rags, apparently villagers from Anafarta. Lambert wrote that "they were engaged in the staple industry—salving the unconsidered trifles from the battle-grounds, tanks, tins, boxes".[25] At the summit of Abdel Rahman the road wound on to the southern side of the hill and then suddenly over the neck between Q (North) and Hill 971. This imposing hill, "the Hill of the Great Pasture", is separated from Q by a steep gap bridged by a razor edge at the back of which the other road—the track up the main range—winds precariously. Our road up Abdel Rahman here ran sharply into it; and at this point, to Lambert's delight, we caught sight of two eagles calmly perched on the big summit—from which the view must have been almost as commanding as any they enjoyed from the upper air. The chance for Lambert to use his revolver was irresistible; but though we halted while he stalked the pair to within pistol range a couple of feathers was his only bag.

On our second visit to the big hill—after Zeki Bey had returned to Constantinople—we were caught in a snowstorm, and raced for home around that narrow ledge at a pace that suited our light horsemen much better than a very amateur rider like myself. As we clattered down one of the long valleys on the Turkish side of Scrubby Knoll we galloped past the small village and minaret of Koja Dere ("Big Valley"—also called Kurija Dere, "Nearly Dry Valley"). There Hughes pulled us up and pointed to an object at the side of the road.

I knew it at once; I had photographed it about three days before the evacuation of Anzac—our old 4.7-inch

---

[25] *Thirty Years of an Artist's Life*, p. 106.

naval gun, actually one that had been used as a land gun in South Africa. At Anzac it had been mounted, as then, with a huge wooden trail, and dragged to a special position high on the right flank for firing at Kilid Bahr Plateau. Just before the Evacuation it was destroyed by bursting a charge in the muzzle.[26] Now it lay by the side of the Koja Dere road, the bare gun with torn muzzle and without the mounting. Apparently the Turks had intended to take it to Constantinople for their War Museum, but had abandoned the task for the present. Hughes and the Mission decided then and there that it should go to an Australian museum, if to any.

---

[26] *See plates 151 and 161 in Vol. XII.* The gun was made in 1896.

Chapter
• XVIII •

THE TURKS
AND THE EVACUATION

AFTER the attempts to seize Hill 60 had ended with the
capture of about half of it, the Anzac and other brigades
on the northern flank were relieved by the 54th British
(Territorial) Division, consisting of troops from the eastern counties—Essex, Norfolk, Suffolk, Bedford, London—
and a Hampshire battalion. The activity was now mostly
in bombing (which gave—or perhaps had already given—
the hill its Turkish name) and mining. On November
20th a big mine there, dug by the Welsh Horse, had
to be prematurely exploded; its crater was rushed and
seized by the Turks. But despite this activity, Zeki Bey
told us, "it was far quieter there—quite different from
the Australian front".

The blizzard which descended on Gallipoli on
November 27th was felt much more severely in the lower
parts of the line than on the Anzac heights. Trenches and
valley beds, previously dry, became flooded and turned
into channels for swirling streams. In Zeki Bey's sector,
"a number of the men of the battalion holding the line
were drowned," he told us. "My regiment was then out
at rest. It had to reoccupy the line there at once and dig
it out again." It so happened that the blizzard coincided
with the last phase of one of the strangest operations
undertaken by the First A.I.F., the so-called "Silent
Stunt" of November 24th-27th. This had been devised
by Brigadier-General Brudenell White, then chief of the
General Staff of the Anzac Corps. Word had just come
through, most secretly, that Lord Kitchener's conference

244

with the commanders at the Dardanelles had recommended that the Allies should abandon the Peninsula. The matter had been discussed in the House of Lords in London, and it was certain that the Turks would be on the alert. Accordingly, to foil their vigilance, General White proposed that there should be periods of complete silence at irregular intervals so that if, and when, the final silence came, it would appear to the Turks as nothing unusual. These silences began at once with a most thorough-going cessation of fire for more than three days. Our troops as far as possible remained hidden and there occurred many strange incidents, in which the Turks were not resisted until they were almost—or sometimes actually—in contact.[1] Zeki Bey told us that they were at first puzzled—as indeed was obvious to us at the time. In the end "we put it down," he said, "to your wanting a quiet period [after the blizzard] to dig out your front trenches also. We were, however, ordered to send out patrols and get into your trenches. Every unit had to send a patrol, but every patrol reported your line held."

Readers of the history of the campaign will remember that on December 6th, after a period of astonishing indecision, in which the fate of the Salonica campaign also was involved, the British and French Governments determined that Anzac and Suvla should be evacuated. Provisional preparations had already been begun. The final order reached the front, although the troops there did not know it, on December 8th. From that time onward those who could best be spared were continuously sent away by night, their transports vanishing before daylight, but some reinforcements and stores being landed by day and fresh tents being added to the hospitals as if in preparation for winter. By this means the force at Anzac had, by December 18th, been reduced from 41,000 to 20,000 and

---

1 See Vol. II, pp. 842-5.

the guns there from 105 to 19 of the older pieces.[2] The 50,000 troops and 91 guns at Suvla were reduced to almost the same extent. The final evacuation was carried out after dark on the two nights of December 18th/19th and 19th/20th. At Anzac the Turks by fighting their way forward for only 300 yards could have looked straight down on North Beach, where an extra pier was built leading to the steamer *Milo*, specially sunk to provide a breakwater. Such conditions made it necessary at Anzac to hide all signs of evacuation until the last moment. This was done—on General White's insistence—by holding the whole Anzac-Suvla front until late on the final night, even though with a skeleton screen of troops, who by various devices kept up the appearance of a normal night. *Normality* was the catchword of the whole operation—a policy for which Brudenell White was responsible, General Godley, then corps commander, backing him stoutly in his opposition to any exception to this rule. In the end a demonstration at Cape Helles on the last afternoon was the only deviation that army headquarters permitted.

Meanwhile during the first of the last two nights half the troops were withdrawn in batches before dawn. On the following night the remaining half were taken off by almost the same steps and in the same small craft. In the small hours of December 20th the whole line at Anzac was held by only 2000 troops. At 1.30 a.m. the line on Zeki Bey's front at Hill 60 was abandoned and the emptying extended progressively southward until at 3.14 the last of our front-line garrison, facing The Nek, withdrew. Sixteen minutes later three mines there including "Arnall's Tunnel" were exploded; though we had then about twenty mines under important parts of the Turkish front, none but these three were to be fired unless the Turks actually attacked. It was the explosion of these

---

[2] For details of the plan and how it was carried out, see *Vol. II, pp 853-906*. For the events that led up to the decision, see *pp. 763-97*.

that first announced to our side that the Evacuation was practically complete. At 4.10 the last man left the Beach.

There had been no interference whatever by the Turks, and it was obvious they had been completely deceived. At dawn, 6.45, they bombarded part of the Old Anzac front,[3] and I myself from the bridge of H.M.S. *Grafton* saw them rushing the trenches with fixed bayonets at 7.15. We had left at Anzac eleven demolished, valueless guns, our hospital tents, and stacks of stores which could not be removed without betraying our intention to evacuate. But at the cost of half a dozen casualties the force at Suvla and Anzac was clear after an operation which at one time had been expected to entail the killing, wounding or capturing of a third of the troops. The transports, trawlers, fleet sweepers, minelayers and other craft carrying them were safe either in Imbros Harbour on the horizon ten miles from Anzac, or on their way to Lemnos.

What had the Turks seen of all this? What had they anticipated? When had they discovered the Evacuation? And what happened when they discovered it? Zeki Bey gave us the answers. "In the summer," he said, "we had been told that sickness—we understood that malaria was meant—would drive your men off the Peninsula. We ourselves had some sickness, but not much. After the fighting at Bomba Tepe [Hill 60] the papers and news agencies began to talk about evacuation. There was a doubt in the air; some thought that you were going, some that you would attack, some that you would go on as we saw you doing, digging for the winter.

"The general view was that you would leave the Peninsula. Towards the end a lot of movement was noticed, but we couldn't make out if you were landing troops or taking them away. Orders had been given to observers to watch the ships and so forth. It was reported, first, that the number of tents was decreasing; second, that

---

3 This bombardment in the dark is shown in *Vol. XII, plate 159.*

the guns were firing less and that fire was being undertaken by the ships instead; third, that there were some days of silence. It was thought that you were abandoning some of the advanced trenches and orders were given to make strong reconnaissances. The report was that everywhere you were holding the front line.

"In spite of the rumours of an intention to leave the Peninsula we were ordered, first, to undertake all sorts of work for the winter, and, second, in consequence of a decision that came to us from Germany, to prepare a very strong attack. As to the winter preparations, the trenches were drained by a gutter inside or out.[4] Dugouts were made deeper and stronger. Fires were generally prohibited because the camouflage of our trenches and stores was of dry brushwood." Presumably the cooks were allowed to make fires in the places provided, for Zeki Bey told us that the food on that side consisted of meat and beans, mainly beans.

Concerning the great attack to be planned, Zeki Bey said that very strict secrecy was maintained. "Some preparations were made in the back area, and orders were given to study the best points of attack and to make plans. But the decision as to the place of attack was not made known; even the ammunition which arrived came labelled so that only those who had to deal with it could read the cypher. The attack would not have been made immediately—not before a month, anyway.[5] An Austrian battery had arrived and been emplaced in prepared positions. Observation posts were at Chunuk and Abdel Rahman Bair; it had four or five observation posts and its fire was well regulated. The first projectiles were fired after the snow, at targets west of Ismail Oglu Tepe ["Hill of Son of Ismail"—the W Hills], and by Lala Baba [at

---

4 Similar steps were being taken on the Anzac side, and the Mission found that the drains had been effective in preserving trenches, terraces, and paths.

5 I take my note of Zeki Bey's statement as meaning not before a month from the day on which we left Anzac, that is, not before January 20th.

Suvla Bay]; and one day either this or another battery fired on your position just west of Chunuk Bair [The Apex or Cheshire Ridge]."

But while these preparations were going on, the watch for signs of withdrawal was constantly keen. The Turkish forces opposite Suvla and Anzac at that time were, I gathered, as far as Zeki Bey could remember them (from north to south):—

12th Division
11th Division
9th Division
6th Division (16th, 17th and 18th Regts)
7th Division (20th Regt on Kaiajik Dere)
           (21st Regt on Asma Dere)
8th Division (23rd and 24th Regts)
19th Division (27th Regt at Nek)
           (57th Regt south of it)
16th Division (125th Regt at Johnston's Jolly)
           (15th Regt and surviving battalion of 47th)
           (48th Regt)
77th Regiment

The order to all local commanders, Zeki Bey said, was that any one of them, upon discovering a withdrawal, should order his troops to attack boldly. This order gave many headaches to the local commanders including Zeki Bey at Hill 60. "It would be impossible," he felt, "to precipitate yourself upon an unknown position, full of wire, unknown trenches and possibly mines." He therefore, after much anxious thought, had decided that his action in such case would be, "to make a demonstration with small arms fire and possibly thus pin down the last of the retiring troops and complicate their operation. I found out later," he said, "that wire *had* been put out by you, and it would have been most dangerous to throw ourselves on your rearguard, especially at night—Turkish troops might even have met and fought each other.

"What specially impressed me," he added, "was that your men were reported to be constructing wire entanglements. They did so nearly to the end. Some nights before the last they were out at midnight working. I had a machine-gun playing on those wiring parties; it was firing that night. I thought that your men were possibly putting out the entanglement by pushing it over the edge of their trench.

"It was reported that your tents were becoming less numerous. But some of us, even at the end, thought that you were preparing to attack. On the last night your troops at Cape Helles made a demonstration. This gave the idea that at Ari Burnu and Suvla something was happening—the idea was possibly awakened in that way.[6] At all events on that evening thirty-five vessels were seen to be gathered at Imbros, with smoke rising from them. The order was given to keep a very good watch. But the first real sign of the Evacuation was the blowing up of the mines at Jessaret Tepe. They killed about seventy men. Why did you blow them up?"

I fancied there was a hint of reproach in Zeki Bey's voice as he said this. I think he meant: "You had completely succeeded in your object—we had come to the end of a long and honourable campaign. Was it necessary to kill these?" I too had often wondered as to that; but the decision whether to fire the mines had been left in the discretion of an officer who, I suspected, must have felt like a child with a huge firework. It was almost inevitable that these mines should be fired; from the purely military point of view there was no reason to hesitate.

"Probably it was to force you to be cautious in following up," I said.

---

[6] The demonstration began at 2.30 p.m., but the firing, which as sometimes happened could be heard at Anzac, lasted till after dark. Zeki Bey's statement shows how wise was General White's resistance to all "abnormalities".

"Well, it was this explosion that really told us of the Evacuation," he said. "I asked my friends on the staff, 'What gave you the first notion?' 'It was the mine that first made us certain,' they said.

"Immediately, a regiment from reserve was pushed up there to occupy the crater," he said, "and these troops got lost and wandered on into your trenches and found them empty. This was reported. Then the fires occurred at Suvla" (two British engineer officers at 4 a.m. set light to the huge stacks of stores on Suvla Beach) "and this gave the show away really.

"At first it was thought that the mine might have been a signal for some action on your part; and even when your trenches were entered it was not yet certain that all the trenches had been left. I had an officer in your trenches by 4 o'clock, and myself went later. The order was given at once to look after the sick, for we saw that you had left a hospital; but we soon found that there were no sick. At first only the [front] companies were ordered to advance; later the troops, some of them, went in without orders. On the first day they were everywhere. Stores abandoned by you were ordered to be collected—sandbags and other material for the trenches were sent to our troops at Helles, but the soldiers at Anzac helped themselves to these very largely. Your booby-traps caught very few men. Some on the right of my regiment were caught by a mine, but none of my regiment. The ships' fire next day did little damage."

Zeki Bey repeated that the limitation of the effect of naval fire on the land was part of the experience of the campaign. "We found that the ships' fire was not so terrible as at first we had thought that it would be. At first we thought that all towns like Maidos would have to be evacuated;[7] but we found that Kurija Dere was

---

[7] Conceivably Zeki Bey meant "as Maidos was"; but I think he meant that even Maidos proved habitable.

quite habitable.[8] The howitzers which you afterwards obtained were very much worse.

"A German cinematographer had just come out to take some pictures" (the Turks themselves, Zeki Bey told us, had no provision for amenities for their troops), "but you had gone and he lost his chance. The authorities wanted exact reports of whatever material was left by you, so as to be able to judge whether you were hurried in your withdrawal or had carried it out easily. The quantity of food abandoned was taken as evidence that you had not got away easily. South of Bomba Tepe [Hill 60] there were 10,000 boxes of biscuits, jam, meat, tea, sugar. Besides these there were some mules which had been left by a doctor with his baggage—this gave the impression that you had withdrawn hurriedly. An order for the Evacuation was found—it allowed for food etc. being left behind."

Zeki Bey found in the Aghyl Dere, quite close in front of his own sector, a considerable dump—evidently the stores which had been left in Australia Valley in a "keep" established there against emergency. He also saw, later, at Suvla "the remains of a great fire"; possibly other stores had been removed from there by the Turks. "Boxes of rubber, all sorts of stores," he said, "were found." Actually the policy of our command had been to avoid imperilling the operation by any attempt to withdraw those stores or guns whose removal might betray the secret; the few guns left were destroyed and at Anzac the stacks were to be set on fire by shelling, after the withdrawal of the troops. The Navy fired at them, but not much seems to have been burnt.[9]

"No one regretted," Zeki Bey told me, "that we hadn't known of your intention to withdraw." Ignorance relieved the local commanders of a very troublesome

---

[8] The Mission, however, found this village largely destroyed.

[9] A photograph of Turks on the abandoned Anzac Beach is given in *Vol. XII. plate 160.*

problem. The Turks at Helles, of course, asked them constantly how it was they had failed to turn the Evacuation into disaster for the Allies. The Turks at Anzac retorted: "Well, you know now that there will be a withdrawal from Helles. So—do what you want to do there." Later everyone knew that we would leave Helles, and the Turks there tried to stop it but failed.[10] The British vanished in one night, that of 8th January 1916.

After the evacuation of Anzac "troops were ordered at once to fortify the places you had left. Possibly this was done in order to occupy the soldiers and not allow them to walk all over the abandoned area." The work then done at Anzac included the construction of the wire entanglement which the Mission had noted on its first day, just above the Beach. But though the Turks apparently at one time feared, or at least considered, the possibility of the Allies' attempting to land again in the same region, the Anzac battlefield had been practically unchanged since we left it in 1915; new trenches were hardly noticeable, and the old ones, wandering everywhere still deep, with their white parapets not yet overgrown, provided us with the constant necessity of jumping them on horseback, a game at which, Lambert wrote, "I am pleased to boast that I more than hold my own, though my gee-gee don't like it." Happily the jumps were narrow and no horse was hurt; I dreaded the thought of an explanation to our good friends of the 28th Division, but, in fact, there was no alternative to jumping; the risk to the horses would have been greater if we had tried to lead them.

---

10 See Vol. II, p. 905; and British Official History, Gallipoli, Vol. II, pp. 472-3.

Chapter
· XIX ·

WHAT THE TURKS COULD SEE

ONE of the questions that we had come to Gallipoli to determine was, "What were the Turks able to see of our men and movements in the Anzac lines?"

What could the Olive Grove batteries, "Beachy Bill", see? Or the lonely spy-post perched on Snipers' Nest? And now that Zeki Bey had told us that his corps commander had a dress-circle view from corps headquarters on Scrubby Knoll, we were particularly eager to find that observation post also. We had not time to do so during Zeki Bey's visit, but on the day that he left Balfour and I walked up the ridges behind our camp to discover the site of that headquarters and sample its outlook.[1]

Just before reaching Scrubby Knoll we crossed a very deep communication trench—really a road, paved with stone. Farther on, the crown of the Knoll was well entrenched; and immediately behind its northern shoulder we found what had obviously been the site of the Turkish zone headquarters, shelf upon shelf dug into the top of a knot of folded gullies, with a well graded road from the Narrows winding up to and round the higher contours. On the shelves were the remains of old and (as my diary says) "very roomy" shelters, the inside littered in some cases with the plaster and cement that had once lined them. One or two of these structures were stone huts. The road ended there at the head of the valleys, but a trench led from that point onwards to the north.

---

[1] We took with us half a dozen men as we were also searching for traces of the advance thither of April 25th.

A few yards up it, in its western side, we found a semi-circular recess with neatly cemented sides—obviously the zone commander's observation post. It gave a perfect pano-rama of our line from about Quinn's to Lone Pine, as well as the chain of crests northwards to Hill 971—except Q, which was obscured by Chunuk. Mustafa Kemal, who originally had placed his headquarters here on the day of the Landing, could possibly have just seen Tulloch's men from there, exactly half a mile to the north-west; certainly he could have seen the Turks firing at them and the fight on Baby 700 and Mortar Ridge. The line on which the Anzacs eventually dug in was farther back, but at three-quarters of a mile Essad Pasha and his observers could see everything that happened above ground on all the vital section of the Old Anzac front.

As Zeki Bey had told us, it was the staff at Scrubby Knoll who first informed him that Greig's men were rushing his front line.

Behind Essad's headquarters, at the bottom of the nearest valley, were what looked to me like carrots and other vegetables, growing wild—possibly provision for headquarters and other messes; and near the crest of the ridge just south of Scrubby Knoll were some old gun-pits. Australian reports suggested to me that this might have been the original position of the mountain battery which accompanied Kemal on the morning of the Landing, but Zeki Bey had told me that Kemal kept that battery by his side near the road north of Scrubby Knoll (that is, about where the observation post had since been built) and that it fired from there on the first day.

Ahead of us, beyond some intervening folds, lay Mortar Ridge with the Second Ridge, from Quinn's to Lone Pine, beyond it. It was from the headquarters of his regiment on Mortar Ridge that Zeki Bey and the regimental commander watched the bombardment of Lone Pine; and the observer beside them had said that he could see through the dust our men crossing No-man's-land. Zeki Bey told me that in Mortar Ridge the Turks had two tunnels in which they emplaced two guns which were to fire through secret openings in the front slope of the ridge; but he added that the moment their first gun fired it was put out of action by a direct hit from a gun of ours. Several years after our visit, on searching the records in Australia, I found that the Turkish observers had evidently detected a similar scheme of our artillery, which had prepared a secret opening in a tunnel at Courtney's Post, directly facing Mortar Ridge at 400 yards distance, and had emplaced there a mountain gun with the object of destroying the Turkish tunnels. Before our gun, which was manned by Indians under Lieutenant J. H. Thom, could open fire the Turkish gunners from their opposing tunnels put several shots straight into his porthole. Thom and his men then managed to place seventeen shots direct into the Turkish tunnels, battering their embrasures and silencing both the opposing guns. Zeki Bey spoke with great admiration of this feat of our Indian friends; but the success was only temporary. We found it difficult to strike at the two Turkish guns in any other way, and this way was too dangerous for repetition. The Turks repaired the emplacements, and Zeki Bey often saw those guns tearing into the sandbags of our parapets and damaging our trench improvements. Eventually one of the guns was hit or damaged and was withdrawn, and the battery was retained for use only in great emergency.

Zeki Bey told me that while commanding at German Officers' he had noticed a patch of freshly excavated earth near the top of Wire Gully, high on its southern side. The work, whatever it was, had been concealed by placing sandbags over it. I told him that it was almost certainly a tunnel, probably associated with the work we called the Tambour, with an opening for a sniper or observer, or for a gun emplaced like those at Mortar Ridge.[2]

Searching Mortar Ridge after Zeki Bey had gone I found the two tunnelled openings near its southern end, with a smaller opening just north of them, almost certainly for a machine-gun. On the rear slope of the ridge were two larger, open emplacements into which the guns were probably run back between their "stunts". Zeki Bey told me what our staff, I believe, also knew, that early in the campaign the Turks had a gun dug in behind Lone Pine—later it fired from behind the Jolly—to shoot at our trenches at the head of Monash Valley, almost from the rear. He also told us that at the head of Monash Valley, in the Bloody Angle, they had a tunnelled opening for a machine-gun, and that it had done much sniping down the valley until we turned a gun upon it. The Mission, searching on February 24th with Zeki Bey, found this opening, four or five yards below the crest-line. The embrasure and parapet were cemented, and showed a startling white against the dark side of the valley; probably during the campaign they had been camouflaged with brushwood.

These works, and possibly one other on Abdel Rahman Bair, were the only tunnelled gun or machine-gun positions that we found in the Turkish defences at Anzac. It is true that some of our artillery commanders thought that the troublesome Olive Grove batteries—that is, "Beachy Bill"—on the southern flank were in tunnels; they inferred this from the way in which these guns used to reopen fire immediately after even the heaviest shoots by our batteries, or the naval ones. One commander told me that he thought the Turkish guns must be run back on rails into tunnels with steel doors, which closed behind them and let them out again as soon as the storm was over.

[2] A photograph of this porthole or one near it, taken in June 1915, is in *Vol. XII, plate 89.* It shows the outlook on Mortar Ridge and Scrubby Knoll.

OLIVE GROVE

I heard the same supposition expressed about batteries on other fronts, and I fancy that the notion occurred to minds on both sides of No-man's-land when the difficulty of hitting the opposing guns, and the bravery of the opposing gunners, made the other side's artillery impossible to suppress.

To look for the Olive Grove guns we rode out on February 27th with Zeki Bey to the southern flank, over the gentle, open undulations in which the Third Ridge ran out on to the plain south-east of Gaba Tepe. We found no signs of tunnels, steel doors and such contraptions but merely what others of our gunners had told me we would find—normal, well sited gun positions. What was unexpected was the number of them. The ground here was covered with something like desert scrub, with shingly patches in between the low shrubs, not unlike saltbush country in the west of New South Wales. The Asmak stream[3] running through this low land into the sea half a mile south of Gaba Tepe had a surprisingly deep bed. South of this again a gentle slope led up to a low crestline from which we found ourselves looking south-westward across a mile and a half of gently hollowed plain to the steep side of the Kilid Bahr Plateau.

The top of this low slope was entrenched, and a few hundred yards down the southern side of it were eight emplacements for heavy guns, with trenches connecting them, and sunken shelters for the crews. Close behind them stood a small house, still partly tiled, and near by, under a tree by a road that ran southwards along the flat, was a grave which, Zeki Bey told us, was that of a corporal of a 15-centimetre (5.9 inch) howitzer battery. He said the Turks called the area Palamut Luk ("The Oak Grove"). Four of the gun emplacements were older than the

---

[3] Asmak appears to be a man's name. There is another Asmak Dere beyond the northern end of the Anzac position, just north of Abdel Rahman Bair, and still another farther north on the Suvla plain. The northern ones are not to be confused with the Asma Dere ("Vine Valley") which lies next to Hill 60.

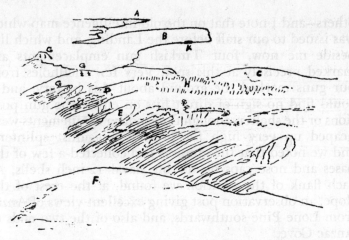

THE SOUTHERN FLANK AT ANZAC, LOOKING SOUTHWARDS FROM SILT SPUR (WHICH PROJECTED FROM THE SOUTH-WESTERN END OF THE LONE PINE PLATEAU)

A. The toe of the Peninsula, Tekke Burnu, 14 miles away.

B. Gaba Tepe, 1½ miles away.

C. Bolton's Hill, the original right flank position. Chatham's Post, to which the flank was extended, lay between this and the Turkish positions which are marked G.

H. The Wheatfield across which the Turks at first tried to rush upon Bolton's Hill.

E. The gully which we found white with the bones of their dead.

D. Leane's Trench, to which the Australians eventually pushed forward.

G-G-G. Turkish positions closing in the southern flank.

F. Silt Spur, showing part of the Australian underground line.

K. Stranded British barge at Gaba Tepe.

others—and I note that on the old intelligence map which was issued to our staff before the Landing, and which lies beside me now, four Turkish gun emplacements are marked precisely at this spot. Very few shellholes from our guns marked the ground about this battery, and I could find no sign of direct hits on either the gun positions or the shelters though the sandbag epaulements were heaped up very high for protection against splinters; and we noted that the gunners had collected a few of the bases and nose caps of our big naval 12-inch shells. At each flank of the position we found, at the crest of the slope, an observation post giving excellent views of Anzac from Lone Pine southwards, and also of the two ends of Anzac Cove.

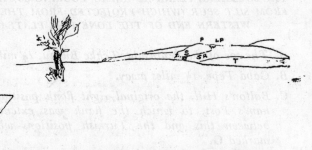

THE VIEW FROM THE OBSERVATION POST AT THE TURKISH 5.9 INCH HOWITZER BATTERY AT THE OLIVE GROVE

P. The Pimple. *SR. Snipers' Ridge (Turkish).*
LP. Lone Pine. *T. Part of Third (Gun)*
S. Silt Spur (Australian). *Ridge.*

A few hundred yards west of this battery position I found, on the same slope, a collection of some twenty-five emplacements for field-guns, or perhaps more, some of them apparently alternative or dummy positions.[4] About

---

[4] At the time I estimated them at about sixteen in number, but later examination of an air photo and of maps makes it appear certain that the number was much greater; for a map of them see *Vol. II, p. 82.*

half were for shooting against Anzac and half against ships. Between these and the heavy battery positions I rode into a gully cratered with our shellholes almost like a battlefield in France, sufficiently to make cantering dangerous; it was the only such area I saw in Gallipoli. I also rode across to the foot of the north-west bastion of the Kilid Bahr Plateau in search of any trace of the position of two old 6-inch pieces which used to fire on Anzac from that direction. I crossed the sunken waggon-road that ran round that foot of the plateau and led towards Maidos, but found no sign of those guns. On one ride across country north of the batteries, however, we ran into a scene that I have never forgotten, a patch of anemones in full spring flower—white, purple, red and, if I remember rightly, yellow. The blooms approached the size of tulips; one could hardly believe that they were wild.

Next to those at the Olive Grove the Turkish battery which most deeply puzzled the Anzac artillery had been the one at Gaba Tepe itself. Gaba Tepe ("Rough Hill") was a grassy, cliff-nosed promontory jutting into the sea at a point just over a mile from our southern flank. On the day of the Landing, incoming boatloads, as well as men on the Beach and in the gullies, were at intervals fired at with shrapnel believed to come from a battery on the saddle leading to the promontory. The big British cruiser *Bacchante* stood in until she must almost have run aground north of the cape, and sent salvo after salvo of 6-inch shell at the flashes of the Turkish guns. The neck of the promontory was covered with shell smoke and the Turkish guns stopped firing for a while, but always opened again when fresh boatloads approached the shore. However, from that day onwards guns rarely, if ever, fired from that position; but a Turkish field-gun was occasionally run out from some fold in the ground on the northern slope of the cape itself and proved most troublesome to our 7th Battery, whose rear, high on Bolton's Hill,

was exposed to it. Eventually one of the Indian mountain
guns was always kept trained on that fold, and the appearance of the arm and shoulder of a Turk around the edge
of it was the signal for the Indian gun to fire. The fire
from Gaba Tepe itself then almost ceased, but the promontory was most useful to the Turks because they could
obtain from it, at two miles' distance, a partial view into
Anzac Cove, including the extremities, but only the extremities, of Anzac Beach. On Gaba Tepe were the observation posts for the Olive Grove field batteries and the
simplest way of stopping these batteries from firing was,
at ordinary times, to shell the Turkish trenches on Gaba
Tepe where the observers were.

Early in the campaign one attempt was made to raid
Gaba Tepe, with a view, if the conditions proved suitable, of possibly attempting its capture at some later
date. The promontory had in peacetime been the site
of a police post, whose white building originally stood
out near the end of it. Below this there had been made,
either in 1914-15 or in the Balkan Wars just previously,
a trench which by the time of the Landing ran along the
whole top of the northern slope and was protected by a
belt of very strong wire of which the inland end ran
down to the beach and actually to the sea. The attempt
to raid the place was made at dawn on May 4th by about
100 of the 11th Battalion and some engineers, under one
of the most famous fighters of the A.I.F., Major Ray
Leane. Destroyers succeeded in shepherding four troop-
filled boats to the shore;[5] but the fire that met the boats
increased so quickly that, though most of the party managed to cross the beach to the shelter of a high bank, they
were pinned down there, both the grassy slope above the
bank and the beach behind being swept by bullets. After
testing the chance of retiring along the beach Leane signalled to the destroyers which, under cover of fierce fire

[5] A photograph of the destroyers bombarding is in *Vol. I, p. 570*.
Photographs of Gaba Tepe are also at *pp. 560-1*.

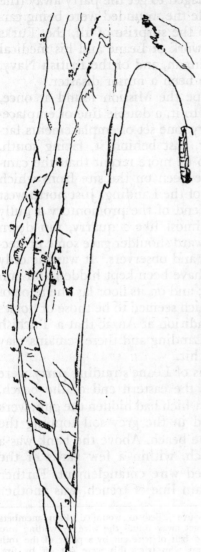

ANZAC AS SEEN BY THE TURKISH OBSERVERS AT GABA TEPE

1. Ari Burnu where the first landing occurred (it was meant to have centred near the point marked 21).
2. Hell Spit (southern arm of Anzac Cove).
3. Shrapnel Valley.
4. Plugge's Plateau.
5. Russell's Top.
6. The Nek.
7. M'Cay's Hill.
8. Shell Green.
9. Bolton's Hill.
10. Baby 700.
11. Battleship Hill.
12. Chunuk Bair.
13. Hill 971.
14-14. Lone Pine.
15. Chatham's Post.
16. Holly Spur.
17. Silt Spur.
18. Snipers' Ridge-Knife Edge.
19. Weir Ridge.
20. Pine Ridge.
21. Southernmost post of Anzac.
22. Scrubby Knoll.
23. Legge Valley.
24. Southernmost communication trench at Anzac.

2-4-1, First Ridge; 9-10, Second Ridge; 22-12, Third Ridge.
Anzac artillery (including Indian mountain guns) had eventually been emplaced at or near 4, 5, 7, 8, 9 and elsewhere.

from their own guns, managed to get the party away (the destroyers ceased fire while the wounded were being carried to the boats—and, to the surprise of all, the Turks did also). The very cool work of Leane and his medical officer, Captain E. T. Brennan, and of the British Navy, avoided what might have been a minor disaster.[6]

On visiting Gaba Tepe the Mission found at once, on the open neck leading to it, a double line of emplacements for a six-gun battery, one set of emplacements facing Anzac and the other, just behind it, facing south. These diggings seemed to be more recent than the campaign, but they may have been on the site from which the guns fired on the day of the Landing. Just north-west of them at the landward end of the promontory a gully with a deep washaway, almost like a quarry, ran down towards the beach. Its seaward shoulder gave some protection from the Anzac guns and observers.[7] It was the only place where a gun could have been kept hidden and run out to fire in emergencies; and on its floor lay the feloe of a wheel and two skulls which seemed to be those of horses or mules. There was a tradition at Anzac that a Turkish gun was hit there at the Landing and these remains may have been results of the hit.

On the beach the signs of Leane's raiding party were still clearly traceable. At the eastern end of the beach, not far below the knuckle which had hidden the gun, were a series of niches scooped in the grey soil topping the high bank that fringed the beach. Above the bank was a grassy stretch across which, within a few yards of the bank, ran a belt of barbed wire entanglement. Farther up the hill, below the main line of trench, was another

---

[6] The party had about twenty-five killed or wounded. Four members sent along the beach managed to get away round the wire by wading into the sea, and then through a second belt of wire cut by a party of the 10th previously sent thither. Two others who tried this were cut off by fire. But the Navy, seeing them, sent in another boat and they succeeded in dashing to it. See *Vol. I, pp. 556-62.*

[7] A photograph of it is in *Vol. I. p. 545.*

belt. The trench behind it ran along most of the hillside, and appeared to have been dug since the campaign, but evidently on the site of the old trench. Above it at one part were the traces of the old police-post building. Close above the beach, but west of our landing place, were two small trenches—probably for Turkish sentry groups, and on the beach near them lay an old barge, washed

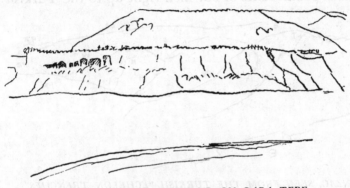

EVIDENCES OF THE RAID ON GABA TEPE

The north-west end of the beach of Gaba Tepe promontory, showing some of the shelters cut by the raiding party under Captain Leane.

thither from Anzac by some storm. Almost at the point where the raiders landed lay one of our mess-tins, and another with some shreds of Australian web equipment lay a little farther west, about ten yards up the hill. The famous bastion of wire that used to run into the sea at the eastern end of the beach had disappeared, but Rogers, examining the place, found the wire still there beneath the sand.

The Turkish observers at Gaba Tepe and the Olive Grove of course looked straight up the valleys and ridges which ran southwards from the southern end of the Anzac position. This flank, like the northern one before the

August offensive, was much less closely shut in by the
Turks than was the centre of the Old Anzac position. For
this reason the valleys and ridges there, into which our
troops could move out with less danger of annihilation,
were chosen for feints to help the operations at Helles—
in particular for the sortie of June 28th by the infantry
to the Valley of Despair and the Knife Edge (where our
Mission found relics of our men right up to the Turkish

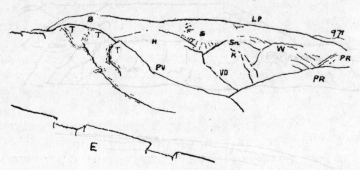

*ANZAC, SEEN FROM THE TURKISH "ECHELON TRENCHES",
WHICH CLOSED IN THE SOUTHERN FLANK*

B. Bolton's Hill.
T, T, T. Turkish trenches.
H. Holly Spur.
S. Silt Spur.
Sn. Snipers' Ridge.
K. Knife Edge.
LP. Lone Pine, showing silt dump from our mines there.
W. Weir Ridge.
PR, PR. Parts of Pine Ridge.
PV. Poppy Valley.
VD. Valley of Despair.

trenches) and by light horsemen to the Balkan gun-pits
down towards Gaba Tepe. Both these feints were costly
expeditions,[8] yet those parts had generally seemed
strangely peaceful. On the sides of the Valley of Despair

[8] *See Vol. II, pp. 292-306.*

the Mission found patches of stunted pine scrub such as had once clothed Pine Ridge.[9] The valley most accessible to the Australians on the right had been the one west of this, Poppy Valley, between the southern end of Bolton's Ridge and Holly Spur (an offshoot of Bolton's) most of which our men seized by ceaseless sapping and mining. Here, according to my diary of the campaign, Major T. A. Blamey, then in charge of the intelligence staff of the 1st Australian Division, "sent out a policeman with two prisoners, who were ordered to gather firewood. He sent them to Holly Spur, and ordered them to get big bundles, hoping they would run away and tell the Turks what a good time they had" and so induce other Turks to give themselves up. "He told the policeman to go to sleep and not watch them too closely.

"The policeman took them to Holly Spur, and let them stroll out, lost to sight. About an hour later they came back carrying the two biggest bundles of firewood ever yet seen at Anzac."

During our stay I made several drawings of this flank showing how it had been extended by tunnelling, and also what the Turks could see of our positions. As far as I could judge, the Turkish observers on Gaba Tepe could not have seen any of the several piers on Anzac Beach, much less the stacks of stores that crowded it. But these could all be seen by observers on the far northern flank at Suvla Bay; and the perfect range which the Turks eventually obtained of the main pier at Anzac, Watson's Pier, which they seemed able to spray with shrapnel whenever men were seen working there, may possibly have been given them by observers four miles to the north. Eventually boxes were stacked along that pier to give shelter from sight and from shrapnel pellets. More probably the Turks guessed both the range and the

---

[9] The Turks had stripped Pine Ridge, possibly after the Evacuation, for its timber.

activity by noting the small steamboats that constantly went from the ships towards the piers and back.

In any case they lost the Suvla observation post when

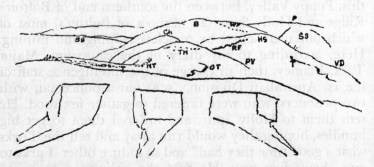

THE SOUTH FLANK AT ANZAC, AS SEEN BY THE TURKS

In the foreground are the "Balkan gun-pits", old earth-
works, probably of the Balkan Wars.

SB. *Suvla Bay.*
B. *Bolton's Hill (our original right flank).*
Ch. *Chatham's Post (our later right flank).*
TH. *Tunnelled Holes (apparently our extreme southern*
works).
OT. *Old Turkish trench, abandoned and filled with barbed*
wire.
NT. *New Turkish trench, made since Evacuation.*
T, T. *Other Turkish trenches.*
WF. *Wheatfield.*
HS. *Holly Spur (occupied from Bolton's by digging,*
sapping and mining).
SS. *Silt Spur (similarly occupied).*
RF. *Right flank of Light Horse on Holly Spur.*
P. *The Pimple (on our side of Lone Pine plateau).*
PV. *Poppy Valley.*
VD. *Valley of Despair.*

the British landed there in August. But they had another and much nearer observing station on the north flank, where they held a prominent knoll close to our lines, looking (at 1500 yards range) at Ari Burnu. This knoll, known to us as "Snipers' Nest", was on the farthest of the four rugged fingers in which the seaward slope of Baby 700 ended. When in August we made our second big effort of the campaign, our columns went out along the beach from our two northern outposts, which were on high knolls just above the strand. The columns then turned inland and seized the spurs of the main range from Chunuk Bair northwards; but the spurs between Chunúk and the Old Anzac position near The Nek were left to be seized a few hours later by the intended pincer movement along the crest, the New Zealanders striking from Chunuk southwards and the 3rd Light Horse Brigade from Russell's Top northwards. When that effort failed, Baby 700 and its fingers (except the extreme end of one at our No. 1 Outpost) remained in the hands of the Turks. And these positions looked down, at anything from a quarter to a half mile, on the beach north of Walker's Ridge.[10]

The result was that we could never safely use that part of the foreshore except the two small areas of it sheltered by the knolls topped by our two posts.[11] Fortunately the Turks had very few men on the seaward slope of Baby 700—in about 300 yards square of thick scrub barely one line of trench was visible to the Anzac observers; and, both in case we might someday have to attack it, and to avoid the increased harassing fire which its full occupation by the Turks would bring about, General White insisted on a policy of leaving that area as far as possible undisturbed. Consequently the Turks held it with the barest force. By day, of course, everyone going from Old Anzac to No. 1 Post had to use the long communication trench except at great risk. But every night our Indian mule train, pack mules and carts, were able to go out

---

10 A photograph of three spurs of Baby 700 is in *Vol. XII, plates 112 A and B.*

11 Nos 2 and 3 Posts were both on the northern knoll, a foothill of Rhododendron and Chunuk Bair, and were practically a single post.

and back across the open flat under the muzzles of these Turks with hardly ever a casualty.

From the scrubby upper part of this seaward slope of Baby 700 the Turks could not see beyond Walker's Ridge, which, leading from North Beach to Russell's Top, most fortunately for us shut off from them all view of Ari Burnu and half a mile of beach north of it. The hidden parts (North Beach) consequently became, after August, a more important landing place and supply centre than even Anzac Cove itself. That it was hidden from observers on the seaward slope of Baby 700 I assured myself by visiting that slope (the Turks called it Kabak Sirta—"Cabbage Slope")[12] on March 2nd. A trench ran part-way down the southern side of the slope, and was continued by a track through the scrub to a short T-head sap just above the precipice overlooking the foreshore far below. There was no trace of snipers in this trench—probably it was used only for observation. Farther north in the scrub along the edge of the precipice were empty cartridge shells where Turks had lain sniping at the beach.

But it was the northernmost of the four jagged prongs projecting steeply from that edge down to the beach that chiefly interested me; for we knew that the Turks had a trench along the top of this razor edge to a knoll 200 yards down it on which they had established an observation post. This was the one we called Snipers' Nest, and it was one from which, some of us had feared, the Turks might hear or see movements that could warn them of our intended evacuation. We knew that the Turks could see from there the northern side of Ari Burnu, and had a machine-gun laid on it for firing at night at extreme range. The path leading from Anzac to North Beach and the outposts crossed Ari Burnu at the point on which this gun was laid, and many times I had passed there with the bullets swishing into the scrub and

---

12 Conceivably because of its shape on a contoured map.

banks around; they hit surprisingly few people but, by an oversight which it is hard to forgive, the white tents of the elderly British labour battalion were pitched within that area, and at least one of those fine "old daddies" was killed. Curiously enough we ourselves had a machine-gun much farther north, high up on Table Top (a lofty offshoot of Rhododendron), which could see into the back of the ridge leading to Snipers' Nest; our Light Horse could often see Turks passing a distant dip in the trench leading to the Nest, and continually sprayed them with bullets.

Now, approaching the Nest for the first time, perhaps, that any one of our side had been there, I quickly found this solitary trench along the razor edge amid a billowing sea of wild, steep spurs. It was revetted with basketwork, the circular tops of the baskets holding up the parapet, and the space between each basket and the next serving as a loophole. I presently came to the dip where the trench lay open to Table Top, whose crest was just visible above Rhododendron, 600 yards to the north. The yellow parapet of the trench was at this point as thick with our bullets as a fruit-cake with raisins; within a minute or two and in the space of a few yards I had picked up at least a hundred for our War Memorial Museum, and they were kept as one exhibit to illustrate their density.[13] Some distance farther on, the trench ended at the observation post, a small excavation about ten feet long, but only three feet deep and three wide. From there another razor edge of gravel, untrenched and along which I could hardly walk, led to a somewhat similar but lower knoll which, lying almost between our Nos. 1 and 2 Posts, had been unoccupied.

Except for Gaba Tepe, it was probably from Snipers' Nest and the slope above it that the Turks kept their closest watch for preparations for evacuating Anzac. The

---

13 The collection of them, perhaps diminished in transit, is in the memorial today.

Nest showed little sign of damage by shell-fire though it
had twice received a merciless basting from the Navy;
White had prevented its being regularly shelled, for the
same reason that prevented the shelling of all this slope.
When the Navy twice attempted to destroy it the guns

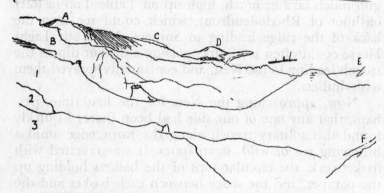

WHAT THE TURKS COULD SEE FROM SNIPERS' NEST

A. *Walker's Ridge.*
B. *Malone's Gully.*
C. *Plugge's or MacLagan's Ridge (First Ridge).*
D. *Ari Burnu.*
E. *No. 1 Post.*
*1, 2, 3. Spurs of Baby 700 (Snipers' Nest was on a fourth spur
of it).*
F. *Part of Camel's Hump (continuation of the fourth spur).*
*The steamer is the "Milo", sunk in the autumn of 1915 as a
breakwater to protect piers at North Beach. A slender pier built
out to the "Milo" just before the Evacuation must have been
visible from Snipers' Nest. It was finished by the 2nd Field
Company A.E. on December 15th. (This pier is shown in
Vol. XII, plate 149.)*

seemed to tear the hill to bits; but apparently, as White
expected, the damage was easily repaired.

Even from Snipers' Nest most of North Beach was
hidden by Walker's Ridge. But you could see the whole
of the steamer *Milo* which was sunk off that beach to

shelter an extra pier for the Evacuation, and which was still there at the time of our visit, as were the old tug *Marsden* opposite No. 3 Post, and several stranded barges. In December 1915 a slender pier had been hurriedly built right out to the *Milo,* and therefore this part of the process of evacuation was carried out under the eyes of the Turks at the Nest—but at night. From the slope of Baby 700 itself one could see only the stern half of the *Milo.*

One other question concerning the Old Anzac position we also settled, the width of No-man's-land and of the opposing footholds on the narrow crest at Quinn's Post. This post was as famous on the Turkish side as on the British. Whereas we took prominent visitors such as H. W. Nevinson up the steep path on our side to Colonel Malone's neat terraces near the top, and into the front line (with a necessary caution not even to speak above a whisper),[14] an American attaché at Constantinople told me that he had been taken with distinguished visitors of the Turks to view Quinn's from the other side—they were generally shown it from Mortar Ridge. They could see the constant bomb-explosions, and were told that bombing never really ceased there. One trench on our side was known as "The Racecourse" because, being within bomb-throw, it used to attract these missiles when anyone made a noise in passing along it. The danger was afterwards met by putting out screens of wire netting. Of course neither these screens nor wire entanglement could be fixed in position by parties working on the surface; they had to be

14 Nevinson deserves rather to be called an habitué. I was with him at the famous interview when Malone, over a pannikin of "morning tea" on his terrace, told him that "the art of warfare was the cultivation of the domestic virtues", and that he would have grown roses there if he had had them. Malone's meaning was clear to anyone who remembered the early days when this post, dominated by Turkish fire and bombs, but still invincibly held, inevitably resembled a stinking rat-run. The improvement became possible when our snipers, from farther down Monash Valley, beat down the Turkish snipers. In Malone's time, as Birdwood often said, "You could eat your dinner off the floor of the trenches."

pushed over the parapet. More certainly than even at other Anzac posts, to show a head at Quinn's was asking for death.

The Mission found that—so far as could be decided by the trenches existing at the end of the campaign— the two front lines were closest to each other at the northern end of the post, where an old Turkish trench, revetted but filled in (probably at the armistice in May), curved within twenty yards of our left trench. It was not easy here, however, to tell which was Anzac trench and which Turkish, for in our attack towards Baby 700 on May 2nd, a week after the Landing, part of the 16th Battalion had dug in along the edge of the Bloody Angle, north of Quinn's, continuing the Quinn's trench intermittently towards the left,[15] and this extension of the trench had afterwards been occupied by Turkish snipers. The actual end of our post seemed to be at a slight break in the trench, just behind a group of four mine craters, apparently blown by us to destroy Turkish tunnels; our trench there was shallow, with one old bomb screen still covering the flank. There were five other discernible mine craters—ours or Turkish—close in front of the rest of our front at Quinn's; a tunnel from our line led to the central crater, and there was a sap leading to another timbered advance post. But No-man's-land was so crossed by sections of old trenches afterwards filled in that it was difficult to decide which ground had been trench and which not. Bits of our kit were everywhere in No-man's-land, torn to shreds probably by the bullets that early in the campaign had shot away even the shrubs. In some places our bullets were thicker than at Snipers' Nest; I picked up for the War Memorial collection those found in one square yard of Turkish parapet near the head of the Bloody Angle.

The Turks along their side of that narrow crest held a foothold about thirty yards deep; ours, I noted, was

---

[15] The new trench was held for a night but abandoned next day.

about eight yards (these figures were noted down a few days later, and were the result of estimate only). The main Turkish communication trench ran up the Quinn's ridge from its southern end in Mule Valley, but there were also approaches from the valley behind the ridge, up which the main trench or track had been metalled. The Turks had been to great trouble to keep their mule train out of sight of our snipers; through the rear end of Johnston's Jolly they had made a trench or sunken road twelve feet deep.

Not the least interesting of our finds at Anzac was made as I was returning to camp along the old curved path from The Nek down Russell's Top. On the gravel I saw a small circular object, and picked up an ancient Greek silver coin. It is conceivable that some villager, or even one of our mounted troops lately in Gallipoli, may have found it in the trench excavations and dropped it on the path; or the last rains or the last boot of some wayfarer may have uncovered it. Ever since the year 550 B.C.—for some 2470 years—the Peninsula had been colonised by Greeks. Their town of Kelia—now Kilia— had been at the nearest point of the Narrows to Anzac, and the famous city of Sestos was on the inner coast just opposite Suvla. Greek pilgrims, or tourists, came in crowds to the supposed tomb of Protesilaus who, according to legend, was the first Greek to leap ashore from the Greek fleet in that earlier "combined operation" against Troy. The tomb was near the southernmost Greek settlement of Elaeus, the Cape Helles of today; from near Helles, looking across the Straits, you can see the mound that covers the remains of ancient Troy. The Bulair Lines, or rather their prototypes, were built by the elder Miltiades at the northern end of the Peninsula to keep out Thracian freebooters. Pericles repaired them. Army after army, navy after navy, had preceded us to the Dardanelles: the Persians in 480 B.C.; Alexander the Great in 334 B.C.; the crusading host under Frederick

Barbarossa in A.D. 1190; the Turkish host in 1354. The traces of those and many other campaigns had passed; under the Turks the Peninsula had reverted to the silent wilderness that we found there. But half the remaining people were still Greek; and on the site of forgotten farms or villas the troops at Suvla had dug up in their trenches one or two stone relics of ancient Greek or Roman tombs or homes.

I knew too little about old Greek coinage to be able to identify this find; that had to be left until the collection arrived in Australia. The relics had to pass through many vicissitudes on the way and alas, when they reached Melbourne, the coin was not among them. So this particular riddle of Anzac remained unsolved.

ANZAC
GETS US DOWN

TOWARDS the end of a week with us Zeki Bey raised the question of his return to Constantinople. I would have liked to take him to Cape Helles, where I intended to spend a couple of days after finishing at Anzac, but something caused me to sense that he was wondering why I was keeping him so long under the cross-examnation to which he so generously submitted. I could see that he was becoming anxious to return, and accordingly at once asked Major Collis if he would kindly arrange for this.

February 27th, the day on which we visited Gaba Tepe promontory and the old Turkish battery positions at the Olive Grove, was his last full day with us. On the way there we rode over the area immediately south of Anzac, where our Army Corps was intended to land, a plan foiled by the sea current which carried the Navy's boats a mile farther north. The hills were much smoother there, and my diary says:

"Zeki Bey was impressed by the fact that if disciplined regular troops (as he said) had landed there, without the great difficulties of the Anzac country, they might have got far enough ahead, and quickly enough, to get across the Turkish communications to Chunuk Bair. But, even so, to carry out the whole day's plans would have been most difficult for a division even in peacetime, he said."

I well remember the look of wonder and interest, and the thoughtful tone, of Zeki Bey, as he gazed over the sweep of those ridges and gave us this opinion. He himself had broached the subject, and with the second part of his comment I agree; but the notion that an opposed landing at that place and in the conditions of 1915 could have been carried through within a time barely sufficient for a practice of it in peace, experience of warfare will lead most Anzacs to reject.

During Zeki Bey's visit to us I had been interested to discover his attitude towards the Germans. It was clear that he wished to counter the impression that German leaders were entirely responsible for the planning of Turkish strategy, or for its success, or that German assistance accounted for the strength of the defence. Without criticising Liman von Sanders, he stressed the German leader's delay in realising the import of the landings at Anzac and Helles and his error in suspecting them to be feints after the Turkish leaders on the spot were convinced that they were main operations. Zeki Bey often told us that the German personnel among the forces in Gallipoli were few. But he was a loyal ally; when someone at the mess-table thoughtlessly said something disparaging the German war effort, he flushed and said warmly: "I think this people made a wonderful effort against their many opponents."

This was interesting as reflecting the attitude of the Turkish officer at his best, for there is no doubt that the Germans and Turks constantly grated on one another in both higher and lower ranks; the casualness and backwardness of the Turks irritated the Germans, and all German soldiers in authority were not as wise as Liman von Sanders. We saw some of them once in Constantinople—it was the first time since before the war that we had lived in a community in which Germans had practically the same status as ourselves. We were in the stately High Street of Pera when an unearthly chirruping, like a canary's but fifty times magnified, suddenly filled the whole air, and down the road came a grey foreign staff-car with some German officers, the exhaust whistle (it was the first time any of us had heard one) turned on, scaring wayfarers off the highway like a present-day fire-engine. The attitude seemed typical. I must add, however, that German officers in Turkey had evidently felt an affinity to our prisoners of war there and in several instances notably befriended them.

At the end of Zeki Bey's stay it happened that our commissariat managed to secure a few bottles of whisky. From my boyhood's days I had understood that strong liquor was forbidden to Mohammedans, and I had, of course, barred from our mess during our friend's stay any ration containing pork in any form; some suggestion among our younger spirits for a practical joke in that connection—possibly not really intended—occasioned the only words I had to speak as a disciplinarian during the Mission. There was, of course, no such objection to having the whisky on the table, though the warning against practical jokes stood. I was much surprised that night when, on a remark from one of our lads, "I suppose you don't take this stuff, Zeki Bey," he asked what it was and then said, "Thank you, I should like to try a little," and let us pour him out a weak glass.

To our surprise, also, as dinner was ending Zeki Bey made us a little speech, in French of course, expressing his appreciation of our countrymen, first as soldiers and now as hosts. We on our side had all come to like and admire him. Strangely enough Lambert, debonair and friendly, had been, I think, the slowest to make a genuine inward accommodation to our one-time opponent. What prevented him was, of course, his memory of the Turkish Government's attempts to exterminate the Armenians. Had he seen what the world has since seen in Germany, Russia, Italy, Poland, Austria, East Asia, Spain and even France, he would probably have drawn from it the same lesson as I—that what separates Australians, English, Americans and the rest of "us" from that life of the wolf-pack and the driven flock is only the chance that we still manage—however precariously—to sustain an inherited and most stubborn tradition of basic freedom. Zeki Bey's friend and hero, Mustafa Kemal, was destined (and perhaps had already determined) to attempt to establish that tradition in his own people.

Our work kept us at Anzac for ten days after Zeki Bey left. By then, as I noted in my diary of Tuesday, March 4th, "pretty well every question which we came here to solve has been settled". I was anxious to leave for Helles and Constantinople, the more so as, since our day among the dreadful heights littered with the wreck of Baldwin's Brigade, Anzac, as it then was, oppressed us, and Wilkins had not been well. He was at work in his iron tank of a dark-room till far into the nights, which were often bitter. He was a born leader and, together with Hughes, who was another, he had been largely responsible for our success. I used to note with amusement that, as we strode and climbed about the hills, the rest of the party unconsciously followed Wilkins' lead. If he used a certain path, climbed a cliff in a particular way, jumped a trench or even went round left or right of a bush, the rest of us usually did the same.

On our last morning at Anzac I took Wilkins to Essad Pasha's headquarters at Scrubby Knoll so that he could get his record of the panorama on which the Turkish staff had looked out. A little farther south I checked and marked with stakes the positions apparently reached by Loutit, and then, returning to Lone Pine, searched the ground which Zeki Bey had said our men reached at the edge of The Cup, above the Turkish battalion headquarters. The cartridges and kit of our men were there, right on the edge of The Cup. The last afternoon I spent in marking for Hughes a number of points—mainly at Old Anzac—the exact location of which he thought might be useful to him. We put in forty-nine numbered pegs, showing the spot in Monash Valley where General Bridges was mortally hit, Birdwood's headquarters, the farthest points reached on the day of the Landing, and so on. In all we had noted about 130 points on our maps and marked them on the ground.[1]

George Lambert and his voluntary Australian orderly, a trooper named Spruce lent to him by Hughes, had been even busier than usual during the last few days. For one sketch, which specially pleased Lambert, Spruce served as a model, lying on the scrub on the rear slope of Johnston's Jolly, posed as one of the Anzac dead. Lambert's health also gave some reason for anxiety as to whether he would be able to complete his work in Gallipoli and later, according to his plans, in Sinai and Palestine. But before leaving Anzac he insisted on going out in the small hours to The Nek, so as to be there in the dawn light in which the charge was made. "Very cold, bleak and lonely," he noted. "The jackals, damn them, were chorusing their hate, the bones showed up white even in the faint dawn and I felt rotten; but as soon as I got to my spot the colour of the dawn on this scrubby, shrubby hill-land was very beautiful and I did my little sketch quite well before breakfast. Ten-thirty saw Spruce and self struggling with a water-colour of a very impressive subject, impressive both in art and military tradition. The worst feature of this after-battle work is that the silent hills and valleys sit stern and unmoved, callous of the human, and busy only in growing bush and sliding earth to hide the scars left by the war-disease. Perhaps it is as well that we are pulling out tomorrow; this place gives one the blues, though it is very beautiful."[2]

It was on one of these last nights, after the whole camp had gone to bed, and the door of the marquee had been laced up to keep the jackals from our boots and mess stores, that a stray kitten (from heaven knows where)

---

[1] The series marked for Hughes (and numbered, on pegs and maps, "A.H.M. 1 to A.H.M. 49") was necessarily separate from the series already marked by the Mission for its own purposes, and numbered 1-75 (and a few odd numbers, AAi and so on); but confusion has been avoided by carefully indexing the Mission's maps and the original diary.

[2] *Thirty Years of an Artist's Life*, p. 112.

was heard to mew outside the tent fly. It was immediately answered by an exactly similar mew from inside the tent —Lambert, of course. At first he imitated each mew of the kitten, but after a short while it imitated him. He seemed to be able to make it say whatever he wished it to. "Me-eaow," said Lambert. "Me-eaow," repeated the kitten. "Me-e-aow" from Lambert. "Me-e-aow" from the kitten. "Mow-ow-aaoow" from Lambert. The same from puss. This went on for twenty minutes, the camp stifling its laughter as best it could in order not to spoil the performance. After five minutes' interval the pair gave another twenty minutes' show and then Lambert allowed puss to go away disappointed. All the time we could hear our fatigue party in their tents bubbling with amusement. Several of the lads there were Welsh, and Lambert, whose forestry service had been in Wales, afterwards gave us their comments to the life. "Tit you hear what the officer sait, Will-yams?" It was like listening to Fluellen over a Gallipoli camp-fire

AT HELLES

On Friday March 7th George Lambert, Wilkins, Buchanan and myself with one groom and an orderly rode out of Anzac in the morning, leaving Balfour to strike and pack up camp and, helped by Rogers and our fatigue party, to cart the sketches, photographs, relics and gear to Kilid Bahr where we would rejoin their party on the 9th. Hughes, who wished, like myself, to follow the tracks of the Australians at Helles, rode with us; and at Kilid Bahr Bigg-Wither, the New Zealander on the Graves Unit, gave us a good lunch and then came with the party.

The day was glorious. We followed a Turkish tramway beside the Dardanelles with the steep side of Kilid Bahr Plateau walling us in on the inland side, until we came to the deep opening of the Soghun Dere, a valley about half a mile wide leading across the Peninsula. We turned up it and then climbed by a very steep, winding waggon-track over the hill forming the opposite or southern slope of the valley. The Turkish reserves had camped there. The country was more open and drier-looking (though probably not actually drier) than Anzac. At the top we came out on a plateau averaging a mile in width and reaching far across the Peninsula. I had expected to find myself on the southern shoulder of Achi Baba peak which we were eager to see at close range, since it had been the unattainable goal always facing the Allies at Helles. The British and French, and our 2nd Brigade and the New Zealanders lent to the Helles force for one very hard fight, had struggled towards it from April till July, most of the troops having the impression that if they could only get there the key of the Dardanelles would be in their hands.

But the plateau on which our party now came out still lay short of Achi Baba though connected with it. We could see that this upland shut out from Achi Baba practically all view of the Dardanelles; and it seemed to provide an additional and most formidable obstacle which the British would have had to overcome before their attack on Kilid Bahr Plateau or the Narrows could be launched. I intended, of course, to visit the peak later in order to ascertain precisely how much we could have seen from that longed-for position and how much the Turks there could see of us.

From the plateau beside the Soghun Dere we descended into another deep valley and then up to another plateau which proved to be the high land forming the shoulders of Achi Baba.[1] The peak itself, though appearing from the Cape Helles side to be a cone rising from two wide, level shoulders, now when we were a mile south of it showed itself as what it is, a long, level pencil-shaped hill, laid on this upland and pointing towards Helles. The plateau, across whose centre it lay, extended four miles across the Peninsula, and formed the top of a slope that descended at first sharply but thereafter always more gently to the toe of the Peninsula, five and a half miles away. Peak, plateau and the long slope were mainly open, with low scrub. The trenches began at the plateau; one road had been sunk four feet, probably to screen transport from observation by the Navy. At Anzac we had often seen the distant warships battering Achi Baba, and we now noticed that the ground was pitted with holes from naval shells—fairly evenly spread but not more thickly than the shellholes on a quiet part of the Western

---

[1] "Father Achi". It is also known as Alchi Tepe which, as Zeki Bey told us, meant "Plaster Hill".

Front. Emplacements for four big Turkish guns lay just to the left of our road.

The country bordering the long road from there to Seddel Bahr village and castle at the northern entrance of the Straits appeared to us, coming straight from France, as being only sparsely trenched. Very soon after we reached the rearmost lines of Turkish reserve trenches we were passing earthworks marked with French names. A French party had been at work identifying the old trenches, and marking them with notice boards. At the top of a rise we found a working party of black Senegalese soldiers—similar to those who held these French lines when I visited them in May 1915, and whom I afterwards saw in the distance attacking, swiftly gaining their objectives, and then all day being driven back and, as they ran, shot down one by one as a man might stamp out disturbed ants. They were now building an obelisk, possibly to commemorate those brave attacks.

We rode down the white road to the slight coastal rise in which the Peninsula ends, and then down its far side to the deserted "V Beach". It was in this terrible corner that the Dublin and Munster Fusiliers and 2nd Hampshire managed to struggle ashore from the beached collier *River Clyde* with dreadful losses from the fire of machine-guns and riflemen on the cliffs and in the village. Only the waves now stirred in that empty harbour enclosed by the hulls of empty ships. I noted: "The *Clyde* has been stripped of all her fittings; I fancy that even her ventilation cowls are lying over some of the dugout roofs in this camp."

"This camp" was the site to which we then turned back, on one of the terraces on the northern side of the coastal rise, a shelf overlooking the beautiful Morto Bay which swept round to the inner entrance of the Dardanelles. It was too early in the year for the gorgeous poppies and daisies that covered this bank when I was here in 1915. But the beautiful cypresses of the old

285

Turkish cemetery were close beneath, and the sweep of the hillside seen through fruit- or olive-trees was seamed with stone huts originally built there by the French, re-built by the Turks after the Evacuation, and now occupied again by Senegalese troops. We pitched our tent on the terrace near a French camp and cemetery and the camp of the British Graves Unit. The French cemetery was a model in lay-out—neat little heaps of earth, regularly grouped—but (we were told) the identification of the graves was far from being as careful as in the British cemeteries.

Next morning I set out with Hughes, Bigg-Wither and the junior British officer in charge at Helles,[2] and, of course, the Australians of our party (Wilkins, Lambert and Buchanan) to go over the ground of the famous advance of the afternoon of 8th May 1915—the one short sharp fight that comprised the whole of the Australian infantry's battle-experience at Helles, but which, in an hour or two, cost our brigade there (the 2nd) over 1000 of its 2900 officers and men. I knew that battlefield better than any in the war—except perhaps Pozières in France—having made the double journey over it, up and back, four times during the afternoon and night of the advance, and once again next day, and once more a few months later when the brigadier (Colonel M'Cay) with Major T. A. Blamey and myself examined it carefully by day after the front there had been advanced another 600 yards to its final position. Battle positions are very quickly forgotten; and M'Cay and I had then found that a trench newly marked "Australian Line", and therefore presumably then believed to be the position seized by our troops, was actually the old British front line that had been crossed by us about half-way through the advance; and that the position reached and dug by our brigade was 550 yards ahead and known as the "Redoubt Line". We

---

[2] A senior officer, formerly of the 29th Division, commanded the whole unit, but was then still at Kilid Bahr.

had found our dead still lying on the open plain behind
that line. But the ground was then still under fire though
at very long range, and one of the chief reasons for my
visit now was to check in comfort the observations that
we had then made.

Accordingly after a night's rest our party spent the
next day, March 8th, and part of the 9th in following and
searching the course taken by our 2nd Brigade on May
8th. Looking up the Peninsula from the hill behind our
camp, the eye met first the rich, low meadows in the
foreground with their belts of mulberry- and olive-trees;
then the long dry plain rising gradually for four miles
to the white stone windmills and ruins of Krithia village
(away to our left front) and finally to the bare Achi peak
straight ahead of us bounding the view there, a mile farther back. This was the scene which, in the early morning of 6th May 1915 had confronted our 2nd Brigade,
as it arrived very shaggy after its first fortnight at Anzac
and perhaps an hour or two of sleep in the fast packets
that ferried it down in the night to Helles. The four
battalions and field ambulance had been landed (under
a few shells from the southern side of the Straits) at the
pier beside the *Clyde*, and after climbing the dusty white
road over the hill at Seddel Bahr, looked out upon what
seemed—after Anzac—a fairyland of meadow and scattered
trees, busy with bright French uniforms, with the battlefield beyond lying like an open map. They were halted in
rich grass-land in the elbow of the neighbouring stream,
and their brigadier, James Whiteside M'Cay, gave them
ten minutes to dig in, as they could be seen, he said, from
Achi Baba. The ground was found too wet for trenching,
but in an incredibly short time the platoons had raised
successive lines of breastworks, made of turfs piled like
walls, about waist high, behind which they could dis-
appear in an instant, completely safe from the long range
shrapnel that occasionally fell there. They stayed for
two days in reserve, spending their spare time making

friends with the French commissariat or crowded on a tumulus near Hadji Ayub Farm to watch the distant battle with its strange, formal—and at that distance unreal—but terribly bloody stages.[3]

It will be recalled that this was the final attempt of Sir Ian Hamilton, the Allies' commander, to seize Achi Baba before a stalemate of trench warfare set in. The Turks had probably not yet firmly entrenched themselves across the Peninsula; Hamilton thought their trenches would then add up to about half the width of the front, and a few patches were being fortified farther back. In this area therefore, Hamilton thought, the Allies' naval and land artillery might still help them to break through and at least seize Achi Baba. Trenches were mainly visible on the right flank, in front of the French beside the Dardanelles, where the sandy parapets could be seen crowning the smooth height south of the Kereves Dere. In front of the British, who held the centre and the left, there existed lengths of trench, at present screened by the scrub, far ahead; except perhaps on the extreme left, they could be seen by few observers, even through glasses. The British advance was intended to be made in three stages, each roughly of a mile and a half —first, to approach the Krithia area; second, to pass Krithia; third, to swing to the right capturing Achi Baba. The French, in shorter stages, would swing across the Kereves Dere into line.

For two days the Australian troops who were in reserve watched the attempts, which, except on the French front, were all made in broad daylight at fixed hours and after sharp bombardments by the Allies' field-guns; but two days, May 6th and 7th, passed and Krithia was not, in fact, closely approached; except on the French front and on the extreme left no trench was taken or probably even sighted. On the third morning, May 8th,

---

[3] This scene, so fantastic to men from the Anzac crags and slopes, is described in *Vol. II, p. 5 et seq.*

the attempt was resumed with the New Zealand Infantry Brigade, which also had been brought from Anzac, replacing part of the 29th Division in the left centre, but the advance was stopped as before. At 4 o'clock that afternoon Sir Ian Hamilton, deciding to make one grand attempt before accepting failure, ordered that the whole line should at 5.30 fix bayonets and advance, the artillery having bombarded for fifteen minutes the ground ahead where the Turks were supposed to be and probably were.

Shortly before noon a message reached the 2nd Australian Brigade in its pleasant bivouac indicating that it would be required to change its position by moving to the left and then some distance forward along the Krithia stream, which ran through the centre of the line; there it was to be ready to support the 29th Division or Indian Brigade if necessary. The battalions quickly fell in and the 6th led off, guided by two officers (Major H. Gordon Bennett and the machine-gun officer, Captain F. V. Hogan) and accompanied by the brigadier. Being in sight of the distant enemy all the way, the battalions marched in "artillery formation". The march was a detour, keeping to the west of the little stream and turning with it where its course led towards the front. After about two miles we reached a fork with fairly high banks, afterwards known as "Clapham Junction". Here the 6th settled down first to its mid-day meal and then to dig shelter for the following night, the other battalions doing the same in rear. Some 350 reinforcements just arrived from Australia—via Egypt and Anzac—joined the battalions during the afternoon. The brigadier went off to see the New Zealanders while a few men of the brigade, scouting around as Australians invariably did, found ahead of them Indians in a long trench which (though the Australians did not know it) was part of the line reached in April and from which the advances started on May 5th. It was now known as the Reserve Line, later as the Eski (old) Line.

289

An hour or two passed and the battalions were just settling to their tea when at 5 o'clock an order suddenly reached them that by 5.30 they must be in line with the New Zealanders and advancing. They had been allotted the central part of the front, about a quarter of a mile wide, between the Krithia stream and the Krithia-Seddel Bahr road. Never, I think, in the history of the A.I.F., was an important attack (as distinct from a counter-attack) started in such haste. Companies and battalions hurriedly shuffled on their equipment and packs, picked up their other gear, and hastened to occupy, as they went, their allotted positions, 7th and 6th in front, 5th and 8th following, each with two companies in line and two following them. The advance started from a slight depression in which the battalions were partly screened by scattered olive-trees and thorn-bushes. While they were crossing this depression the Allies' artillery thundered out behind them, the French 75's throwing quick salvos which tore fountains of brown earth and smoke from the distant scrub ahead. As the Australians passed over the Indians' trench, which, so far as the hurrying battalions knew, was the front line, they looked over a bare level plain covered only with shrubs ankle high and reaching ahead to some low growth nearly a mile away. At the same time Turkish artillery observers somewhere beyond that expanse also saw the Australians. The expected result came presently in salvo after salvo of shrapnel, bursting in fleecy little clouds over the 7th Battalion and whipping up other clouds of tawny dust close below,

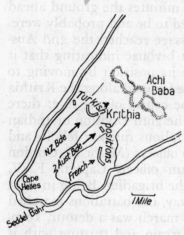

where the hissing pellets struck the dry plain, sometimes obscuring with haze the hurrying platoons. Bullets from long range began to whistle past thickly or peck the dust like scattered drops heralding a thunder-shower. It was, I thought, like walking against a dust storm in Sydney. The bang of the guns at this stage relieved us from the tension caused by the whiz of passing bullets.

WHERE THE 2nd BRIGADE'S ADVANCE ON KRITHIA BEGAN

A. Achi Baba (Krithia lay under its left shoulder).
B. Bivouac of Indian troops by the Krithia Nullah.
The brigade advanced from the creek in the foreground, deploying to the right as it moved up the depression. It began to come under aimed fire as it topped the rise. The rise was held by a line of Indians. The distant high ground on the right lay ahead of the French sector.

After what seemed an age the swift advance across the apparently endless open came suddenly and quite unexpectedly upon a trench across its whole front, garrisoned by Lancashire troops. From that moment it was known to all Australians as "the Tommies' Trench". The hurrying Australians, who had thought that only Turks were ahead, let themselves down into it or lay down behind it, getting their breath. Many wondered if their task was to reinforce it; but within a few minutes of each company's reaching it their leaders, calling "On Australians", climbed out and the men scrambled after them. At this stage the fire from ahead became intense, the bullets splashing more thickly in the dust. The brigadier had jumped out to give the signal to the first line, which was led on by Major R. W. Wells and Lieutenant R. C. Keiran on the left and by Major W. E. H. Cass, the brigade-major, on the right. Major Gordon Bennett— then a red-headed slip, little more than a boy—led on the second line of the 6th, its colonel, W. R. McNicoll, the fourth. The brigadier, M'Cay, who with his small party had led the advance to the Tommies' Trench, was still conspicuously putting his driving force into it, constantly hoisting himself on to the parapet and waving onward each batch of men with his periscope. But even those who so exposed themselves could see little of the troops ahead

THE "TOMMIES' TRENCH", HELLES

A. *Achi Baba.*
X. *Where General M'Cay crossed.*

except a few moving figures, quickly dwindling in the distance, a sprinkling of dead amid the grass and shrubs, and here and there a wounded man limping or crawling back to the Tommies' Trench. The fire was terrific. M'Cay was opposite the left centre of his front where some old track, or hedge, evidenced by a thin line of scrub and three or four wild olive-trees, crossed the Tommies' Trench. A twig of olive lying beneath the trees was sent spinning into the air as though the bullets were playing tipcat, and earth from the parapet was constantly showered on to the heads and bodies of the troops in the trench. But the advance could not be controlled from there; and after parts of the 5th and 8th Battalions also had come up and passed, M'Cay could not wait for the rest of the 8th, which was not in sight, but, taking

Staff-Sergeant Jack Monks and two men with a telephone reel (one now a volunteer from the 8th, who took the place of a wounded signaller) he went on with the intention of keeping the attack in motion, as ordered, until "the ridge beyond Krithia" was reached. He ordered me to stay where I was, in the Tommies' Trench. At the same time, knowing that in face of such fire the line could be kept going only if constantly reinforced, he sent his orderly officer, Lieutenant Tom Hastie, to find and hurry forward the rest of the 8th. Captain Hogan was sent on some other errand and was quickly wounded.

I had watched from the Tommies' Trench line after line of men scramble to the parapet, stand there for a moment astride of the trench, with rifle and bayonet clutched across their chests, glaring to the front with eyes puckered to pick up any trace of where the tempest of bullets came from. I noted in my diary: "Their faces were set, their eyebrows bent, they looked into it for a moment as men would into a dazzling flame. I never saw so many determined faces at once." Then they threw themselves, heads bent, as if into a thunder-shower, here and there one holding a shovel before his head like an umbrella. I had felt for my camera to get what I thought must be the finest photograph of the war, only to find that in our haste I had left it at our starting point. On a hill a mile to our right I could see Turks lumbering off from their trench in front of the French Senegalese who were also attacking and were now fifty yards away making for the parapet with their long, spiky bayonets. One Turk stood nestling his rifle to his cheek as he aimed until the Senegalese were thirty yards from him, and then ran back. A few seconds later the first black soldier or two reached the parapet and stood on it lunging down in a curiously matter of fact, slow-motion manner at whatever was below the parapet. I couldn't help wondering what horrid scene was being acted there; but almost immediately afterwards French and Senegalese were standing all along that parapet, apparently talking cas-ually. The next time I looked the Senegalese were trotting slowly back from the trench, with French officers, swords drawn, trying to rally them. At that stage I heard my name called near by, and along the trench came a scrap of paper from Lieutenant Hastie: "Shot through both hands. Please inform brigadier."

There is no rule against war correspondents' carrying a message like that, and, whatever the message said, I should have felt forced to take it. So I went on, following the telephone line which the signaller and the volunteer from the 8th, marching behind the brigadier, had un-rolled as they went forward and which I knew must lead to him. It trailed along the ground, leaving Tommies' Trench immediately east of the olive-trees and·heading towards Achi Baba. Here and there I passed a dead or wounded man, and, about 250 yards out, was surprised to hear myself again called: "Hallo, old man; you up here?" and saw near me Colonel McNicoll lying badly wounded, behind a couple of packs placed there by his men. I had seen him hit already once, but slightly, at the Tommies' Trench, and my diary says that, as he now lay out, "he was awfully plucky and cheerful". Going on, I presently saw ahead a little earthwork, about nine feet long by three deep, with a parapet of up to two feet. Sitting behind the parapet were M'Cay and his signaller and the volunteer. "We couldn't reach the ridge behind Krithia," M'Cay said to me when I joined them. "They set us an impossible task." Staff-Sergeant Monks was not there. On the way forward M'Cay had heard a bullet strike someone behind him. He turned and asked Monks if he was hit. "Yes, I'm hit through the heart," came the quiet reply and that splendid soldier fell dead. After dark M'Cay searched for him, lighting matches to scan the face of each dead man who lay near, but he was never found.

The front line of the 6th Battalion lay about 100

yards ahead of M'Cay's post. By the crack of the Turks'
bullets one might guess that their line lay perhaps another
300 yards beyond that, but our line was now stopped.
We afterwards learnt that Major Gordon Bennett, who
really led and directed the left of this attack and mirac-
ulously escaped unscathed, had to give up the notion
of pressing farther without strong reinforcement, inas-
much as the line was then so thin that with further progress its extinction would have been merely a matter of
arithmetic. The brigade-major, Cass, who had directed
the 7th battalion on the right had been badly wounded.
Bennett was the only combatant officer of the original
6th Battalion then left unwounded, and four of its former
N.C.O.'s, promoted to officers since the Landing, had
been killed in this advance; except him, every leader mentioned in this chapter was hit, half of them killed. The
rear lines coming up dug a support trench after dark;
and during the night touch was found with the New
Zealanders who had attempted a similar advance west
of the Krithia stream. After dark the ground was fairly
safe, despite frequent storms of Turkish fire, and daylight found the line well dug in. Just towards the end
of the advance a few officers had detected Turkish parapets in the scrub at some points about 350-400 yards
ahead, but the fire seemed to be coming from closer, and
especially from both flanks, the Australians being then
ahead of other troops.

This flanking fire had been mentioned to me by
Major Cass when I saw him late that night as he lay, twice
shot through the chest and critically ill, among the
crowd of wounded within the dim light of the distant
lanterns at the collecting station. He realised his condition, but between breaths he questioned me.[4] "Bean,
old man, do you know about our right flank?........
Is that safely up?........It was that........which was
........worrying me. I was over there........I could

---

[4] I quote his words from my diary of 8th May 1915.

. . . . see the. . . . . see the bullets. . . . . striking the road. . . . . the Krithia road [it was raised about a foot]. . . . . from the east. . . . . and I thought. . . . . they must be getting. . . . . round our right flank." He had managed to tell passing officers of the 5th, and, though he could not yet know it, that battalion had since thoroughly secured that flank.

This advance had been famous among the troops then on the Peninsula. Sir Ian Hamilton wrote: "A young wounded officer of the 29th Division said it was worth ten years of tennis to see the Australians and New Zealanders go in."

Our Mission had now to identify on the ground the successive stages of the 2nd Brigade's attack and make certain where it began and ended. We started our investigation much farther back, at the old camp site in the meadows 250 yards south of Hadji Ayub Farm, where we found the low walls of mud and turf still standing where the Diggers on arrival at Helles had so quickly raised them to shelter their bivouac. Thence we followed roughly the old detour of their march till we cut a wheel-track leading to Krithia stream.[5] To the left of the track was a slight swelling of the plain, and behind this, I think, the 2nd Australian Field Ambulance had had its collecting station, where I had seen Cass and hundreds of other wounded lying on the grass under some trees in the light of two dim stable lanterns. A little farther on, where the banks of the Krithia stream began to rise to perhaps eight or ten feet, was where the 5th Battalion had been settling down to its tea when the attack order arrived. It was on the eastern bank there that, on the morning after the fight, Captain G. C. M. Mathison, medical officer of the 5th, had been sitting after a night

5 We struck this track a little farther back than the Brigade had done, just where the stumps of some trees marked the site of the old headquarters of the Royal Naval Division (Major-General A. Paris). It was under this division—though few of the troops knew it—that the brigade was operating.

of tense, continuous work when one of the half-spent bullets that lisped everywhere entered a brain that would have been precious in the future of Australian medicine.[6] It was difficult for the Mission to identify the precise slit-trench in the eastern bank in which Brigadier-General M'Cay had temporarily placed his headquarters before the sudden order reached him. Several such trenches existed there. However its general position was certain, and from there began the Mission's real "search" following, as I could remember it, the course taken by the brigadier and the head of the 6th Battalion.

Working out of the shallow dip, at about 350 yards we came across the line where we had passed over the Indians. It was deeper than when we crossed it in 1915. From there our course took us (to quote the Mission's diary) "a long way over the open—without shelter of any sort—only the low, rounded, grey-blue and green shrubs like saltbush, with the dry light pinky earth between them." About seventy yards out we passed an old shallow line, barely dug and evidently held only briefly, perhaps for a few hours. After we had gone a few hundred yards I could pick out ahead the four olive-trees that marked where M'Cay had crossed the Tommies' Trench; one of these trees grew actually at the parados; two were in line with it ahead, and the fourth in rear of the trench, in the "hedge" or higher scrub marking the edge of some old track to Krithia along which they stood. There was no doubt in the Mission's identification of this place. The old Tommies' Trench afterwards officially known as the Australian Line, lay, says the diary, "almost exactly as it was—with a meaningless collection of holes behind it". These were the shallow pits in which—and also in the trench itself—as that cruel night wore on the wounded and dying had collected by scores from the plain about,

---

6 It would, however, have been strongly against his wish had he been kept out of the line, and he was to be there for only a short tour.

and had lain waiting, some of them desperately, for stretcher-bearers.

At the risk of undue discursion I cannot forbear quoting from my 1915 diary one passage describing the scene there when shortly before dawn I reached it on one of my journeys. I was carrying a tin of water which was acutely needed farther forward. Though the stretcher-bearers had toiled continuously all night their carry was so long that many men who had been hit still lay out on the plain ahead with (as daylight would soon be near) dwindling hope of rescue. "The cries of the wounded," says my diary, "were heart-rending. The Tommies' Trench was full of them—little Mathison had been there attending to them. The poor chaps there badly wanted water........Although the water was for the men at brigade headquarters one could not help giving the poor chaps a drink. I told them I had very little to spare and they must be content with a little. We got a mess-tin and handed a little down to everyone in the trench or under the parapet.[7] Each fellow took about two sips and then handed it back—really you could have cried to see how unselfish they were. One fellow said, 'Here, sir, I think this man would like a drink'—not himself but the man next him. I went over to him and bent over the wrong man in the dark—but he pointed me out his mate— 'Him, sir,' he said. The man he meant was hit in the head or back and was lying on his face—and at first we didn't think he would be able to move his head to get at the drink—he didn't seem to think he could himself; although he was barely articulate I could understand that much. I moistened his lips first and then we managed to get his head into a position from which he could suck at the tin.

"It was late—4 o'clock nearly—and there was not a great deal of water in the tin—so I decided to leave it

---

[7] I think this means "behind the parados", where many were lying, on the surface immediately behind the trench.

at the Tommies' Trench with two Lancashire Fusiliers[8]
—to give to the wounded every now and then."

The Mission found that many of the holes behind
this trench had since been filled in as graves, probably
of the men who had lain there; others had been buried in
the trench itself, and a number in the low scrub of the
"hedge" where the rearmost olive-tree stood.

I described to George Lambert the advance across
the Tommies' Trench as I remembered it, and at mid-day
he settled down there to his sketching. "Achi Baba makes
a fine contour in the background," he wrote afterwards,
"and the plain is covered with bushes of heather and sage-
brush, with a few small thorn-trees and olives . . . The
whole landscape is a dull mauvy grey with a sage green
admixture and very delicate if sombre in tone. The dead,
or rather their bones, spoil it, of course. I got . . . a panel
ready to get a quick shot at the evening light . . . made
a very carefully considered landscape from which I can
do a big one, if necessary. I was left alone and didn't
really mind it; the work was very absorbing and the
weather perfect" (*Thirty Years,* pp. 113-14).

The rest of us, searching in an extended line forward
of the Tommies' Trench, found the remains of Australians everywhere on the plain, as far forward as the
two trenches of the Redoubt Line, 400 and 500 yards
ahead respectively. We found Australian kit, and the
arm patches of the 6th Battalion, red and purple, and
the bronze "Australia" from the shoulder strap, right
up to the front Redoubt Line. Two communication
trenches had since been dug from the Tommies' Trench
right up to the final British front line; and between them,
just behind the Redoubt Support Line, was a small detached pit which I recognised as the one in which I
found M'Cay and his signaller. I had visited it more than

---

[8] The 1st Lancashire Fusiliers of the 29th Division were holding the
Tommies' Trench together with the Drake Battalion, Royal Naval Division,
and they behaved magnificently throughout.

once during the battle and on the last occasion found
M'Cay's signaller with his leg broken by a bullet but
still at his telephone, and the poor chap from the 8th
mortally wounded. Before the Landing my brother had
given me two opium pills for such emergencies. Fumbling
in my purse in the dark I now dropped one of them but
fortunately not the other, which I gave to him. Shortly
after this Mathison and I heard that the brigadier was
wounded, all the brigade staff that took part in the advance having thus been hit. The Mission now noted that
in the parados of M'Cay's little trench a man had been
buried, and apparently another in the parapet. Doubtless one of them was the poor chap to whom I gave the
opium pill.

The extent of that advance, famous in at least Australian military history, had now been placed beyond
doubt,[9] and the main object of our visit to Helles was
thus accomplished.

Wilkins, Buchanan and I now rode on a mile and a
quarter to Krithia village which we found a complete
ruin, all woodwork having been taken by the Turks for
their trenches. We rode back by the Gully Ravine, close
to and parallel with the Mediterranean coast—the ravine
ran to beyond Krithia and in sharp contrast to the rest
of the country, was as rugged as the Anzac valleys,
though not as deep. Then, while Wilkins went back to
work on his photographs, Buchanan, Bigg-Wither and I
returned to the position reached by the 2nd Brigade
and explored the ground ahead of it with the object of
determining where were the Turks who fired at them

---

[9] The visit was not unnecessary. Not only had French surveying parties
marked the trenches wrongly—the Tommies' Trench, for example, as being
held on April 30th (actually it was reached and dug on May 5th) and the
Redoubt Line as held on May 4th (actually May 8th)—but the excellent history
of the Royal Naval Division by Douglas Jerrold shows the Australian
advance as ending at the Redoubt Support Line; actually the Redoubt
Front Line was dug by Australians that night and the Support line by their
supports on the same night. On the Mission's return to Australia an
examination of the records and further inquiry among the surviving leaders,
some of whom had made a survey of the lines, confirmed this.

and of finding the positions reached by the British later in the campaign.

We could not finish this search by nightfall, but Bigg-Wither noticed some rifle-pits behind a slight bank from which the Turks had—to judge by the cartridges—been firing very heavily. With his advice I returned to search for these next day. For about 220 yards ahead of our final Australian firing line we found no sign of Turks. Then just beyond a tiny plantation of twenty-four baby firs, we came on a British trench, marking the line to which the 42nd (East Lancashire) Division advanced by night, losing hardly a man, exactly three weeks after our terrible experience in daylight. Ian Hamilton had wished to adopt that plan of a night approach in the earlier battle also; but, as in the greater crisis in August at Suvla, he refrained from breaking the usually sound military rule, and allowed the commander on the spot (in this case Major-General A. Hunter-Weston) to pursue his own method. Eighty-five yards beyond that trench was a very old boundary between two former patches of cultivation. It had all long since reverted to heath, but the ridge between the two fields was still visible, and along it the Turks had dug a dozen shallow rifle-pits. From one of these, which we examined, 100 shots had apparently been fired, and a line of similar "pozzies" straggled across country to either flank. There were card-board ammunition packets at some points immediately south of this line and two or three rifle-pits immediately north of it, with Turks buried in them. All these Turks can only have been firing at our men; no previous attack came close enough. But the fire of such a line of skirmishers could not account for the fusillade that met the 2nd Brigade, or the casualties;[10] this must, I think, have come from the first Turkish trench-line, which lay about

---

[10] Bullets lay everywhere on the ground we had passed, but a large proportion of them would be "overs" fired at targets farther ahead.

100 yards behind the rifle-pits, along the near side of the small patch of vines known as the Vineyard.

In the Vineyard, a level field about 100 yards in width and 185 in depth, lying between the new Krithia road on the east and the old road on the west, the vines and some small olive-trees were still growing. One line of fire trench passed along its southern side, another through its centre, and a third, partly dug and, I judged, never continuously held, along its northern edge. Clearly in the last part of the campaign, this last trench had been in No-man's-land, or held only by British listening posts or some such light groups. The Turkish front line was only 17 yards beyond. The French surveyors had marked it as "English position of June 21st". There were signs that the British might have reached it in some attack. I picked up an English water-bottle and other gear beyond it; but there was no sign that this trench beyond the Vineyard had ever been held by us for more than an hour or two, and every sign to the contrary.

That day, Sunday March 9th, I paced out for the second or third time all the distances between trench-lines from the start of the 2nd Brigade's advance to the front held by the two sides at the end of the campaign. By this means I judged (summarising our main observations in this area) that from where the brigade staff started, just behind the 6th Battalion[11] and in front of the 7th, 5th and 8th, the brigade had advanced 350-400 yards to the British reserve (Eski) line; 498 yards from there to the Tommies' Trench; 515 yards farther to where the attack was stopped (or 410 yards in the case of the supports)—a total of some 1400 yards. Ahead of the line then reached other lines had since been dug at 240 yards, and at 135 yards beyond that. Next, apparently, a main Turkish line had been captured at the edge of the Vineyard, 60 yards farther on (or 435 yards beyond the line

---

[11] M'Cay and his staff hurried forward and led the advance as far as the Tommies' Trench, Cass similarly leading the right.

reached by the Australians). A second Turkish line had been taken 100 yards beyond this. There, so far as the marks on the ground allowed us to judge, the main front appeared to have lain at the end of the campaign, though the Turks had also been driven from another trench at the far end of the Vineyard, 85 yards on, and perhaps small British posts subsequently maintained there. The Turkish trench 17 yards beyond this had probably at some time been rushed, or even temporarily passed, by the British but had remained Turkish at the end. I may add that the British Official History, when published in 1931, and other accounts confirmed these observations. Apparently the Vineyard was approached by the 42nd (E. Lancs) Division in night advances on May 27th and 28th. In the great thrust of June 4th, under the splendid cover of the French "75's" the Manchester men seized the Turkish front along the southern edge of the Vineyard, and went on to its northern edge and 200 yards beyond—some even, it is said, 600 yards beyond—but eventually had to withdraw to the southern edge of the Vineyard. In the disastrous feint made at Helles on August 6th and 7th to divert attention from the offensive at Anzac, the Lancashire territorials again took the trench at the northern edge of the Vineyard as well as the one through its centre. These were the only gains that were held when that battle ended, and they were held despite a decision of the higher commanders to withdraw. On August 12th the northern edge of the Vineyard was again lost, and according to the British maps it belonged to neither side from that time forward.

We noted down for Hughes Australian graves near the Tommies' Trench. Everything that we planned to do at Helles had now been finished except to survey the battlefield from that goal of so many hopes, the top of Achi Baba. I wondered how many British wives, mothers and sweethearts for how many months had grown used to those cheery letters, "and then for Achi Baba", "We may get the place at the next go", "Achi Baba seems as far off as ever, but here's hoping", only to receive the telegram that told of the writer's final effort to win the next furlong of that distance in the shell- and mine-torn ground where we had found those relics beyond the Vineyard. Wilkins and Buchanan joined me at the Vineyard, and we rode straight on to Achi Baba. Lambert stayed to finish a sketch of the *River Clyde* and would come on to Kilid Bahr by Bigg-Wither's Ford car.

The "peak" of Achi Baba we had found, as I said before, to be really a ridge, about a third of a mile long, rising from several square miles of plateau that form its shoulders. The ridge points towards Helles, and therefore appears narrow from the front, and it was about half covered with low scrub. Around the whole summit was a deep, well traversed trench in which were several big, deep observing stations, one of them containing parts of a large range-finder, either never completed or else partly removed by the French. We saw no sign of damage by our naval guns, though probably some had been done and repaired; on both sides of crest and plateau were shellholes, some of them big, but they were widely distributed. On top the Turks had gathered a collection of shell fragments, some from 12-inch guns.

Turning round to obtain the view of the southern battlefield which had been enjoyed by the Turkish defenders throughout the campaign, we found the toe of the Peninsula exhibited like a raised plan. We could pick out every detail, Seddel Bahr, the Hadji Ayub mound, the Krithia road, the olive-trees by the Tommies' Trench, the patch of little firs, the Vineyard, and Krithia close below us. But one condition may have been in our favour on May 8th: the sun and its bright reflection on the sea would be in the Turkish observers' eyes, and may have accounted for their not catching us more severely with their shrapnel. However, the two things

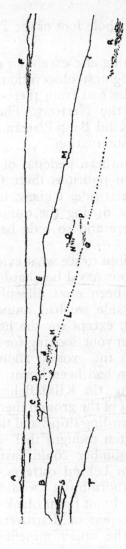

WHAT THE TURKS SAW FROM ACHI BABA LOOKING SOUTH-EAST

A. Tenedos Island.
B. De Tott's Battery (in the French sector overlooking Morto Bay).
C. Seddel Bahr, old fortress.
D. "V" Beach (hidden by cliffs).
E. Lancashire Landing (hidden by cliffs).
F. Part of Imbros Island.
J. Meadows and trees.

K. Mound of Hadji Ayub.
L. The Krithia road.
M. Gully Beach (hidden by cliffs).
N. Olive-trees by the Tommies' Trench.
O. Krithia Nullah. R. Krithia.
S. Turkish trenches overlooking the Kereves Dere.
T. South-east shoulder of Achi Baba.

The French attack of 8th May 1915 took place on the height between B and S. (Only features related to the 2nd Brigade's story were noted in this sketch.)

that immediately struck us on the top of Achi Baba were, as I noted in my diary:

"(1) that it commanded the whole foot of the Peninsula;

"(2) that it commanded nothing else except an excellent view of Anzac. Not the slightest observation over Chanak or the Narrows could be had from there—only a featureless little triangle of the Narrows. The big shoulder to the south, and the Kilid Bahr Plateau, completely shut out any further observation."

Crossing a swamp on the southern pedestal of Achi Baba, and passing some old gun positions there (there were similar ones on the northern side, I knew, for we had seen the flashes from Anzac during the campaign) we dipped into the Soghun Dere and so rode back to Kilid Bahr.

At Kilid Bahr fort I was anxious to see what evidence existed of any damage done by our naval bombardments to the forts, which must have been most difficult targets to reach. On the Chanak side we had found the fortifications almost undamaged, except for the hole in the old Turkish castle, though anyone looking for shell-craters could find a number in the ground about the earthworks, and part of the town had been burnt. Now, so far as we could see in passing, the Kilid Bahr forts showed no sign of damage.[12] Most of the ground there was entirely screened from our bombarding ships; and though I am no soldier I have since often thought that with a few field-guns, of which any number could easily be screened up the many gullies or behind cottages, huts, forts, or even behind any handy thorn-bush, I would have felt confident of knocking out at almost point blank range any flotilla whether of minesweepers or destroyers that tried to clear a way through the upper minefield, or perhaps even part of the lower one. But our minesweepers

---

[12] A photograph of one is in *Vol. XII, plate 51.*

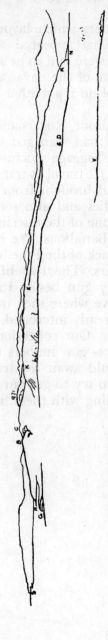

WHAT WE WOULD HAVE SEEN, LOOKING NORTH-EAST, IF WE HAD CAPTURED ACHI BABA

N. *Narrows.*
G. *Gaba Tepe.*
H. *Hell Spit, Anzac.*
S. *Suvla Bay.*
B. *Battleship Hill.*

C. *Chunuk Bair.*
K-K-K-K. *Kilid Bahr Plateau.*
SD. *Soghun Dere.*
V. *Valley leading to Suliman Bey Farm.*
971. *Hill 971 (Koja Chemen Tepe).*

never reached the narrow waters which favoured such action. In the fort we saw what appeared to be two portable torpedo-tubes. There were said to be such tubes at the Soghun Dere at the time of the naval attempt to force the Straits, but I know of no report that they were ever used.

At Kilid Bahr we found Balfour, Rogers and the men and gear from Anzac. Balfour had managed to arrange for the Mission with its own baggage (pictures, photographs, records and personal kit) to travel by transport next day to Constantinople. He had brought from Anzac 26 ammunition boxes full of relics and also some of the old timbers from Lone Pine—one of them scribbled with names of the 23rd and 24th Battalions. We had found that the Turkish huts at the back of the Pine had largely been built from these timbers. The two lifeboats on Anzac Beach, and the old 4.7 gun beside the road at Koja Dere, we had had to leave where they were in the hope that Hughes, who was greatly interested, could get them to Australia for us later. Our collection together with a number of larger relics—gun limbers and water carts—collected by James would await sea transport at Kilid Bahr. James promised to try to get our collection with his own to Egypt, travelling with them, if possible, himself.

Chapter
· XXII ·

BY CATTLE-TRUCK
THROUGH THE TAURUS

WE boarded the Greek steamer *Spetsai* at 11 o'clock,
March 10th, waving to our good friends Hughes and
James and the fatigue party, which was there with our
horses, as the tender took us out to her. She was full of
Greeks, Turks, Armenians and French native soldiers in
the waist and cheery French officers and their women-

*THE ANZAC HILLS SEEN FROM CHANAK AS THE MISSION
LEFT, 10th MARCH 1919*

folk in the saloon; we did not get away till 5 o'clock, but
the French were all very gay and particularly friendly
with us Australians. Next day Constantinople again wel-
comed us with gusts and bitter sleet.

I had intended to take the Mission back to Egypt by
sea; several of its members suggested that we should ask
for transport overland by the newly opened Turkish railway across the Taurus and Amanus mountains, linking
the Anatolian railway across Asia Minor with those of
Syria and Palestine. The last link, through the mountains, had been open for only a few months; Allenby
had come to Constantinople that way, and the Turkish
Army from Palestine and Syria was being repatriated by

that route. However, for us it would be purely a joy ride and I saw no justification for putting the Australian Government to the expense of sending us that way. In Constantinople, however, Wilkins had made several firm friends on the British transport staff; and when one of these offered to take us back on some of the returning rolling stock I agreed.

As we had to lay in some stores for the journey I hurried with Balfour and Lambert to the British ordnance office on the wharf at Constantinople. It chanced that our very good friend, General Croker of the 28th Division at Chanak, happened to see us and followed us into the office to ask if he could help, and I have no doubt that his interest smoothed our way, although we always found the British ordnance and supply admirably helpful and efficient. We gave our order for bread, blankets, tins of fruit and milk and the like, to be ready for putting on a lighter on Friday 14th, when we and all our gear would be ferried across the Bosporus to Scutari on the Asiatic shore to entrain at Haidar Pasha Station.

At the comfortable Officers' Rest House I wrote the second part of the report on Gallipoli graves which the Australian Government had asked me to cable, the points of which are summarised later. I had also—by producing whatever authority I could and with Cameron's help—to try to get transport for James and the relics to Egypt. Furthermore I had received a telegram from Australian headquarters in London based, I think, on reports from our light horsemen lately in Constantinople, that guns and other things left by our troops at Anzac were in a museum at the Turkish capital. I was asked to see if I could procure these for the Australian museum. The reports were true, for I met in Constantinople a man who had seen in the famous Arms Museum two guns and limbers of, he thought, a Tasmanian battery. They were certainly some of the demolished guns that we had left behind at the Evacuation. Strangely enough, General Birdwood had directed that every gun left behind—all were worn and worthless—should be "so completely blown to bits as to ensure its worthlessness even as a trophy". General White, to whom the vital consideration was that the Turks should not learn of the Evacuation by hearing or seeing anything unusual, had insisted that the charges used to crack the gun-barrels should not be heavier than would sound like a gun firing. Evidently they had not been destroyed as trophies. I left with Major Cameron a letter asking him to do what he could to get them for us, and indicating that a formal request would probably be sent later.

I have a notion, however, that the British command was diffident in making our request to the Turkish Government; possibly Cameron felt (though I did not at the time) that the presence of these guns in a Turkish museum provided an exhibit of which we, too, might be proud; and that if the Turkish Army had a few trophies of Gallipoli, it unquestionably deserved them. We had not then heard, as has since been reported, that Captain Lalor's sword, left at The Nek, was in a Turkish museum. It was a family heirloom, and the Turkish staff might have agreed to return it, at least if we could have offered some exhibit in exchange. I have since felt that the British staff, if it did hold this view, was right with regard to the guns.

Also the Turks had given our Mission a generous measure of help. The Chief of the Turkish General Staff, Kiazim Pasha, who had been Chief of Staff to Liman von Sanders, had himself undertaken the answering of the questionnaire that I had been allowed to submit;[1] and he himself saw me for a few minutes on my return to Constantinople. I recall him as a keen faced, lightly built officer, who might have been Italian or Greek, with big, bright, sensitive eyes. He was obviously

---

[1] Kiazim Pasha's answers, which were of great value to the Australian history of the war, are printed in *Appendix I*.

intelligence itself, but I wondered whether he had the exceptional strength needed for his position.

By Friday our task had been completed; the graves report cabled; Kiazim Pasha's answers translated by the British staff. We had eaten our last afternoon tea at the Greek café and made our last trip through the crowded, wicked-looking alleys where we noted the names of light horsemen scribbled on the door-post of an eating-house. Ordnance had for once forgotten our bread and blankets, but we rushed them to the lighter in time and, after waddling for half an hour across the water to Scutari, landed them at Haidar Pasha. Our friend on the transport staff had been as good as his word: the railway transport officer knew all about us, and two long, enclosed wooden horse- or cattle-trucks in a mixed train, partly assembled but waiting for its engine, were shown us as our home for the first week of our 1500-mile journey to Egypt

Our first job was very thoroughly to scrub down the trucks with pails of water and scrubbing brooms. Lambert and Rogers, who were looking after the baggage, volunteered to turn the rearmost truck into a mess-room and kitchen. A Turkish carpenter and two of his "off-siders" were sent to do the actual work, but Lambert and Rogers found that they could do better and quicker themselves. Dismissing their assistants, borrowing a hammer and some nails, and getting hold somehow of some wood, they made in no time a table and two benches and a meat-safe; and they were so proud of their work—and we so appreciative of it—that they forthwith volunteered to stay there and cook for us during the trip. We were turned out to doss in the other truck; it would be our sleeping quarters—our two cooks insisted on sleeping in their kitchen.

For me, with our safe delivery of ourselves to our cattle-trucks and to the care of the omnipotent railway, the war seemed over. We didn't know when the train

would start—and I'm not sure that the authorities did—
and we didn't care. After a good dinner from our cooks
the rest of us bedded down in our sleeping quarters, I,
for one, thoroughly worn out. We were awakened about
9 o'clock next morning by the racing shafts of sunlight
and the jolt of the springs as we bumped over the railway points on the outskirts of Scutari.

It was a journey of extraordinary interest and, in
parts, through scenery both grand and beautiful, in
country with a history going back much farther than
St Paul; where Assyrians, Lydians, Greeks, Romans,
Egyptians, Arabs, Turks, Crusaders—and in these very
modern times Napoleon and ourselves—had marched and
fought. In that one journey there was ample matter for
an entrancing book. But just then I was writing no more
books; at last we were free to enjoy sights and scenery for
the sake of the enjoyment, an indulgence that we had
felt impossible even in the most beautiful rest areas of
France and Belgium while men were killing one another.
Scene after scene swam before us, drunk in with delight,
but leaving the impression of a dream. Nearly all the
first morning we were slipping through rich lowlands
past the Gulf of Ismid, where we passed the German
battle-cruiser *Goeben* whose clever flight to the Dardanelles did so much to bring Turkey into the war. In
the afternoon for an hour we skirted Lake Sabandscha
and wound along a river valley; and night found us
watching the moonlight on the mountains as our slow
train curled itself round their slopes. Eskischehir, the
junction for Angora (150 miles to the east) we passed in
the small hours—no one was interested in Angora then
though in a few months it was to supplant Constantinople
as the nerve centre of Turkey.

Next morning brought us, through rather dry
country, to the immense outstanding rock and low-
clustered houses of Afiun Kara Hissar ("Opium Black
Castle"). This was the junction for the only railway

313

running in from the Aegean to join the Anatolian railway—the line came up 200 miles as the crow flies from the great port of Smyrna where, though less than half the population was Greek, the old Ionian Greek community still flourished on despite the Turkish conquest 500 years before. The chief tongue spoken there was Greek; and so Greek were the neighbouring districts that some of us war correspondents, on holiday at Mytilene during the Gallipoli Campaign, had been ferried over by an English volunteer motor boat patrol and lunched a mile inland under the mulberries and vine-pergola of a hospitable Greek farm in Asiatic Turkey. We had made good friends among the Mytilene Greeks, and I hoped that the happy end of the war had delivered our hosts from the fear that was never far from them during the evil regime of the old Sultan Abdul Hamid.

But neither the Turkish castle on the great rock nor the busy Greeks at Smyrna, 200 miles down beside the sea, occupied our thoughts at that moment. It was near midday and my chief memory of the Black Castle of Opium is of the bunch of shallots that we had time to buy from a vendor on the dusty edge of the town almost in the shadow of the great height. Lambert and Rogers quickly converted the shallots into part of a delicious lunch. On this journey they often gave us three courses—soup and entrée, which they served to us in due succession on the top of our plates, and sweets, for which we turned the plates over and ate from the backs.

Lambert's stories enlivened the meals. Some of them were fruits of his recent attachment to the Light Horse as their official artist in Sinai[2] and Palestine. He never tired—nor did we—of the description of some earlier British expedition to close some wells in Egypt as told, apparently at Shepheard's or the Ghezireh Club, by an

---

[2] Lambert had not been present during the Sinai campaign, but he made sketches there afterwards for his "Romani", and other pictures. He was present during part of the campaign in Palestine.

BRILLIANT WILDFLOWERS NEAR GABA TEPE,
February 1919.   *G1750*

NO. 1 OUTPOST NEAR THE SHORE
north of Walker's Ridge. It looks up at The Nek and Baby 700, which were held
throughout the campaign (after the first day) by the Turks.   *G1814*

SEDDEL BAHR AND THE HARBOUR
at "V" Beach. The *River Clyde*, the *Massena* and another French ship sunk for
a breakwater; in the distance, dimly seen, is the southern entrance of
the Straits.   *G1857*

THE OLIVE-TREES AT THE TOMMIES' TRENCH.
On the horizon on the extreme right is seen the end of the northern shoulder of
Achi Baba.   *G2041 A*

ALL THAT WAS LEFT OF KRITHIA.
The main street in 1919.   *G2057*

THE SUMMIT OF THE RAILWAY
through the Taurus Mountains at Bozanti.   *G2140*

THE T
Troops crowded into trucks for
Deaths from ac

EMOBILISING.
urus tunnels near Adana.
were frequent.   G2134

VIEW FROM THE MISSION'S TRUCK
at a tunnel entrance in the Taurus.   G2145

HADSCHKIRI, NEAR THE FAMOUS CILICIAN GATES.
In the middle distance is the German cemetery. At this place was also a
cemetery with the graves of twelve or more British, Australian and New Zealand
prisoners.   *G2130*

ON TO THE CILICIAN PLAIN.
The old road, route of so many armies, passes through the Cilician Gates, but the
railway veers down the ridge west of them and emerges on to the plain near
Dorak.   *G2131*

A BRITISH PATROL,
and demobilised Turkish soldiers, in Adana. The "Tommies" were well liked in
the Levant.   G2152

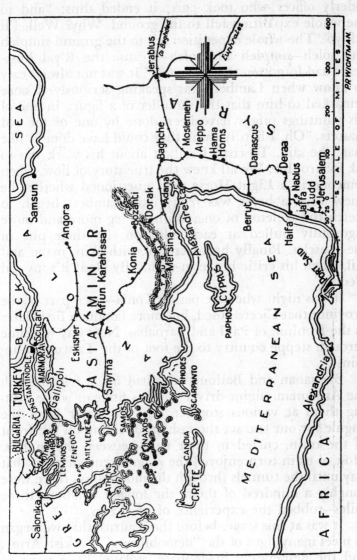

THE TAURUS RAILWAY AND ITS SOUTHERN EXTENSIONS

PR WIGHTMAN

elderly officer who took part; it ended thus: "and so the whole exp'dition fell to the ground. Why? Well, I'll tell yo'. The whole expedition fell to the ground simpleh and soleh—*simp*leh and *sol*eh—b'cause the R'yal Engineers had forgotten the spannahs!" It was not always easy to know when Lambert was speaking seriously. I once remarked to him that the shoulder of a figure in one of his paintings might have been done by one of the old masters. "Oh, I hardly think they could have done it like that," he said. To chaff Lambert about his work was to ask for trouble. We all knew the true story of how, when someone in a Light Horse mess questioned whether he knew what a horse was *really* like, Lambert began to sketch the skeleton of one. With his leg more and more vigorously pulled at each addition, he then put in the muscles. Finally he covered it with skin, mane and tail, when his critic broke in with: "By God! it's my old Neddy."

It was night when we passed Konia—once part of the province that Cicero ruled, but more famous a little later as the Iconium of Paul and Barnabas. Next day we came through steppe country to the foot of the Taurus Mountains.

Buchanan and Balfour, who had made friends with the Armenian engine-driver and his fireman while visiting them at various stops to beg hot water from the engine for our tea, set the fashion of riding on the front of the train, curled in their rugs between the buffers. Most of us in turn enjoyed the magnificent views in that way until the tunnels through the mountains—there were roughly a hundred of them, the longest of about three miles—robbed the experience of its charm.

It was at this stage, before the Taurus, that we began to meet many signs of the "demobilising" Turkish Army, and the desperately inadequate, isolated little posts of British or Indian troops that were supposed to be supervising and enforcing the demobilisation. Once or twice a day we met trains similar to our own but going the other way and literally tasselled with Turkish soldiers; they overflowed from every carriage, out of the windows, sometimes on the steps and even the roofs. We were told that men had been brushed off and killed in the tunnels. At one or two centres we saw Turkish officers—stalwart fellows, well enough dressed, one of them a fair, red-haired youngster directing the men from the train, and doubtless telling them where to pile their arms for handing over to the Allies.

But a cheerful British officer lad, Lieutenant Mackinnon, whom we found with his lonely handful of Indians, anything from 50 to 100 miles from the next similar post, doing his best to look as if his orders must be obeyed, told us that he could really do little more than bluff, outnumbered as he was, perhaps 100 to one, by the retiring Turks. And two old Anzac friends whom I met next day at Adana, Lieutenant-Colonel W. H. Hastings and Major W. H. Cunningham—who as captains had been with Malone on Chunuk Bair, Cunningham in the advanced trench—confirmed Mackinnon's statement. They were now the commander and second-in-command of the 92nd Punjabis; and from what they and Mackinnon told us it seemed that the Turks were now playing something of a game with the Allies. Instead of being demobilised, part of the retiring army, or at least part of its weapons and equipment, was being sent into the interior of Asia Minor, possibly for future use. A British officer had been sent after them to demand that a battery of guns which had gone thither should be handed over. He found the Turks very polite, but they did not give him the guns and he had no force with which to take them. Two thousand miles away a British Prime Minister was talking of freeing part of Turkey from the Turks but was not game to ask the tired British people to provide the men or money for doing it.

From Eregli (the Turkish version of the ancient

Heracleia) the train climbed the Taurus Mountains, heading for the famous Cilician Gates, one of the few passes in this rugged barrier. We were soon up to 4500 feet. Through gorges, and crawling and winding from tunnel to tunnel, we reached, about 4 o'clock one afternoon, if I remember rightly, a bleak stopping place, high up in the mountains beyond Bozanti: Hadschkiri. The tunnel from which our train had just emerged was one of the last to be completed, and an English officer on the railway platform told me that some Australian prisoners had been among the men working in the tunnel, and that the graves of some were in a cemetery not far above the railway. He pointed the way to me; beyond was a much more prominent German cemetery, standing out with its circular stone wall. Our engine was puffing and blowing, but had to take in water; so I scrambled 200 yards along the line, and then 200 up the hill to the right—and there, derelict and overgrown with grass, were a dozen or twenty graves: "Pte. B. Calcutt, 14 Bn., A.I.F., died 1/1/17"; "Kightley, Auckland Bn., N.Z., died 25/10/16"; and a few names of British soldiers also legible.[3] The British officer at Hadschkiri, to whom I hurried back after photographing the graves, told us that, by comparison with other prisoners, those working on the Taurus tunnels were not badly treated; the work was being done by a Swiss company. Other prisoners suffered, not by cruelty so much as by the casual, neglectful methods of the Turks, and the task on the tunnels was generally preferred.

I shall not attempt here to describe the great Cilician Gates now by-passed by a detour of the railway, but through which so many of the greatest leaders of all ages

---

[3] Calcutt's name appeared to me to be inscribed as "Pte I. Calcutt, 17 Bn", but the carving or painting had weathered. An inquiry of his father later showed that he had been duly informed that Pte Brendon Calcutt was buried at Hadschkiri; he had been wounded in the Battle of Sari Bair on Gallipoli. His brother, Lance-Corporal Gerald Calcutt, 7th Bn, A.I.F., had been killed at Anzac on 24th May 1915.

passed their armies towards Europe or Asia—whichever was the bait that drew them. Our train carried us, with an ease unknown until the previous year, down to the plain which was spread like a map below. There, at Adana, twenty miles from St Paul's city of Tarsus, we were able to stretch our legs visiting the shops, where for the first time I saw a potter's wheel in ceaseless use, and the bazaar. The crowds in the streets were strangely sprinkled through by *poilus* in French khaki and helmets, but who spoke English with an American accent, and who proved to be Armenians, enlisted, if I remember rightly, in the French Foreign Legion. We heard that they were causing some headaches to the British control, who, having come to Turkey with a duty of protecting the Armenians against the Turks, found themselves at that time and place more worried as to how to protect the inhabitants against some of these Armenians. The Armenians were not popular with our army, or, apparently, with any westerners who mixed with them for long—but they had their reasons. Adana had been largely an Armenian town until 1909 when a great massacre of them happened there; and no one who had studied the attempts by some Turkish leaders to exterminate this people, and the dreadful means used before and during the war, could wonder at the Armenians' ruthlessness or, what was much harder for us outsiders to tolerate, their shrillness.

A curious sight in this half-modern town was, in the open market, the counterpart of our "chemist and pharmacist". His whole stock lay on a tray, perhaps three feet square, placed on a trestle in front of him amid the constant stir of the crowd circulating through the sellers of vegetables, professional letter-writers, water sellers and others. Our druggist's tray was divided into small squares by low wooden partitions, and in each square was a tiny heap of some commodity—small dry leaves, powdered bark, and other substances doubtless of medical significance, at any rate psychological, but resembling chalk, brick dust, salt, yellow ochre and so forth. As each patient came to him he weighed out in a pair of very light brass scales an infinitesimal dose of one or more of his drugs and solemnly handed it out in return for apparently good cash. The string of his patients was constant, and we stood fascinated behind him, especially when once—and only once—he raised his eyes to us with a wicked confiding twinkle and a flash of smile which we all interpreted as: "You and I know this is humbug, but it does them good and me good, and you won't give away the show."

I don't know whether it was while we watched him, or when we were in the thronged streets, but at some time that day a hand stole into and out of my right-hand trouser pocket without my observing it and got away with two golden sovereigns—the only two that I took from the £50 in my money-belt between England and Australia. Quite illogically, we all strongly resented the fact that in the Middle East the English pound notes (they called them "Bradburys" from the signature in the corner) had fallen in value since 1914—though they still stood astonishingly high; and, still more illogically, I was determined not to leave there any good British gold if it could be avoided. But as we might need some supplies in a hurry I had transferred £2 to my pocket that day, and probably my uniform served as a "good mark".

At Bagtsche, beyond Adana, our train began to climb the second great range, Amanus, and then, rounding at about forty miles' radius the extreme western angle of the Mediterranean (at Alexandretta), headed south to the Syrian plain at Aleppo. Aleppo is a city of a quarter of a million people; and, as at Hama and Homs, the two big towns of about a quarter of its size that we came on successively south of it, the civil city appears to have grown up about the foot of the citadel. In Aleppo the citadel lies on a hump rising from the midst of the city, and said to be artificial—there is a similar hump, 130 feet high, in Hama, but the citadel that once stood there has vanished. The Crusaders fought in all these places, and at Aleppo we met, to our great surprise and pleasure, the first signs of an army that had come as far as the Crusaders —the split red-and-white pennant outside a corps headquarters in which I found Sir Harry Chauvel, the lieutenant-general commanding the A.I.F. in the Middle East who was acting here as the most advanced representative of Allenby's army. I found that he had the latest news of Mustafa Kemal, who had taken over from Liman von Sanders the command of the Turkish armies retiring from Palestine and Syria and had proved a stubborn and difficult man to deal with in the "enforcement" of the Armistice terms. Chauvel also had initial difficulty with the Arabs, who had suddenly rushed into Aleppo on the heels of the retreating Turks and just ahead of the British cavalry. Even when we were there Arab staff officers, with their apparently British-made khaki uniforms and gorget patches—but with white Arab burnouses, cloak and hood, held on their heads by circlets— seemed everywhere. Chauvel did not like the unreliable Arab methods; few regular soldiers did; and perhaps he underestimated the military value of their achievement almost as much as, I suspect, some others have overestimated it. But this wise, good and considerate commander was far from the stupid martinet that readers of Lawrence's *Seven Pillars of Wisdom* might infer or whom his artist has lampooned.

At Chauvel's headquarters our cook, George Lambert, was among clean linen, wine glasses and serviettes again, and next day his job in our mess-truck ended. After passing down the valley between Lebanon and Anti-Lebanon, through the dry, dead, overgrown stubble of ancient cities, which looked as though adders and scorpions lurked in every crevice, past the lovely pillars of Baalbek, we came to Rayak Junction, where the broad-gauge line from Constantinople runs up against the French-

Syrian narrow-gauge line from Beirut to Damascus, and ends. We had had warnings that our two cattle-trucks might be requisitioned and ourselves transferred to a passenger compartment, but by scrawling the Mission's name in large letters outside the trucks, by pleading the amount and value of our baggage, and chiefly, I am sure, by the friendliness and kindness of our British friends along the railway, we had managed to retain them until then. But here was a break of gauge, and we had to transfer to a couple of compartments on the narrow-gauge line which quickly brought us to Damascus.

There all roughing it—if the luxury in which we had slept and, thanks to Lambert and Rogers, eaten can be so mistermed—ended. In that wonderful oasis of luscious green and blossom against pink desert under the eternal snow of Mount Hermon, we were driven by cabs to our hotel near the Barada River. Next day saw us in train for Jerusalem with only one hitch, at the broken bridge across the Yarmuk chasm, where about thirty Egyptian porters carried the Mission's baggage without loss along the airy track to another train beyond the break. Jerusalem, with its exquisite mosque and the sickening venality of most of the human element around that and other shrines—largely the poor relations of the great Christian churches—absorbed us for a day; and the next train carried us in one night's sleep over the coastal plain and Sinai Desert which had taken Murray's and Allenby's army—with our Light Horse most of the time as its advanced troops—two years to win.

The Light Horse was back in Egypt by now, or on its way to Australia. But as the sun set that evening, along a track near the railway we saw a handful of tall, thin fellows, with slouch hats, and pipes, and sleeveless vests showing their long bare arms, riding quietly to some camp or village. I could have sworn they were light horsemen, but someone told me they were British engineers, who had adopted the Australian felt hat. If so, they were also unquestionably adopting the Australian manner. My thoughts flew back to the weeks before the Gallipoli Campaign when many of our troops, the Light Horse and Artillery foremost among them, were consciously imitating the British uniform and manner. It had been the worship of the new soldier for the veteran, and apparently the wheel had turned full circle.

It was not till next morning when the train sped through the teeming Nile Delta that we really encountered any of the Light Horse regiments which in March 1916 after Gallipoli, had stayed in the Middle East. We had lately heard that riots threatening the lives of Europeans had broken out in Cairo and other towns, and the sailing of the Light Horse and New Zealand Mounted Rifles on their longed-for voyage home had been interrupted, embarkation suddenly countermanded, and a number of regiments told off to picket the towns and railways. They cheerfully gave up the dream of their immediate homecoming. Never did I see morale more clearly expressed in the faces and behaviour of troops than among those laughing, confident, clean-looking youngsters whose little groups were camped on or beside the railway platforms that swam past.

In Cairo, Hector Dinning, of the Australian War Records Section, told us that he had as yet no word of the shipment of our relics from Gallipoli. He was getting for the memorial museum one of the pontoons in which the Turks—after dragging it across Sinai—tried to cross the Suez Canal in 1915, and a light railway engine since used by us on one of the desert railways; and the section appeared to have secured its strangest relic, a mosaic that had formed the floor at one time of a small ancient Christian church but more recently of a Turkish trench in that graveyard of forgotten civilisation, the border area of Sinai and Palestine. The mosaic was, from its inscription, at first thought to be the tomb of St George and had been saved from oblivion largely by the enthu-

siasm of Chaplain Maitland Woods. Rumour had it that
Woods telegraphed in great excitement to the D.A. and
Q.M.G. of his division: "Have found grave of Saint
George at Shellal." That officer (who had heard of the
find) signalled back: "Can't trace this man. Wire regimental number and unit." The George whose little
church was thus disturbed was not the dragon-slayer but
a good priest of the diocese of Gaza. Nevertheless, when
Maitland Woods and Anzac engineers, using methods
recommended by archaeologists in Cairo, had packed the
mosaic without losing one stone, powerful objections were
made by some archaeologists in Great Britain to its transfer to the Antipodes; and it was only the determined
fight put up by young Major Treloar in the War
Trophies Committee in London and the support of Senator Pearce in Australia that secured permission for shipping it. The New Zealand commanders generously agreed
to its going to some place in Australia where it would be
accessible to New Zealanders.

On 2nd April 1919, saying good-bye on Cairo railway
station to Wilkins, who had duties in England, and Lambert, who, in spite of ill-health, was determined to make
for the memorial more sketches in Sinai, we embarked
in the *Kildonan Castle,* a corner of whose saloon became
for the next four weeks the office in which the Mission
worked on its papers for the war history and also of the
museum, of which I was to act as director until more
permanent arrangements were made.

Chapter
• XXIII •

THE FUTURE
OF ANZAC

THE final part of the report on the Gallipoli graves and the future treatment of the Anzac area was sent from Constantinople. It informed the Australian Government and our representative on the War Graves Commission in London that Hughes had already located and surveyed 4700 graves[1] and others were still being found; that he would practically have finished this part of his task in five weeks from that time and would then go to Helles to help a British officer to locate Australian graves there. Large wooden temporary crosses were being inscribed and were to be erected over every grave found. The putting up of the crosses, making up of mounds, and fencing, would then presumably be carried out by fatigue parties of British troops while waiting for demobilisation.

As the temporary work on the graves and cemeteries was so soon to be begun, I urged that the Australian Government should as soon as possible express its wish as to whether graves should be retained in their present positions, and men's remains be buried where they lay, or whether graves and remains should be concentrated in a few of the large existing cemeteries. I had already recommended the former system and I now urged that this could well be carried out at Anzac provided that the whole of that area was vested in the Imperial War Graves Commission. At Helles, where the ground occupied by the Allies had been much larger and the country was agricultural and not wild scrub as at Anzac, this method

1 These would include British, New Zealand and other graves.

325

might not be possible; in any case the decision as to Helles obviously rested with the British whose forces and losses there had been immensely greater than ours. If they retained a number of separate cemeteries, then the Australians in that region should be buried behind the Tommies' Trench and the Redoubt Line, where most Australians fell.

I also urged several reasons why the work on the graves should be completed quickly. As on all battle-fields, the remains of the dead lay scattered everywhere until burial, and it would be inexpressibly distressing for their relations to see Anzac or Helles in their then con-dition. The Turkish dead also, I urged, should be buried before visitors were allowed in the area. But the Graves Registration Unit on Gallipoli seemed to me far too small and short of labour even for its own task.

I may here add what was not in the report, that the officer in local charge,[2] a major of the 29th Division, seemed rather old for the requirements of such a job. His seniority and service probably justified him in ex-pecting some comfort, and at Kilid Bahr he told me that he had no intention of going on horseback to Helles, to rough it and sleep on the ground. But Hughes and his men, from a sense of obligation to their old comrades and the people at home, were riding and working in all weathers, and camping as best they could, and had prac-tically finished the finding of graves at Anzac at a time when the work seemed little more than begun at Helles, and at Suvla had not started. Yet Hughes and Bigg-Wither, though the requests of the Australian and New Zealand governments were responsible for their presence on Gallipoli, were actually only part of the small staff of the Graves Unit there; Bigg-Wither was employed in administering his headquarters, and Hughes, as soon as he had completed the first stage at Anzac, would probably be charged with the British work at Suvla.

---

[2] Not Major R. C. Everett, the assistant director for the Middle East.

It was not my duty to report on any but Australian interests, but they were clearly involved here. I accordingly represented that the British portion of the Unit was "not a quarter large enough to cope with the work in reasonable time". Hughes and Bigg-Wither, I urged, should be made representatives of their Dominions on the Graves Registration organisation, responsible to their respective governments for the work in the Middle East. The task at Anzac would involve not only establishing the cemeteries but converting the tracks into roads and paths for supplies and, ultimately, for visitors; and, at Hughes' suggestion, I asked that he should be given, not fatigue parties of British troops awaiting demobilisation, who were unsuitable for these tasks and probably felt they had not enlisted for them, but, say, 100 Macedonian or Egyptian labourers. Finally, as Hughes intended to take up civil employment in Egypt, I suggested that he should then be made Australian representative on the eastern section of the Imperial War Graves Commission, with the duty of visiting once yearly all cemeteries in Palestine, Egypt and Gallipoli on behalf of the Australian Government.

This report,[3] like the first, envisaged the whole Anzac area as one big graveyard, which would probably be visited by thousands of Australians and others yearly, and in which the dead, merely by being buried where they fell, or where their comrades had carried them, would commemorate their achievement better than any inscription. Thus anyone standing by the graves on Baby 700, or Quinn's, or The Nek, or Chunuk Bair, or the line of them on Pine Ridge—especially if he knew the story of the campaign—could not fail to grasp something of what these men, and indeed those opposed to them, had done and were. After perhaps all great wars—certainly after all modern ones—soldiers and relatives and, later, interested visitors have flowed to the battlefields; and one's mind

---

[3] It is given in full in *Appendix V*.

could see Anzac, the most striking battlefield of that war, being the goal of pilgrimages from Britain and the Anzac countries, a calling place on Mediterranean tours, a regular stopping place for those who visited Egypt and the Holy Land and thence made their way by Damascus and the Taurus to Asia Minor, Constantinople and Greece. Here was a battlefield in which, though the trenches could not be preserved—as was being done in some parts of France—the graves themselves would mark the front line and even the farthest lines reached in the struggle, so heroic on both sides.

For Anzac this plan commended itself to all of us, Hughes, Wilkins, and Box and the War Graves Commission, and the work went ahead with astonishing speed. Whether my report affected the immediate measures I have no direct knowledge; but nine days after it was handed to G.H.Q. Hughes was promised fifty Greek and Turkish labourers instead of the troops, while another party under a special officer was to arrive for Chunuk Bair, a sub-section of the Graves Unit was sent to begin work at Suvla, and two additional officers with parties of Greeks and Turks were being sent to Helles. Hughes asked that the ground covered by Australian troops at Helles should be left untouched until he visited it. The British at Helles eventually concentrated their many cemeteries into six; as it happened, one of these had originally been established just behind the rearmost of the two Redoubt trenches dug by our 2nd Brigade in its famous advance, actually very near to M'Cay's little headquarters. Hughes wrote to me in November 1919 that all the Australian remains had been discovered and were buried there "practically where Colonel Gartside was buried".[4] Only a few were identified as he was—probably

---

4 Lieutenant-Colonel Gartside, a man of 53 years, an orchardist of Castlemaine, Victoria, was commanding the 7th in the advance. He is said to have been rising to lead one of the final rushes, saying "Come on boys, I know it's deadly, but we must get on," when he was hit in the abdomen by machine-gun bullets.

200 or more are among the unidentified men whose graves are here, but as six other cemeteries were afterwards transferred to this place the nameless Australians lie among some 1200 of their British comrades whose names also are unknown.[5]

Some time after our Mission left, the cemeteries were visited by the War Graves Commission's principal architect for that region, Sir John Burnet, and his assistants, Captains D. Raeburn and G. S. Keesing (an Australian). They conferred with Hughes and others at the cemeteries, approved the general plans, and began work on the details. Meanwhile the two cabled reports on our Mission had reached Alan Box in London and the Australian Government. Box has since told me that the account given of Hughes' work, and the knowledge that such a man was on the spot, greatly reassured Sir Fabian Ware (Vice-Chairman of the Commission) and himself, both of whom were deeply disturbed by the risks to these cemeteries and most anxious to get them finished and protected. Hughes was called to England, and Box induced the Australian Government—which in this matter was guided almost entirely by him—to suggest that an Australian and New Zealand staff should undertake the construction, on behalf of the Empire, of the Gallipoli graveyards. Sir Fabian Ware and New Zealand supported the proposal. When it was put to the Commission in session, Winston Churchill, then Secretary of State for War, at first saw difficulties—the Anzacs were not the only forces on Gallipoli. Edward, Prince of Wales, in the chair, was hesitant. But Winston finally gave way and, as always when he does so, gave way handsomely. When next Hughes wrote to me, in November 1919, he was back in

---

5 Those Australians who are buried, but not named, in this cemetery are, together with others missing in this area, commemorated by name on the great British memorial near Cape Helles lighthouse. The New Zealanders who fell in this area are largely buried at the Twelve Trees Cemetery near which they fought, and their missing are commemorated at that cemetery. The Pink Farm Cemetery is close to the slight dip where was the collecting station at which I saw Major Cass.

Gallipoli as lieutenant-colonel and Director of Works, in control of the Commission's task there—the establishment and maintenance "in perpetuity" of all the cemeteries, on which the preliminary work of the Graves Registration Unit would soon be complete. He had been allowed to select and take out his staff comprising ten officers and five sergeants, almost all Australians, and a dozen civilian experts and clerks, mostly English.[6]

The Graves Commission had picked a forceful man. Cyril Emerson Hughes, then twenty-eight years old, was a Tasmanian, born at Launceston, educated at the Grammar School there and at Sydney and by profession a civil engineer and surveyor. At Anzac he had eventually transferred from the Light Horse to the Engineers, but at that stage was for the second time sent away sick. In Egypt, finding himself in danger of being invalided to Australia, he managed to get lost for the time being in a company of the British Royal Engineers, and eventually—somehow—to rejoin the Light Horse. In the 1st Field Squadron he won a commission and a Military Cross and, though ultimately pronounced by a medical board to be unfit for active service, was still actively engaged in the Suez Canal zone when the opportunity came for him to go to Gallipoli with the Graves Registration Unit.

And now when, eight months after our Mission's visit, Hughes was in control of the Commission's work in Gallipoli there was a singular absence of hesitation or delay. His methods were breezy and effective. The mixed Turkish, Greek, and White Russian working party that had arrived after we left could not (he told me in his letter) speak English, "but my mixture of Arabic, Turkish and Greek seems to impress them, and the fact that I'm an

---

[6] Captain Keesing, the assistant architect, had to return to his practice in Australia; Captain Raeburn took his place at Anzac. Captain Bigg-Wither also was on the staff for a time. Sir John Burnet and Captain Keesing on return to London had, I believe, confirmed the opinion that I had expressed as to the work of Hughes.

Australian is better still". He placed his headquarters in huts at Kilia Liman, made roads for his Thornycroft lorries, drew tools and wire from the Turkish dump at Ak Bashi Liman, put in pumps and a sawmill, developed for monumental stone an old quarry on the Straits' side at Ulgar Dere—stone of "the same class," notes Mr Pemberton, "as that of which the Homeric walls of Troy were built." When the lorries could not get the stone over the roads, he bought a motor-caique and built a slip to repair it on, loaded the stone on barges, and hauled it round to Anzac by sea, built a pier under shelter of the old wreck of the *Milo* at North Beach, and lifted the stone from there by an aerial ropeway to near Baby 700 and thence south along Second Ridge to Lone Pine and other posts. "Thank goodness," he said, "all my fellows can do about fifteen things."

Meanwhile at Anzac the Graves Unit had erected the temporary wooden crosses in the cemeteries and wherever the bodies of the dead lay. On Anzac Day 1920 for the first time a considerable party of visitors—British civilians and soldiers from Kilia and Chanak—drove out on the Commission's five trucks and cars to Hughes' old camp, and then walking over that ridge towards Second Ridge across the valley, came in sight of the graves and cemeteries of Anzac as we had hoped some day to see them. There were the Anzacs still, as in 1915. "One thought of that Sunday five years ago," Hughes wrote. "You could see the handful of men who pushed down Owen's Gully . . . the little white crosses down on the slope of Pine Ridge and of Legge Valley. . . . How they must have fought down there. . . . Right over Lone Pine we went, past Colonel Onslow Thompson's grave and down Bridges' Road, with the 3rd Battalion cemetery on our left and the 4th just on the right . . ." and so on down to the Beach where they held their memorial service.

But that was probably the only formal occasion on

331

which the graves were seen just as we had envisaged them. The final design of the cemeteries rested with the architects, and after careful inspection Hughes and Raeburn concluded that the isolated graves and also some of the cemeteries, which had been endangered by the rush of rain in the recent winter, could not well be maintained. Accordingly the scheme we had suggested was modified though its principle was maintained; the men whose bodies or graves were found at Baby 700, The Nek, the terrible slopes about The Farm, Chunuk Bair, Hill 60, and the remains from No-man's-land in front of Quinn's and other posts, were gathered each in some safe space at or near which most of the bodies were found. At Old Anzac six of these cemeteries were made along, or ahead of, the old front line, and nearly all the original cemeteries also remained, making a total of twenty-two. North of Old Anzac, in the area of the August offensive (where the relics of the troops, largely British, and the little cemeteries had been sprinkled amid wild gullies and slopes) front-line cemeteries were made only at Chunuk Bair, The Apex, The Farm and Hill 60; and at Suvla two, at Chocolate Hill and the Asmak watercourse.[7] The many other cemeteries on the flats north of Old Anzac and at Suvla were concentrated in a few—four at Anzac and two at Suvla—not far from the beaches. Eventually there were 29 cemeteries at Anzac (containing 4300 graves), 7 at Helles (5900 graves), 4 at Suvla (4300 graves). Only one isolated grave was preserved, that of Lieutenant-Colonel Doughty Wylie, V.C., of the Royal Welsh Fusiliers, who was killed at Seddel Bahr leading the 29th Division's most difficult landing.

On these cemeteries, when Sir John Burnet and his assistants had delivered their plans, the work went quickly. Visitors were firmly kept away. "One old chap

---

[7] These two Suvla cemeteries give a general notion of the position of the old front line. The Asmak is not to be confused with the Asma Dere near Hill 60.

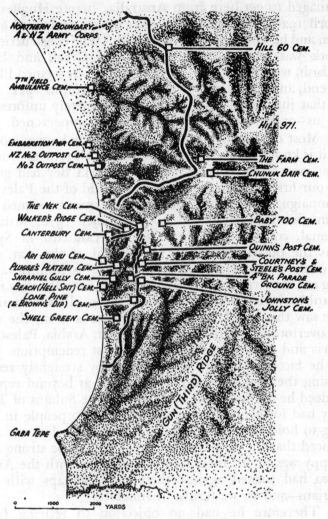

NORTHERN BOUNDARY of
A & NZ ARMY CORPS

HILL 60 CEM.

7TH FIELD
AMBULANCE CEM.

HILL 971.

EMBARKATION PIER CEM.
NZ No2 OUTPOST CEM.
No 2 OUTPOST CEM.

THE FARM CEM.

CHUNUK BAIR CEM.

THE NEK CEM.
WALKER'S RIDGE CEM.

CANTERBURY CEM.

BABY 700 CEM.

QUINN'S POST CEM.

ARI BURNU CEM.
PLUGGE'S PLATEAU CEM.
SHRAPNEL GULLY CEM.
BEACH (HELL SPIT) CEM.
LONE PINE
(& BROWN'S DIP) CEM.
SHELL GREEN CEM.

COURTNEY'S &
STEELE'S POST CEM.
4TH BN. PARADE
GROUND CEM.

JOHNSTON'S
JOLLY CEM.

GUN (THIRD) RIDGE

GABA TEPE

0   1000   2000 YARDS

THE ANZAC CEMETERIES

*This shows the completed scheme. The black line marks
the Anzac Corps front at the end of the campaign.*

managed to get here from Australia," wrote Hughes, in April 1920, "looking for his son's grave; we looked after him and he's pushed off to Italy now." The constructional work was given to contractors, first Greek and later British, working under the Commission. It seemed likely to end, and the stream of pilgrims to begin, in 1922. But at that juncture a turn of events, completely unforeseen by us—or by the British Government—supervened.

Most of the story has become publicly known—so far as it is known—only long afterwards. It all centres around that same Mustafa Kemal of whom Zeki Bey had given us our first vivid impression. By the end of the Palestine campaign, when the Sultan's Government signed an armistice in Lemnos on 30th October 1918, Mustafa Kemal, commanding the Turkish rearguard in Syria, was the outstanding Turkish general of the war, and Liman von Sanders handed over control to him. In carrying out the Armistice terms he proved, from the very first, a stubborn, determined opponent of the Allies' demands.[8] He saw that the Turkish Empire—that is to say the rule or overlordship of the Sultan in Egypt, Arabia, Palestine, Syria and Mesopotamia—had gone past redemption. Just as he faced each crisis in Gallipoli by straightly recognising the facts, he accepted that loss as beyond repair; indeed he did not want to repair it. The Sultans of Turkey had for generations wasted their own people in trying to hold these misgoverned appendages. He was convinced that the only way for the Turks to be strong and happy was to cut their losses—have done with the Arabs who had turned against them, and perhaps with the Syrians—and to westernise themselves.

Therefore he had no objection to retiring from

---

[8] In this account I have relied largely on H. C. Armstrong's brilliant biography of Mustafa Kemal, *Grey Wolf*; on *Briton and Turk*, by Philip Graves; and to a less degree on *Turkey Faces West*, by Halide Edib. So far as concerns the events at the Dardanelles during this crisis I have been guided also by T. J. Pemberton's *Gallipoli Today*, and by Colonel Hughes' letters to me at the time.

Lebanon; but he was determined that not a foot of Turkey itself should be given up. From the first he seems to have felt that this would have to be fought for; or at all events the Turks must show themselves to be in a position to fight for it. Accordingly he made every delay that he could in the carrying out of the Armistice terms so far as they affected his withdrawing and demobilising troops. He refused to give up the vital port of Alexandretta until threatened with an armed landing. He set on foot the local creation of committees of resistance, and sent officers into the Taurus Mountains with arms to organise guerilla bands. In December 1918 he was summoned to Constantinople by Turkish leaders who wanted to put more backbone into the new Sultan, who seemed simply the tool of the Allies. But in Asia Minor, doubtless by his instructions, the same tactics continued. However, Allenby was not an opponent to be trifled with; and we now know that it was to force the Sultan to end these prevarications that the British leader hurried to Constantinople (where Wilkins and I saw him in February). The British now had their way—the Sultan, his ministers and parliament, and indeed the exhausted Turkish people, were for peace at any price. Cilicia including Adana soon afterwards was occupied by the French. In the weeks when we were at Anzac and Constantinople Mustafa Kemal, disappointed and resentful after futile negotiations with a spineless sovereign and politicians, was living privately in the suburbs, chafing at inaction. The British were sending "dangerous" opponents to temporary internment in Malta, and he was on their list of those likely to be sent thither.

Nevertheless in May in Anatolia the demobilisation of troops and handing over of arms, of which we noticed the early difficulties in the Taurus, was still miscarrying to such an extent that the Sultan decided to send some personal representative to force the performance of the Armistice terms. The Grand Vizier believed that Mustafa Kemal was the man to go—"he is a gentleman," it was said, "he can be trusted." Against their earlier judgment, British and Sultan were persuaded, and Mustafa Kemal was sent. He sailed to Samsun, 400 miles along the Black Sea coast, 200 miles farther back than Angora. Before he arrived there the Grand Vizier heard that he planned resistance, and orders were sent to intercept him, but too late. From Samsun he moved his headquarters sixty miles inland where the hated English could not get at him; and there, under pretext of defending from them both the Sultan and his country, he set about organising all Turkey for resistance.

It was high time for him to do so if Turkey was to be kept for the Turks. Even we in our few days at Constantinople had seen how the Greeks longed to regain that great city; at the time of our visit it was announced by the Allies that Constantinople was to be left to Turkey. But the Greeks were hopeful of obtaining by the peace-terms at least their ancient foothold at Smyrna and along the western coast of Asia Minor; Smyrna had been the bait held out when the great Greek leader, Venizelos, brought his people at last into the war on the Allies' side in 1917; part of the bait for Italy had been a similar foothold farther south. Against the will of their Allies the Italians had now taken this. Venizelos was urging the Allies' peace conference at Versailles to give him Smyrna, and at this juncture, probably fearing that the Italians might any day occupy Smyrna also, the Allied governments agreed to the landing of a Greek force there.

This was the last news that Kemal had heard before leaving Constantinople. He was now convinced that the Turks must fight if the nation was to survive. From levies, and regular troops from the East, he organised an army and called representatives of all Turkey to a congress at Sivas, farther inland and therefore less open to interference, to discuss the nation's defence. The Sultan had by then dismissed him; but though many of those he gathered were suspicious of his intentions and opposed to breaking with the Sultan, the actions of the British Government under Lloyd George often helped him at crucial moments, and so did those of the Greeks. War between Middle Eastern nations was always an affair of murder, rape, pillage, burnings and massacres on both sides. At Smyrna shots fired by Turks at the Greek landing had set off the Greeks, and at once the flames of enthusiasm in Kemal's cause leapt higher. Encouragement given by the Sultan, and apparently in a bad moment by the British, to the wild Kurdish tribes to launch attacks upon Kemal and the congress at Sivas, sent the national feeling still higher. The congress had laid down in the "Pact of Sivas" its basic terms for peace; and, after new elections, most of its members returned to parliament in Constantinople, where, in January 1920, the "Pact" was published. Its basic principle was that all parts of the Turkish Empire containing a Turkish majority must be left to the Turks. The Allies tried to quieten feeling by the announcement that under their terms Turkey would not have to give up Constantinople.

But with Turks now drilling, seizing arms from dumps, ignoring Allied orders, insulting and even raiding Allied troops, the Allies had at last to act strongly. As politicians and troops were eager for quick demobilisation, garrisons had been thinned or withdrawn; only at Constantinople could strong force be exerted. So they occupied the capital, closed parliament, and interned many leaders in Malta. Mustafa Kemal had warned his congress against going to the capital, and he himself had stayed at Angora. Now many Turkish leaders fled to him. The Sultan, still seeing in British support the only hope for himself, tried to crush him by a religious war.

But again just at this time fuel was added to the nationalistic furnace. The Greeks were pushing farther; and Mr Lloyd George and his colleagues at Versailles presented the Sultan with their terms of peace—known as the "Treaty" of Sèvres. This would carve Turkey into pieces—and the announcement gave Mustafa Kemal the reaction that he needed to stir the National Assembly which he had now rallied at Angora. His troops smashed the Kurds, beat the Sultan's, killed a French garrison in the Taurus, temporarily stopped the Greeks, forced the British handful in sheer prudence to withdraw from Eski-schehir, and came up against the British garrisons near the Marmora. The French already repented the terms they had laid down—one French leader hinted they were as brittle as other Sèvres ware. By that time, May 1920, French, British and Italians had too few troops in Asia Minor to deal with the Turks. When at this stage Veni-zelos offered the help of the Greek army Lloyd George and his colleagues rashly, as events proved, accepted it.

Venizelos was thrown out at the Greek elections and later banished, but his successors maintained the army at Smyrna and in July 1921 attacked. Mustafa Kemal had to order withdrawal almost to Angora; but there in August, now as commander-in-chief and with powers of a dictator, in a twenty-two days' battle on the Sakaria River he forced them back. Exactly a year later he struck the Greeks again on the line to which they had re-tired at Afiun Kara Hissar, and followed their rout to Smyrna, each side in turn pillaging and murdering right to the Smyrna water-front. On 9th September 1922 the city was taken; the Greek army climbed on its ships under the guns of the British fleet, which, however, could not protect the people on shore. The Greeks had also driven into European Turkey almost to Constantinople; for some time even Gallipoli had been policed by them. Mustafa Kemal now turned northwards to drive them out. The Marmora, the Bosporus, and the Straits stood between; but the French were now anxious to get out; they had practically made a separate peace with Mustafa Kemal and given up Cilicia. The Italians were no obstacle—they constantly went behind the backs of both their allies. And even the British had thinned their garrisons till they held Chanak with one weak battalion.

Mustafa Kemal did not want to fight the British. "They are a nation with character," he once said to a friend of Philip Graves. They seemed resolute. Lloyd George said they would fight for the freedom of the Straits. Winston Churchill was Secretary of State for the Colonies, and it was at this stage that the governments of the British Dominions received from London an apparently totally unexpected call for military help at the Dardanelles. According to a semi-official summary issued at the time, it invited the Dominions "to be represented by contingents in defence of interests for which they have already made enormous sacrifices, and of soil which is hallowed by immortal memories of the Anzacs". To say that they were astonished is to put the reaction mildly; the summons was a typical Churchillian gesture, of a kind that might succeed—once. In spite of embarrassment New Zealand replied next day that she would send a contingent; and Australia "was prepared, if circumstances required it, to send a contingent of Australian troops".[9] The British Government privately explained that it intended to insist on the Turks' discussing the issues at a conference. Mustafa Kemal faced the possibility that with an ill-equipped, half-organised army, and an exhausted people behind him, he might well be crushed. Apparently he decided to try bluffing his way through without fighting, but at that stage an offer to compromise reached him through the French. On September 29th, by an armistice arranged with General Harington at Mudania (on the southern shore of the Marmora), it was agreed that the Greeks should leave Turkey and a peace settlement should be discussed with the other Allies who, as soon

---

9 South Africa did not reply before this crisis passed. Canada asked if the Dominion Parliament should be summoned and the appeal discussed. The British Government did not desire this to be done.

as a satisfactory treaty was signed, would also withdraw
their forces from the country.

A conference was immediately held at Lausanne in
Switzerland. There Mustafa Kemal's chief-of-staff, Ismet
Pasha, Lord Curzon and Venizelos, in a tussle lasting till
July 1923, during which time the atmosphere at Chanak
was often electric,[10] fought out the terms. These left Turkey to the Turks but "demilitarised" the Dardanelles
and Bosphorus under a "Straits Commission" with a
Turkish president. Gallipoli was to be neutral ground.
Turkey gained a peace satisfactory to Mustafa Kemal, but
on no point did Lord Curzon stand more firmly than on
the demand of the Allies—especially Australia and
New Zealand—that the war cemeteries on the Peninsula
should be given to the War Graves Commission, representatives of both sides determining the areas and the
whole of Anzac being considered as one graveyard.

The work of completing the cemeteries had continued throughout the crisis, though for several months
little could be done owing to the melting away of the
Greek labourers while, on the other hand, British troops,
ships and guns poured into the Dardanelles. The Greeks
had already fled from Asia Minor; and, by a wise term
of the settlement in which Mustafa Kemal and Venizelos almost cordially co-operated, this withdrawal was
extended and made permanent in the form of a general
exchange of Greek and Turkish populations except in
Constantinople and western Thrace. Thus it came about
that, in these years while the cemeteries were being
finally established, the Gallipoli Peninsula and parts of
Asia Minor, which from the earliest dawn of western
civilisation had been largely Greek, became purely Turkish. A few months later, in October 1923, all Allied troops
also withdrew.

So Hughes, who began his task with working parties

---

[10] In Constantinople the Sultan was forced by Mustafa Kemal's police
into a final flight from his throne, escaping in a British warship.

of British troops, and then employed Greeks, Armenians and White Russians, finished it in Turk-administered (though neutral) territory with Italian masons and Turkish workers some of whom had fought at Anzac. Nurseries for trees and shrubs, including some from Australia and New Zealand, were established under a British expert from Kew Gardens. The intense cold of the winter of 1923 split many of the stone monuments and walls, but the trouble was cured by 1924, when as many as 300 men were at work, some of them living in our old dugouts at Shell Green and elsewhere.

By the end of 1924 the task was practically finished. The grave of each soldier whose name was known was marked by a low headstone. The unknown, of whom there were even more, especially in the new cemeteries in which the bodies that lay close around were collected, were buried among and beside the known; but often, owing to the difficulty of identifying the remains as those of any one body, they were marked by no headstone but covered only by the green lawn of the plot, the lines of these graves being sometimes marked by rosemary. Thus in some cemeteries, where there were few known graves, the plot of lawn itself, surrounded by plantation and partly by wall and memorial stone, was the cemetery.[11] The names of those whose individual graves were not known, and of those who were not found or who were buried at sea from the hospital ships or transports, were carved on stone memorials: those of New Zealanders on the walls of the cemetery nearest to which they fell and where they probably lie;[12] those of British and Indian soldiers on the beautiful monument at Cape Helles; and those of Australians at our main memorial at Lone Pine,

---

11 The same method was adopted at V.C. Corner Cemetery in France where, under a beautiful rectangular lawn, were laid many of the Australian dead from the battlefield of Fromelles.

12 This was the method that I recommended for the Australians, but it was not adopted in their case. I still think that it would be possible to record at each cemetery—or at least in a register at the Commission's office at Chanak—the names of those who are probably buried at each cemetery.

or else at Helles with the British. A New Zealand memorial was raised on Chunuk Bair. The Turks, who did not attach any comparable importance to the burial of their dead, cleared the battlefield by cremating the remains found after our dead had been gathered. Even today, it is said, the rain still uncovers some Turkish bones.

The Australian Prime Minister, Mr Bruce, visited the graves in 1924, and next year the pilgrimages began. In May 1925 arrived the *Ormonde* with 400 including the High Commissioner for New Zealand to unveil the New Zealand memorial. A few months later came Sir Ian Hamilton and Sir Roger Keyes, and in 1927 the Prince of Wales, afterwards King Edward VIII. In 1935 the *Lancastrian* was still bringing pilgrims, among them General and Lady Birdwood, Sir Roger Keyes again, and Captain E. Unwin, V.C. In charge of all the cemeteries as area superintendent for the War Graves Commission was a Tasmanian, Mr Tasman Millington, who went to Anzac in 1915 with our 26th Battalion, returned with Hughes in 1919, and has remained since, living with his wife at Chanak.

The upkeep of the cemeteries was, by all accounts, admirable. Visitors could stroll along Second Ridge, past cemetery after cemetery, each with the name of the post, marking the site of the old front lines. At Lone Pine, Johnston's Jolly, Steele's and Courtney's and Quinn's they walked among the graves of those who fell there; and in the cemetery at Baby 700 they could stand where Kindon's line lay, look towards where Tulloch fought, and know that almost certainly among the graves at their side lay the relics of Lalor, and possibly those of Mordaunt Reid. At The Nek, though the 316 unidentified graves were marked by no headstone, there lay certainly nearly all the dead of the Light Horse Brigades that charged there; and not far from them the modest memorial of the Turks marked the place where they stopped that charge, the place from which, indeed, after the brave stand of Hairi Bey (with Mustafa Kemal close behind him) on the first night, we were never able to drive them. On this monument was a tablet to a Turkish sergeant who, in the days of fierce fighting at The Nek, held out in some crevice near our lines until his mates heard his last call: "I die happily for my country, and you, my comrades, will avenge me." A Turkish pilgrimage visited this spot, and British wreaths were laid there. At the cemetery at Chunuk Bair visitors stood where the Turks buried the foremost New Zealanders after the struggle there, a little on the inland side of the ridge. Here and near here lie, probably, most men of both sides who fell in the fighting from The Apex to Chunuk Bair. On the seaward slope, high on The Farm shelf, are the dead of Baldwin's Brigade and its neighbours. On the low top of Hill 60 lie most of the New Zealanders, English, Irish and Australians who fell there.

With the neutrality of the Straits guaranteed by the League of Nations, and with the habit of travel fast growing, it seemed to Hughes and Wilkins and the rest of us likely that this interesting centre in so interesting a region would become increasingly a calling point for travellers—possibly a regular one for voyagers between the southern Dominions and Europe. The attitude of the Turks was chivalrous, as it had long been with regard to the British cemetery at Haidar Pasha where lay some of the dead of the Crimean War. Though they did not keep up their own cemeteries they respected ours. Turkish officials attended our memorial services. I had had one letter from Zeki Bey[13] after he had checked, as promised, some of his statements to me at Anzac. He was writing in Constantinople nine days after the Turks had been shocked by the announcement of the terms to be imposed

13 A translation is in *Appendix III* of this book.

on them by the "Treaty" of Sèvres. "I write to you," he said, "recalling to myself the days most honourable for both sides, and at the same time seeing my poor country perish." When we next heard of him, some years later, he was Chief of Police under Mustafa Kemal while that unexampled leader carried out the second and more difficult part of his task in westernising the Turkish nation. In those years Hughes, who was then senior British representative on the Anglo-Turkish War Graves Commission, and chief administrative officer of the I.W.G.C. for the Middle East, with headquarters at Cairo, had only to let Zeki Bey know that he wished to make one of his inspections in Turkey and the way was immediately smoothed for him by our generous friend. Our dream seemed to be coming true.

But Hitler and Mussolini changed all that. Visions that were realisable with the League of Nations as guardian of peace and of the neutrality of the Straits became only visions again when by 1935 Germany and Italy were out of the League; and in October of that year Mussolini's infamous attack on the Abyssinians quickly proved that, in existing circumstances, the system built with so many hopes gave no safeguard. Naturally Turkey had asked to be allowed to re-establish her forts and garrisons on Gallipoli. Russia and Britain agreed, and by a treaty again made in Switzerland, at Montreux, with Colonel Hughes present as adviser to the British Government so far as concerned the cemeteries, the Dardanelles was remilitarised. But the ownership and maintenance by Britain of the cemeteries, including the two and a half square miles at Anzac, which had been granted in perpetuity by the Treaty of Lausanne, was equally assured under the Montreux Convention; and throughout the Second World War which followed so soon after, the cemeteries were controlled directly by the Imperial War Graves Commission and were excellently attended to, despite the establishment of Turkish concrete machine-gun posts along the Anzac foreshore within the Commission's area.

During the war, though Turkey was neutral and friendly, few visitors, except from the British embassy in Angora, were allowed there.[14] After the war the situation remained somewhat tense owing to the desire of the Russian Politbureau to control the Straits. In August 1946 the Russian leaders proposed to the Turks that the Montreux Convention should be revised and Russia and Turkey become jointly responsible for the defence of the Dardanelles. The great Atatürk, "Father Turk" as Mustafa Kemal had himself called, had died in 1938 and had been succeeded as President of the Turkish Republic by his former chief-of-staff, Ismet (known as Inönü); but the Turks, now confining themselves to their own borders, held as firmly as ever the principle that their nation and soil should be inviolate whether it was a British opportunist, like Lloyd George, or a Russian one, like the Politbureau, that threatened encroachment. They therefore refused.

So long as big national groups grate upon one another in the Middle East the Dardanelles is likely to be an area of great military importance. And it may therefore be that the "war to end wars" in 1914-18 produced a vision which cannot yet be fully realised even under the safeguards of the United Nations. Nevertheless the rights of access as laid down in the Straits Treaty are recognised by the Turks, and pilgrimages organised under those rights are (it is said) freely allowed. In August 1947 a British squadron visited Helles and was warmly entertained by the Turkish military authorities.

---

14 An Australian writer, Frank Clune, was allowed to visit Anzac in 1942, and immediately after the war Ian Bevan of the *Sydney Morning Herald* went there. Both noted that the remains of Turks were again becoming visible, probably uncovered by the rains.

The graves of Gallipoli, exquisitely maintained, where Anzac folk can walk amid thousands of names as familiar as those along Collins or Pitt Streets, do call for visitors. As the area superintendent, Mr Millington, said in his report for 1946, it is a pity that more facilities for visiting them are not yet available.

In Australia the memorial collection for which our Mission and Hughes and James helped to obtain the Gallipoli exhibits, was established in Canberra as the basis of the Australian War Memorial. The conception of that memorial is that it should impress the visitor with the feeling: "Here is their spirit, in the heart of the land they loved; and here we guard the record which they themselves made." Accordingly the centre of the memorial is a quiet courtyard open to the sun and surrounded by cloisters which will contain the names (inscribed under those of their home-towns or districts) of all Australian servicemen and women who died in or through the two World Wars; and in the galleries surrounding the cloisters, already visited by thousand on thousand, lie the records and relics. Among the relics are the 4.7 gun from Koja Dere and one of the old ships' boats from Anzac Beach, duly sent out by Hughes; part of the bomb-shattered, corrugated iron head-cover from Quinn's and a fragment of wire entanglement from there; bullet-spattered loophole plates from the Pine and Russell's Top; a bullet-pierced water-bottle from far out on Pine Ridge; the badges of some of Baldwin's men and others found on the wild hills about The Farm; fragments of bombs and bullets from Quinn's and a whole heap of bullets from a patch of parapet at Snipers' Nest; a mess-tin and knapsack from The Nek; an Australian hat from Hill 60; an arm patch of the 6th Battalion from Helles; a timber from Lone Pine with our men's names scratched on it. On the walls are Lambert's many sketches and his big pictures of the Landing and the charge at The Nek.[15]

The Canberra memorial has been so devised that visitors to that quiet Court of the Roll may, when the roll is eventually inscribed there, almost feel the presence of the 120,000 individual men and women whose names will be marshalled in their last parade on the surrounding walls.

---

[15] Lambert's many other commissions for the War Memorial, and his great work in sculpture during the post-war years (including the Lawson Memorial in the Sydney Domain, the Recumbent Soldier in St Mary's Cathedral, and the Geelong Grammar School War Memorial) prevented his undertaking the picture of the 2nd Brigade's advance at Helles, which was painted instead by Charles Wheeler.

Appendix
· I ·

ANSWERS OF KIAZIM PASHA TO QUESTIONS
FROM THE AUSTRALIAN OFFICIAL HISTORIAN

1. Where were the Turks expecting us to land?
2. Did they expect us to land troops at Gaba Tepe?
3. Did they expect a landing at Ari Burnu?
4. What did they think our intentions as to landing were?

Answer, 1-4: The landing was expected from Seddel Bahr and Gaba Tepe; also landings were expected on the Asiatic side and

---

[1] Kiazim Pasha was in 1919 Chief of the Turkish General Staff. He had been C.G.S. of the 5th Army at Gallipoli from 25th March 1915 (he was at first lieutenant-colonel, but was promoted to colonel on 14th December 1915). Eighteen months later he was appointed to command the XIX Army Corps in Smyrna, but a few days later became again C.G.S. of the 5th Army. On 21st February 1918 he was made C.G.S. of the famous Yildirim (Lightning) group of armies in Palestine, and next month was promoted to major-general.

Together with Kiazim Pasha's answers to the historian's questionnaire, our friends in Constantinople sent some notes of a talk with Kiazim Pasha recorded by one of them. As these were not, like his answers to the writer, a contribution by Kiazim Pasha to the Australian history, I do not feel at liberty to quote them. I think I may say, however, that they indicated that Kiazim Pasha believed that, if the first attack on the Straits had been made by the Army and Navy together, it would have succeeded; and also that the naval attack on March 18th would have forced the Straits if it had been continued for a day longer. Kiazim Pasha also thought that landings at certain parts of the Gulf of Saros would have succeeded in cutting Turkish communications with the Peninsula; and that a landing on the Asiatic shore might have resulted in the destruction of the forts guarding the Straits, a method of attack which Liman von Sanders expected.

Needless to say the opinion of this fine soldier commands great respect, but probably no other authority would agree with him as to *all* the probabilities above mentioned.

I should add that the footnotes in this appendix are the writer's. Furthermore the English version of the questions is not identical in wording with that submitted by the writer, which was inadvertently lost at G.H.Q. Constantinople. The British Staff had sent a translation of it to Kiazim Pasha, and afterwards kindly retranslated for me the Turkish version. The questions here printed are the retranslated ones with some revision by myself. C.E.W.B.

349

on the north of the Peninsula in the Gulf of Saros. No landing was expected at Anzac. The Turkish Staff thought that the British intention had been to land at Gaba Tepe, and that the landing at Anzac was made in error.

Our appreciation of the situation was that attempts would be made to take the forts by surprise attack and so open the Straits.

5. Approximately at what date did they first hear of our intention to land troops?

6. What was their expectation as to the date at which the forces at Mudros would land?

Answer, 5-6: The Turkish General Staff considered that after the failure of the naval attack on March 18th a combined naval and military attack would be made to endeavour to open the Straits, join the Russians, and separate the East from the West. We had information by the end of March that 50,000 British, Australian and New Zealand soldiers under General Hamilton, and 30,000 French under General D'Amade, were concentrating in Mudros, but the date or week of the landing was unknown.

7. What forces were between Ari Burnu and Gaba Tepe on April 25th? and where were they?

8. How many troops did they amount to in all? What numbers were in reserve? Where were the reserves?

Answer, 7-8: On April 25th between Anzac and Gaba Tepe— in other words, between Anafarta Asmak and Kum Tepe— there was the 2nd Battalion [of the] 27th Regiment, with its centre at Gaba Tepe. One Q.F.[2] Mountain Battery of the 8th Artillery Regiment was attached to this battalion. The other two battalions formed the reserve. They were under cover of the Olive Trees in Maidos. The 19th Regular Division was in the area Boghali-Mal Tepe. At Ari Burnu point there was a company of the 2nd Battalion, 27th Regiment, and the whole of the above-mentioned mountain battery.

9. What forces faced the British at Cape Helles on April 25th?

10. Where were the reserves and in what strength?

Answer, 9-10: Two regiments of the 9th Infantry Division

---

2 "Quick firing"; the term is now obsolete.

formed the garrison at Helles. Their line extended from **Gaba Tepe** to Morto.

11. On April 25th what was the first report of the Ari Burnu landing?
12. Were our troops seen in the boats before reaching the shore?
13. What was the first sign seen? How was the alarm given?
14. How did the news reach the reserves?

Answer, 11-14: The first report was that the British troops were landing at Gaba Tepe and to the north of it. This report reached A.H.Q., Gallipoli, at 6 a.m., April 25th. An hour or two later news arrived that landings were also being made in the Gulf of Saros, Seddel Bahr, Morto Bay, Sighin Dere, Kum Kale and Besika. The report of the landing at Besika was false.

15. What, and where, was the reserve which was sent to Ari Burnu, and when was it put in?
16. How far did our troops advance at Ari Burnu on April 25th, and how did they fight?
17. What were the casualties of the Turks?
18. What reserves were sent to Cape Helles and what was the strength of these reserves?
19. What Turkish artillery was there at Helles?
20. What Turkish artillery was there at Ari Burnu on April 25th? How many land guns and ships' guns were used respectively?
21. How many guns were put in afterwards at Ari Burnu? and where?

Answer, 15-21: At first the two battalions of the 27th Regiment at Maidos were sent to Ari Burnu *via* Koja Dere. They started at 7.30 a.m., after the Australians had landed. A mountain battery of the 19th Division was sent from Boghali towards Chunuk Bair. The Australians that day advanced as far as the western hillocks [?foothills] of Kemal Yere [Scrubby Knoll], and in the direction of Chunuk Bair as far as the line between Dus Tepe [Battleship Hill] and Chunuk Bair. The Australians succeeded well in throwing back our advanced troops and in reaching the points they did. Their first effort in this difficult country was beyond praise. But when the 27th and 57th Regiments began to make their counter-attack the advance was checked and the first attack broken. On counting the casualties of these two regiments it was realised how well the Australians[3] had fought in their efforts to hold the line they had reached. The casualties of these two regiments during the day and the following night were 50 per cent of their strength. The two regiments were together slightly more than 4000 strong. The three Australian brigades which were landed were estimated at 12,000.

The Turkish artillery in Ari Burnu consisted of two mountain batteries, of which one was captured but retaken in the counter-attack. Two field batteries took up positions in the afternoon but remained in observation. On April 26th two more mountain batteries took up positions in [on] Kemal Yere. There were no naval guns.

[Relating to the landing at Helles]: Reserves were at first sent to Helles from the 7th Division, which was at Gallipoli; afterwards, the battalions from the 11th and 3rd Divisions from the Asiatic side. Our guns on April 25th were the field and mountain guns forming the divisional artillery. Divisions, as they reinforced, brought their divisional artillery into the line. There were no other artillery reinforcements.

22. What was the Turkish estimate of the effect of our artillery?
23. Was its fire accurate?

Answer, 22-23: The effect of the British naval artillery was moral without being material. The effect of the land guns was to force our infantry to keep out of view in the centre, and also prevented free movement

24. What were the first counter-attacks delivered by the Turkish force at Anzac? On April 25th? April 26th? April 27th-May 1st? What was their main tactical object?
25. What was the Turkish Staff's appreciation of our plan and motive in attacking at Ari Burnu?
26. When did they estimate that our attack was checked?
27. What expectation had they of further attacks?

Answer, 24-27: No demonstration or counter-attack was made

---

[3] Needless to say, in the Turkish replies the term "Australian" often covers action by the New Zealanders also; "Anzac troops" also is used. Among themselves the Turks always called both Australians and New Zealanders "English".

by us on April 26th. Real counter-attacks were made on April 25th and 27th and May 1st, the aim being to drive the Anzac Corps into the sea. In all these attacks the Anzac troops were superior in number, and consequently no decisive result was obtained, though the Anzac troops were pressed back to the line that they remained in up to the evacuation of the Peninsula. The distance between opposing trenches was very small. During the counter-attack of April 25th, 5 more battalions were put into the line, and on April 27th, 6 more were put in, making a total of 16 battalions against the 6 British brigades.[4]

In the counter-attack of May 1st, 5 more battalions joined the line. By that time the British Naval Brigade had also landed.

The tactics of the Turks were to prevent the British from landing, or, if not, to prevent lodgments being made.

We imagined the tactics of the Anzac landing to be as follows:— By landing in two different places the result would be more of a surprise and the allotted task effected quicker. Further, by drawing more troops to Anzac the task at Seddel Bahr would be more easily effected. By holding the Kavak Tepe [Anderson Knoll]—Sandjak Tepe [Scrubby Knoll]—Chunuk Bair—Koja Chemen Tepe—Abdel Rahman Bair line, communications between Gallipoli and the rest of the Peninsula would be cut. The command of the Straits would also be gained. The above-mentioned line was marked on maps found on dead Australian or New Zealand officers.

It was realised that the attack was checked in April, but it was always expected that further attacks would take place.

28. *See after 31.*
29. What importance was attached to the head of Monash Valley, Baby 700, Pope's Hill, and Quinn's Post?
30. What importance was attached to our attack in the Bloody Angle and on Baby 700 on May 2nd?
31. When did the Turks begin to mine?

Answer, 29-31: Monash Valley, Baby 700 and Pope's Hill were looked upon as very important positions if Koja Chemen mountain was to be menaced. It was always realised that the British

---

[4] Presumably the two Dominion divisions were estimated to have three brigades each. Actually the N.Z. and A. Division then had two.

effort was to take Koja Chemen. Quinn's Post was looked upon as a poor position, as it was commanded. The attack on May 2nd was evidently made to better this position.

Mining was started near Quinn's Post after the attack on May 11th,[5] and the mine exploded on the morning of May 29th.

28. When did the Turkish Staff realise that the British attack at Helles had been checked?

32. What was their estimate of the result of the offensive of May 6th, 7th and 8th at Helles?

Answer, 28 and 32: The Turkish General Staff considered that the British attack at Helles was broken by the middle of June, but even after this date there were other attacks on this front. At first attacks were made every four or five days, later every fortnight. It was considered that the object of these attacks was to break through on the Krithia side. The last real attack was made 23 days after the June attack.

33. What troops were holding the Turkish front during this attack?

Answer, 33: The troops used in defence were:—

1st and 2nd Battalion	29th Regiment
2nd „	56th „
2nd „	19th „
1st and 4th „	26th „
2nd Corps[6]	15th „

34. What was the effect of the attack towards Krithia on May 8th?

Answer, 34: The advance against Krithia on May 8th was checked by the fire of the front line troops.

35. What regiments were in front of Krithia, and what batteries opened upon the troops advancing to that attack?

Answer, 35: Opposite Krithia there were the

2nd Battalion	25th Regiment
1st „	20th „
2nd „	56th „

---

[5] The attack referred to is evidently that on the night of May 9th; there was no attack on the 11th. In the attack evidence of mining was reported.

[6] This is the answer as received. It is possible that the British translator may have written "2 Coys" and the typist misread it. Further, if the answer to Question 35 is correct, the forces mentioned may be only those that faced the initial attack on May 5th.

According to the disposition of the Turkish troops at Cape Helles on 9th May 1915, there were seven Q.F. field batteries [and] one 12-centimetre howitzer battery of six guns, but it is not known how many batteries actually took part in the fighting.

36. Why was there no counter-attack?

Answer, 36: There was no counter-attack as the casualties had been heavy and there was insufficient strength to make one.

37. What was the Turkish appreciation of the position before their great counter-attack of May 19th at Anzac, and why did they choose Anzac for this attack? When did this plan originate?
38. What was the plan of attack?
39. What units were employed in it and who commanded them?
40. What was the quality of these units?
41. What was the Turkish estimate of the result?
42. What were the Turkish casualties?
43. Against what part of our line was the attack most strongly directed?
44. What were the objectives? What was the Turkish estimate of the defence? What guns were employed in the preparation? What was the reason for the tremendous outburst of rifle-fire just before midnight on May 18th?

Answer, 37-44: The position at Anzac was without parallel in history. The opposing trenches were so close together and the Anzac Corps line was very close to the sea; consequently they were much confined and would make every effort to enlarge their positions. It was therefore better for the Turks to have the initiative and attack before the Anzac troops attacked. This they did on May 19th. If this attack succeeded a force of some 4 or 5 Turkish divisions would be freed, and available to deal with Seddel Bahr. The proximity of the trenches was an advantage in making a surprise attack.

The plan was to attack before daybreak, drive the Anzac troops from their trenches, and follow them down to the sea. The following troops were used in this attack:

Facing the British left: 19th Division (12 battalions—O.C.

Lieutenant-Colonel Mustafa Kemal Bey).
Facing the left centre: 5th Division (9 battalions—O.C. Lieutenant-Colonel Hassan Basri Bey).
Facing the right centre: 2nd Division (9 battalions—O.C. Colonel Hassan Askeri Bey).
Facing the right: 16th Division (12 battalions—O.C. Colonel Rushdi Bey).

The whole force was commanded by the III Army [Corps] Commander, Major-General Essad Pasha. The total force numbered about 30,000 rifles. The divisions were good. The 2nd and 16th were fresh divisions; the other two had taken part in all the previous fighting. Everywhere the British trenches were entered, but the attack was held up by machine-gun fire from the flanks and became abortive. The Turkish casualties were much heavier than was expected. More importance was attached to the capture of [the position facing] Lone Pine and the ground north of it. In this attack the worth of the Anzac soldiers in defence was realised; they shot well and used their machine-guns to the best advantage. Our artillery was small—only 6 mountain batteries, 4 field batteries, and 1 howitzer battery without much ammunition, and one mortar [heavy howitzer] battery, being available for the preparation of the attack.

The outburst of fire before midnight, May 18th, was due to the excitement of the troops. Similar outbursts used to occur on both sides.

45. What was the situation at Ari Burnu after May 19th as viewed from the Turkish standpoint?
46. What were the Turkish tactics at Quinn's Post? and
47. Was our bombing severe or negligible at that stage and later?
48. Were our snipers in the trenches or the scrub found to gain superiority? If so, at what stage?
49. How did the Turks interpret our demonstrations in firing and cheering at night?
50. Were they able to patrol the ground in front of our trenches?
51. Generally, what did the Turkish Staff think of the situation at Quinn's Post?
52. What was their estimate of the Australian mining?

Answer, 45-52: After May 19th it was realised that the British defence at Anzac was too strong to enable us to effect anything against it without heavy artillery with plenty of ammunition; and, realising that our position was also very strong in defence, two weak divisions were left in the trenches and the other two divisions were withdrawn.

The bombing was severe and caused most casualties in the late afternoon and evening. Anzac snipers were very annoying. Sniping was very effective when the sun was in our faces.

The cheering and firing at night at first caused the idea that an attack was impending, but after a while it was realised that it was only a demonstration and was waste of ammunition.

Regular patrolling was impossible. The small valleys between trenches were patrolled every night but nothing was done when the trenches were very close. At Quinn's Post both sides used the same tactics. It was thought the Australians were endeavouring, firstly, to improve their tactical positions at that point, and, secondly, fighting took place there because the trenches were so close.

The ground was very suitable for mining and bombing. The mining of the Australians[7] was very good. They seemed to make every effort to gain the upper hand. Apparently they were well provided with the necessary machinery and implements.[8]

53. What was the Turkish estimate of our sortie at Anzac on June 4th?

54. Did this demonstration prevent assistance being sent at the time to the Turkish forces facing the British attack at Cape Helles?

55. What was the Turkish estimate of the forces employed in the sortie?

---

[7] New Zealand miners, as well as Australians, worked at Quinn's and Russell's Top.

[8] Zeki Bey said that the Turks considered our entrenching tool—a miniature pick with one head flattened like a spade—particularly suitable for mining, and the Turkish miners were given these tools which had been found on the dead or otherwise captured. Australian mining machinery was, by the initiative of Professors Edgeworth David and E. W. Skeats, proposed for use at Anzac, but action was taken too late. It was ultimately brought to France and is stated to have been the first of its kind used at the fighting front.

Answer, 53-55: The attack on June 4th was not heavy. The Australians[9] took our trenches during June 4th/5th, and by the morning of June 5th our counter-attack retook them. The strength of the Australians was estimated at 2 companies. No troops were taken from the Seddel Bahr front on account of this attack.

56. What estimate was made of our sortie of June 28th?

57. What reserve, if any, was used in meeting this attack?

Answer, 56-57: The attack on June 28th was made by day and directed against our left flank. The strength of the attack was estimated at one brigade, a new force—the dismounted cavalry brigade.[10] No reserves were necessary to stop this attack.

58. Was any Turkish attack planned between May 19th and June 28th?

59. What was the intention of the Turks in attacking at The Nek on June 29th?

60. What was the plan of this attack?

Answer, 58-60: A plan of attack was made to take the "high mounds" [Russell's Top—apparently called so from the gun positions there] on June 28th. It was determined to increase our heavy artillery and artillery preparation. The attack was made on June 29th with the object of taking the "high mounds" and, if possible, to reach Khain Tepe [Plugge's] and thus command the landing place. The Australian demonstration on June 28th forced the attack to be postponed to the 29th.[11]

61. Did the Turks expect the offensive which we launched on August 6th? If so, when did they expect the attack to be made?

62. Did they observe our landing of troops during the first days of August?

63. Had they any prior information of the attack?

---

9 This attack was made by New Zealanders.

10 The sortie, a pure feint, was made by strong detachments of infantry and Light Horse. The reference in the Turkish answer to "a new force" might lead the reader to imagine that the Turkish Staff believed there was only one dismounted brigade at Anzac when there were actually at this time four. But the Turks certainly knew that dismounted troops had long been on the left and centre. They were, however, "new" in the right sector.

11 Actually it occurred just after midnight on June 29th/30th.

64. Did they expect it to the north or to the south of Anzac?
65. What was their estimation of the situation of our left flank?
66. What steps did they take to meet the attack?
67. What troops were facing Anzac on August 6th before the attack began?
68. What was the strength of the Turks at Helles at this date (August 6th)? and at Suvla (Anafarta)? What was the total force on the Peninsula?
69. What reserves were at Anzac during the attack on Lone Pine?
70. What units were brought up? and from where?
71. What reserves were brought up during the attack on Chunuk Bair?
72. What reserves were moved to Suvla?

Answer, 61-72: The attack on August 6th was unexpected, but it was known that a general attack was being prepared, and that a new landing would take place about the beginning of August. The landing was not seen from Anzac, but the movements of the ships awoke suspicion. There were two possibilities as to the point of landing and the direction of the attack:

1. From just north of Anzac or else directly on Anafarta because the activity of the Australian left wing was noticeable.

2. Between Anzac and Seddel Bahr because the British had always tried to obtain a decisive result at Seddel Bahr.

All preparations were made to meet either eventuality.

Before the attack of August 6th the 19th and 16th Divisions were in the Anzac trenches. A regiment of the 5th Division was between Aghyl Dere and Sazli Dere. A regiment was in Kurt Dere [south of Hill 971] and another was on our left flank south of Koja Dere. Altogether the total force was 38 battalions. All units were unseasoned[12] soldiers. The strength of battalions averaged 500 to 600. The Anzac reserve consisted of the 13th Regiment of the 5th Division, in position south of Koja Dere, and the 15th Regiment of the same division in Kurt Dere. When the attack was made towards Lone Pine those two regiments were sent to check it, and a battalion of the 19th Division

---

[12] There may be some mistake in the translation; on the other hand it is possible that the meaning is that units included many recruits.

in divisional reserve was sent to face the attack around Baby 700.[13]

On the morning of August 7th when the attack was made at Chunuk Bair the following troops were sent to face the New Zealanders, Indians, and British who were advancing between Sazli Dere and Aghyl Dere on Chunuk Bair:

1	battalion	64th	Regiment
1	"	25th	"
1	"	10th	"
1	"	11th	"

These units formed part of the general reserve of the Peninsula. Afterwards two more battalions were sent from the 28th Regiment, and the 23rd and 24th Regiments were sent from Seddel Bahr.

The 7th and 12th Divisions were sent to Suvla from Gallipoli and the 127th Regiment was also sent in the Suvla direction.

On August 6th there were—

4 infantry battalions and 11 guns at Suvla.[14]

At Cape Helles there were—

1st Division	9 battalions	8 machine-guns	
4th "	12 "	8	"
8th "	9 "	6	"
10th "	9 "	8	"
11th "	9 "	3	"
13th "	12 "	4	"
14th "	12 "	8	"

The artillery [at Helles] consisted of 163 guns and howitzers of various calibres.

73. What was the Turkish Staff's first impression as to the objects of these attacks?

74. When did they realise what were the real objectives?

75. What troops opposed our attack on Abdel Rahman Bair on August 8th?

---

[13] Apparently Zeki Bey's battalion (the I/57th) is not here mentioned, possibly because it was not regarded as part of the reserve. The battalion sent to Baby 700 was presumably the II/72nd which was eventually used by Mustafa Kemal next morning for Chunuk Bair and Battleship Hill.

[14] The Turks called the Suvla area the "Anafarta" zone, and Anzac "Ari Burnu".

76. What was considered the main danger to the Turkish positions during these attacks?

Answer, 73-76: From the attack at Aghyl Dere and the landing at Suvla it was deduced that the main objective of the British was Suvla.[15] The Lone Pine attack accomplished its object well, as most of our troops were sent there to reinforce.

On August 8th the Australian attack on Abdel Rahman Bair was opposed by the—

4th Division
$$\begin{cases} \text{11th Regiment} \\ \text{33rd Regiment} \\ \text{1 battalion, 31st Regiment} \\ \text{1 battalion, 32nd Regiment} \end{cases}$$

The main danger to the Turkish position was the [possible] loss of Abdel Rahman Bair and consequently the loss of Koja Chemen.

77. What troops were facing the sea from Hill 971 to Anzac on August 6th?

78. What troops made the final attack when the British were driven back on Chunuk Bair on August 10th? What was the plan of this attack?

79. What was the number of troops attacking? What were the casualties?

80. What was the strength of the Turkish force at Anzac, Suvla (Anafarta), and Helles, respectively, on August 10th?

Answer, 77-80: On August 6th the 14th Regiment was defending the line Koja Chemen to Ari Burnu. The 2nd Battalion of the 72nd Regiment was holding south of Sazli Dere. Sazli Dere was the dividing line between these units.

On August 10th, when the British were driven off Chunuk Bair, the 23rd and 24th Regiments of the 8th Division and the 56th Regiment of the 13th Division were the attacking troops (total strength 5000, approximately). The object of the attack was to push the British off Chunuk Bair and consolidate it, as Chunuk Bair was considered one of the most important points on the front.

The casualties were not heavy.

On August 10th the 19th Division, consisting of the 56th,

---

15 "Suvla" is probably the British interpreter's translation for "Anafarta".

27th, 18th and 72nd Regiments (12 battalions), and the 16th
Division, consisting of the 125th, 47th, 48th and 77th Regiments
(12 battalions), also the 13th, 15th and 33rd Regiments (9
battalions), making a total of 33 battalions, were all at Ari
Burnu.

At Anafarta, i.e., from Hill 160[16] south of Chunuk Bair to
Ege Port, the following troops held the line:—The 8th Division,
consisting of the 23rd, 24th, and 28th Regiments (8 battalions);
the 4th Division, consisting of the 11th, 31st, and 32nd Regiments
(9 battalions); 9th Division, consisting of 64th and 25th Regiments
(6 battalions); 7th Division, consisting of 20th and 21st Regiments
(6 battalions); 2nd Division, consisting of 31st, 35th, and 36th
Regiments (12 battalions), and 11th Division, with 127th Regiment and Broussa Gendarme Battalion (5 battalions)—a grand
total of 47 battalions.[17]

All these units had had heavy casualties in the previous
fighting and were not up to strength.

The fighting strength at Suvla and Ari Burnu was 45,000.

(Strength at Helles, August 10th—

> 39 infantry battalions
> 19 field batteries
> 2 mountain batteries (not Q.F.)

81. What was the Turkish appreciation of the attack at Suvla
(Anafarta)?

82. What was the Turkish appreciation of the attack on Sari
Bair?

83. What was the Turkish appreciation of the attack on Lone
Pine?

Answer, 81-83: From these attacks the Turkish officers appreciated
the ability of the Anzac troops to act on their own initiative, to
profit by the shape of the ground, and to operate in difficult
country.

84. What was the Turkish appreciation of the attack at Helles?

Answer, 84: It was thought that if the British attack at Cape
Helles was successful the result would be more decisive than an

---

[16] Hill 160 is presumably Hill 261 (south shoulder of Chunuk); Ege Port
(or Liman) is Ejelmer Bay.
[17] There is some error here; the figures as received total 46.

attack in another part of the front; also that the cramped nature of the Anzac position would prevent free movement in attack.

85. What was the Turkish Staff's estimate of the position after August 10th?
86. Where did they estimate the most critical position to be?
87. What was the effect of the attack on Hill 60 across the Kaiajik Dere?

Answer, 85-87: After August 10th it was thought that the British would continue their attack, but after the attack of August 21st the situation became more easy.

The most important consideration was the impossibility of driving out the British from their positions with the means available to the Turks at the time.

The attacks on Hill 60 opposite Kaiajik Aghala had no effect except the shedding of blood.

88. What were the Turkish intentions after September?
89. What preparations were made for winter?
90. What opinions were held as to the probability of an evacuation by us of the Peninsula?

Answer, 88-90: After September the policy was to obtain heavy artillery and ammunition from Germany to beat down the opposition. The same line would be held throughout the winter. The general opinion was that the British would not evacuate their positions on the Peninsula.

91. How did the Turkish Staff interpret our cessation of fire on November 27th, 28th and 29th?
92. Did they think it might be due to our evacuating?
93. When did they first begin to suspect that an evacuation was probable?

Answer, 91-93: Owing to the bad weather on the 27th, 28th, and 29th it was not realised that the fire had slackened.[18] This bad weather had affected both sides.

On November 28th we made a sudden bombardment for 10

---

[18] This is almost certainly incorrect; in the early hours of November 27th the Turks sent out patrols from most parts of their line; and other reactions were also noticeable. Possibly no record of them existed at the Turkish War Office.

minutes. At first the British artillery replied lightly but increased their fire later, the Navy joining in.[19]

Some British units were known to have been sent to Macedonia. The mining of our machine-gun emplacements gave no indication of an early evacuation.

94. What did the Turks suspect in December as to our evacuation?

95. Did they notice any movement on our part, and, if so, to what did they attribute it?

96. Was there any report of evacuation at Suvla or Anzac during the last two days or nights of our occupation?

Answer, 94-96: In December the front was quiet. Two days before the Anafarta evacuation hostile aeroplanes were very active and bombed the back areas. Hostile artillery also visibly decreased.

97. To what did the Turks attribute the conflagration that occurred at Ari Burnu three nights prior to the evacuation? Question 97 was not answered.[20]

98. What was the first news of the evacuation of Anzac?

Answer, 98: The 19th Division reported as follows to the Fortress Group Command at 4.30 a.m. on 20/12/1915: "The enemy exploded three mines in front of trench No. 18. Part of our front trenches has been destroyed. A company commander on his own initiative occupied the craters with his company and met with no opposition. He therefore sent a patrol forward to the enemy trenches and found them empty. This fact was reported to the Division, who ordered the trenches on the divisional front to be occupied.[21]

99. Where did the Turks attack on the morning following our evacuation?

---

[19] This presumably refers to the bombardment of Lone Pine and neighbouring posts by the Turks on November 29th. But that bombardment lasted from 9.10 a.m. till 11.40 and was resumed from 11.55 till 12.15 (*see Vol. II, pp. 848-50*).

[20] Zeki Bey, however, said that it was thought the fire (*see Vol. II, p. 885*) had been caused by a shell.

[21] The translation of the Turkish reply does not make clear where the quotation of the report ends. Probably the final inverted commas should be at the end of the answer.

Answer, 99: The Northern Group Command gave the general advance order to all divisions at 6.40 a.m. on 20/12/1915.[22]

100. What was the total number of Turkish casualties on the Peninsula? How were they distributed between Suvla (Anafarta), Anzac (Ari Burnu), and Helles (Seddel Bahr)? When did the bulk of them occur?
101. What were the casualties through sickness at these places respectively?
102. When was ammunition most and least plentiful?

Answer, 100-102: The heaviest losses on the Peninsula were at Seddel Bahr, then Ari Burnu and Suvla.

Most casualties occurred in the early counter-attacks. Casualties from sickness were very small in comparison.

Ammunition was always tight.

103. What big guns were there at Anzac before October?
104. What heavy German and Austrian batteries were placed in position before December?
105. In what positions were they placed?
106. What was the object of placing them there?

Answer, 103-106: At Ari Burnu before October the largest calibre gun was the old pattern 21-cm. mortar. There was very little ammunition. In November an Austrian 24-cm. mortar [howitzer] battery arrived at Suvla and took up a position in Manik Dere [behind Hill 971]. The maximum range of the mortar was 6000 metres.

107. Which of the battles did the Turks consider the most severe?
108. Which of our attacks, and of theirs, did they consider the most brilliant?
109. What was the Turkish estimate of our generals?
110. What German forces were present?
111. What German commanders were present?

Answer, 107-111: The fighting in the Dardanelles campaign from beginning to end was very difficult and severe. The performances of both sides were brilliant.

---

22 Watching from H.M.S. *Grafton* the writer saw the Anzac trenches bombarded heavily by the Olive Grove guns at 6.45 a.m., and the Turks swarm over them at 7.15.

From the Turkish point of view the best British operations were:

1. The Landing and establishing positions on the Peninsula.
2. The brilliant attack on Chunuk Bair on August 6th.
3. The attack on Kanli Sirt [Lone Pine].
4. The Evacuation.

The Anzac commander (General Birdwood) was recognised as a very active commander.

There were no German units during the campaign, except—

Machine-gun detachment off the *Goeben*.
Personnel of three batteries.
A weak engineer company.

In the early days at Anafarta and Suvla there were two German officers commanding divisions, and one officer commanding a regiment. Later there were one army corps commander, one divisional commander, and some artillery officers.

ARMY AND CORPS COMMANDERS (the successive commanders of the five groups are given)
5th Army.

G.O.C.: Field-Marshal Liman von Sanders Pasha.
Chief of the Staff: Colonel Kiazim Bey.

Group of Xeros (Saros)
1. G.O.C.: Col. Feyzi Bey.
   C. Staff: Lt-Col. Hairi Bey.
2. G.O.C.: Maj.-Gen. Faik Pasha.
   C. Staff: Lt-Col. Selaheddin Bey.
3. G.O.C.: Maj.-Gen. Back Pasha (German).
   C. Staff: Lt-Col. Yassim Hilmi Bey.
4. G.O.C.: Maj.-Gen. Mehmed Ali Pasha.
   C. Staff: Maj. Eckert Bey (German).

5. G.O.C.: Maj.-Gen. Mustafa Hilmi Pasha.
   C. Staff: Lt-Col. Mustafa Ilhami Bey.

Northern Group (Ari Burnu)

1. G.O.C.: Maj.-Gen. Essad Pasha.
   C. Staff: Lt-Col. Fahreddin Bey.
2. (The last two months):
   G.O.C.: Maj.-Gen. Ali Riza Pasha.
   C. Staff: Maj. Eckert Bey (German).

Southern Group (Seddel Bahr)

1. (First 2½ months):
   G.O.C.: Maj.-Gen. Weber Pasha (German).
   C. Staff: Lt-Col. von Toweney Bey (German).
   C. Staff: Lt-Col. Selaheddin Bey.
2. G.O.C.: Maj.-Gen. Vehib Pasha.
   C. Staff: Col. Nehad Bey.
3. (The last two months):
   G.O.C.: Maj.-Gen. Jevad Pasha.
   C. Staff: Lt-Col. Shefik Bey.

Anafarta Group (Suvla)

1. (For few days):
   G.O.C.: Col. Feyzi Bey.
   C. Staff: Lt-Col. Hairi Bey.
2. G.O.C.: Col. Mustafa Kemal Bey.
   C. Staff: Maj. Izzeddin Bey.
3. (The last month):
   G.O.C.: Maj.-Gen. Fevzi Pasha.
   C. Staff: Maj. Izzeddin Bey.

Asiatic Group

1. G.O.C.: Col. Feyzi Bey.
   C. Staff: Lt-Col. Hairi Bey.
2. G.O.C.: Mehmed Ali Pasha.
   C. Staff: Maj. Eckert Bey (German).
3. G.O.C.: Maj.-Gen. Faik Pasha.
   C. Staff: Lt-Col. Selaheddin Bey.

Appendix
· II ·

NOTE FROM ZEKI BEY
ON RANKS OF TURKISH OFFICERS

2nd Lieutenant was Mulazim sani.

Lieutenant: Mulazim.

Captain: Yusbashi (Yu, hundred; bashi, head of).

Major: Bimbashi (Bim, thousand); titled as Effendi, or, if on staff, Bey.

Lieut.-Colonel: Kaimakam (Bey).

Colonel: Miralai (Mir, Emir; alai, regiment); titled Bey.

Brigadier: Mirileua (Mir, Emir; leua, brigade); titled Pasha (first grade).

Major-General: Ferik (commanded division); titled Pasha (second grade).

Lieut.-General: Biringi Ferik; titled Pasha (third grade).

Field-Marshal: Mishir.

Zeki Bey added that Mustafa Kemal Pasha was Mirileua (presumably at the end of the Gallipoli Campaign). He should have been Ferik if he had had the rank appropriate to the position he occupied.

Ahuni Bey (the commander of the 57th Regiment) was at first a major and later a colonel.

Zeki Bey, when commander of both battalion and regiment, was Bimbashi.

Liman von Sanders was at first Ferik but later Mishir.

Appendix
· *III* ·

LETTER FROM ZEKI BEY

Zeki Bey's letter, amplifying or correcting certain details of his account, is here given in the original French.

Cons/ple
20 Mai 1919

Mon honorable Monsieur,

Comme je n'ai pas eu l'occasion de vous revoir, j'ai du vous donner les explications suivantes pour compléter et corriger l'histoire racontée, par coeur, durant notre voyage a Anzak.

(1) La première nouvelle de débarquement arrive à notre division à 5.30 a.m. par 9ème division; mais, d'abord, pas clair.

(2) Le premier engagement (feu) a eu lieu à 10.30 a.m.

(3) Nos attaques principàles sont suivant:

    (a) 25 Avril.

    (b) 26 Avril votre attaque qui nous oblige à nous retirer jusqu'à Dus Tepe sur l'aile droite et jusque dans la vallée de Kara Yeuruk (l'est de Lun Pein) a l'aile gauche, un jour défavorable pour nous a Anzak (pas de réserve sous la main).

    (c) 27 Avril, notre 2ème attaque que nous a fit gagner le terrain perdu 26 Av.

    (d) 1er Mai notre troisième attaque que nous a fit gagner les positions dernières.

    (e) L'attaque de 19 Mai n'a pas fait beaucoup de changement dans les positions.

(4) Le 25 Avril au soir 77ème Rég/ent avait fait la complication racontée. 3ème bataillon de ce régiment avait été envoyé, 24 Avril, à Souvla pour remplacer le bataillon de gendarme. Ce dernier bataillon avait été envoyé 25 Avril à

Helles. Le 72 Rég/ent, avec deux bataillons, le 25 Avril au soir, était comme réserve derrière de l'aile droite et a la suite de l'attaque Australienne 26 Avril au matin ces deux bataillons étaient venus a l'est de Lun Pein et avaient arreté le retir. Seulement un bataillon de 72 Régiment avait renforcé l'aile droite le 25 Avril au soir. En résumé, la complication, à l'aile gauche, a été faite par deux bataillons de 77ème régiment.

(5) Le combat dans la fossée devant mes tranchées que j'avais raconté à 29 Juin à 10 heures 20 avant midi s'était passé.

(6) A Kanli Sirt (Lun Pein) le 3ème jour de démonstration nous avions repris la tête du vallée que j'avais montré sur le terrain (8 Août) et 4ème jour (9 Août) j'avais quitté avec mon bataillon Lun Pein pour aller à l'est de Edirné Sirt.

(7) Le jour de démonstration mon bataillon à 5.50 après midi avait reçu l'ordre d'aller à Lun Pein (il me semble que j'avais dit à 2 heures).

(8) Moustaf Kemal Bey était allé à Anafarta la nuit 8/9 Août. Il avait fait l'attaque 9 Août. La nuit 9/10 Août il était revenu à Djonk Bair. L'attaque de Djonk Bair a été faite 10 Août à la bonne heure. Grâce à cette attaque on avait pu repousser les Australiens jusqu'à Chahin Sirt.

(9) 19 Mai les vraies pertes de 19 Division:

$$339 \text{ mort}$$
$$755 \text{ blessé}$$
$$\overline{1094}$$

A ce compte là le total ne depasse pas, maximum, 10,000.

Je vous écris en me rappelant les jours les plus honorables pour deux côtés et en même temps voyant périr mon pauvre pays.

Major Zéki.

Translation

My Honourable Sir,

As I have not had the opportunity of seeing you again, I ought to give you the following explanations to complete and correct the story which I gave you, relying on my memory, during our tour at Anzac.

370

· A P P E N D I X   III ·

(1) The first news of the Landing reached our division at
5.30 a.m. from the 9th Division; but at first it was not clear.

(2) The first engagement (fire) took place at 10.30 a.m.

(3) Our principal attacks were as follows:

   (a) April 25th.

   (b) April 26th came your attack which forced us to
retire as far as Dus Tepe (Battleship Hill) on the
right flank and to Karayuruk Valley (Legge Valley)
east of Lone Pine on the left flank, an unfavourable
day for us at Anzac (no reserve in hand).

   (c) April 27th. Our second attack, which regained for us
the ground lost on 26th April.

   (d) May 1st. Our third attack, which gained us our final
positions.[1]

   (e) The attack of May 19th did not make much change
in the positions.

(4) On the evening of April 25th the 77th Regiment
caused the confusion of which I spoke to you. The 3rd Battalion
of this regiment had been sent on April 24th to Suvla to replace
the Gendarme Battalion. This last battalion had been sent on
April 25th to Helles. The 72nd Regiment, with two battalions,
was on the evening of April 25th acting as reserve behind the
right flank, and following the Australian attack on the morning
of April 26th these two battalions came to the east of Lone Pine
and stopped the retirement. Only one battalion of the 72nd
Regiment had reinforced the right flank on the evening of April
25th. As said before, the confusion on the left flank was caused
by two battalions of the 77th Regiment.

(5) The fight in the crater in front of my trenches, of which
I spoke to you, took place on June 29th at 10.20 a.m.

(6) At Kanli Sirt (Lone Pine) it was on the third day of the
demonstration that we retook the head of the valley which I

---

[1] Actually, though the Turks pushed forward their line on the Second
Ridge, this merely meant approaching closer to our line, not driving us out
of it. The Turkish interpretation of the fighting of the 26th is also erroneous
—the rather complicated facts are as stated in the Australian history. But
evidently two battalions of the 72nd Regiment were brought round to the
east of Lone Pine at the time of our 4th Battalion's mistaken attack.

371

showed you on the spot (on August 8th), and on the fourth day (August 9th) that I left Lone Pine with my battalion to go to the east of Edirna Sirt.

(7) On the day of the demonstration my battalion at 5.50 p.m. received the order to go to Lone Pine—I think I told you it was at 2 p.m.

(8) Mustafa Kemal Bey went to Anafarta on the night of August 8/9th. He attacked (there) on August 9th. On the night of August 9/10th he came back to Chunuk Bair. The attack at Chunuk Bair was made on 10th August early. Thanks to this attack we were able to throw back the Australians as far as Shahin Sirt (Rhododendron Ridge).

(9) On May 19th the actual losses of the 19th Division were:

339 killed

755 wounded

———

1094

At that rate the total (Turkish loss in that attack) did not exceed at most 10,000.

I write to you recalling to myself the days most honourable for both sides, and at the same time seeing my poor country perish.

Major Zeki

Appendix
· IV ·

TURKISH PLACE NAMES AT ANZAC
AND HELLES, AND THEIR MEANINGS

The name by which we knew each place (often the Turkish name)—or else the location—is here generally given first; the Turkish name, as pronounced to me by Zeki Bey, next; his translation of it last. The general order is from north to south; but since many of the places lie on about the same latitude they are taken in successive belts, each belt being followed from west to east. (In a few cases Zeki Bey's readings seemed different from those on our maps.)

Southern Part of Suvla Area

(S.W. edge of W. Hills)—Yeni Chesme—New Spring.

W. Hills—Ismail Oglu Tepe—Hill of Son of Ismail.

Karghrele Kesik Mevke—(noted down as) Karglikusuk Mevki—
    The Position of Karglikusuk.

Aire Kavak—(noted down as) Erikulak—Inverted Ear (possibly
    referring to shape of river-bend at this point).

Chakajik Kuyusu—Well of (Proper Name).

Kavaklar—Poplars.

(S. of Chakajik Kuyusu)—Shukri Effendi Kuyusu—Well of Shukri
    Effendi.

Sosak Kuyusu—Well of (Proper Name).

Dervish Ali Kuyusu—Well of Dervish Ali.

N. end of Abdel Rahman Bair
$\left\{\begin{array}{l}\text{Yeshil Tepe—Green Hill.}\\ \text{Furka Dere—Division Valley.}\\ \text{Top Tepe—Gun Hill.}\end{array}\right.$

Northern Anzac Area

Kazlar Chairi—Geese Meadow.

Kabak Kuyu—Cabbage Well.

Hill 60—Bomba Tepe—Bomb Hill.
Asmak Kuyusu—Well of (Proper Name).
Damakjelik Kuyusu—Well of (Proper Name).
Damakjelik Bair—Spur of (Proper Name).
Kaiajik Dere—Valley of the Little Rock.
(S. of Hill 60)—Kaiajik Aghyl—Sheepfold of the Little Rock.
(Wheatfield area S.E. of Hill 60)—Nahim Sirta—(Proper Name) Spur.
Hill 90 (where 4th Bde was caught by m.g.'s)—Yaivan Tepe—Level Hill.
Asma Dere—Vine Valley.
(Hill whence Turk m.g.'s fired)—Alai Tepe—Regiment Hill.
(Valley leading N. from Hill 971)—Tauk Juluk Dere—Poultry Valley.
Aghyl Dere—Sheepfold Valley.
Walden's Point—Utch Tepe—Three Hill.
Australia Valley—Chukur Dere—Ditch Valley.
Hill 100—Musellas Tepe—Triangle Hill.
Abdel Rahman Bair—Abdel Rahman (Proper Name) Spur.
Aghyl Dere North (leading to Hill Q)—Kara Aghyl Dere—Black Aghyl Dere.
Hill 971—Koja Chemen Tepe—Hill of the Great Pasture.
(N.E. Spur of 971)—Chifte Tepe—Double Hill.
(Valley S. of Chifte Tepe)—Obus Deresi—Howitzer Valley.
(Valley E. of Obus Deresi)—Manik Dere—(Proper Name) Valley.
Bauchop's Hill—Yaila Tepe—Meadow Hill.
Chailak Dere—Creviced Valley.
The Farm—Aghyl—Sheepfold.
The Farm Plateau—Sari Tarla—Yellow Field.
No. 2 Outpost—Mahmus Sirta—Spur Ridge.
Old No. 3 Post—Haliden Rizar Tepesi—Halid and Rizar Hill.
Table Top—Pilaf Tepe—Rice Hill.
Rhododendron Ridge—Shahin Sirta—Falcon Spur.
Chunuk Bair—Dchonk Bair—(Proper Name) Ridge.
Hill Q South—Besim Sirta—(Proper Name) Slope.

Old Anzac Area

Fisherman's Hut—Balijke Damleri—Fisherman's Hut.

No. 1 Outpost—Chatal Tepe—Fork Hill.

Sazli Beit Dere—Seaweed Valley.

Baby 700 (seaward spurs)—Kabak Sirta—Cabbage Slope.

Baby 700—Kulich Bair—Sword Hill.

Battleship Hill—Dus Tepe—Straight Hill.

S.E. Spur of Chunuk Bair—Suyata—Watercourse.

Achinga Tepe (next hill along this spur)—Third Hill.

(Valley S. of Hill 971)—Kurt Dere—Wolf Valley (or Mazi Choukuri Dere).

(Next Valley to East)—Kuchuk Dere—Little Valley.

(Valley leading to Koja Dere, continuation of Manik Dere)—Chailar Dere—Stream Valley (lower down it was called Koja Dere, the Big Valley, or Kurija Dere, the Nearly Dry Valley).

(East of Chailar Dere)—Sivari Sirta—Cavalry Slope.

Walker's Ridge—Sercha Tepesi—Sparrow Hill.

Russell's Top (and Nek and Turk's Point)—Jessaret Tepe—Hill of Valour.

(S. Spur of Battleship Hill)—Top Bair—Gun Ridge.

(Next Ridge to East)—Inje Bair—Thin Ridge.

(Next Valley)—Dik Dere—Steep Valley.

(Next Ridge)—Usun Sirt—Long Ridge.

(Next Valley)—Usun Dere—Long Valley.

Third or Gun Ridge—Top Chelar Sirt—Guns' Ridge.

(Next Valley)—Kuru Dere—Dry Valley.

Ari Burnu—Bee Point.

Watson's Pier—Irajis Gelesi—Landing Pier.

Plugge's Plateau—Khain Tepe—Cruel Hill.[1]

The Sphinx—Yuksek Tepe—High Hill (or Point 122).

(The Cliffs by the Sphinx)—Sari Bair—Yellow Ridge.

Quinn's Post—Bomba Sirt—Bomb Spur.

Courtney's Post—Boyun—The Nek.

Mule Valley—Kesik Dere—Broken Valley.

Mortar Ridge—Edirna Sirt—Adrianople Spur.

Behind Mortar Ridge—Chatal Dere—Forked Valley.

Scrubby Knoll—Sandjak Tepe—Standard Hill (also known as Kemal Yere, Kemal Hill).

Gezel Dere (E. of Scrubby Knoll)—Beautiful Valley.

---

[1] Others have translated this "Traitorous Hill".

(Next Valley to East)—Uran Arda—(Proper Name).

Hell Spit and Queensland Point—Kuchuk Ari Burnu—Little Ari Burnu, Little Bee Point.

Shrapnel Valley—Kuruku Dere—Valley of Fear.

Wire Gully—Gedik Dere—Hole Valley (the nick at Bridges' Road was Gedik, the "hole").

German Officers' Spur—Merkez Tepe—Central Hill.

(S. shoulder of Scrubby Knoll)—Kehal Bair—(Proper Name).

Victoria Gully—Kikrik Dere—"Tommy" Valley.[2]

M'Cay's Hill—Yeshilik—The Green Things (probably our gun emplacements).

Johnston's Jolly—Kirmezi Sirt—Crimson Slope.

Owen's Gully—Djemal Dere—(Proper Name).

Fondaluk Sirt (Spur E. of Legge Valley)—Brown Spur.

(Valley E. of that spur)—Mersin Dere—Mersina Valley.

Adana Bair—Adana Spur.

(S. shoulder of Scrubby Knoll)—Haidar Tepe—(Proper Name).

(Valley S.E. of this)—Mibairak Dere—Blessed Valley.

Koja Dere Village—Kurija Dere (Nearly Dry Valley) or Koja Dere (Big Valley).

(S.E. of Koja Dere)—Nepunari—(Proper Name).

Clarke Valley—Chakal Dere—Jackal Valley.

The Wheatfield—Yeshi Tarla—Green Field.

The Pimple—Shuheidlar Tepe—Martyrs' Hill.

Kanli Sirt—Bloody Slope—Lone Pine.

Legge Valley—Karayuruk Dere—The Valley of Black George.

Bolton's Hill—Kel Tepe—Bald Hill.

Valley of Despair—Kars Deresi—Kars Valley.

Cooee Gully—Kara Dere—Black Valley.

Wanliss Gully—Gulnar Dere—(Proper Name).

Pine Ridge—Al Bairak Sirta—Ridge of the Red Flag.

(The pine wood on this ridge)—Karayuruk Ormana—Wood of Black George.

(Valley N. of Anderson Knoll)—Keklik Dere—Partridge Valley.

Deirman Tepe (S.W. of Koja Dere)—Mill Hill.

Chatham's Post Ridge—Sungu Bair—Bayonet Ridge.

Anderson Knoll—Kavak Tepe—Poplar Hill.

---

[2] Zeki Bey said that the British soldier was nicknamed "John Kikrik"; the French soldier "Tango" (after the dance); and the Italians "Makarnaji" (presumably "Macaronis").

(Valley E. of this)—Kavak Dere—Poplar Valley.

(S. end of Koja Dere Valley)—Keui Deresi—Village Valley.

(S. end of Harris Ridge, i.e. of Bolton's Hill Spur)—Kuchuk Tepe—Little Hill.

(Foothill of Gun Ridge N.E. of this)—Hotchkiss Tepe—Hotchkiss Hill.

(Foothill of Gun Ridge N.E. of Gaba Tepe)—Baghdad Tepe—Baghdad Hill.

Gaba Tepe—Kaba Tepe—Rough Hill (Karakol—Police Post).

Hadji Abdi Chiftlik—Farm of Hadji Abdi.

(Track 1½ miles E. of Gaba Tepe)—Sirsofur Yolu—Sirsofur (village) road.

Damlar (on this road)—Ruins.

Asmak Dere—(Proper Name).

Kum Tepe—Sand Hill.

Southern Zone (Helles)

Achi Baba (S.W. shoulder) Er Oglu Sirta—Hero's Son Ridge.

Achi Baba—Father Achi (also Alchi Tepe—Plaster Hill).

Ali Bey Chiftlik—Ali Bey Farm.

Krithia—Kirte.

(W. Branch, Krithia Nullah)—Kuchuk Kirte Dere—Little Krithia Gully.

(S. Spur of Achi Baba)—Hilal Sirta—Crescent Hill.

Gully Ravine—Sighin Dere—(Proper Name).

(Near Fir Tree Wood)—Yusuf Effendi Tepe—Hill of Yusuf Effendi.

Krithia Dere—Kirte Dere.

(Spur up which 2nd A.I.Bde advanced)—Surreya Effendi Bair—Surreya Effendi Spur.

(Valley E. of Vineyard)—Shuheidlar Deresi—Martyrs' Valley.

(Minor Spur E. of this valley)—Rejib Bey Bair—Rejib Bey Spur.

(Main Spur E. of valley)—Kutsi Bey Tepe—Kutsi Bey Hill.

Pink Farm—Sotiri Chiftlik—(Proper Name) Farm.

(E. of Pink Farm)—Harablar—Ruins.

On Krithia Road—Kuyu—Well.

(S. of Pink Farm)—Harablar—Ruins.

(W. of Kanli Dere)—Tombak Tepe—Round Hill.

(E. of Kanli Dere)—Suhaz Nesi—Water Depot.

(Main Spur E. of Kanli Dere)—Kemal Bey Tepe—Kemal Bey Hill.
Kereves Dere—Celery Valley.
Observation Hill—Hadji Ayub Chiftlik—Hadji Ayub Farm.
(At bridge over Krithia stream)—Chesme—Spring.
Water Towers—Su Terrazileri—Water Towers.
Kanli Dere—Bloody Valley.
Zimmerman's Farm—Hadji Husseinar Chiftlik—Hadji Husseinar
   Farm.
Hill 114—Karajaoglu Tepe—Hill of Karaja's Son.
Tekke Burnu—Shrimp Point.
Lancashire Landing—Tekke Koyu—Shrimp Bay.
Head of Lancashire Landing—Kuyular—Wells.
Cape Helles—Ilias Burnu.
V. Beach—Ertoghrul Koyu—Ertoghrul Bay (after first Ottoman
   Sultan).
Ertoghrul Tabia—Ertoghrul Fort.
Old Fort—Harab Kale—Ruined Fort.
Seddel Bahr—Barrier of the Sea.
Morto Koyu—Morto Bay.
Suleiman Reis Dere—Suliman Reis Valley.
De Tott's Battery—Eski Hissarlik—Old Fortress.
Hissarlik Burnu—Fortress Point.
Signal Station Hill—Eumercoptan Tepe—Captain Eumer Hill.

South of Straits' Entrance

Kum Burnu—Sand Point.
Kum Kale—Sand Fort.

Appendix
·V·

REPORTS ON GRAVES AT GALLIPOLI AND THE FUTURE OF ANZAC

First Report

The first report of the present writer after inspection of the Old Anzac cemeteries was sent on 17th February 1919, the day after inspection. It has been printed at the end of Chapter V except for the third, fourth, and fifth paragraphs, which ran:

"The following are details of my examination made in company with Hughes. No evidence exists at Anzac of any systematic desecration of graves. Four cemeteries, (1) Brown's Dip North, (2) Shrapnel Gully, (3) Beach, (4) Ari Burnu Point, have been interfered with. At Brown's Dip North six or seven graves unquestionably have been dug up and replaced recently by mounds wrongly sited. In the other cemeteries mentioned there is no evidence of any grave having been dug up though there are signs that two or three have been opened, probably by inhabitants of the Peninsula or soldiers searching for loot; there are also a few signs of interference by dogs.

"What is certain is that at some time early in 1916 Turkish authorities ordered these cemeteries to be put in order. Previously thereto all wooden crosses had disappeared—it is almost certain that they were taken by the local garrison for firewood. The Turkish officer detailed to rectify this made up numerous mounds bordered by stones, similar to the mounds in the Turkish cemeteries, on the site of the old cemeteries; but both (the boundaries of) the site and the direction of the rows are in every case wrong.

"Very careful examination by Hughes and Woolley, however, located with complete certainty the positions of every original grave. These lie beneath the later Turkish constructions. These have been checked with the plans and proved exactly accurate. Two or three inscriptions on stone, bronze or tin which are still

379

in position afforded final proof. An examination of one grave in each cemetery is now being made at my request in order to obtain a definite test as to whether the bodies in the original graves are undisturbed. I will later report the result. In the case of the Shell Green cemeteries, new fortifications dug on the edge of the hill appear deliberately to avoid them; four graves here were disturbed at some period. The remaining cemeteries of the Old Anzac position have, since the disappearance of the crosses, been apparently unrecognised and are untouched by the Turks. Although completely overgrown they can be recognised with certainty by the methods worked out by Hughes.

"Of the 8000 Australians killed during the campaign, about 2000 were buried at Egypt, Malta and Lemnos; 6400 are definitely recorded as having been killed at Gallipoli. Of these about 3500, recorded as having been buried with (sometimes) vague locations, will be identified with certainty; respecting the graves at Cape Helles I will report later. The remainder at Anzac number about 2500. Of these some can be located with certainty beside men of the same unit killed the same day, of others the graves are probable but not certain, and the remainder were killed in No-man's-land and either were buried during the armistice or lie there today recognisable as Australians by their kit."

Second Report

The final report, handed on 13th March 1919 to British G.H.Q. at Constantinople for cabling to the Department of Defence, Melbourne, and the High Commissioner for Australia, London, was as follows:

"In continuation of my previous report, during the past three weeks I thoroughly inspected the graves at Anzac and Helles, and completely confirmed the opinion that the graves had not been systematically desecrated. At some period after the Evacuation the graves were unprotected and local inhabitants and individual soldiers dug up a certain proportion, searching the pockets and money-belts of the dead. Some cemeteries were not discovered by the marauders and remained untouched until rediscovered by Hughes. In other cases Turkish and Australian dead have been dug up indiscriminately. Turkish governmental control was always weak. If in future the Dardanelles is administered by Turkey, special care will be necessary to prevent a recurrence of depredations by the inhabitants who are now returning and salvaging the Anzac area for wood, tanks, etc.

"Anzac has now been almost completely searched by Lieutenant Hughes, about 4700 graves having been definitely located and surveyed while others are still being found. Within five weeks Hughes will have located and surveyed the exact position of nearly all graves of which reports exist, and will then proceed to Helles to help a British officer locate Australian graves there. Large temporary wooden crosses are now being inscribed for every located grave. Erecting the crosses, making up the mounds and fencing will then presumably be carried out by fatigue parties of British troops supervised by the Royal Engineers.

"It is therefore necessary that the Australian Government should as soon as possible express its wishes with reference to the rival policies, namely (1) that crosses should be erected over the men where they fell, or (2) that the remains should be collected in a few large existing cemeteries. The former policy can be perfectly well carried out if the whole of Anzac is vested in the Imperial Graves Commission but only if this is done. At Helles the case is different, because the Helles area is larger and more agricultural. There it clearly rests with the British Government whether to express a wish to retain the whole battlefield. The Australian advance (there) on May 8th covered about 1000 yards square. Possibly 200 Australians are buried all over the area, especially (1) just behind the Tommies' Trench, and (2) behind the support trench dug by the Australians after the advance. Hughes has not yet completed this area, but will certainly identify many graves near these points besides others in British cemeteries. At Helles, therefore, even if the British decide to concentrate the bodies into the main cemeteries, two small Australian cemeteries might be placed at the Tommies' Trench and the line reached by the Australians. If there is only one cemetery, the Australians should be transferred to a special portion.

"Throughout Anzac and Helles, similarly to all battlefields, numerous skulls and bones of both sides remain on the surface until work is completed. These sights would be unspeakably distressing to soldiers' relations if they visited the place prematurely. This is one of many reasons why it is necessary to complete the work. In my opinion the British portion of the staff of the Graves Registration Union [*sic*][1] here is not a quarter large enough to cope with the work in reasonable time. Suvla is completely untouched; the New Zealand representative is occupied in administering the British headquarters; the Australian representative, after locating the graves at Anzac, will probably be required to locate British graves at Suvla. In my opinion he should be charged solely with the completion of the Australian graves at Anzac and Helles including any British graves within purely Australian areas. For the British work at Suvla, Helles and Chunuk Bair the present staff should be quadrupled.

"Work is also perpetually hampered because it is attempted with soldiers in process of demobilisation; Europeans are not suited for summer work and also probably feel that they did not enlist for this duty.

"As regards salvage, several large relics at Anzac should certainly be removed, including two lifeboats and the barrel of our 4.7-inch gun which Hughes found near Koja Dere. If not removed they will become a Turkish war trophy. Also there are quantities of loophole plates, and smaller relics which would form a basis of exchange with foreign museums or could be sold for the benefit of the museum funds.

"With reference to the roads, Anzac is accessible by Ford car during fine spells even in winter, and (the journey) would easily be practicable in summer. Hughes estimates that the laying out of the cemeteries, and fencing them with salvaged material within three months, with Egyptian labour would cost £1000 in wages, sustenance and materials. The laying out of paths to eight principal points within Anzac would cost £200, and the annual upkeep by a working party each spring £110. The first cost or repair of motor roads from Boghali to North and South Anzac and around the Beach would be about £600 and the annual cost £200. Hughes bases the above on the cost of labour in Egypt and Palestine.

---

[1] I should have written "Directorate". "G.R.U." stood only for its Units, such as the one on Gallipoli.

"On the basis of the above facts, I recommend that, in order to meet Australian and New Zealand sentiment, the Peace Conference be asked to vest the Anzac area in the Graves Commission; if this is conceded, that all Anzac graves should be retained in their present positions, namely:

(1) all cemeteries remain on their present sites, strongly fenced with salvaged material, the paths made up and the cemeteries planted with small Australian trees, not altering the appearance of the battleground;

(2) outlying graves be made where still lie the remains of men who penetrated furthest on the first day;

(3) miscellaneous remains in No-man's-land be buried before each post and a monument erected containing the name of the post and the names of all men who have fallen there;

(4) Australian graves at Helles should be treated in conformity with whatever principle is adopted by the British, namely, if the area is taken over they should be retained in situ; if several cemeteries are retained Australian cemeteries should be placed at Tommies' Trench and the line reached by the Australians; if only one cemetery is made the Australians should be transferred to a special portion of it;

(5) after the Australians and British are all buried the Turks should all be buried, but not until the burial of our men is completed, because if the Turks begin work before we are finished they are certain to confuse Australians with Turks;

(6) visitors should be prohibited with the utmost rigour, whatever their pretext, until all remains are buried and the work entirely completed;

(7) it is most urgent that this work be completed as soon as possible;

(8) with this object all official and semi-official tourists should be strictly barred;

(9) representations should be made that the British staff should be greatly increased in order to deal with Helles, Suvla and North Anzac in reasonable time;

(10) Australian and New Zealand officers should be confined to work on the areas covered by Australian and New Zealand fighting including British graves only within those areas;

(11) these officers should be made representatives of Australia and New Zealand on the Graves Registration Union[2] responsible to their respective governments for the eastern theatre. Now they are simply employees of the Graves Registration Union for use in any work the Union desires;

(12) in order to finish the Australian graves as soon as possible, I urge that Hughes should be allotted a working party of, say, 100 Macedonian Labour Corps or Egyptian labourers;

(13) after the Anzac graves and paths are completed, these should make the quickest and most comprehensive salvage of the whole area in order to remove national relics;

(14) arrangement should be made with the future authority controlling the Peninsula for the repair, every springtime, of the motor road to Anzac in accordance with Hughes' plans;

(15) if, as is probable, Hughes resides in Egypt, it is desirable that he should be appointed, on appropriate conditions, Australian representative on the Eastern Section of the Imperial Graves Commission, with the duty of visiting once yearly all cemeteries in Palestine, Egypt and Gallipoli on behalf of the Australian Government."

---

[2] This should be Graves Registration Directorate (see previous note).

Appendix
·VI·

LESTER LAWRENCE'S VERSES,
"THE GRAVES OF GALLIPOLI",
FROM *THE ANZAC BOOK*

The herdman wandering by the lonely rills
    Marks where they lie on the scarred mountain's flanks,
Remembering that wild morning when the hills
    Shook to the roar of guns and those wild Franks
        Surged upward from the sea.

None tends them. Flowers will come again in spring,
    And the torn hills and those poor mounds be green.
Some bird that sings in English woods may sing
    To English lads beneath—the wind will keen
        Its ancient lullaby.

Some flower that blooms beside the Southern foam
    May blossom where our dead Australians lie,
And comfort them with whispers of their home;
    And they will dream, beneath the alien sky,
        Of the Pacific Sea.

"Thrice happy they who fell beneath the walls
    Under their father's eyes," the Trojan said,
"Not we who die in exile where who falls
    Must lie in foreign earth." Alas! our dead
        Lie buried far away.

Yet where the brave man lies, who fell in fight
    For his dear country, there his country is.

---

1 Lawrence was Reuter's Correspondent on Gallipoli. This was at the time when we were leaving these graves—to what future we knew not. (In *The Anzac Book* the poem contains misprints due to faulty editing— "ranks" for "Franks" and "keep" for "keen".)

And we will mourn them proudly as of right—
　　For meaner deaths be mourning and loud cries.
　　　　They died pro patria!

Oh, sweet and seemly so to die indeed,
　　In the high flush of youth and strength and pride.
These are our martyrs, and their blood the seed
　　Of nobler futures. 'Twas for us they died.
　　　　Keep we their memory green.

This be their epitaph: "Traveller, south or west,
　　Go, say at home we heard the trumpet call,
And answered. Now beside the sea we rest.
　　Our end was happy if our country thrives.
Much was demanded—Lo! our store was small:
　　　　That which we had we gave—it was our lives."

Appendix
·VII·

A MEMORIAL TO SOLDIERS WHO FELL
AT THE DARDANELLES IN 440 B.C.

After the war of 1914-18 there came to the notice of some
Australians the existence in the National Museum at Athens of
a memorial to members of an earlier force which had served its
country at the Dardanelles. On a marble monument are the
names of twenty-eight Athenians, grouped under the names of
their "tribes" (that is, of their electoral divisions), as well as of
others who fell at Byzantium (which 750 years later became
Constantinople) and elsewhere. In the *Manual of Greek
Historical Inscriptions* (Hicks and Hill, Clarendon Press, Oxford,
1901) the editors conjecture that the fighting at the Dardanelles
(or Hellespont) took place in 440 B.C., when the people—or
aristocracy—of Samos revolted against the Athenian democracy,
and the Greek colony of Byzantium also took the opportunity to
revolt. In a sea and land war, in which Pericles and the poet
Sophocles both served as leaders, the Athenians won.

On a slab of Pentelic marble across both columns of the
monument is the following inscription:

'οίδε παρ' Ἑλλήσποντον ἀπώλεσαν ἀγλαὸν 'ἥβην
βαρνάμενοι, σφετέραν δ' εὐκλέϊσαν πατρίδα,
'ὥστ' ἐχθροὺς στενάχειν πολέμου θέρος ἐκκομίσαντας
Αὐτοῖς δ' ἀθάνατον μνῆμ' ἀρετῆς ἔθεσαν.

This has been translated, I believe by the late Christopher
Brennan, as follows:

These by the Dardanelles laid down their shining youth
  In battle and won fair renown for their native land,

387

So that their enemy groaned carrying war's harvest from the field—
But for themselves they founded a deathless monument
of valour.

Australians who fell on the same shores 2355 years later are
commemorated in the Memorial Town Hall at Tamworth, New
South Wales, by a shortened version:

They gave their shining youth, and raised thereby
Valour's own monument which shall not die.

·INDEX·

Ranks shown after the surnames of officers and men are in general the highest held by them during events referred to in this volume.

Page numbers followed by *n* indicate that the reference is to a footnote on the page specified.

389

·INDEX·

·INDEX·

Other titles from ABC Books, Spoken Word and Video

To order by mail,
contact ABC Mail Order,
PO Box 10 000,
Willoughby NSW 2068,
or call 406 0233 in Sydney
or 008 02 3333 from
anywhere in Australia.

THE BOYS WHO CAME HOME

Recollections of Gallipoli

Harvey Broadbent

Paperback 160 pp

It was partly for king and country… on the other hand there was a certain element of adventure…'

'I was keen…100 per cent keen… British Empire, you know, very much so…'

'King and country nothing! No, adventure, adventure, that's all, I'd say.'

Over the last seventy-five years, the Anzac story – the disastrous landing on the narrow beaches of Gallipoli, the terrible fighting at Lone Pine, the miraculous withdrawal that somehow turned a defeat into a victory – has become the stuff of Australian legend.

In this book, the recollections of the 'boys who came home' from Gallipoli present a picture of Australian character quite different from the popular myth of the Anzac hero. It is a picture of heroes of another kind, of ordinary men caught up in a wave of patriotic chauvinism, who fought in a war they sometimes did not understand and then learned to live with the memory of the horror and the realisation of the futility of it all.

Harvey Broadbent has made a number of ABC radio and television documentaries about the Gallipoli campaign, including 'Gallipoli: The Fatal Shore', presented by Chris Masters, which won the 1988 Media Peace Award.

an
ABC
BOOK

Available from ABC Shops, bookshops and ABC Mail Order

CHANGI PHOTOGRAPHER
George Aspinall's Record of Captivity
Tim Bowden

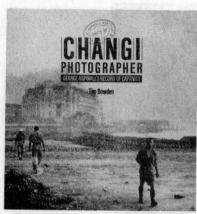

Paperback 144 pp

Even before he became a prisoner-of-war of the Japanese in Singapore in 1942, George Aspinall was nick-named 'Changi' Aspinall by his 2/30th Battalion mates. At lights-out time in Birdwood Camp, George was invariably 'down at Changi Village' helping to process photographs he and his friends had taken of their new and exotic tropical surroundings.

After captivity that hobby became a private obsession that saw George not only taking secret photographs in the Changi area, but up on the appalling Thai–Burma Railway. He not only took photographs at great personal risk, but processed them on the spot, using chemicals smuggled in medicine bottles from Singapore. The ingenuity and resourcefulness of this teenage Australian private soldier have resulted in a unique visual diary of captivity.

'the recollections and observations o an ordinary man are more dramati than any "official" history could hop to be.'

Melbourne *Hera*

'a beautiful book – all the more re markable because of the stinging tra gedy that lies behind the surface of it sepia photos.'

Sydney *Telegrap*

'one of the bravest and most inger ious photographers in Australia wartime history.'

Australasian Pos

'The words, Aspinall's own, recorde with great skill by Bowden, are vit to the pictures. The story is told wit understatement and economy c words . . . a deeply moving account.
Far Eastern Economic Revie

'. . . records with a poignancy tha cannot be equalled by words alone – it is a splendid, unique collection, mute tribute to the courage and in genuity of a teenage amateur, wh tackled successfully problems t daunt the professional, often in th face of mortal peril.'

Canberra Time

'. . . a more poignant reminder of th sufferings of Eighth Division soldie than the official war historians.'
Rupert Lockwoo

'the old Australian capacity for wr and irreverent humour in adversity displayed on every page.'
C. J. Koc

an
ABC
BOOK

Available from ABC Shops, bookshops and ABC Mail Order

THE WAR AT HOME
1939 Australia 1949
Daniel Connell

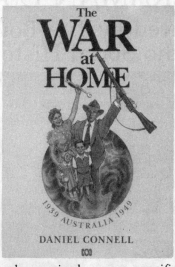

Paperback 144 pp

those Australians who remained
ome, World War II was an extra-
nary period, a time of excite-
t, anxiety, austerity and glamour.
, women and schoolchildren all
to deal with a range of experi-
s for which nothing had pre-
d them.

sing the words of people of all
who remember the home front,
el Connell has assembled a
aic of life in Australia during
e years. Material for *The War at
e* comes from interviews and let-
collected for an ABC Radio series
86, and deals with a wide range
ubjects: home and school life,
, the problems of aliens, war-
bureaucracy. Some people have

more specific recollections—the
Knackeroos, for example, an elite
group of men sent to the Northern
Territory to learn how to live off the
land in case of invasion; and witnesses to the bombings of Sydney
Harbour, Darwin and Broome.
Events that have hitherto been paragraphs in history books lift off the
page in their immediacy; some stories
are told here for the first time.

 The War at Home is not an official
history but a human document about
a time in Australia that profoundly
affected a generation. As one inter-
viewee says: 'It was a hard rite of
passage ... we will never forget it and
it should not be forgotten when we're
gone.'

an
ABC
BOOK

ilable from ABC Shops, bookshops and ABC Mail Order

ABC Spoken Word Cassettes

NEIL DAVIS, COMBAT CAMERAMAN 1934-1985
Produced by Tim Bowden, ABC Radio Social History Unit

2 x C60

'As I lay there half-reclining with blood streaming down my head and hands, a North Vietnamese soldier appeared literally a metre away over a slight rise.

'My first reaction was, "What a fantastic shot!" I looked down to adjust the focus and the swing of the turret of the camera onto a wide-angle lens. I mean, there was this man coming to kill me and my first reaction was to get on to the right lens to get this dramatic shot.'

Such was the professionalism of Neil Davis, the Australian camerman who covered the conflict in Indo-China for eleven years, and whose camera captured world news events for twenty years until he was kille September 1985 in Bangkok, w filming an unsuccessful Thai coup

In 1976 Tim Bowden, a friend former colleague who worked v Neil Davis in Southeast Asia and V nam in 1965-67, began taping Dav reminiscences. In the months be he died Davis sent tapes to Bow from Japan or the Philippines, wherever he was on assignment the American NBC network. In *Davis, Combat Cameraman*, Da speaks of his attitudes to fate death, and of his experiences companying Asian soldiers i battle in Vietnam, Cambodia Laos.

ABC
SPOKEN
WORD
CASSETTE

Available from ABC Shops, bookshops and ABC Mail Ord

ABC Video

GALLIPOLI: THE FATAL SHORE

Presented by Chris Masters, Producer Harvey Broadbent

Duration approx.
92 minutes.
Beta and VHS

nine months during 1915, 12 000 stralian and New Zealand sol-rs, known as the Anzacs, were ed fighting in a land most of them I never heard of, for a country st of them had never seen.

This award-winning documentary cribes the Gallipoli campaign of rld War I from both the Anzac and kish perspectives. It explodes ne old myths and reveals new s.

Through interviews with Anzac and Turkish veterans, archival foot-age and reconstructions, the film provides a greater understanding of the tragedy and of the complex truth behind the campaign. It does not glorify war, but rather commem-orates the young soldiers who served in a campaign that became part of Australian legend.

Winner of the 1988 United Nations Media Peace Award.

ABC
VIDEO